D0369847

TWO SISTERS IN THE SPIRIT

HANS URS VON BALTHASAR

TWO SISTERS IN THE SPIRIT

Thérèse of Lisieux
&
Elizabeth of the Trinity

IGNATIUS PRESS   SAN FRANCISCO

Title of the German original:
Schwestern im Geist:
Therese von Lisieux und Elisabeth von Dijon
© 1970 Johannes Verlag
Published with ecclesiastical approval

Therese von Lisieux translated by
Donald Nichols and
Anne Elizabeth Englund

Elisabeth von Dijon translated by
Dennis Martin

Cover calligraphy by Victoria Hoke Lane

The most fervent Christians, the priests, find that we are too extreme, that we should serve with Martha instead of consecrating to the Lord the vessels of our lives with the ointments contained within them. But what does it matter if the vessels are broken, since Jesus is consoled and since, in spite of itself, the world is obliged to smell the perfumes flow forth, perfumes that serve to purify the poisoned air the world never ceases to breathe.

THÉRÈSE OF LISIEUX

CONTENTS

Elizabeth of the Trinity

FOREWORD TO
THE NEW EDITION

W HEN THE TWO WORKS that make up the present book
were published in 1950 and 1953, the meaning of contemplative life was, for the most part, not a matter of debate in
the Catholic Church. Today that meaning has become so obscure that even the orders living the contemplative life, including the Carmelites, have become uncertain. For most people
"openness to the world" makes sense only in the form of dialogue and directly experienced "sociability" accompanied by
practical goals and measurable successes. Yet did not the great
contemplative tradition, when it was fully Christian and evangelical, live out of a much deeper insight?—the insight that all
social actions smash into the same barrier Jesus encountered in
his active life, the insight that the world's steadily mounting
resistance can only be overcome when one gathers one's entire
existence together into a unitive yielding to God so that God
can ceaselessly marshal them on behalf of all men and women
in the service of his cosmic plan of salvation. Passion and contemplation, which are closely linked to each other, would thus
become an inward continuation of action, indeed, they would
become through the incarnation of God not merely the humanly extorted aim of action but the goal God planned from
the very beginning, the goal that Jesus freely affirmed in all
his activity. For God does not give himself in Christ merely
for the sake of a bit of dialogue and action among men and
women, rather God eucharistically pours himself out endlessly
in absolute love. His surrender "to the end" in crucifixion,
abandonment by God, and the path through hell took upon
itself all the world's resistance, destroyed it from within, and
buried it in the abyss. Anything shaped, spoken, or done first
bears fruit out of the Son's final, formless Yes to the Father,

9

a Yes in which the incarnation itself took place (Heb 10:7), a Yes that also fills the thirty hidden years, the forty days in the wilderness, the many nights of prayer-vigil, and the last struggle in Gethsemane. Finite man, including the man Jesus, has no other way to respond fully to the infinite will of God except with an absolute readiness, with a boundless *Fiat!* that permits one to be made more and more profoundly limitless, with the will to let oneself be led "where you do not wish to go" (Jn 21:18).

This forms the center of every Christian contemplative vocation, a vocation received first by the Mother of the Lord, who answered it with her own *Fiat!* Since her Son needs followers not only for the actions and organizations of his church, but to help complete his hidden position before the Father, there will always be a Mary who "chooses the best part" and desires to live solely to hear and carry out the divine word.

Far from being a flight from the world, Carmel and all purely contemplative forms of life in the church extrapolate the encounter between the world and the living God of Jesus Christ to its most radical point. In the language of scripture, "wilderness" means the dumbfounded nakedness and demonic decadence of a world stripped of her green finery, on the one hand, and a place of undistorted, unmitigated encounter with the living God, on the other hand: "a land naked and pitted, dried up and darkened, a land through which no man passes and in which no man dwells" (Jer 2:6) yet a land toward which God still "seductively" redirects his Bride in order to "speak to her heart-to-heart" (Hos 2:14). Origen and Antony already realized that the decisive battles of the Kingdom of God would be fought out in this "wilderness". How can it be that such a clear insight should be threatened with obscurity again and again through the centuries? Has there ever been a time when monastic communities have not needed reform? Yet oddly enough, the closer one comes to modernity and the more one considers both apostolic openness to the world and the fusion of contemplation and action to be exemplary even for religious orders, that much more clearly does the biblical basis for a purely contemplative life emerge from various spiritual and individualistic obscurities. Anticipated by the Rhenish and Spanish mystics, a final breakthrough, a quiet elucidation, takes place at the end of the nineteenth century in the two figures appearing here side-by-side as "sisters in the Spirit".

Thérèse of Lisieux and Elizabeth of the Trinity, who died at the age of twenty-four and twenty-six, respectively, understood the act of total surrender to the triune God as the highest possible form of engagement on behalf of the world's salvation. They knew that this calling burrowed itself into hiddenness even as roots disappear into the ground. Above ground the visible church and her activity feed from these roots. How foolish it would be to pull roots out of the ground "so that for once they can be exposed to light and sunshine"—for the tree would then wither away. Fully agreed in this basic realization, Thérèse and Elizabeth engage in an odd and fruitful opposition to each other inside their consensus. Their common concern is to devote their lives entirely to the reality of faith, to live "theological existences". But Thérèse wants scripture and dogma to take on flesh and blood in her existence, and this brings the accompanying risk that objective truth might disappear into existential truth, thereby reducing the framework of the church's great doctrine to the framework of an experienced "little way". In contrast, Elizabeth permits her entire existence to disappear into the truth of the Gospel to the extent that the overpowering objectivity of divine truth threatens to destroy her subjectivity. Each tries to be fully obedient to her own task but each actually remains dependent on a task that complements the task of the other. Each points to the other; they construct hemispheres that, fitted together, make Carmel's spiritual world round. Thérèse is subjectively stronger. Elizabeth knows her and builds on her but it is in Elizabeth, the one who is subjectively weaker and objectively stronger, that contemplative faith expands to its full biblical dimensions.

Missions that emanate from the center should not be eval-

uated by weighing them against each other. Ignatius expressly
forbids this (*Spiritual Exercises*, 364). One ought, however, to
confront them with each other, as Mary and Elizabeth, Francis
and Dominic encountered each other. Out of such encounters, by comparing spiritual things with spiritual things (1 Cor
3:13), one can gain joyous surprises and unhoped-for fruit.
Moreover, precisely in recent times, the Carmelite world has
been a favored place for encounters: Benedictines (Dom Vandeur wrote a celebrated commentary to Elizabeth's prayer),
Dominicans (Fr. Valléd, Fr. Petitot, Fr. Philipon and others),
Jesuits (e.g., E. Przywara), representatives of other orders and
of the secular clergy were able to feel at home and close to the
Carmelites. This is a sign that many branches can be nourished
from the same roots if the same task is faithfully carried out in
differing ways:

> Like a root out of dry ground,
> he had no form or comeliness that we should look at him,
> and no beauty that we should desire him.
> He was despised and rejected by men, . . .
> (Is 53:2–3a, RSV)

In the present edition the texts from Thérèse's *Story of a Soul*
have been reworked to correspond to the critical edition of her
autobiographical writings that has since appeared. Both parts
of the present book were carefully revised and improved in
many instances. I owe renewed thanks to Miss Cornelia Capol
for her assistance in that work.

HANS URS VON BALTHASAR

Thérèse of Lisieux

✤

ABBREVIATIONS

WORKS BY SAINT THÉRÈSE OF LISIEUX:

Ged   *Gedichte* [Poems]. Quoted from the French prewar edition of the work (Office Central, Lisieux), translated into German by the author.

GC   *General Correspondence.* Translated from the original manuscripts by John Clark, O.C.D. (Washington, D.C.: Institute of Carmelite Studies). Volume I: 1877–1890 (1982); volume II: 1890–1897 (1988).

H   *Histoire d'une âme* (Lisieux, 1923).

LC   *St. Thérèse of Lisieux: Her Last Conversations.* Translated by John Clarke, O.C.D. (Washington, D.C.: Institute of Carmelite Studies, 1977).

N   *Novissima Verba* (Office Central, Lisieux).

S   *Collected Letters.* Edited by Abbé Combes, translated by F. J. Sheed (New York: Sheed & Ward, 1949).

SS   *Story of a Soul: The Autobiography of St. Thérèse of Lisieux.* A new translation from the original manuscripts by John Clarke, O.C.D. (Washington, D.C.: Institute of Carmelite Studies, 1976).

T   *Saint Thérèse of Lisieux, the Little Flower of Jesus.* A revised translation of the definitive Carmelite edition of her autobiography and letters, together with the story of her canonization and an account of several of her heavenly roses, by the Rev. Thomas N. Taylor (New York: P. J. Kenedy, 1926).

Works about Saint Thérèse:

Co   André Combes, *Introduction à la spiritualité de sainte Thérèse de l'Enfant-Jésus.* Etudes de théologie et d'histoire de la spiritualité, I (Paris, 1946).

Esprit   *L'Esprit de la bienheureuse Thérèse de l'Enfant-Jésus.* D'après ses écrits et les témoins oculaires de sa vie (Office Central, Lisieux). For the most part, as quoted by Görres.

G   I. F. Görres, *Das verborgene Antlitz: Eine Studie über Therese von Lisieux* (Herder, 1944). (ET: English translation of the 8th revised edition: Ida Friederike Görres, *The Hidden Face: A Study of St. Thérèse of Lisieux* [Pantheon, 1959].)

P   Summary of the Process of beatification and canonization. As quoted by Görres.

Ph   M. M. Philipon, O.P., *Sainte Thérèse de Lisieux*, 2d ed. (Paris: Desclée, 1946).

Pl   Mgr. Paulot, *Le Message doctrinal de sainte Thérèse de l'Enfant-Jésus à la lumière de saint Paul* (Cerf, Juvisy, 1934).

Pt   H. Petitot, O.P., *Sainte Thérèse de Lisieux: Une Renaissance spirituelle* (Paris: Desclée, 1925).

NOTE ON
THIS TRANSLATION

I N HIS FIRST EDITION OF THIS WORK, von Balthasar quoted
from the early French editions of *Histoire d'une âme* and
Novissima Verba, translating these passages into German. In the
first English translation of this work, Donald Nichol also translated the passages from *Histoire d'une âme* and *Novissima Verba*
directly from the early French editions. In the third German
edition of this work, von Balthasar made revisions based on
the new, definitive French edition of *Histoire d'une âme* (see
footnote 21 in his Introduction to the section on Thérèse of
Lisieux for further information). Mr. Nichol's translation has
accordingly been revised to reflect these changes. For the English reader's convenience, footnote references have been given
to the most recent English edition of both works (*Story of a Soul*
and *Last Conversations*), although, in most cases, the translation
given here is somewhat different.

Von Balthasar used the Combes edition of the *Collected Letters*. In his English translation, Mr. Nichol quoted the Sheed
translation of that edition. Since von Balthasar made no changes
in these passages for his revised edition, the Sheed translation
(with occasional editorial revisions) has been retained in this
edition as well. For the English reader's convenience, however, references to the more recent ICS translation of the *General Correspondence* have been given as well.

INTRODUCTION

T HE CHURCH OF CHRIST, according to Saint Paul's words, is founded on "apostles and prophets" (Eph 2:20), on office and charisma—or, more precisely, since office should not be without charisma—on objective and subjective charisma, objective and subjective sanctity. It is because the Church has received the promise of objective sanctity (against which the gates of hell will never prevail), in her foundation and tradition, her sacraments and orders, that her divine mission is guaranteed until the end of time. But this in no way eliminates the obligatory vocation to subjective and personal sanctity, which is indeed the ultimate reason for her whole institutional and objective side. The office of the priest is for the sake of the community; the wellsprings of grace, the sacraments, are there for those who receive them; the word of God is there for its hearers. And the nearer a man is placed to the Church's springs of objective sanctity, whether as a priest or member of an order or as a custodian of some sacramental grace, the stricter is his obligation to conform to and prepare himself for that objective sanctity that he administers and preserves.

But the reverse is also true. Just as the subjective sanctity of her members is the aim of the institutional Church, similarly the Church is the only place where this aim can be realized. In the Church, and for the Church, which is herself for the world. Since the Church is the Body of Christ for all, and this Body is informed by the spirit of Christ in all its members as they conform themselves to the love of God and their fellow-men, to the complete expropriation of self. "God has proved his love to us by laying down his life for our sakes; we too must be ready to lay down our lives for the sake of our brethren" (1 Jn 3:16). Christ has no other motive in "sanctifying" himself than "that they also may be sanctified through the truth" (Jn 17:19). Subjectively, sanctity is identical with the

love that prefers both God and man before itself and therefore
lives for the community of the Church. "Love seeks not its
own" (1 Cor 13:5); a sanctity that sought its own and made self
its aim would be a self-contradiction. Yet, as a member of the
Church, the individual is not left to choose the way in which
he will surrender his self for the sake of the whole community;
otherwise something like a chaos of love would sweep over the
body of the Church. And the characteristic of love lies in its
interior order, just as the spirit of love that produces subjective
sanctity within the Church's objective framework at the same
time produces order within her offices and charismata.

> And yet there are different kinds of gifts, though it is the same
> Spirit who gives them, just as there are different kinds of service,
> though it is the same Lord we serve, and different manifesta-
> tions of power, though it is the same God who manifests his
> power everywhere in all of us. The revelation of the Spirit is
> imparted to each, to make the best advantage of it. One learns to
> speak with wisdom, by the power of the Spirit, another to speak
> with knowledge, with the same Spirit for his rule; one, through
> the same Spirit, is given faith; another, through the same Spirit,
> powers of healing; one can perform miracles, one can prophesy,
> another can test the spirit of the prophets; one can speak in dif-
> ferent tongues, another can interpret the tongues; but all this is
> the work of one and the same Spirit, who distributes his gifts as
> he will to each severally (1 Cor 12:4-11).

The mission that each individual receives contains within
itself the form of sanctity that has been granted to him and is
required of him. In following that mission, he fulfills his appropriate capacity for sanctity. This sanctity is essentially social and outside the arbitrary disposition of any individual. For
each Christian, God has an idea that fixes his place within the
membership of the Church; this idea is unique and personal,
embodying for each his appropriate sanctity. There is no danger that it will not prove high enough or broad enough in any

instance. Indeed, it is so sublime, so intimately bound to divine infinity, that it is perfectly achieved by no one except Mary. The Christian's supreme aim is to transform his life into this idea of himself secreted in God, this "individual law" freely promulgated for him by the pure grace of God.

In the prayer of Saint Thérèse: "I wish to fulfill your will perfectly and attain the degree of glory you have prepared for me in your Kingdom. In a word, I desire to be a saint".[1] The "fulfillment of God's will" does not mean carrying out an anonymous universal law that is the same for all; nor does it mean the slavish imitation of some fixed blueprint—like a child reproducing a pattern on tracing paper. On the contrary, it means freely realizing God's loving plan, which presupposes freedom, and is, moreover, the very source of freedom. No one is so much himself as the saint, who disposes himself to God's plan, for which he is prepared to surrender his whole being, body, soul and spirit.

In conceiving this idea of sanctity for us, God reckons with the unique nature, strength and capacity of each individual. Nevertheless, he deals with us freely, as a painter with the colors on his palette. We cannot foresee in advance which colors the painter will prefer, which he may use up, while scarcely touching others, or what mixtures he may decide upon to produce his overall effects. No more is it possible, by simply assessing a man's nature, to predict God's gracious intentions for him, the idea of sanctity to which he must conform or the sacrifices it will require of him—though we can predict quite certainly that sacrifices *will* be demanded of him, since all love involves self-denial. Each one of us has to experience and grow attentive to God's sanctifying will in prayer and meditation; outside prayer there is no means of discerning our path to sanctity. This is the foundation upon which the whole structure of the Ignatian Exercises rests: there each of us is told to "contemplate

[1] SS 276.

his life, to investigate and to ask in what kind of life or state his divine Majesty wishes to make use of us . . . and how we ought to dispose ourselves in order to arrive at perfection in whatever state or kind of life God our Lord shall propose for our election."[2]

But, besides the infinite shadings of personality displayed in the mission to sanctity, there are also certain typical differences. Without splitting sanctity up into crude divisions, one can say that there are two types. On the one hand, "customary" sanctity, by which the Christian fulfills his vocation through the normal, unspectacular round of the Church's life; on the other hand, a special type of sanctity, by which God singles out some individual for the good of the Church and the community as a model of sanctity. An example of the latter is Saint Paul, so convinced of his mission that he called upon the Church to look to him and imitate him as he himself imitated the Lord. He could do this because he was certain that he had not cast himself for this role but, contrary to all expectations, had been chosen as a "vessel of election" to occupy this vanguard position; indeed, he was aware that it would be disobedience for him not to respond to this command to "play"[3] and shine before the whole Church. Since Saint Paul, all those called to representative sanctity have enjoyed the same awareness about themselves: they are simply attending to a strict command of the Holy Spirit when they grasp their special mission and accomplish it in the face of the whole Church. Before anyone is singled out in this fashion, it is generally presupposed that he has made the evangelical renunciation that Jesus demands of all who wish to be his disciples in the strictest sense: to sell all they have and follow him, to enter by the narrow gate, receiving what only a few can receive. It means abandoning one's life, without any reserves, to the will and Kingdom of God. Abandoning every earthly attachment in this way trans-

---

[2] *Spiritual Exercises*, no. 155.   [3] I Cor 4:9.

forms one's life into that plastic material required by the hand of God if his hand is to form it freely. Moreover, one essential for these special missions is that they should be sanctioned by the Lord's words: "It was not you who chose me. It was I who chose you. The task I have appointed you is to go out and bear fruit, fruit that will endure" (Jn 15:16). Cases are not lacking in the Church's history of those who, without any call, have taken upon themselves a special mission; but they overreach and strain themselves, and their unauthentic note always betrays them. They always have to look outside God for the source of the energy they deem necessary to their peculiar mission. By contrast, those who are really singled out by God for a special purpose are obedience itself. In a word, they are not highflyers who have achieved more than most, simply through exceptional talents or efforts, or who have created an impression by their personal courage, leaving others to hesitate and stagnate in mediocrity. Not that even this aspect is devoid of truth, for sanctity demands courage, and many who were called have failed to respond through lack of it. But a more essential note in the office of special representative sanctity, such as was bestowed, for instance, on the great founders of Orders, is that it comes as a pure gift of God, which the receiver must appropriate to himself, for better or for worse.

This distinction between "customary" and "representative" sanctity is bound up with another distinction, though the two do not quite coincide. Within the Church, the Body of Christ, there are certain sanctifying impulses and missions that proceed from the body to the head and others that flow from the head to the body. And, although head and members form one single body, although Christ and the Church equally draw upon the same unique grace, the holiness of God, yet there remains a polarity within this unity. And this is demonstrated precisely within the varied types of sanctity. There are missions that flash across the dome of the Church like lightning from heaven and light up unmistakably some unique point of God's

will for the Church. On the other hand, there are missions
that arise from the womb of the Church, from the community
and the Orders, becoming a model for others through their
purity and fruitfulness. The first come from God and penetrate into the Church, which, in obedience to these stirrings
of the Holy Spirit, receives them and uses them to fertilize her
sanctity. The others, rooted in the Church, are like blossoms
nurtured in the graceful garden of the Church, which offers
them as first fruits to God. Both types of saint live upon the
same Holy Spirit, both belong to Christ and the Church; both
alike prove their Christian inspiration by their adherence to
the Church. But the first group is incomparably more distinc-
tive than the second. It includes those unmistakable types of
saints whom God sets as cornerstones of the Church, whom
he selects to serve for centuries as living interpretations of the
gospel. They are irrefutable, beyond questioning, as indivisible
as prime numbers. They proclaim whatever the Spirit of God
wishes to declare at that precise moment; for the Spirit of God,
blowing where it wills, discloses ever-new vistas of the endless
revelation. When those in the first group are canonized, it is
rather the Church bowing before the Lord; when the second
group is canonized, it is rather the Lord complying with the
just desires of the Church. And, because it is more important
for the Church to accept God's wishes than to seek his com-
mendation of her own, it is more important to light upon those
saints whom God has without question sent to serve as models. She must receive them and herself embody their message,
imploring God in virtue of the universal holiness of his Church
to send more such divine messengers, while at the same time
conceiving numberless similar saints of her own.

These direct missions from God all share the divine quality
of being perfectly concrete yet beyond comprehension. Comparable in this respect to God's nature, they are absolutely de-
terminate and unchangeable, while harboring boundless interior riches that ultimately transcend adequate definition or

determination. Which is precisely why they kindle such burning love within the Church and among the faithful in general.
Each of us discovers in them some quality that particularly attracts us, so that we penetrate more deeply into the meaning
of holiness, especially when theologians—and, indeed, anyone
who studies manifestations of holiness—reveal the fresh lights
that they are constantly seeing in them. Those saints who do
not belong to this group do not present this paradox, or at
least only insofar as all Christian living does. They represent
an intensification of customary virtues and are examples of the
Christian virtues brought to perfection; consequently, they are
set before the faithful in another manner, since these saints stem
from them and reflect them insofar as one can compare a natural
and a supernatural environment. Nevertheless, it is the saints of
the first group who become favorites of the faithful. Although
they are much less directly imitable, the Christian community
knows instinctively that they are God's great gifts to them—
not only as "patrons" whom one invokes for certain needs but
as the great warm centers of light and consolation sunk into the
heart of the Church by God. For the faithful, they are, above
all, a new type of conformity to Christ inspired by the Holy
Spirit and therefore a new illustration of how the gospel is to
be lived. For theologians, on the other hand, they are rather
a new interpretation of revelation; they bring out the scarcely
suspected treasures in the deposit of faith. Even when the saints
have not been theologians, nor themselves very learned, their
sheer existence proves to be a theological manifestation that
contains most fruitful and opportune doctrine, the directions
of the Holy Spirit addressed to the whole Church and not to
be neglected by any of her members. Not that anyone is bound
in conscience to have a devotion to some particular saint or
to believe in certain miracles or private revelations; nor are we
bound to accept the words or doctrine of some saint as the
authentic interpretation of God's revelation. But here we are
not dealing with that negative limitation that safeguards the

absolute uniqueness of Christ's revelation. In these saints, we are faced with a living and essential expression of the Church's tradition; it is true that this tradition is animated by the Holy Spirit, which in every age prompts those in apostolic office or in the hierarchy to *interpret* the scriptural revelation of Christ, but we should not forget that this prompting is equally urgent in the saints, who are the "living gospel". The objection that the Bible suffices is most superficial, for who is to measure the sufficiency of God's word? Who can withdraw his attention from those interpreters whom the Holy Spirit itself sets before the Church as authentically representing the meaning of Scripture? Our answer inevitably raises a demand for the most intimate penetration of hierarchy and holiness, as of speculative Scholastic theology and a theology of the saints. Only they can understand and interpret God's word who themselves live in the world of the saints. All the Church's theology is rooted in the period that stretches from the apostles into the Middle Ages, when the great theologians were also saints. Then life and doctrine, orthopraxy and orthodoxy were wedded; the one fertilized the other, and they brought forth much fruit. In modern times, theology and sanctity have become divorced, to the great harm of both. Except in a few cases, the saints have not been theologians, and theologians have tended to treat their opinions as a sort of by-product, classifying them as *spiritualité* or, at best, as *théologie spirituelle*. Modern hagiographers have contributed to this split by describing saints, their lives and their work almost exclusively from a historical and psychological viewpoint, as though they had no bearing upon the task of theology. This task, however, demands corresponding alterations in method: rather than consider the psychological unfolding from below, it should work out a sort of *supernatural phenomenology* of their mission from above. The most important fact about any great saint is his mission, the new charisma bestowed upon the Church by the Holy Spirit. The person who receives the mission is simply its servant—and a weak one at that—up to the very moment of its fulfillment. It is not the person but the witness, the office, that matters: "He himself was not the light but simply came to give witness to the light." All the saints—they especially—realize how inadequately they fulfill their mission, and they are to be taken seriously when they insist on their inadequacy. What matters about them is not their personal "heroic achievement" but the resolute obedience with which they have utterly surrendered themselves to serving a mission and have come to see their very existence in the light of it. We must bring to light what they wished to bring to light, what they were bound to: their representation of Christ and the Scriptures. We should leave in obscurity what they wished to leave in obscurity: their poor personalities. Therefore we should strive to penetrate through their holiness to understand their message from God to the Church, trying as far as possible to distinguish between their holy mission and their inadequate realization of it. Not that the two can be separated, for the mission's incarnation takes place precisely in their persons, their history and psychology, and in all those little anecdotes and details that characterize saintly lives. The living, concrete reality must not be transformed into a series of abstract concepts, into a depersonalization of what is uniquely personal, for we can only reach toward a person's essence [his *Gestalt*] by means of the phenomenological method, discerning it in its concrete manifestations, *intelligibile in sensibili*. And we must remember that here the *intelligibile* is something supernatural, the discernment of which presupposes faith or even a participation in the life of sanctity.

In a saint, it is primarily the mission that is perfect; only secondarily is he himself described as perfect, insofar as he integrates the whole of his gifts and strength into fulfilling his mission. Many have grasped their mission joyfully, taking it, so to speak, on the wing; others have undertaken it hesitatingly, almost reluctantly—but the mission proved too strong and compelled them to serve it. Some, at the cost of their flesh and blood, have allowed its complex demands to lay hold on every single fiber of their persons; others have been content to accept the essential demands, leaving many corners of their selves untouched and empty. For the kingdom of the saints knows many degrees, from the lowest limit, where the integrity of a mission is just preserved, to the highest level of all, where the mission and the person become indistinguishable. The Mother of God alone has reached that level.

There can be no doubt that Thérèse of Lisieux was directly entrusted by God with a mission to the Church. The very first sentence of Pius XI's speech at her beatification expressly refers to it: "The voice of God and the voice of his people have joined in extolling the Venerable Thérèse of the Child Jesus. The voice of God first made itself heard, and the faithful, recognizing the divine call, added their voices to the anthem of praise. We repeat, the voice of God was the first to speak."[4] One may even say (although all such formulations are somewhat dangerous, because they skirt the shadowy limits where the two types of sanctity run together) that Thérèse and the Curé d'Ars were the only two perfectly evident instances during the nineteenth century of a primarily theological mission, in the sense that we have so far given to this term (Catherine Labouré and Bernadette were both entrusted with a more restricted task, while Don Bosco and Gemma Galgani do not quite achieve the fullness of a primarily theological mission). And, as no other instances have occurred since, the judgment of the faithful agrees with the saying of Pius XI that Thérèse is the greatest saint of modern times.

Thérèse's mission, at the very first glance, displays the marks of a clearly defined and quite exceptional character. This is much less due to the personal drama of the little saint than to the sacred form into which the trickling grains of petty anec-

[4] T 267-68.

dotes are compressed, into a hard, unbreakable block, by a firm, invisible hand. It is contrary to all expectation that the simple, modest story of this little girl should eventually culminate, as it irrefutably does, in the enunciation of theological truths. Originally she herself never dreamed that she might be chosen to bear some fundamental message to the Church. She became aware of it only gradually; in fact, it did not occur to her until her task was almost completed, after she had already lived out her teaching and was writing the last chapters of her book. Suddenly, as she saw it all laid out before her, she recognized its strangeness, that in her obedience she had unwillingly conceived something beyond her own personality. And now that she saw it, she also understood it and seized it with a kind of violence. Ever since her childhood, Thérèse had shown a striking inclination to meditating and reflecting upon herself. Which meant that when she discovered her mission, she became intensely conscious of it in a manner rare among the saints. At that moment she realized she was to be set on a pedestal and that every bit of her life, even its smallest details, would be used as a pattern for many of the "little ones". She scrutinized her relationship to others who also had great missions and aligned her own mission with that of Joan of Arc. "For my mission, as for Joan of Arc's, the will of God will be carried out despite the envy of men."[5] She defined the content of her message ever more exactly, searching for more and more compact formulae for her doctrine of the little way. She attached great significance to the publication of her manuscript; she knew "that all the world will love me" and that her writings "will do a great deal of good".[6] During her last months, as if making her last will and testament, she repeated constantly: "One must tell souls. . . ." Exactly the same expressions recurred in reference to the mission she was soon to begin in heaven: "I feel that my mission will soon begin—to teach souls to love God as I love

[5] N 94-95 (LC 113).   [6] N 107-8 (LC 126).

him, to give them my 'little way'. If my wishes are realized, I shall spend my heaven on earth until the end of the world."[7] And, when her sister Pauline asked her what this little way was into which souls must be led, she answered with the deepest sense of her responsibility: "It is the way of spiritual childhood, the way of trust and total surrender. I will bring to them the little means that have served me so perfectly. . . ."[8] Similarly she recognized the function within the Church of her mission. She not only foresaw the proclamation of her own sanctity— she was always aware of being "a saint" and never pretended otherwise, as is shown in her distributing her own relics, or at least not objecting to their distribution, as she lay on her deathbed; crucifix, pictures, rose petals, even her hair, nails, tears and eyelashes. But she also, as it were, foresaw the canonization of her doctrine. The two are not separable—it is not so much her writings as her life itself that is her doctrine, especially since her writings speak about her life more than anything else. Nor did she hesitate to propose her life as an example for the Church, because it was in her life that she saw the realization of that doctrine that "can do so much good". She is to be counted as one of those who, in the phrase of Marie-Antoinette de Geuser, are "expropriated in order to be ready for public use". So her life only contains exemplary value for the Church insofar as the Holy Spirit possessed her and used her in order to demonstrate something for the sake of the Church, opening up new vistas onto the Gospels. That, and that alone, should be the motive for the Church's interest in Thérèse. That, and that alone, should engage the attention of those who feel themselves put off by many features of her cultus, or even of her character, or who experience indefinable objections to them. In fact, there are few other cases in which it is so prudent to distinguish between the mission of a saint and its inessentials. For instance, I have already mentioned one of Thérèse's

[7] N 81 (LC 102).   [8] N 82–83 (LC 257).

permanent characteristics—her self-reflection: this cannot be counted an essential. Indeed, I hope to show how unfortunate circumstances to some extent intensified this habit and how she came to resemble a patient in the demonstration-theater, who follows and takes to heart the observations that the professor is making to his students about the case. She became inclined, therefore, to forget that she had to remain a neutral object and not to take everything personally; she took as personal what was meant to be simply objective. This means that the spectator's vision may momentarily become blurred; which proves irritating to many. It will be shown later how far Thérèse was responsible for her "self-canonization" and how far it was her own family who laid the foundations for her cult in Carmel during her very lifetime. But it is all the more important not to indulge Thérèse's inclination to self-reflection by conducting prolonged psychological, perhaps even psychopathological, analyses—rather, to stand off a little in order to keep one's gaze on the objective mission. Clearly Thérèse makes this no easy task. But, as I have insisted, it is no solution to seek for explanations solely at the personal and psychological level. That would prove vain with every saint; but it is doubly impossible with Thérèse, whose mission it was to expound her "way". The only sure procedure is painstakingly to allow each detail of her biography to sketch out the trajectory of her mission. And this movement from the biographical and personal to the dogmatic level in the exposition of Thérèse's sanctity rests upon the authority of the Church. I have quoted Pius XI's statement on her divine mission; he goes on to describe her as "una cosa venuta di cielo in terra a miracolo mostrare". And he puts the question: "What is the word that God wishes to say to us? What does the little Thérèse wish to say to us, who allowed herself to be transformed into a word of God? For God speaks in her work. . . ."[9] Pius XI goes a step farther in his homily

[9] T 270.

at the Mass of her canonization; after having referred to the
Gospels as the basis for her doctrine of spiritual childhood, he
continues:

> The new saint, Thérèse, had thoroughly learned this teaching of
> the Gospels and translated it into her daily life. Moreover, she
> taught the way of spiritual childhood by word and example to the
> novices of her convent. She set it forth clearly in all her writings,
> which have gone to the end of the world and which assuredly no
> one has read without being charmed or without reading them
> again and again with great joy and much profit. . . . In her cate-
> chism lessons, she drank in the pure doctrine of faith; from the
> golden book of *The Imitation of Christ*, she learned asceticism; in
> the writings of Saint John of the Cross, she found her mystical
> theology. Above all, she nourished heart and soul with the in-
> spired word of God, on which she meditated assiduously, and the
> Spirit of Truth taught her what he hides as a rule from the wise
> and prudent and reveals to the humble. Indeed, God enriched
> her with a quite exceptional wisdom, so that she was enabled to
> trace out for others a sure way of salvation.[10]

In a similar sense, the day after her canonization, Pius XI spoke
of a "new message" or "new mission",[11] and the canonization
Bull itself refers to "a new model of sanctity";[12] in a letter,[13]
the Pope speaks of her as a "master" in matters of spiritual
teaching; the *decretum de tuto* for the canonization had already
laid it down that the canonization "extends beyond the person
of Thérèse".[14]

For a long time, these words of the Pope have gone un-
heeded. The best-known and most impressive studies devoted
to Thérèse in recent times have confined themselves mainly
to the categories of history and biography or psychology and

---

[10] T 273. The concluding words are a quotation from the address of Benedict
XV on August 14, 1921.

[11] T 276.   [12] T 278.

[13] Letter to Cardinal Vico, papal legate in Lisieux, May 14, 1923.

[14] March 29, 1925, 180f.

asceticism. Along these lines, a number of well-known books have been produced that attack the sugary, sickly descriptions of the little saint in order to reveal her genuine stature but that, on account of their method of study, have restricted themselves to unearthing what they conceive to be "historical truth". This literature displays two constant tendencies. The first is toward making "revelations". In the not unjustifiable belief that many painful and bitter incidents in Thérèse's convent life had been glossed over by her sisters on grounds of charity, a veritable storm of protest has arisen against the "deceptions" of the official biographies, and people have outbid one another in presenting tragic and, in some ways, shocking, scandalous details. The second tendency follows directly from the first: the picture of Thérèse seemed to acquire depth and strength if one penetrated behind the smiling, modest "little way" to the superhuman and tragic aspects of her destiny and suffering, nakedly unfolding before the reader's eyes the bloody sacrifices that Thérèse herself, out of Christian forgiveness, had preferred to conceal.[15]

This psychological approach has been so much overdone

[15] The first to attempt this method of "psychological revelation" was the Capuchin Father Ubald d'Alençon in his "Sainte Thérèse comme je l'ai connue" (Barcelona: Estudios Franciscanos, 1926). His essay would have been buried forever in an inaccessible Catalan review if Lucie Delarue-Mardrus had not reedited it along with a bilious commentary of her own (La Petite Thérèse de Lisieux [1937], a follow-up of her Sainte Thérèse de Lisieux [Paris, 1925]). Using the same psychological method, Ghéon and Bernoville, each after his own fashion, conducted a campaign against the sugary piety issuing from Lisieux. Bernoville did so by dramatizing certain episodes in Thérèse's life; Ghéon, philosophizing over pious excrescences, tried to show why Thérèse had to hide behind this façade and accommodate herself to contemporary fashion, although the real person behind the mask was quite different. In two later works, this psychological method was taken to its farthest limits—so far, indeed, as to make it obvious that the limits of profitable research along these lines had been reached. These are the important studies by Ida Friederike Görres (Das Verborgene Antlitz [Herder, 1944]; new, revised and enlarged edition: Das Senfkorn von Lisieux [Freiburg, 1957; and as a pocketbook by Herder, no. 192]; English translation: The Hidden Face [New York: Pantheon, 1959]), and Maxence van der Meersch (La Petite Sainte Thérèse [Paris: Albin Michel, 1947, 1950: 55 thousand]). Van der Meersch, who was

that it needs complementing and correcting by the principles of theology. The way for this was already skillfully prepared by the balanced pioneering work of H. Petitot, O.P.: *Sainte*

Léon Bloy's grandnephew, depicts an impressionistic portrait of Thérèse on which the apocalyptic figure of Bloy throws its shadows. Like the masterly storyteller that he is, van der Meersch introduces racial and temporal considerations into his dynamic biography, making every possible use of "revelations" in order to present Thérèse as if she were the grandiose heroine of some classical tragedy. The whole story is feverishly intensified and therefore, despite its striking effects, falsified. To appreciate this, one only needs to read the passage in which he tries to distill the essence of the "little way": "In our opinion it means, quite simply, this: to accept one's weakness, even to accept one's ruin; and finally, for all the remorse, to accept one's very denials and sins. Let the strong pursue victory, let them strive to override obstacles; it is their privilege and their duty. But the weak ones have, in their very weakness, to make their poor efforts, hesitating and powerless, even though they know beforehand that it will mean defeat in the end. Their defeat will be their victory. To human eyes, they are ruined—yet God will not notice either their denials or their sins but only their efforts. That seems to us the true meaning—unadorned but unquestionable— of the little way of childhood." No argument is necessary to prove that Thérèse (who herself does not speak of sin, for instance) would never have recognized her own thought in this passage!

Literary gifts of the same high order have also been placed at the service of the little saint by Ida Görres. She too places most stress upon biographical and psychological factors, and her handling of them constitutes the main strength of her work. Görres has drawn upon every available source and document in order to fill out the picture of Thérèse, to which she adds both depth and richness. So carefully and minutely does she portray the family milieu (which has formed the subject of a separate study by P. Piat, O.F.M.: *Histoire d'une famille*) and the convent background that Thérèse seems to spring to life in the midst of it; and many aspects of her writings that had previously seemed colorless are suddenly thrown into unexpected relief. But, whereas van der Meersch dresses Thérèse up as a rabid revolutionary of the gospel in the Léon Bloy style, Görres sees her in the light of German personalism.

Both these authors take her rejection of "great deeds" and "great asceticism" as their starting point, stressing this negative thesis of the "little way" to set off the positive side of the picture. As far as van der Meersch is concerned, this negative thesis is an expression of the way Thérèse unmasks Phariseeism, that of one's own heart above all—its "profound and irremediable perversity", "for

Thérèse de Lisieux, une renaissance spirituelle (1925). This author reaches to the heart of Thérèse's life by the exemplary care with which he proceeds from one point to the next in accordance with the plan of her own doctrine. Nor does he succumb to the temptation of allowing the ideal of his own Order to color his picture of Thérèse; the hand of the experienced follower of Saint Thomas is only to be traced in his prudent description of sanctity as the "golden mean".[16]

P. M. Philipon, O.P. (in *Sainte Thérèse de Lisieux, une voie*

---

unknown monsters lurk in the depths of us all". Thus Thérèse is the supreme genius in self-knowledge, the most profound psychologist of recent times (180, 187, 189). In accordance with the ideals of the *Jugendbewegung*, Ida Görres takes as her negative thesis the breakaway from ecclesiastical and ascetical formalism and the rediscovery of personal integrity. With a tremendous liveliness, and touches of genius, Görres pours out her criticism of the bourgeois piety prevalent in the family milieu and the reactionary convent and of the threadbare theological teaching on the states of life. She especially criticizes the practice by which girls of seventeen had to make a choice for life between the convent and marriage. But, since Görres does not introduce the distinction between the person and the mission, she has to resort to depth psychology in order to bring out her heroine's greatness. This leads to obvious misinterpretations, so that, in spite of her brilliant account of Thérèse's personal life and milieu, Görres' work is inadequate on the theological side. In the new, revised and expanded edition of her book, I. F. Görres takes into consideration the original texts that have appeared in the meantime. She finds they do not vary significantly from the earlier versions. Therefore, she has not changed the basic features of her earlier interpretation. Her intention can be clearly inferred from the motto from Nietzsche's "Will to Power" with which she begins her book: "What am I protesting against? That one does not take this little, peaceful mediocrity, this balance of a soul, which does not know the powerful impetus of great exertions, as something lofty, possibly even as the measure of the person."

[16] One other study of the saint primarily concerned with her doctrine is that from the pen of an anonymous Benedictine, *Sainte Thérèse de l'Enfant-Jésus, considérée comme amante de la Bible, docteur de la voie d'enfance spirituelle et Seraphin d'amour* (Bruges: C. Byaert, 1934). But the author of this attractive volume shows few signs of synthesizing ability, and his work is inferior to Petitot's. His chief title to praise is that he was the first to call attention to Thérèse's use of

toute nouvelle, 1946),[17] has laid down the principles that will
have to be followed if an objective exposition is to replace this
exaggerated psychologizing of Thérèse. The first need for all
serious hagiography is a delicate awareness of the theological
issues. "Everyone naturally demands that a neurologist who
is telling us about one of his patients should know his psy-
chiatry, but no one seems to assume that a person has to be
a theologian before speaking of God's workings in the souls
of saints."[18] He goes on: "Theology's task is not only to an-
alyze the articles of the Creed; it must seize upon all the de-

---

Scripture, though his exposition contains no critical evaluation. A volume in the
series *Présences, Une Sainte parmi nous* (Plon, 1937), contains homage to Thérèse
from several contemporary writers. One does not need to be told that contribu-
tions by such men as Stanislas Fumet, Gustave Thibon, J. Maligne, J. Madaule,
Daniel-Rops, etc., afford a wealth of insights into Thérèse's importance to the
contemporary world and to France in particular. Several vital points in Thérèse's
theological development have been clarified for us by André Combes in his studies of Thérèse. In his *Introduction à la spiritualité de sainte Thérèse de l'Enfant-Jésus*
(*Études de théologie et d'histoire de la spiritualité*, ed. Gilson and Combes [Paris:
Vrin, 1946] [English trans.: *The Spirituality of St. Thérèse: An Introduction* (New
York: P. J. Kenedy, 1950)]) and in *Sainte Thérèse de l'Enfant-Jésus et la souffrance*
(Paris: Vrin, 1948), Combes has produced a series of detailed, careful studies
of what Thérèse means when she speaks about love, vocation, the apostolate,
prayer and meditation and of how her conception of suffering and the little way
develops. Combes' studies are of the first importance on account of his scholarly
method and concern for chronology; unfortunately, an excess of rhetoric often
obscures the real point of his discoveries. Combes' 1954 work, *Sainte Thérèse de
Lisieux et sa mission. Les Grandes lois de la spiritualité thérèsiennes* (Paris-Brussels,
Editions Universitaires) is a kind of theological synthesis. Msgr. Paulot, Vicar
General of Rheims, wrote a dogmatic work in 1934: *Message doctrinal de sainte
Thérèse de l'Enfant-Jésus à la lumière de saint Paul* (Juvisy, Ed. du Cerf). This study,
which begins well but then becomes rather lost in edifying panegyric, calls for
an investigation into the relationship between Thérèsian and Pauline theology,
by a comparison not only of isolated expressions but of the whole structure of
their theology.

[17] Presented in a shorter, more popular form as *Le Message de Thérèse de Lisieux*
(Bonne Presse, 1946).
[18] Ph 8.

tails in the long history of God's revelation to the world and awaken in us a conception of God's plan not only in the external events of the world but also in his secret guiding of souls. It extends into the whole history of the Church's life of grace and of the whole Mystical Body of Christ." And it is precisely the advances in psychology that call the theologian to take the results of this science into account in order to open the way to a new theological hagiography. "Our Scholastic theology, which only too often remains abstract and schematic, would greatly profit from more profound research into the psychology of the saints, provided that its explanations are based on theological principles and not simply on external description. This is true, above all, where the mission is not only that of a holy life but also of a doctrine, as with John of the Cross, Francis de Sales and many of the founders of Orders." The appropriate method is difficult—indeed, it has yet to be worked out—"In order to understand the souls of saints, one must see them with the vision of God himself"[19] —and this requires a certain indefinable combination of love and criticism, of intimacy and distance, of sympathy and abstraction. And Philipon sees clearly that "with the saints, as with all great masters, even their remotest visions may be traced back to a few decisive, original insights that serve to integrate their souls in the way that first principles unify a science. Once they are grasped, one has the key to the whole."[20]

On the one hand, therefore, we have the psychologists dramatizing Thérèse's life, intensifying its incidents and casting its blackest shadows over her surroundings and into her darkness and anxiety. On the other hand, the theologians seem frequently to leave everything in a well-lit world without shad-

[19] Ph 23.

[20] "In Thérèse's spirituality, these principles can be reduced to four or five themes whose all-embracing influence reaches into the smallest acts of her life. These are littleness, love, trust and self-surrender, fidelity, . . . all themselves reducible to the essence of Thérèse's mission: spiritual childhood" (Ph 13).

ows, to which her life serves as an introduction, a perfect illustrated guide to the theology of the "virtues".

This very contrast does perhaps reveal that both sides share a common assumption that goes unnoticed but makes it impossible for them to bring their subject to life without affectation. I mean the assumption that, because a saint is canonized and is declared to have practiced the virtues in a "heroic" degree, all his actions and thoughts, and even more his life as a whole, must be accorded the epithet "perfect", an epithet that is taken to mean the same, and have the same richness and application, for every single saint (for the moment we will not mention what Thérèse herself had to say about this criterion in her own teaching). Even when it is admitted that there are different paths to sanctity, different characters and destinies among the saints, people still feel obliged to assert that this wealth of possible forms of sanctity in no way affects their notion of sanctity, since, for them, sanctity and complete perfection are synonymous terms, and to say "perfect" is to fix a *non plus ultra*. But, as I have said before, this is not the case—as one quickly realizes if one thinks of the common sinners and the canonized saints and brings to mind the untold shades of grey separating the black from the white sheep; this continuous gradation makes it impossible to say at what point in the "scale of perfection" a Christian actually becomes worthy of canonization. This being so, the scale will continue through many gradations even among those who are canonized. God forbid that we should attempt to work out these gradations! But it is a help simply to recognize that the saints themselves retain their weaknesses, perhaps even their sins; and, what is for the moment more important, the truth that their missions are not always the same enables us to see the drama of their lives, and the light and shadow in their characters, much more authentically than we could do by misplaced psychologizing. There are saints who are canonized on account of a single act —the martyrs. Even among those not martyrs, there are some who by a single act of surrender to God in the middle of their lives have then been borne along to the end of their lives by the very force of that single act, which, so to speak, took control of them. There are some who have heard their call as a ringing trumpet blast and have remained faithful to it even in the face of the solid phalanx of worldly or ecclesiastical opponents—Joan of Arc, for instance. But there are others whose mission, being so arranged as to require the sympathetic cooperation of their fellows in order to come to fruition, has been corrupted by their sins and hardheartedness. Not that this corruption was able to reach the core of their mission; it has, however, visibly hindered its healthy growth and final fruition.

In the case of Thérèse of Lisieux, the dramatic tension between her mission and her person needs especially to be borne in mind and to be appreciated primarily in theological terms (without of course excluding the application of psychology). This has been the aim of the following study: an attempt at theological phenomenology. I believe, with Philipon, that few things are so likely to vitalize and rejuvenate theology, and therefore the whole of Christian life, as a blood transfusion from hagiography. Yet this must be done as a work of theology; the essence of sanctity has to be grasped as truly evangelical, as belonging to the Church, as a mission and not simply as an individual ascetical, mystical manifestation. And even if the present attempt comes to be regarded as a failure, still that would not invalidate the method employed. But, if it proves successful, then it may be of some importance for the mind of the Church and for the Church's saints in the present and future. For not only has reverence for the saints among the people of most countries suddenly become very slight; even *knowledge* of them has almost vanished. And very little is being done to refresh the memories of the people. The old accounts of saints, even when they are obtainable, would not satisfy the Christians of today and tomorrow. The artificial isolation into which saints were thrust by their sentimental baroque hagiographers has alienated our contemporaries. Moreover, it is not just because of contemporary "needs" but because of the depth of revealed truth that portraits of the saints must in the future be remodeled, so that the saints can again live among us, and in us, as the best protectors and inspirers of the *Communio sanctorum*, which is the Church, but one that reaches beyond the visible to the redemption of the world.[21]

---

[21] After the first edition of this book, which had to utilize the earlier editions of the *Story of a Soul*, appeared in 1950, the critical edition of the *Manuscrits autobiographiques de Sainte Thérèse de l'Enfant Jésus* finally appeared in print in 1956. Under the careful direction of the indefatigable, prematurely deceased Father François de Sainte-Marie, O.C.D., it appeared simultaneously in a four-volume facsimile and in a one-volume printed edition (Carmel de Lisieux). This edition was very accurately translated into German by Otto Iserland and Cornelia Capol (*Selbstbiographische Schriften* [Einsiedeln: Johannes Verlag, 1958]). This brought an end to the painful uncertainty about the main texts. In this new edition of my book, all quotations from the autobiographical text, insofar as they appeared there, were rewritten to correspond to the authentic original text. As far as the letters are concerned, A. Combes had already provided a critical and complete edition in 1948. Some uncertainty remains as to the degree of authenticity of those sayings collected from persons around Thérèse and then added to her writings: (1) the "Novissima Verba"; (2) the report of Thérèse's death (the twelfth chapter of the *Story of a Soul*; (3) the collection entitled "Counsels and Reminiscences"; (4) a few scattered bits in chapters 1–11 of the *Story of a Soul*, which cannot be found in the definitive edition but nevertheless give the impression of being authentic. They were presumably added here and there by the Sisters, from their own recollections. This additional material, of which we cannot be entirely certain, generally fits perfectly into what is known to be authentic, without adding anything really new.

Just a few of the "Novissima Verba" sound a little forced. After the appearance of the critical edition, Father Victor de la Vierge, O.C.D., brought out a balanced portrait of Thérèse's life and doctrine: *Réalisme spirituel de Sainte Thérèse de Lisieux* (Lethellieux, 1956). Only after my second edition was completed did I become aware of the comprehensive work by Conrad De Meester, O.C.D.: *Dynamique de le confiance. Genèse et structure de la "voie d'enfance spirituelle" chez Ste. Thérèse de Lisieux* (Paris: Ed. du Cerf, 1969). It contains a comprehensive bibliography. A discussion of my book is found on pages 185–89.

I

THE ESSENTIAL

TRUTH

T HÉRÈSE OF THE CHILD JESUS seems like a person whom we can see summoning all her energies in order to wrestle against something whose form is only dimly outlined and whose hostility we scarcely perceive. Not until the last years, when she herself came to realize that she had conquered in the fight, does the face of the enemy become visible to us, and perhaps also to her: it is the great lie. Lying in all the forms it can assume within Christendom, the veneer of truth overlaying deep deception, genuine spiritual poverty mingling with contemptible weakness, pious trash beside real art, sanctity and bigotry, all inextricably bound together. It was Thérèse's destiny to have to thread her way through all this; she was not only committed to being misunderstood both in life and death but often enough gave occasion for that misunderstanding. She had to fight against her time with the weapons of her time, fighting against pious trash with the aid of trashy pictures and words, throwing off her false skin without, however, being either willing or able to abandon her hereditary background.

And so her life becomes a continual battle, which she readily and frequently compares with the battles of her friend Joan of Arc yet which (apart from the heresy trial) was far harder to conduct than any battle with material weapons. Thérèse fights with the sword of the spirit against the powers of darkness, with the sword of truth against the serried ranks of lies that secretly encompass her about on every side. A tender plant with weak roots, she yet manages to force her way through the hardest rocks and finally to split them apart. Truth is the touchstone of her love, which is therefore brought into the province of theology. But truth in her case has all the richness, strength and decisiveness that one finds in the words of Holy Scripture: truth as a witness to the light of God illuminating the farthest reaches of one's being. Her whole life becomes an exposition of God's word, a sacrifice of all her own truth to the unique

truth of God within her. That is her obedience, and it bestows
her mission upon her.

"In Carmel, one is not allowed to strike false coins in order
to buy souls."[1] Here, where the truth of love is in question,
no "form" can suffice; there can be no confidence in the efficacy of "forms". "Do you think you can satisfy our Lord with
one of your nicely composed devotions? No. Words are not
enough. In order really to be a victim of love, one must utterly
surrender oneself."[2] Truth must be realized in action. "The
most beautiful thoughts are nothing without good works."[3]
In this way, Thérèse protected herself from ever writing any
statement that she herself had not tested and that she was not
translating into deeds as she was writing. She had lived her "system" before formalizing it.[4] "I am writing about sisterly love,
which gives me plenty of opportunity to practice it. Mother,
love of one's neighbor is everything in this world. We only love
God insofar as we practice love of our neighbor." "Just now I
was writing about charity, and very often the nuns came and
disturbed me. I tried not to become impatient, so as to put into
practice what I was writing."[5] She not only achieves truth, she
suffers it and is grateful for the opportunity to witness through
suffering to the truth of her teaching. "Everything that I have
written about my longing to suffer is really true."[6] "Now I
feel that everything I have said or written is in every respect
true. It is true that I wished to suffer much for the good God,
and it is true that I still wish it."[7] That is the crucible of truth.
"O Mother, what does it mean to write down beautiful sentiments about suffering? Nothing—nothing. We must suffer
if we are to know what all these longings are worth."[8] "I,
who have desired for myself every imaginable way of martyrdom—oh—we have to be in that way before we know what it

[1] N 57 (LC 82).   [2] H 282 (T 311).
[3] SS 234.   [4] G 285 (ET 229).
[5] N 36 (LC 66).   [6] N 194 (LC 205).
[7] N 187 (LC 200).   [8] N 186 (LC 199–200).

means."[9] That shows how seriously God takes the love of truth on the part of his saints.

This search for truth had been her lot from the beginning. Even as a child, she could not bear to be in a false situation. Twice she insists that she used to see her faults immediately and just as quickly seek forgiveness.[10] The same love of truth characterizes her later account of her youth; she desires "to tell quite simply what the good God has done for her without attempting to conceal his gifts, . . . not maintaining, under the pretext of humility, that she was without charm and sweetness . . . while knowing the contrary all the time".[11] Later she was to become well known for speaking the truth without any trimmings: "What does it matter if people don't love me on that account? If people don't want to hear the truth, then they should not come to me."[12] She draws aside all the veils that are intended, either from sympathy or worldliness, to conceal the realities. "I have never behaved like Pilate, who refused to hear the truth. Always I have said to the good God: O God, I will listen to you gladly; I beg of you to answer me when I humbly ask you: What is the truth? Make me see things as they are. Let nothing cause me to be deceived."[13] And, in Manuscript B, when she unfolds her tremendous vision of love in the Church, of that total love into which she herself desires to be transformed, it is as though the vision takes away her breath for a moment, and she has to test the radiance of what she has seen in the lens of truth: "But is this pure love truly in my heart? Is my infinite longing not a dream and an illusion? Oh, if it is, then enlighten me! You know that I am seeking only the truth."[14]

She penetrates straight through all triviality and counterfeit to the simple, naked truth of the gospel.

[9] 2 P 828 (G 469 [ET 374]).   [10] SS 18–19, 22.
[11] SS 15.   [12] H 297 (T 324).
[13] N 87 (LC 105).   [14] SS 197.

> What does me a lot of good when I think of the Holy Family is to imagine a life that was very ordinary. It wasn't everything they have told us or imagined. Such as the story that the Child Jesus modeled a little bird out of clay and breathed upon it, so that it came to life. . . . In that case, why were they not transported to Egypt by a miracle—that would at least have been useful and not at all difficult for the good God. They would have been there in the twinkling of an eye. But no, that did not happen. Their life was the same as ours.[15]

Here the truth of the Incarnation is in question and therefore the truth of our whole life, which is only true when it is lived through to its utmost depths as it comes to us from its source, the Savior. Men always believe that they are supposed to attribute to the Lord every imaginable, superhuman "perfection"; and the fact that they do so may even be a token of their admiration. Yet ultimately this perfection lies in that very humility and love by which he became like us in everything except sin. For he was obedient unto death, learning this obedience through suffering.

And what pious nonsense has been talked in the name of Mariology! Rather as if she herself were wielding the thong of cords at the purification of the temple, Thérèse ruthlessly kicks aside all the heaps of pious, well-meant untruths that have been wished upon the Mother of the Lord and in the end leave souls unnourished and prevent them from drinking the living waters.

> All the sermons on Mary I have heard have left me cold. . . . How I should love to have been a priest in order to preach about the Mother of God! I believe that just *one* sermon would have been enough for me to show what I mean. I would begin by showing how the life of the Mother of God is, in fact, very little known. One should not relate improbable stories about her, such as, for instance, that she went to the temple when she was a child of only three years in order to offer herself to God, because she was so full of burning love and extraordinary fervor. Perhaps she

[15] N 148–49 (LC 159).

went there quite simply out of obedience to her parents. . . . If a sermon on Mary is to bear fruit, it must give a genuine picture of her life, as we are allowed to glimpse it in the Gospels, instead of something imagined. And it is surely easy to sense that her life in Nazareth and later must have been perfectly ordinary. "He was subject to them." How simple that is! The Mother of God is depicted as unapproachable. Whereas one ought to show how she is to be imitated by the practice of hidden virtues; one ought to say that, just like ourselves, she lived by faith and cite the references for this in the Gospels, where we read: "And they did not understand what he said to them." Or again: "His father and mother were amazed at the things that were said of him."[16]

A priest had written in a letter that Mary had known no physical pain. Thérèse's love of the truth could not stand that kind of "homage".

This evening as I was contemplating the Mother of God, I realized that it is not true. I realized that she suffered not only in soul but also in body. She suffered a great deal from cold, heat and weariness during their journeys. Frequently she must have fasted. Yes, she knows well enough what it means to suffer. And good Saint Joseph . . . admittedly his work prevented him from fasting. But I see him wielding his plane and wiping the sweat from his brow now and again. How much trouble and disappointment he had to face! How often people reproached him. And how often they refused to pay him for his work. We should be amazed if only we knew what they had to put up with.[17]

And once more she protests against a meaningless way of honoring Mary.

We know well enough that the Mother of God is the Queen of heaven and earth; but she is more Mother than Queen. One ought not to say—as I have heard it—that she so outshines the radiance of other saints with her privileges that she makes them invisible, as the rising sun extinguishes the stars. My God, what an idea! A mother who extinguishes the glory of her children! I hold just the opposite: I believe that she will make the crowns

[16] N 154–55 (LC 161).   [17] N 147–48 (LC 158, 159).

of the elect shine more brightly than ever. It is perfectly right to
speak of her privileges; but one should not stop there. If someone preaches about the Mother of God in such a way that the
congregation is compelled to gasp Oh and Ah from beginning
to end, it only produces weariness. Who knows whether some
souls would not finally succumb to a feeling of alienation in the
face of such a superior creature? . . . The unique privilege of
Mary is that she remained free from original sin.[18]

Her attitude toward the saints was the same. Someone had
proposed to read to her extracts from the life of Saint Francis.
All that about the dear birds and the little flowers would please
her. "No; not for that reason. I need nourishment for my soul.
I need examples of humility."[19] For her, humility is synonymous with truth, and truth alone can nourish her. Anything
that fails to provide food for the soul, no matter how piously
presented, is for her indigestible, sugary trash. A Sister prophesied that a company of radiant white angels would be present
at her deathbed. Her answer: "All these images mean nothing
to me. I can only nourish myself upon the truth."[20] But just
as she recoiled from prettifying the truth, she also refused to
have it made hateful. "Death will carry you off", someone
said. "No, not death. The good God will come to take me.
Death is not a ghost, a horrifying figure such as one sees in
pictures. It says in the catechism that death is the separation of
body and soul—nothing more."[21] It is almost as if she had a
mania for stripping everything of the trappings in which it was
given to her, in order to see what it was really like. Curiously
enough, even visions fell beneath her mistrust; for she feared
that attachment to images might blind one to the unvarnished
truth. "I can only nourish myself on the truth. On that account I have never sought after visions. On earth we cannot
see heaven or the angels as they are. I would rather wait till
after death."[22] This unusual fear will have to be discussed later;

[18] N 156–58 (LC 161–62); Mt 12:50.   [19] N 44 (LC 72).

[20] N 177 (LC 134).   [21] G 476 (ET 380).

[22] N 117 (LC 134).

in any case, it is clear that Thérèse did not expect the complete truth this side of heaven. All earthly things, even the best, remain objects of suspicion for her, and she is unhappy when it happens that her lack of education hinders her from arriving at the full truth: "Not before coming to heaven shall we be aware of the full truth in everything. Here on earth, as in the Holy Scriptures, there is a dark and incomprehensible side. I am troubled by the differences in the various translations. If I had been a priest, I should have learned Hebrew, to be able to read the word of God in the language in which he was pleased to express himself."[23]

Truth is humility. Thérèse holds to that also, and especially when it affects the truth about her own life. Her judgments on herself are in line with those of all who have been proclaimed saints by their fellows and by the Church; the distinction between her own nothingness and God's fullness in her is crystal clear. "Truly, you are a saint!" "No; I am no saint. I have never performed saintly deeds. I am a quite little soul upon whom the good God has heaped graces. What I say is the truth. You shall see in heaven."[24] Though truth is humility, there is yet this difference, that one can see the truth but cannot see humility. Which accounts for the astonishing statement: "It seems to me that humility is truth. I do not know whether I am humble. But I do know that I see the truth in everything."[25] But when a soul becomes so permeated with the truth of God as to live by that truth alone, not darkening it with its own preconceptions, then it becomes possible to express its humility; for then this humility is simply a participation in divine truth. "Yes, I believe that I am humble. The good God shows me the truth. I feel certain that it all flows from him."[26] And on the day of her death: "Yes, I believe that I have always sought after truth. Yes, I have understood lowliness of heart."[27] Such

[23] H 289 (T 317).　　　　　　[24] H 266 (T 297); N 133 (LC 143).
[25] H 266 (T 297).　　　　　　[26] N 114 (LC 132).
[27] N 193 (LC 205).

is humility, which sustains one on the narrow ledge between the abyss of truth on one side and that of lying on the other. Such humility is no virtue but rather the sign that one possesses no virtue, since "it all flows from him". This is the point at which Thérèse engages in her desperate battle against the great and even more pernicious misunderstanding of her virtue and sanctity. "No; I am no saint. I have never performed saintly deeds."[28] She does not produce light, she reflects it. "I leaned forward and, looking through the open window, saw the dying sun casting its last rays upon nature; the tops of the trees appeared transformed into gold. Then I said to myself: What a difference if one remains in the shadows or, on the contrary, if one exposes oneself to the sun of Love. Then we appear all golden. In reality, I am not this, and I would cease to be this immediately if I were to withdraw myself from Love."[29] There is only One who is light. Others may all stand in the light of the One and bear witness to the light. People praised her patience. "I have not yet had even one moment of patience! It is not my patience! People are always deceiving themselves."[30] And when the doctor joined in the hymn of praise to her: "How can he say that I am patient? It is a lie!"[31] And, the brighter the truth of her humility, the darker grew misunderstanding about her. "*I said to her that I would later get the true worth of her virtues properly recognized.*" "One should simply get the true love of God properly recognized. My poor nothingness leaves nothing to be eliminated."[32] She almost bristled when she was asked to dispense "edification". "*I suggested to her that she might address a few edifying remarks to the convent doctor.*" "Oh, Mother, that's not my way. Let Monsieur Cornière think what he likes, I only like simplicity, and I have a horror of acting otherwise."[33] In the end, when she realizes that the struggle is in vain, she wearily deflects compliments. "*I said to her that she must have*

[28] N 133 (LC 143).
[29] N 93 (LC 239).
[30] N 143 (LC 153).
[31] N 182 (LC 193).
[32] 2 P 911 (G 462 [ET 369]).
[33] N 50–51 (LC 77).

had a hard fight to reach the degree of perfection where we now saw her. With an indescribable expression, she simply answered: 'Oh, it's not that. . . .' "[34] "Why should people be constantly talking about these 'virtues' and 'degrees of perfection', instead of paying honor to God alone in his saints?" *"What a comfort it must be for you to do so much good and promote God's glory. How much I wish I were so favored!"* "What has it to do with me if the good God uses my soul rather than another's to promote his glory? What has it to do with the instrument? In the last resort, he has no need of creatures."[35] *"What do you think of all the graces that have been showered upon you?"* "I think: the Spirit of God blows where it will."[36] She does not deny the graces nor the burden of them: "This ear of corn is an image of my soul. The good God has weighed me down with graces, for myself and also for many others."[37] But this does not imply that she became a "blueprint of sanctity" from which other saints could be mass-produced.

It is precisely this danger she strives to avert. She knows well enough that she is the first to tread a path that is to become a path for many and will be recognized by the Church. And she picks her way cautiously so that those who follow after will not be frightened or discouraged but will be inspired to go on. Everything in her little way has to be "ordinary" and "imitable". And yet: there must be something unique in each of them. In her it was truth, but in others it might be empty convention or dangerous presumption. She surrendered herself to God by a special Act of Consecration; therefore, one of her Sisters suggests that she should send the Act of Consecration to all her devout relatives in the world and thereby perhaps launch a "movement". Thérèse prohibits this. "People might easily mistake it for Quietism."[38] "To offer oneself as a sacrificial victim does not mean offering oneself sweetness

[34] N 112 (LC 129).
[35] H 269 (T 300–301).
[36] H 299 (T 325).
[37] N 114 (LC 131).
[38] G 348 (ET 281).

and consolation; it means abandoning oneself to every fear and torment and bitterness; for sacrifice is the food of love."[39] She who had written the story of her life under obedience advised against autobiographies. "It is more in accordance with humility to write nothing about oneself. Even without writing, you can no more forget the great graces of your lives than that of your vocation, and it is more salutary for you to meditate on them in the memory rather than on paper."[40] Her warnings against imitating her correspondence with priests was even sterner. "Anyone at all could write what I have written, and they would receive the same expressions of praise and the same trust. . . . Correspondence must be very infrequent and should not be permitted at all to certain nuns who would become preoccupied with it, believing they are doing marvels when they would in fact only be bringing harm to themselves and falling perhaps into the subtle snares of the devil. Mother, what I am saying about this is very important; do not forget it later."[41] In supervising the novices, Thérèse had learned how different are the ways by which God leads souls.[42] It is this reverence toward the ways of God that restrains her from advocating a universal "school of perfection". Truth is not something that can be learned once and for all and then simply repeated. Truth means lovingly accepting the will of God from moment to moment and carrying it out.

For anyone to base his whole attitude toward life so firmly upon the concept of truth is itself sufficiently striking. That a young girl should do so is quite amazing and cannot be explained without some fundamental inner experience—or, better still, some gift of understanding that can have no other source than a unique, personal mission. Such a supernatural source has to be assumed if we are to understand how someone like Thérèse, with her many-sided personality, became so single-minded—almost cranky—in her set purpose. By no

---

[39] G 335 (ET 270); T 211.   [40] 1 P 132 (G 391 [ET 314]).
[41] N 56 (LC 82).   [42] SS 239-40.

means the least confirmation of which is that Thérèse herself begins to make so much of the word "truth" and its implications at the very moment when her mission unfolds itself out of her unconscious into the clear light of her consciousness; that is, during the last two or three years. Which in no way implies that the astonishing persistency with which she had schemed to enter Carmel has to be taken as a symptom that she was fleeing from a "false" to a "true" life. "Truth" and "falsity" are concepts that to her mind cut across the boundaries between the cloister and the world. Indeed, at the very time when she herself interprets her unquenchable thirst for the Absolute as her will for the truth, it is much more the "falsity" of the convent atmosphere that prompts her on her course—rather than a general "existential feeling", which would have been equally valid if she had remained in the world. The truth in her heart, and the falsity that she fights against to the bitter end, are not philosophical concepts but the landmarks dominating the Christian's supernatural destiny within the Church. Again, this resolute and fearless wrestling with truth and falsity proves unmistakably that it is a vital part of her mission.

EXISTENTIAL THEOLOGY

I F WE CONSIDER THIS FIRST, unmistakable *motif* in Thérèse's mission and then ask ourselves what was the body of the doctrine she defended, what its content and scope, we experience a great surprise. "Truth" refers to doctrine, as doctrine is taught within the Church, and therefore is related to the sources of the Church's teaching: the revelation as it has been recorded in Scripture and tradition, then interpreted by the teaching authority and the consensus of theologians. Yet Thérèse had no contact with theology, either in its scientific, technical aspects or even in its less technical mode of *spiritualité*, or spiritual literature. It is true that she had read a great deal besides the Holy Scriptures; but the more conscious she became of her own theological mission, the more radically she withdrew from all books or spiritual teachers. "Later", that is, after the age of eighteen, "spiritual writers left me dry, and they still have the same effect to this day. When I open a book, no matter how fine and wonderful it might be, my heart contracts, and I read without understanding it, or, if I do understand it, then my mind goes blank and I cannot meditate upon it."[1] "I can find nothing in books any more."[2] Once she was gazing at the convent library: "How distressed I should be to have read all those books; I would just have got a splitting headache and lost precious time, which I have simply spent in loving God."[3] And, since she now attaches no importance whatsoever to books, she is also quite indifferent to the fate of her own: "If our Mother were to throw the whole thing into the fire? It would not worry me in the least. It would not cause me the slightest doubt as to my mission. I would just believe that the good God intends to fulfill my longings in some other way."[4] It has been pointed out that much of her teaching was already to be found in the

[1] SS 179.
[2] 2 P 240 (G 313 [ET 251–52]).
[3] Pt 67–68.
[4] Pt 141.

54

tradition of the *Ecole française*, that, before her, Marguerite de
Beaume, a seventeenth-century Carmelite, had recommended
devotion to the Child Jesus and used the expression "the little
way". Others have instanced Bérulle and Condren's insights
into the "spirit of childhood"; some have maintained that she
had a predecessor in Saint Francis de Sales, whose Order has
recognized Thérèse's thought as "its own".[5] But, on the same
score, these parallels have to be supplemented by observing that
Thérèse was not aware of them, that one cannot trace a direct
line from any of these writers to her; moreover, she felt herself
to be the accredited messenger of something definitely new.[6]
In fact, she takes some pains to point out this absence of any
external guidance: "Jesus alone has been my sole instructor. I
have not been taught from any book nor from theology, and
yet I know from the bottom of my heart that I am grounded
in the truth. I have received encouragement from no one as I
have from Mother Agnes of Jesus. When the opportunity has
arisen to open my heart, I have been so little understood that I
have repeated with Saint John of the Cross: 'Send me no more
messengers who cannot say to me what I long for.' "[7] The
sole person who she once felt understood her—Father Alexis
—encouraged her to continue along the path on which she
had struck out. He confirmed her conviction that her thinking conformed to the mind of the Church. But he taught her
nothing. "This assurance filled me with joy. . . . I felt at the
bottom of my heart that this was really so."[8]

Just as Thérèse received no theological formation, so also
she never had a spiritual director who acted as her authority in
spiritual matters. The priests who met her all bring out "how
perfectly simple and modest Thérèse proved during their conversations; she wanted to have things elucidated and to hear the
sober truth. . . . She wanted to see things aright and distinctly

[5] G 429–32 (ET 344–46).   [6] G 432 (ET 345–46).
[7] 2 P Anidmadv. 22 (G 432 [ET 346]).
[8] SS 173–74.

and to have her illuminations, presentiments and desires tested by the irrevocable standards of the Church. . . . Her own conviction that her way was the right one did not suffice for her any more than it has for almost any saint."[9] But, although she constantly requested expert opinion about her way, yet to no one did she owe the essentials of it. She adheres to the *Magister Interior* and appropriates to herself the Lord's words to Margaret Mary Alacoque: "I will allow you to read in the book of life, which contains the science of love." "Without showing himself, without letting his voice be heard, Jesus teaches me in secret; not through books; for I do not understand what I read."[10] The antitheses in the following quotation are worth noticing: "Spiritual directors are in the habit of prescribing a multiplicity of acts in order to draw people to perfection, and they are right to do so. But my spiritual director, Jesus, does not teach me to count my acts; he teaches me to do everything out of love, to refuse him nothing and to be content when he gives me the opportunity to prove my love; and all this in the peace of complete surrender. Jesus does it all, and I do nothing."[11] "I hold and know from experience that 'the Kingdom of heaven is within us.' Jesus needs neither books nor teachers in order to instruct souls. He, the teacher of teachers, gives his guidance noiselessly. I have never heard him speak, and yet I know that he is within me at every moment. He instructs me and guides me in whatever I say or do. Just when I need it, I find certain lights I had not seen until then."[12] Indeed, Thérèse is convinced that the divine Master is instructing us from within just as surely as he instructed the apostles by the spoken word: "I am certain that the Lord didn't say to the apostles by his instructions and his physical presence anything more than he communicates to us by the interior promptings of his grace."[13] Of course this extreme formula was not intended in

[9] G 394 (ET 316).   [10] SS 187.
[11] S 190–91 (GC II:796).   [12] SS 179.
[13] N 128 (LC 140).

any "modernistic" sense. No one could have possessed a more unquestioning faith in the Church than Thérèse. She was never touched by the temptation to substitute an interior certainty for the Church's external authority; this is proved by the very naïveté with which she writes about the subject. Alike in her family and in the convent, she is firmly rooted in the living, unwritten tradition of the Church and never makes the slightest attempt to separate or free herself from it in any direction. Nevertheless, she does permit herself some astonishingly independent judgments on the great figures of tradition—on the Fathers of the Church as well as on the two great pillars of Carmel, Teresa of Jesus and John of the Cross, to whom as a young girl she was presumably taught to look up in sheer reverence devoid of any vestige of criticism. Not that she is irreverent; rather, she is not cowed by any authority, and she candidly measures each of them, without any preconceptions, by the one ultimate standard—which for her is the word of God. There is no spiritual book, as far as she is concerned, that could ever begin to rival the word of God. Nor does she allow anyone to prescribe for her a "way of perfection" if this way does not coincide with the way that she has already found for herself.

> Many times when I read certain treatises where perfection is described as if it were surrounded with untold hindrances and endless illusions, my poor little mind quickly wearies. I close the learned book that gives me a splitting headache and a dried-up heart. . . . I abandon the fine books, which I can neither understand nor translate into practice, to those with superior intellects and great souls. . . . Luckily the Kingdom of heaven consists of many mansions; for I should never arrive there if there were only those whose description I cannot understand and the entrances to which appear impassable.[14]

When someone as authentic as Thérèse behaves with this extraordinary self-confidence toward all spirituality—even the

[14] S 332 (GC II:1093-94).

traditional spirituality of her own Order—it can only arise out of the sort of inner experience that inspires the great founders of Orders and spiritual movements. Thérèse, then, was granted that inner experience, that "science of the saints", who are taught directly by the Holy Spirit;[15] but with her, since her preparatory formation had been slighter, one finds a marked stress upon experience at the expense of tradition. Consequently, the authenticity of her teaching needs to be subjected to particularly rigorous tests; yet it emerges triumphantly, displaying all the features that are derived from the presence and workings of the Holy Spirit—freedom, mastery, penetration, fullness and joy.[16]

But we have not yet mentioned the most decisive factor of all. Thérèse lived before she wrote. She strove to satisfy her need for the truth by achieving it in her own life and translating the word of God into the heart of her own being. Just as a painter in the grip of his purest vision will try to realize it in a single work upon which he lavishes all his skill, so Thérèse labored with every ounce of energy she could raise in order to perfect one unique work—her own life. Her being was to be the expression of truth—so that she should herself eventually be transformed into the truth welling up inside her. "To do the truth, to be transformed into truth"; this injunction of Saint John's is the starting point of her theology. Therefore she stands in exactly the same relationship toward her own existence as the writer does toward his novel or a sculptor his statue. She labors at it in complete self-forgetfulness. Occasionally she steps back in order to inspect it, viewing it critically and objectively, impartially, completely detached from herself. She is just like the true artist, who works away without any thought for his own fame but simply listens to his inner voice, striving to shape the objective idea confronting his vision, something

[15] Pl chapter 8: "Thérèse a puisé sa doctrine au-dedans par la suggestion du Saint Esprit" (100–104).

[16] Pl 109.

more real to him than his own self; such an artist would gladly abandon everything for the sake of his work, content to die unrecognized and unknown if only his work might become famous and its riches be revealed to men. With the same passion, Thérèse works away at her masterpiece, her own life, without any backward glance upon her poor, struggling self. This self has long since been absorbed into her mission, has become a scarcely noticed instrument; for all her attention is fixed upon her task: to embody the Word of Love in her life. Her mission finally takes possession of her on Christmas Day 1886, when the Lord casts his net for her and gives her the mission to become a fisher of souls. "I felt love penetrate my heart and the need to forget myself and to please others; from then onward, I was happy."[17] It is as though there were two Thérèses; one is a means and an instrument, oblivious of itself, and the other is an aim and destiny. One recedes ever deeper into the shadows; the other comes forward into the light. The one wears herself out to the very bone until a horrible, slow death squeezes the last drop of blood from her; it is a cruel transfusion that leaves behind only a hollow doll upon the deathbed. The other comes to fruition in the exact measure that the first wears away, blossoming ever more beautifully, more deeply conscious of the divine light. She comes to life, like the statues of Prometheus and Pygmalion, and one no longer needs to walk around her to examine her, for she herself begins to turn around to allow her heavenly features to be observed on every side—almost like a mannequin, who is not showing off herself but her clothes— here, the clothes of grace.

Scarcely anything, perhaps, in the whole history of Christendom gives one such a jolt as this duplication. In all the other great missions, their content has been something primarily objective: some task, some foundation, the formulation of a doctrine or the objective exposition of certain aspects of revelation. In these cases, the self became Christian precisely inso-

[17] SS 99.

far as it was overshadowed by its objective mission. The mission, in Thérèse's case, seems to be called "Thérèse". Every action, every gesture, each hidden recess of her life, the subtlest, scarcely perceptible vibrations of her personality—all are subjected to her unwavering examination. Everything is drawn out into the almost unbearable light of consciousness; not for its own value, but because it is a means that must be perfected; and, since it has to serve as a model "for all little souls", its perfection needs to be scrupulously tested and made available for all. Here we have an anatomy of sanctity; and, what is quite unparalleled, a self-canonization pronounced with great deliberation and firmness. Leaving aside the Mother of God and her *beatam me dicent* (which is in a wholly different category), the one comparable case, and a significant one, is that of Paul. He, also, draws attention to himself and takes every opportunity to recommend himself for imitation, because *he* is the most concrete representation of the Lord to the Church. As the type *kat' exochen* of the apostles, having striven so much harder than the others, and as the type of the personified mission, he is authorized to put his own life forward for display, to demonstrate the faith by allowing the full light of God's countenance to shine upon his own being. It is not only his teaching, nor his deeds, that is the content of his mission but himself, his life and the trajectory of his destiny.

There is simply no tradition of proposing oneself for imitation in this way. One can find it in Gregory Nazianzen (in whom, however, it is marred by intellectual vanity), and traces of it are also visible in such a positive, downright person as Saint Teresa of Jesus. Yet in none of these cases do we encounter it in such a highly self-conscious and fundamental form as with Saint Thérèse. In this respect, Paul and the two Teresas are ranged together on one line of sanctity, while the opposite line includes John, Francis and Ignatius. The contrast does not arise, of course, from the latter's lives' being devoid of theological interest; their lives, also, radiate the most tremendous theological truths. But there is a contrast in that they neither look at themselves nor point to themselves, whereas Paul and Thérèse are clearly aware of their sanctity. But no matter how pronounced this awareness may be, it cannot in the least be described as vanity and self-satisfaction. It is a sign that these outstanding saints feel themselves called to interpret the teaching embodied in their lives. Indeed, we may regard it as the touchstone of Christian humility to be able to treat oneself as a separate object, an instrument of the gospel. There is a difference, however, between Paul and Thérèse. For, besides having his own life to preach about, Paul also ranges over the whole universe of Christian doctrine, the Trinity and the Incarnation, the Old and New Testaments, the Church and the world, while Thérèse, who was no theologian, was restricted to her own life for the material out of which to shape her teaching. This has been taken as a symptom of intense "self-preoccupation": "Despite all that she had attempted, and accomplished, in the way of self-stripping, how heavily burdened with self her nature remains! In spite of sticking to her intention of maintaining silence, . . . every page of her book, her every poem and letter, betrays the passionate intensity with which she observes and commends herself, analyzing and dissecting her own life. How often and how long a person must have gazed into the mirror of self before producing a self-portrait of such precision and subtle nuances!" This is supposed to be "the deep wound in her being, never touched by the healing knife";[18] the natural, and dangerous, disposition of her character that was never completely illuminated by grace and absorbed into the light of grace; it is the "typical defect of *really* 'little' souls". Later, we shall consider how far this judgment is just. First, we must try to see this fundamental feature of Thérèse's character quite clearly. For Thérèse, a thing is not true unless it can be realized in practice. She simply would not dare to recommend a doctrine that she had not already tried out on herself with all its painful consequences. But once she has tested it, then this

---

[18] G 504 (ET 404).

part of her own being ceases to belong to herself; it has become a part of the stream of grace and power of Christ within her. No longer belonging to the earthly Thérèse, it is appropriated to that heavenly Thérèse whose name she had deciphered in the stars while still a child;[19] thus she is dispossessed of it and has placed it at the disposal of the Church to serve as the common good of this Church. She releases this part of her self from herself once she has examined it and given it a good passing mark. She is constantly giving herself these good marks: "The flower that is telling its story rejoices to announce the unmerited graces of Jesus. . . . Out of his love, he wished to preserve his little flower from the poisoned breath of the world."[20] "He also sent much love into my little heart, which he made warm and affectionate."[21] She quotes one of her mother's letters: "But still she has a heart of gold; she is very lovable and frank; it's curious to see her running after me, making her confession: 'Mamma, I pushed Céline once, I hit her once, but I won't do it again.' "[22] She further recounts: "Without drawing attention to myself, I used to notice everything that was going on around me or whatever was said in my presence. I believe that my judgments on things were the same then as now."[23] To her, the famous "I choose all"[24] represents the essence of her life. "At that time, I already possessed the same kind of disposition as I do now; for I displayed great self-control in all my actions."[25] This did not involve any effort; it came perfectly naturally. She tells about the growth of her love of God. And about her Christian insight: "The first [sermon] I did understand and that *touched me deeply* was a sermon on the Passion preached by Father Ducellier, and since then I've understood all the others."[26] Without any trace of affectation, she displays before her readers' eyes: "The exercise of the virtues

[19] SS 43.
[20] SS 15-16.
[21] SS 17.
[22] SS 22.
[23] SS 20.
[24] SS 27.
[25] SS 29.
[26] SS 42.

became sweet and natural to us."[27] Confessing how she had previously feared to encounter evil, before her pilgrimage to Rome, she then adds: "I had not yet learned that, to the pure, all things are pure, that a simple, modest soul sees evil in nothing."[28] After entering the convent, she recounts: "We were no longer walking, we were all five flying along the way of perfection."[29] "I especially practiced little virtues, since I didn't have the capability of practicing the great. For instance, I was glad to fold up the mantles the Sisters had forgotten, and I took every opportunity to do them little favors."[30] In the following announcement of the retreat, we can perhaps imagine an amused smile: "In the year following my Profession, I received great graces during my retreat. Ordinarily preached retreats are more painful to me than the ones I make alone. But this year it was otherwise. I had made a preparatory novena with great fervor, in spite of the inner feeling I had that the preacher would not be able to understand me, since he seemed to be more suitable for helping great sinners than cloistered religious. God wanted to show me that he alone was the Director of my soul, and he made use of Just this Father, who was appreciated only by me."[31] And, in the evening of her life: "He has not willed that I have one, single desire that is not fulfilled, not only my desires for perfection but those too whose vanity I *understand* without having experienced it."[32] "I have noticed that it is the holiest nuns who are the most loved. . . ."[33] During her last months, reverence and admiration for her were greatly intensified. Not only her own sisters but also many of the other nuns in the convent began to regard her as a saint.[34] The doctor also used to express his admiration afresh at every visit.[35] The Sisters conducted a novena "because we did not know

[27] SS 104.
[28] SS 123.
[29] SS 157.
[30] SS 159.
[31] SS 173.
[32] SS 174-75.
[33] SS 245.
[34] H 229 (T 217).
[35] H 248 (T 234).

how we should manage if we lost this treasury of virtues".[36]
The smiling Thérèse readily joined in this canonization of the
living. During her illness, she had demonstrated more openly
than ever the truth of her teaching, the Christian life. "I always see the good side of things. Some people take everything
the way that will cause them most trouble. With me it is the
opposite. Even when I have nothing but suffering . . . well,
I make this my joy."[37] "It took me a long time before I was
established in this degree of abandonment. Now I am there."[38]
She was asked what she would do if she could begin her life
again. "I believe that I should do just what I have done."[39]
"One must take our Lord by caresses; that is what I have done
and why I will be so well received."[40] And finally, to crown
all these statements, she says: "Yes, I believe that I am humble.
The good God shows me the truth."[41] Moreover, she does
not confine herself to private conversations with the Sisters as
occasions on which to propose herself for imitation; she does
the same in her official instructions to the novices. Whenever
she dispenses advice, she always illustrates it by some example
from her own life that gives it the seal of authenticity: "We
must be constantly bent upon mortifying ourselves, so that as
soon as the bell rings or there is a knock on the door, we do
not do another stroke before calling 'Come in'. This has been
my practice, and I assure you it is a source of peace."[42] She puts
forward a truth about littleness and adds an anecdote from her
younger days: "The one sure method of making rapid progress
in the way of love is this: to remain quite little always. That is
what I have done." *"How well you understand all this! Have you
always behaved like that?"* "Yes, I have always forgotten myself and tried not to seek myself in anything."[43] She always
has a recipe from her own experience at hand; when a novice
is disturbed at her many distractions, "I have many as well,"

[36] H 240 (T 225).   [37] N 20 (LC 51).
[38] N 50 (LC 77).   [39] N 65 (LC 237).
[40] N 83 (LC 257).   [41] N 114 (LC 132).
[42] H 276 (T 306).   [43] H 261-62 (T 293, 306).

she says, "but, as soon as I notice them, I pray for the people who keep coming to mind, and so my distractions are turned into blessings for them."[44] When her cousin is tormented by scruples: "I can hear you saying, 'Thérèse only says so because she is ignorant of them!' Yet she knows well enough . . . , she herself has endured the martyrdom of scruples; but our Lord granted her the grace to make her Communion nonetheless."[45] And, at a time when Céline was suffering temptations: "Your difficulties do not surprise me. Last year I had to go through it all [j'ai passée par là]—and I know what it is."[46]

Who could fail to find such a manner of teaching curious or to sense the peril of self-deception in this constant posturing and display of perfection? The most obvious danger in display-ing one's virtue and humility in this way is that at any mo-ment it may turn into unconscious exhibitionism. But there is an even greater danger that the subjective limitations of one person's experience will be taken as the measure for the ob-jective truths of revelation. The critical observer is liable to find himself concentrating more upon the person than upon the divine truth beyond the person. Admittedly, it needs to be put into its context to be properly understood, yet one state-ment made just before she died makes the danger clear: "I have lights only to see my own little nothingness. But that does me more good than lights on the Faith."[47] At least it is a case of double vision: "One glance at Jesus, and the recognition of one's own poverty compensates for everything."[48] The danger of becoming self-righteous and pharisaical is only intensified when we remember that it is fulfillment of the "letter" that leads to self-satisfaction and that Thérèse is never tired of in-sisting on *literal* fulfillment. In this respect, she reminds one more of John Berchmans, the "model novice", than of Aloy-sius or Stanislaus. Berchmans himself might have written the

[44] H 287 (T 315).   [45] S 108 (GC I:568).
[46] S 234 (GC II:870); cf. S 297 (GC II:1017).
[47] N 139 (LC 148).   [48] Esprit 185 (G 424 [ET 339]).

note preserved by Sister Mary of the Sacred Heart that ends:
"I must leave you, nine o'clock is stri. . . ."[49] He too would
have left the parlor with a friendly farewell as soon as the hour-
glass had run out, whereas the others would have quickly completed whatever they were doing.[50] And, in the end, she also
confesses her grief to her nurse: "Oh, how little fidelity to the
Rule, how many souls in the convent who casually do nothing
. . . who just make the best of it!" She takes the Rule literally,
as she has taken everything literally from her tenderest years,
including the slightest impulses of the Holy Spirit. Not for her,
the "broadmindedness" and elasticity in interpreting the Rule
that is so favored in convents; without criticizing the others
who take a different view from herself, she allows no one to
deflect her from her course, even by example—not even her
Prioress. Nor is it the dead letter of the Old Testament that
she fulfills, but the living, spiritual letter of the Lord—the law
of love that she faithfully carries out to the last jot and tittle.
Moreover, she does not do it through her own inclination but
rather through pure obedience, freely transgressing all the laws
of natural sympathy. The person whom she favors with her
most loving smile is the one whom she finds the least congenial; as her companion in recreation, she chooses the one
who grates on her nerves; she bestows her confidences on the
Sister who most mistrusts her, winning her over by charm.[51]
Her mastery in this Christian art of arts is so perfect that even
her own sisters are deceived, when grace seems to be her very
nature—not *seems* but *is*—when that split between nature and
grace (so plain in most of us and traceable even in the great
masters) vanishes completely from Thérèse's life. At each moment, her sole concern is to carry out the will of God as it is
revealed to her from second to second.

She had a deep distrust of making surveys and standing back
to take her bearings or working out the theoretical implica-

---

[49] S 50 (GC I:427).   [50] G 286 (ET 230).
[51] G 295–308 (ET 237–47).

tions of every move. To make a survey, one has to separate oneself from the concrete reality of the truth here and now; for Thérèse, a survey means "theory", and theory leads one into the world of "problems", where untruth begins. From a distance, everything facing one seems a problem. "When I was a child, the great events of my life seemed like unscalable mountains. When I saw the young girls going to their First Communion, I thought, 'How shall ever I make my First Communion?' And later—how shall I manage to enter Carmel?, or again— how to receive the Habit and make Profession? And now I am saying the same to myself about dying."[52] But the solution is: to live in the immediate present, to tread the narrow ledge of the present moment that runs between two unbridgeable abysses. "People tell me that I shall fear death. That may well be so. If only they knew how unsure of myself I am. Yet I will cherish the feelings that the good God sends me *now*; there will be plenty of time to bear the other kind."[53] "We who run in the way of love should never think of the pains that may afflict us later. That would signify a lack of trust and would mean meddling in God's creative work."[54] Thérèse never tries to dominate the course of events. In a very womanly fashion, she simply tries to receive everything, and to receive it lovingly. For her, every moment comes so fresh and immediately from the hand of God that the thought of separation never arises. "In the convent, we should behave as though we had only two days to spend here."[55] Consequently, she was unacquainted with the cares that come through setting oneself apart. "We who are journeying along the path of love should never allow ourselves to be burdened with cares. Did I not have sufferings to bear at each moment, it would be impossible for me to exercise patience. But I just keep concentrating on the present moment. I forget the past and preserve myself from worries about the

[52] N 29-30 (LC 58).
[53] N 12 (LC 46); [italics are von Balthasar's].
[54] N 89 (LC 106).   [55] Pt 48.

future. When people become despondent and fainthearted, it
is because they are thinking about the past and the future."[56]
The Christian, whose "heart is filled with the will of Jesus",[57]
has no room left for care or abstractions. He does not need to
ponder each moment about what he should do; he only needs
to attend faithfully at each moment to God's will; in faith, he
will discover what this is just as surely as the divine Son at all
times perceives the will of the Father and, without reflecting,
fulfills it. Therefore, Thérèse suffers without reflecting; and
one can suffer so much in this way. "There is so much to suffer from moment to moment."[58] "I suffer from one moment
to the next. When one thinks of the past and the future, one
loses courage and falls into despair."[59] "In regard to bodily
suffering, I am just like a tiny child. I am without thought, suffering from one minute to the next."[60] This fulfillment of the
divine will in its momentary uniqueness embodies the theologically exact conception of time and duration. To turn away
from this reality is to fall out of God into nothingness, into
care and sheer impotence. And, if one sets up some scheme of
one's own besides the will of God, one loses all guarantee of
being maintained in the truth. "The good God grants me just
as much as I can bear."[61] "I would never ask God for greater
sufferings, . . . because they would then be *my* sufferings, and
I should have to bear them; and alone I have never been able
to do anything."[62] On the contrary, "The good God gives me
courage in the same measure as he gives me sufferings. At the
moment, I feel that I could not bear any more; but I do not fear,
because, if he increases them, he will at the same time increase
my courage."[63] The total fulfillment of God's will rests ultimately with God. "I am glad that I have never prayed to God
for suffering, because now he is bound to give me courage."[64]

[56] H 235–36 (T 222).   [57] H 236 (T 222).
[58] N 34 (LC 64).   [59] N 145 (LC 155).
[60] N 163 (LC 170).   [61] N 160 (LC 168).
[62] N 136 (LC 145).   [63] N 141 (LC 149).
[64] N 162 (LC 169).

Thérèse, who had such a gift for seeing into other souls and discerning their destinies, used no other guiding star for herself than that of the moment. It is this that enables her to reach the heights of trust and self-surrender. "The good God gives me no premonition of an early death—only greater sufferings. But I do not trouble myself—I prefer to think only of the present moment."[65] "It is as if my eyes were blindfolded. What people say to me about death being at hand makes no impression on me. Doubtless the good God wishes me not to be concerned about it. . . . He wishes me to abandon myself like a tiny child who does not worry what is going to be done with him." In fact, Thérèse would have regarded a philosophy based upon care as a philosophy of disobedience. So she forbids herself to intervene at all in her true destiny, in God's will for her: "I have prayed to the good God not to listen to any prayers that might hinder his plans for me."[66] This is the spirit of her "Song of Today":

> My life is a moment, a passing hour.
> My life is a moment that flits away from me.
> O my God, you know that for loving you on earth
> I have only today!
>
> Oh! I love you, Jesus! . . . my soul is drawn to you. . . .
> Be my sweet support for one day alone!
> Come reign in my heart, give me your smile
> Just for today!
>
> What does it matter, Lord, if the future is bleak!
> I cannot pray for tomorrow's needs. . . .
> Keep my heart pure, keep me in your shade,
> Just for today!
>
> If I think of tomorrow, I fear my inconstancy,
> And feel stirrings of sadness and boredom in my heart;
> But I gladly accept the trial of suffering, O my God,
> Just for today!

[65] G 472 (ET 377).   [66] N 135 (LC 240).

Living Bread, Bread of heaven, Eucharist divine,
Moving mystery that is the work of love!
Come dwell in my heart, Jesus, my white Host,
Just for today!

I have only this passing day in which to form
This cluster of loving souls. . . .
Oh! Jesus, give me the flaming spirit of an apostle,
Just for today!

Soon I shall fly away to sing his praises,
When the endless day dawns upon my soul
Then I shall sing on the angelic lyre,
THE ETERNAL TODAY![67]

"Today", a fundamental concept of revelation, does not
mean evanescent time as opposed to eternity. "Today" is the
God-given, supernatural mode of created time by which it is
possible to express the simultaneity of eternity (for which our
term "timeless" is quite inadequate). In the same way, the incarnate Son reveals himself as dwelling in the Father by fulfill-

---

[67] H 377-78. Ma vie est un instant, une heure passagère, / Ma vie est un
moment qui m'échappe et qui fuit./ Tu le sais, ô mon Dieu, pour t'aimer sur la
terre, / Je n'ai rien qu'aujourd'hui!

Oh! je t'aime Jésus! . . . vers toi mon âme aspire . . . / Pour un jour seulement
reste mon doux appui! / Viens régner en mon coeur, donne-moi ton sourire /
Rien que pour aujourd'hui!

Que m'importe, Seigneur, si l'avenir est sombre! / Te prier pour demain, oh!
non, je ne le puis . . . / Conserve mon coeur pur, couvre-moi de ton ombre /
Rien que pour aujourd'hui!

Si je songe à demain, je crains mon inconstance, / Je sens naître en mon coeur
la tristesse et l'ennui; / Mais je veux bien, mon Dieu, l'épreuve, la souffrance,
/ Rien que pour aujourd'hui!

Pain vivant, pain du ciel, divine Eucharistie, / O mystère touchant que l'amour
a produit! / Viens habiter mon coeur, Jésus, ma blanche Hostie, / Rien que pour
aujourd'hui!

Cette grappe d'amour dont les grains sont les âmes, / Je n'ai pour la former
que ce jour qui s'enfuit . . . / Oh! donne-moi, Jésus, d'un apôtre les flammes,
/ Rien que pour aujourd'hui!

Je volerai bientôt pour dire ses louanges, / Quand le jour sans couchant sur mon
âme aura lui: / Alors je chanterai sur la lyre des anges / L'ETERNAL AUJOURD'HUI!

ing his Father's will simultaneously on earth and in eternity. In this respect, Thérèse is following the Son: "I have often noticed that God will not give me provisions. He nourishes me at each moment with totally fresh food; I discover it within me without knowing how. I believe quite simply that Jesus himself, hidden in the depths of my poor little heart, grants me the grace of working in me and that he suggests everything to me that I should do according to his will at the present moment."[68]

The term "existential theology" affords the best description of the truth that Thérèse is realizing in her own life and being. As far as she is concerned, a thing is not true unless it can be perfected in the moment-to-moment fulfillment of God's will. As she herself points out, this gives such fullness to her whole life that even her "little failings" do not make her feel any separation between the will of God and herself. The "little failings" are immediately consumed in the furnace of divine love; there is no time even to count or consider them; the separation is overcome in the lightning mercy of God's grace. In her utter surrender, Thérèse experiences something of the peace and serenity that the poets and troubadours longed for in vain: eternity in the moment of time. For, unlike them, she does not seek the enjoyment of her experience but forgets herself in God. And whatever fulfillment he sends, she receives with gratitude: "I will cherish the feelings that the good God sends me now; there will be plenty of time to bear the other kind."[69]

But, by concentrating the whole content of revelation into the passing moment, Thérèse does, in consequence, neglect certain objective, timeless aspects of the revealed truth. While she succeeds in realizing the gospel truth quite concretely by her method, she restricts its breadth, and even its depth. True, this concreteness is the very essence of her mission, and she achieves it with all the burning energy of her ardent soul. Yet every Christian mission does include the possibility of dimly

[68] SS 165. [69] N 12 (LC 46).

sketching the whole universe of divine truth. Naturally many truths and dogmas receive greater stress than others, which are implied rather than explicit; yet they can be appreciated in their wholeness, without being distorted. In this respect, Thérèse is an exception. She is, as it were, absorbed into the present moment of God's grace and her own complete response to his presence. And her whole teaching springs from this primary intuition; she translates her life into words—as far as that is possible. She can lay hold of anything she can trace to this primary intuition and can place it within reach of other people. But anything else remains beyond her horizon. She does not deny that there are other aspects; if she is told to believe in them, she believes them without difficulty. But they do not move her; they do not form part of her "existential" system.

This is particularly noticeable in the way she speaks about God and the next world and of what lies beyond the senses. She is fully aware of being at the heart of the supernatural when she allows herself to be guided at each single moment by the will of God and allows his will to do its work in her. She lives out of love, through love, for love; a love that is not her own but God's within her.[70] This love includes faith and hope (for "love believes all things, hopes all things" [1 Cor 13:7]); it is the outpouring of the Holy Spirit into our hearts (Rom 5:5) and therefore a participation in the very love of God: "Whoever believes . . . has eternal life" (Jn 3:36). Because she already realizes that she is sharing concretely in eternal life, Thérèse finds no difficulty in interpreting the laws of the next world in terms of the circumstances and factors surrounding her love in this world. Instead of devoting herself to idle speculations about the next world, she infers its laws from the eternal love dwelling in her at the moment. Nor do these inferences lead her to abstract generalizations about "grace", for she expresses them in terms of the concrete, personal love binding her soul to God and of the personal mission bestowed upon her by God.

[70] Cf. SS 256.

She knows that her love and her mission are essentially beyond time, in eternity; only in the next world will they come to full fruition—even her mission, which she feels stirring within her as death comes closer. More intensely than a mother feels the movements of the child she is soon to bear, Thérèse feels her mission stirring within her; she already knows its features, its members and its every expression. "Jesus has already disclosed to our souls what no eye has seen. Yes, our hearts feel beforehand what the heart of man cannot conceive, for at times we are without words to express I-know-not-what-it-is that we feel in our souls."[71] Even now she knows what work on earth she will carry out from above. She constructs her vision of her eternal happiness from the truth she has learned through her indwelling love.[72] "If our Lord calls me to himself soon, then pray this little prayer daily, for my desires will be the same in heaven as on earth."[73] In the light of this vision, there are some conceptions of eternal life to which she can assent with certainty and others that she excludes with equal certainty. "I feel that my mission will soon begin. . . . I shall have no rest so long as there are souls to be saved. When the angel shall cry, 'Time is no more', then I shall take my rest and rejoice, because the number of the elect will be complete and all will have entered into joy and rest. . . . The good God would never inspire me with this desire to do good on earth after my death unless he meant to fulfill it; otherwise he would give me the desire for rest."[74] Without hesitation, she rejects all conceptions of heaven that do not correspond to her vision of love: "I cannot think for long of the gladness that awaits me in heaven. One expectation alone makes my heart beat faster—the love that I can receive and can return. I think of all the good I can perform after death, getting children baptized, helping priests and missionaries and the whole Church. . . ."[75] "How unhappy I

---

[71] S 154–55 (GC II:713).
[72] S 313–14 (GC II:1060).
[73] S 313 (GC II:1060).
[74] N 81–84 (LC 102).
[75] N 68–69 (LC 94–95).

should be in heaven if I could not do little favors for those on earth whom I love."[76] Céline is propounding some lesson about eternal bliss when Thérèse quickly interrupts her: "That does not entice me." "*What does, then?*" "Oh, love. To love and be loved, to return to earth and make love loved."[77] It is as though heaven were a garment that has to fit her and that, in consequence, she measures according to her own Christian stature. She knows the law of her own love; to pour out her own life, to suffer, to suffer unconditionally so long as there is anyone else suffering. If some circumstance were not to correspond with this interior law of her love, then she would sooner come back here:

> I count with certainty upon not being inactive in heaven. My desire is to work still more for the Church and for souls; I pray to God for this, and I am certain he will listen to me. . . . If I am leaving the battleground, it is not with the selfish intention of seeking repose! The thought of eternal bliss scarcely makes my heart beat faster. Suffering has long since become my heaven here below, so that I find real difficulty in imagining how I should acclimatize myself to a land where joy reigns untouched by sadness. Our Lord will have to transform my soul and endow it with the capacity for enjoyment, otherwise I could never bear eternal joys.[78]

And again: "It is not only that the thought of heavenly bliss affords me no joy; the fact is that I often ask myself how it will be possible for me to be happy without suffering. Surely our Lord will transform my nature; otherwise, I would be nostalgic for the sorrows in this vale of tears."[79] At the heart of her existential theology, Thérèse rediscovers the ancient patristic conception of heaven, one to some extent shared by the Middle Ages and according to which the saints in heaven are in a transitory state until the Last Judgment. Not until all the members of the Mystical Body are gathered together can

---

[76] N 38 (LC 68).   [77] N 85 (LC 217).
[78] S 353 (GC II:1142).   [79] S 358 (GC II:1152).

the whole Body of Christ rise again; not until the last of the
awaited brethren enters into the Kingdom can the heavenly
throng cease to bend over the earth with care. No more than
the Fathers does Thérèse doubt that even this transitory state
before the Last Judgment is really and truly heaven. But it is a
heaven whose most beautiful feature, perhaps, is the eager love
that sacrifices itself for the sake of the brethren still struggling
on earth. At least this applies to souls of Thérèse's stamp, for
whom joys are unbearable so long as any other single person
is still suffering. She goes as far in this direction as a Christian
existentialist can go in a letter to Céline that, though bold and
even defiant, was the result of long consideration. One step farther and we should be in the position of Ivan Karamazov, who
will not accept an eternal bliss on the grounds that it would be
immoral to slide into an all-too-smooth "total harmony" while
there is still suffering in the world. But in the vision of the beyond that Thérèse derives from the springs of her own existence, she does not go so far as to criticize God's dispositions;
her conviction that it will entirely come up to her expectations
is too firmly rooted. She knows what it will be like during the
time before the Judgment; as to what will happen afterward,
she has no analogy within her own experience, she can only
leave it to God to transform her suffering love into an utterly
joyful love: "Our Lord will have to transform my love completely, otherwise I could never bear the joys of eternity." Her
imagination can reach as far as the Judgment, which gladdens
her endlessly; but after that, she faces an impenetrable mystery.
"When will the Day of Judgment come? Oh, how I wish it
were here already! And what will there be after that . . . ?"[80]
Thérèse has this much in common with Rilke, that they both
give us visions of the world to come based on their experiences
here below. The poet writes:

> How much there is to suffer! Who could guess
> there'd once been time for laughter and repose?

[80] N 49 (LC 76).

And yet I know, better than most of those
that knew a resurrection, blessedness.[81]

But the poet remains enclosed within natural perspectives.
Thérèse speaks from the supernatural evidence of the love indwelling her heart, the outpouring of the Holy Spirit that is
the pledge of our promised home. And, finally, she hands it all
back to God to dispose of as he wills. "Even if I were never
to reach those lofty regions of love for which I have aspired,
I should still have tasted more sweetness in my pain and folly
than if I had been in the bosom of eternal joys, unless you extinguish the memory of my earthly hopes by a miracle. Allow me
then, during my exile, the delights of love. Allow me to taste
the sweet bitterness of my pain."[82] Céline said to her, a month
before her death: "Just think, the Sisters at the Carmelite Mission in Indochina will still believe that you are coming out to
them!" And Thérèse: "So I shall, I shall be there very soon. If
only you knew how quickly I shall make the journey. And the
plans I am making, and how I shall arrange things when I get
to heaven!"[83] Moreover, since she is convinced that God will
do her will completely after her death, because she has done
his will completely here below,[84] the plans she is working out
are perfectly real to her—"I shall allow the good God no rest
until he has given me everything I wish."[85] Nor are these plans
extravagant hopes or vague surmises; they are very simple but
compelling conclusions drawn from evident premises. It is not
so much God's promises that she takes as primary evidence
but rather the essence of the love she lives and experiences—
which dwells within her, whose laws she knows and whose
fruits she can already envisage.

Consequently, without knowing it, she conceives a new idea
of the next world. Christians had imagined it primarily in terms

[81] Rainer Maria Rilke, *Later Poems*, trans. J. B. Leishmann (London, 1938),
178.

[82] SS 197.   [83] G 479 (ET 382).

[84] N 66 (LC 91).   [85] S 351 (GC II:1140).

of "happiness"—and, what is more, an individual, personal happiness that is the final state toward which human beings, of their very nature, must inevitably strive. And this final state was regarded as synonymous with the cessation of all movement, as "resting in God" after the "restlessness of this world". This classical conception of the next world, shaped by Augustine and Thomas, was originally derived from the Platonic philosophy of Eros and the Aristotelian view of finality. Thérèse knows no philosophy. Even her simplest Christian notions remain uninfluenced and uncorrupted by current generalizations or clichés. She heeds only the laws of heavenly love within her; by them she is guided to her conclusions about the nature of heaven. The notion of earthly labors being rewarded does not come within her reckoning: "The crown she is to receive did not interest her at all. She said to me that it was a matter she left to the good God."[86] She was no more interested in getting to heaven as soon as possible: "I would not have picked up a single straw in order to avoid the fires of Purgatory. Everything I have done I have done in order to give joy to the good God and to save souls for him."[87] And, responding to the remark that she should rejoice to be released soon from the troubles of this life: "I who am such a brave soldier!"[88] It is not "happiness" that draws her toward heaven. Although she will accept all the joy God may send her with overflowing, childish gratitude, she herself longs, not for "happiness", but only for love. "Eternal love", not "eternal happiness", is the center of her being in God, and the laws of love are infinitely richer and deeper than the laws of happiness, to say nothing of the laws of repose.

To envisage the next world through love as she has experienced it is a typical example of the existential method that Thérèse always employs. Not a concept, but her own small experience provides the starting point from which to realize

---

[86] 1 P 50 (G 341 [ET 275]).   [87] N 98–99 (LC 118).
[88] N 85 (LC 238).

God's love. A Sister had caused her pain and came to apologize. Thérèse is very moved. "If only you knew what this means to me! Never has it been made so clear to me with what love our Lord receives us when we seek his pardon for some fault. If I, his poor little creature, am filled with such tenderness the moment you come back to me, what must happen in the heart of God when we go back to him!"[89] Thérèse is not forgiving her in the strength of her own natural love; she lives upon our Lord's love within her; and so her remark, far from being an inference, expresses an immediate experience. With her, everything she thinks and does is completely real; her future meeting with God will bear the stamp of her present meeting with him, because the reverse is also true: she lives the present in the light of the future. Her whole being is so bent upon the transcendent that she seems even now to be living in heaven rather than upon earth. No image recurs more frequently in her writings than that of the ship hurrying toward its harbor. She arranges rendezvous in heaven with all her friends and acquaintances as if they were going there the next day, and it is a glowing picture of heaven that she paints for them.[90] Whatever is not eternal is a "mirage and a daydream".[91] And yet she wishes not to leave here; on the contrary, she wishes to come back here from above. Just as she spends her earth in heaven, similarly she will spend her heaven on earth. Love, in whose compulsive rhythms she lives, is a circling movement between heaven and earth: "I came into the world, I go to the Father, I go there and am coming back to you." And just as she wishes to return to earth in the fullness of heavenly life, likewise she wishes to appear before the God of heaven in the fullness of her earthly life: "In the hour of death, when I shall really see how good the good God is, and how he means to bestow his tenderness upon me for all eternity, while I can no longer make him any sacrifice to prove my love—would that not be unbearable if

---

[89] H 280 (T 310).   [90] S 95–96 (GC I:546).
[91] S 132 (GC I:630).

on earth I had not done everything in my power to give him joy?"[92]

In this sense, her foreknowledge of heaven can no longer be described as conjecture (even though in faith) about something the sight of which is hidden from the believer; it is a genuine participation in what already *is*, and truly *is* (though still obscure). The young Bellière, a priest of peasant stock, dejectedly complains of his awkwardness in spiritual matters, and she folds him into her love as if she were a guardian angel from heaven. "Yet I am here, and I am not your little sister for nothing; I promise you after I pass into eternal life that I shall secure for you the greatest happiness anyone can enjoy, the comfort of a friend's presence by one's side."[93] She makes the same promise to her Sisters. And, as if she were already gazing down from above, she knows in advance the concerns of the heavenly hosts: "I believe that the blessed have a great sympathy for us poor souls; they remember that they themselves were once fragile and mortal, committed the same faults and endured the same struggles, and their brotherly affection will be even deeper than it was on earth."[94] And Thérèse also knows that one can pray for the blessed: "For it seems to me that they receive great glory from the prayers directed to their intention, which they can dispose of for the benefit of souls in suffering".[95]

Seen in this perspective, Thérèse's "existential theology" acquires a significance that might otherwise remain unsuspected. It is apparent that there is a danger that her method of testing all Christian truth and doctrine by living it might lead to the narrowing and impoverishment of divine truth, which can never be completely represented by anyone except the revealed Word. Yet the fact remains that she follows so close to Christ, who is himself both Word and Life, theory and practice, objective and subjective truth, that she casts all the purely theoretical as-

---

[92] Esprit 50 (G 342 [ET 276]).
[93] S 361 (GC II:1163).
[94] S 367 (GC II:1173).
[95] S 333 (GC II:1094).

pects of Christianity into the fiery crucible from which everything emerges new. She thinks of faith in the primitive gospel
sense, as a concrete act of love, as putting God's truth before
one's own truth, because "I love him more than myself and
feel that this is true from the depths of my heart; for I belong
to him more than to myself".[96] Only a life of such intensity
could have modestly and skillfully dissolved traditional notions
of spirituality and mysticism, submerging them in the original
life of the gospel, from which they might be born again.[97] Only
such intensity could produce an unlimited increase in "the poor
stock of her works and deeds"[98] and lend that stock an incalcu-
lable perspective—even for professional theologians. It is the
startling uniqueness of her mission that allows one to overcome
one's distaste at her canonizing herself and spotlighting herself,
to overlook the amazing way in which she displays herself, her
sufferings included. "I have suffered much here below. Souls
must be told of this. . . ."[99] This deposition she regards as part
of the obedience she owes to God and her mission. In her eyes
it would have been an offense against love to have shut all this
up within herself. "For the good God has entrusted me with
graces . . . for the sake of many."[100] She wishes God to grind
down every single particle of her being until she becomes his
wheat.[101] Her mission is to praise God with her whole being
in the presence of the Church. And, since this *confessio* cannot
be a confession of sin—because God has preserved her from
sin—it has to be a *confessio* of God's grace in her. For Thérèse,
to display herself is a token of her own poverty.

---

[96] S 139 (GC I:652).

[97] The whole of Petitot's study is woven around this theme of being born
again.

[98] G 502 (ET 399).   [99] N 102 (LC 123).

[100] N 114 (LC 131).   [101] N 134 (LC 144).

THE WORD OF GOD

THÉRÈSE'S EXISTENTIAL METHOD should not lead one to assume that she sets herself up as the measure of the word of God. The fact is that she only dares to make her achievement a standard of divine truth because she herself has received her measure from God. This prevents her from falling away from the truth of God, into which she penetrates more deeply without having to abandon her own method. Her "lack of tradition" (which she shares with certain dominating figures of Church history such as Francis and Ignatius—without ever attaining their stature) is automatically remedied by the Holy Scriptures. It is not her mission to continue interpreting and developing the tradition (as, say, Thomas Aquinas did) but to press back unflinchingly to its sources in the Scriptures, from which the tradition can derive fresh inspiration. She quotes our Lord's words to Saint Gertrude:

> "My daughter, search out for yourself those of my words that breathe most love, write them down, treasure them as a sacred relic and read them often. When someone wishes to rekindle in his friend's heart the fire of their first love, he says to him, 'Remember how you felt on the day you said that to me', or, 'Do you still recall your feelings on that day at that time in that place?' Believe me, then, when I say that the most precious relics I have left behind on earth are the words of my love, the words that proceeded from my tender heart."[1]

The Scriptures, for Thérèse, are her direct contact with God and his word. And so she abandons all other books in order to devote herself entirely to the study of Scripture. At the age of fourteen, she was inseparable from *The Imitation of Christ*; no matter where she opened it, she could recite to the end of the chapter by heart. "It was the only book that helped me, for I had not discovered the treasures that are hidden in the

[1] Ged 386.

81

Gospels. I knew almost all the chapters of my beloved *Imitation* by heart. This little book never parted company with me."[2] In her development, it acted as a preparation for the Scriptures and remained the one other book she could read: "In this helplessness, Sacred Scripture and the *Imitation of Christ* come to my aid; in them, I find a pure and strong nourishment."[3] At the age of seventeen or eighteen, there comes an intermezzo; she discovers Saint John of the Cross: "What light have I not been granted from the writings of Saint John of the Cross. At seventeen or eighteen, I had no other nourishment."[4] The novice mistress is amazed at her understanding of this mystic.[5] A novice testifies that Thérèse could recite long passages from the "Living Flame" and the "Spiritual Canticle" by heart. Yet, in spite of the readiness with which she later quotes John of the Cross, she does so only in order to express her own thoughts or—even more frequently—to adopt his allegorical interpretation of the Scriptures. She never adopted his "System"; this simply served her as a guide to the Scriptures and enabled her, above all, to understand how the Old Testament foreshadows the Gospels.

And so all that remains eventually is Scripture. "It is from here that I derive everything my poor little soul needs. I constantly receive fresh illuminations and detect new, hidden meanings." "I can find nothing in books any more; the Gospels are enough for me. Is it not implied, for example, in the words of our Lord, 'Learn of me, for I am meek and humble of heart'? How sweet to learn nothing except from the mouth of Jesus."[6] And she asks the Lord: "Reveal to me the hidden mysteries of the Gospels! Oh, that golden book is my most precious treasure."[7] Once more, as with the *Imitation* and Saint John of the Cross, her knowledge of it seems rather mechanical at first; she simply learns it by heart. "Quotations from the Gospels

[2] SS 102.
[3] SS 179.
[4] Ibid.
[5] Pt 69.
[6] 2 P 240 (G 313 [ET 252]).
[7] H 389.

used to come pouring out whenever she wished to drive home something she was telling me. She seemed to know them by heart."[8] The novices whom she instructed tell the same story, of how she used at all times to amaze them by her display of scriptural knowledge. She always carried a copy of the New Testament around with her. In her cell, she used to write out passages and work out a sort of concordance of her own. In her writings, she shows a startling freedom and mastery in handling the texts not only of the New Testament but of the Old as well, of the Sapiential Books especially, of the Psalms and Isaiah. In a special study, "Thérèse, a Lover of the Scriptures", a Belgian Benedictine has gathered together all her scriptural quotations and set them into their context; according to the index in the latest edition of her works (1947), 117 come from the Old and 250 from the New Testament. And this number is considerably greater if the new edition of the letters is also taken into consideration.

Yet this gives no indication of *how* Thérèse reads and interprets the Scriptures. It is clear that she will never try her hand at interpreting whole passages of Scripture; she almost always quotes isolated verses, and this simply in order to confirm or clarify some opinion she has already put forward. And one notices that it is Thérèse's own favorite thoughts that she underlines by scriptural quotations—her selection is most personal and original. By no means does she merely repeat such familiar sentences of the Lord as would have impressed themselves on her mind after hearing them in sermons or conferences. She reads independently and unexpectedly finds what she needs. In fact, she finds what she is looking for. And she looks for confirmation of what she knows. Consider the striking and very characteristic manner in which she describes her "little way". Thérèse desires to be a saint. But her first experiences in Carmel are bitter. She breaks down upon the road that the Lisieux Carmel had come to consider as *the* road to sanctity:

[8] Pt 72.

great mortifications prove too much for her. She feels herself rejected. Her very *raison d'être* is called into question. "I will look for a means of reaching heaven that offers a perfectly straight, short and completely new little way."[9] The way, in fact, of an "elevator" that simply avoids the "steep steps toward perfection". She knows now exactly what she needs. Secure in this knowledge, she approaches the Scriptures:

> I looked for the desired elevator in the Sacred Scriptures and found the words coming from the mouth of Eternal Wisdom, "Whoever is a little one, let him come to me" [Prov 9:4]. I drew near to God, rightly suspecting that I had found what I sought; and, because I wanted to know, O my God, what you would do to the very little one who answered your call, I continued my search, and this is what I found: "As a mother caresses her son, so will I comfort you; on my breasts I shall carry you and upon my knees I shall caress you" [Is 66:12–13].[10]

Now it is quite true that the Scriptures contain special sayings appropriate to each mission and are, so to speak, waiting to be interpreted by that mission. Thérèse was led to this particular passage by the Holy Spirit, and she found confirmation in it for her mission. But what distinguishes Thérèse is that she looks for confirmation when she already knows her mission. Just as her confessors never really tell her anything she does not already know—although she is grateful for their authoritative approbation—similarly Scripture seems to her a guarantee for what the "teacher within" has taught her. And the very same procedure by which she confirms her little way serves to ratify her mission to the Church. Again it begins with her personal desires and aspirations: she wishes to unite every form of Christian life and martyrdom in her own person so as to glorify God. But, as she is no more than human, and a nun, her mission is narrowly restricted. This dilemma "became a veritable martyrdom. So one day I opened the letters of Saint Paul to find some kind of answer. The twelfth and thirteenth chapters of

[9] SS 207.   [10] SS 207–8.

the First Letter to the Corinthians caught my eye."[11] And what Thérèse reads there—not to say reads into it—is the answer to her problem. In the "pure way" of love, which outstrips every particular calling, Thérèse discovers something that Paul certainly did not intend directly: her calling is both a special and a universal one. In exactly the same way, she takes the "double spirit of Elias"[12] as referring to herself and interprets the obscure passages of the Song of Songs likewise. Or again, when a picture of the Crucified slips out of her missal, she has a sudden intuition of her calling to suffer with our Lord, so as with him to save souls; she understands our Lord's thirst and his words to the woman of Samaria, "Give me to drink."[13] She can read through fifty chapters of Isaiah without a single sentence striking her; then, in the fifty-third and sixty-sixth, she suddenly stumbles on what she is seeking and rejoices over it like the woman who found the drachma she had lost. She reads the Scriptures in the light of her mission; anything that corresponds to her mission immediately becomes luminous and essential to her. The proof of this lies in the fact that she never makes the slightest effort to harmonize texts that do not fit in with her special mission. Nor does she attempt to broaden the scope of what she takes to be her task; she leaves aside anything not directly bearing upon it. She plays about with the words of Scripture like a child who knows that they all belong to her, so that she can select the ones she pleases. There is a sort of naïveté about her conviction that Scripture is there for her service. She gladly employs the device of "Bible-pricking"; she opens the Bible at random and expects the verse upon which her eye first falls to solve a problem or clarify some doubt. This is what she does when she is given the order to write her biography, and she comes upon the text: "And going up a mountain, he summoned those he desired"(Mk 3:13). That reveals to her the kernel of her life.[14] She repeats the process

[11] SS 193.   [12] SS 195.
[13] SS 99.   [14] SS 13.

when tormented by doubts about her mission and comes upon the above-mentioned passage in Corinthians. Or she wishes to write to Céline and consults the Bible at random to discover an appropriate scriptural opening. On another occasion, she is cast into deep gloom and temptation as to her vocation; the light breaks through in the words of a chance note from Mother Agnes . . . , and yet her last doubts are not dissipated —perhaps those words only express Pauline's love? "At once I felt an impulse to consult the Gospels. And, when I opened them at random, my attention was caught by a verse I had never noticed previously, 'For he whom God has sent speaks the words of God; for God does not give the Spirit by measure' " (Jn 3:34).[15]

Leaving aside the rather colorless quotations that any nun will insert into her letters or greetings, we find that her distinctly personal quotations fall into three groups.[16] (I use the Vulgate texts as does Thérèse):

1. *Quotations in which Thérèse relates some scriptural passage to herself, her surroundings, experience and destiny.* Such quotations serve to illustrate the authenticity and Christian inspiration of the experience Thérèse is relating. To give some examples: Psalm 22 is interpreted in the prologue entirely in terms of her life (as also in a letter to Father Pichon that has been lost). Psalm 70:17: "You have taught me, O God, from my youth: and still I will declare your wonderful works." Psalm 117:23: "This is the Lord's doing"—is applied to her father's illness. Psalm 125:5–7 —sowing in tears and reaping in joyfulness—is often used to describe her and her family. Psalm 118:141—"I am very young and despised, . . . but have become wiser than the old"—is applied to her faithful remembrance of God's interior graces. Psalm 91:5: "Lord, through all that you do, you overwhelm me with joy": is related to an interior trial; a similar trial calls forth

<hr />

[15] H 237–38 (T 223–24).
[16] The following texts are translated the way Thérèse quotes them.

Psalms 17:5 and 22:4: "The sorrows of death surrounded me: and the torrents of iniquity troubled me"; "For though I should walk in the midst of the shadow of death, I will fear no evils, for you are with me." Psalms 17:3 and 22:4 are also directed to her own death struggle. Song of Songs 2:11—"For winter is now past, the rain is over and gone"—is applied to her miraculous cure; Song of Songs 2:1—"I am the flower of the field and the lily of the valleys"—to Jesus, when she received him at her First Communion. Song of Songs 8:1—"That I may find you without, and kiss you, and now no man may despise me"—is used to describe the pious conversations and hours of delight that Thérèse had along with Céline in Les Buissonets; Song of Songs 2:3—"I sat down under his shadow whom I desired"—her entry into Carmel; and Song of Songs 2:9—"Behold, he stands behind our wall, looking through the lattices"—expresses her soul's experience of God's withdrawal into the shadows. Isaiah 52:11—"Purify yourselves, you who carry the vessels of the Lord"—is applied to the period when she was sacristan. "I will cry like a young swallow" is Thérèse's cry to God. She also ascribes to herself the first part of Ezekiel 16, the chapter where God later goes on to heap terrifying reproaches upon the faithless Jerusalem. But Thérèse only shares the endearments, not the reproaches. Proverbs 1:17—"But a net is spread in vain before the eyes of those who have wings"—is related to herself, because she allows no net to ensnare her. Ecclesiastes 2:11—"All is vanity"—is frequently applied by Thérèse to her inner experience. Wisdom 4:12—"For the bewitching of vanity obscures good things and the wandering of concupiscence overcomes an innocent mind"—is the description of a journey that she made after her miraculous recovery. Sirach 24:21— "They who drink me shall yet thirst"—corresponds to one of Thérèse's spiritual experiences; 1 Kings 16:7—"For man sees those things that appear, but the Lord beholds the heart"—fits her relationship to the Prioress; 2 Kings 16:10: "Let him alone and let him curse, for the Lord has bid him curse David"— this phrase of David's about Semei's curses comes to her mind after an encounter with a novice. Of Job 13:15—"Although he should kill me, I will trust in him"—Thérèse said: "I recognize that it has taken me a long time to reach this degree of abandonment. But now I am there." Matthew 3:10—"For now the axe is laid to the root of the trees"—is used of a demand made on Céline. Matthew 5:11–12—the blessings on the persecuted —is again applied to Céline. Matthew 5:48—the perfection of the Father in heaven—must be Céline's goal. Matthew 8:26— "Then, rising up, he commanded the winds and the sea, and there came a great calm"—describes the calming of a storm in her soul. Matthew 25:40: "Amen I say to you, as long as you did it to one of the least of these my brothers, you did it to me"—this comes to her mind when she is looking after a tiresome old Sister. At another time, she uses it of herself: "The least—that is me." Matthew 25:36—"I was sick and you visited me"—is referred to her desire to become a nursing Sister. Matthew 27:46—"My God, my God, why have you forsaken me?"—is repeated when she is overcome by Léonie's leaving the cloister for the second time. Mark 1:2: "Behold, I send my angel before you"—Pauline precedes Thérèse. Luke 1:49 —"Because he who is mighty has done great things to me" —she applies to herself on three occasions. Luke 5:5: "Master, we have labored all the night and taken nothing"—"*I also could say this with the apostles. And Jesus, even more merciful to me than to the apostles, took the net himself, cast it and drew it in full of fish.*" Luke 5:32—"I came not to call the just but sinners to penance"—is taken as referring to herself in a most peculiar sense: the call to her does not so much free her from sins committed as preserve her from committing them. Luke 7:47 —"But to whom less is forgiven, he loves less"—is referred to Thérèse, to whom everything is forgiven beforehand. Luke 15:31—"You are always with me" (the father's words to his eldest son)—is quoted three times in reference to herself. Luke 18:13—"O God be merciful to me, a sinner"—is her vicarious prayer for sinners. Luke 19:26—"To every one who has shall be given, and he shall abound"—is her gloss upon a grace to which she was faithful and that led to an abundance of graces. Luke 22:28—"And you are they who have continued with me in my temptations"—Thérèse and Céline can appropriate to themselves. John 1:5—"And the darkness did not overcome it"—is quoted in reference to a temptation against faith. John 8:10—"Has no man condemned you?"—Thérèse asks herself after committing a fault. John 8:10: "Where are those who accused you?"—these words to the adulteress struck her when she had been guilty of some small fault and had thankfully accepted the humiliation of it. John 11:4—"This sickness in not unto death"—is related to the severe illness she suffered when she was ten. John 16:5–7: "Now you are sad", said the dying Thérèse to her sorrowing Sisters, "but I shall come back." John 21:16—"Feed my lambs"—is taken as appropriate to her office with the novices, as is John 10:12: "But the hireling sees the wolf coming and flees." Galatians 2:20—"And I live now not I, but Christ lives in me"—is quoted in order to express her feelings at her second Holy Communion. Titus 1:15— "All things are pure to the pure"—is applied to herself as she was about to set off on her pilgrimage to Rome. Philippians 4:7: "The peace of God, which surpasses all understanding" flows over her at her Profession, which had been preceded by a violent interior struggle; 1 Corinthians 4:3—"But to me it is a very small thing to be judged by you or by men"—she repeats after a small incident that took place at recreation. Ephesians 6:17: Thérèse teaches her novices to be armed with "the sword of the Spirit"; 2 Corinthians 12:5: "But for myself, I will not boast except of my weaknesses"—this is the art that Jesus teaches to Thérèse.

2. *Quotations meant to clarify the little way.* Psalm 35:5: "O Lord, your mercy is in heaven"; Psalm 49:13–14: "Shall I eat the flesh of bullocks? or shall I drink the blood of goats? Offer to God the sacrifice of praise: and pay your vows to the Most High"; Psalm 75: "When God arose in judgment to save all the meek of the earth"; Psalm 90: "In their hands they shall bear you up

lest you dash your foot against a stone"; Psalm 93:18: "If I said, My foot is moved, your mercy, O Lord, assisted me"; Psalm 102:13–14: "As a father has compassion on his children, so the Lord has compassion on those who fear him. For he knows of what we are made; he remembers that we are dust"; Psalm 112:1: "Praise the Lord, you children; praise the name of the Lord"; Isaiah 49:15: "Can a mother forget her infant . . . and if she should forget, yet will I not forget you." Isaiah 53— the song of God's suffering servant—is frequently quoted by Thérèse in connection with her devotion to the Holy Face. Isaiah 50:4–5, 54:2–3, 55:8; 59:1–11 and 66:19 are also cited; and again Isaiah 66:13: "As a mother caresses her son, so will I comfort you, and you shall be comforted in Jerusalem"; Proverbs 9:16: "Whosoever is a little one, let him turn to me"; Proverbs 1:4: "To give subtlety to little ones"; Proverbs 16:32: "The patient man is better than the valiant; and he who rules his spirit than he who takes cities"; Wisdom 6:7: "For to him who is little mercy is granted" (Thérèse quotes this twice); Sirach 11:23: "For it is easy in the eyes of God suddenly to make the poor man rich"; 2 Esdras 4:1: "With one of his hands he did the work, and with the other he held a sword"; Matthew 9:13: "I have not come to call the righteous but sinners." Matthew 5:48: "Be perfect, therefore, as your heavenly Father is perfect" (and in no other way, not even in the manner of angels); Matthew 8:24: "But he [Jesus] was asleep"; Matthew 11:29: "Learn of me, for I am meek and humble of heart; and you shall find rest for your souls"; Matthew 19:14: "Suffer the little children, and forbid them not to come to me, for the Kingdom of heaven is for such as these"; Matthew 20:23: "But to sit at my right or left hand is not mine to give you but to them for whom it is prepared by my Father" (Thérèse relates this text to the little children, since the "great saints" and martyrs were not given these places). Matthew 26:39—"My Father, if it be possible, let this chalice pass from me, nevertheless, not as I will but as you will"—is taken as direction for the way of weakness. Luke 6:37: "Judge not, and you shall not be judged"; Mark 7:28: "For the dogs also eat under the table of the crumbs of the children"; Luke 7:47: "But to whom less is forgiven, he loves less"; Luke 10:21: "I confess to you, O Father, Lord of heaven and earth, because you have hidden these things from the wise and prudent and have revealed them to little ones"; Luke 12:32: "Fear not, little flock, for it has pleased your Father to give you a kingdom"; Luke 22:32: "And you, being once converted, confirm your brethren" (upon which Thérèse comments: "This means, tell them the story of your soul, show them from your own experience how necessary it is to trust in God alone"); John 4:6 (Jesus is weary from the journey); John 4:7: "Give me to drink"; John 14:2: "In my Father's house there are many mansions"—not only for the great saints but also for the little children; John 21:5: "Children, have you any fish?"—"*and the good Saint Peter realized his powerlessness*"; Romans 8:26: "For we know not how to pray as we ought"; 2 Corinthians 8:9: "Being rich, he became poor for your sakes"; 2 Corinthians 12:5: "For myself, I will boast of nothing except my weaknesses"; Philippians 2:7: "But [Christ] emptied himself."

3. *Scriptural phrases Thérèse adopts in order to weave them into some meditation of her own.* Here Thérèse seems very much a pupil of Saint John of the Cross in his manner of interpreting Scripture. She takes over his allegorical method, chiefly in interpreting certain celebrated verses of the Song of Songs, and she does this with such graceful confidence that one is sorry not to have a sustained work of scriptural commentary from her pen. There is a special charm about her letters to Céline, which she used to begin with some quotation from Scripture that she then went on to interpret as the answer to her sister's personal problems. First of all, one should notice the allegories on John 4:35: "Behold, I say to you, lift up your eyes and see the nations; for they are already white for harvest", which, to begin with, she interprets in the traditional sense as applying to the contemplative life but then weaves into her own thought in an original

way. In her charming gloss upon Song of Songs 2:1—"I am the flower of the field and the lily of the valleys"—she takes Céline to be the little drop of dew. She is just as independent in dealing with the story of Zachaeus, who climbed the sycamore tree and was called down by the Lord (Luke 19:5). It is proof of how these texts only serve as a starting point for Thérèse's own reflections that she occasionally starts in the same series of letters from favorite symbols of her own, such as the lyre or the peach. She takes Saint John of the Cross as her authority in her repeated commentaries upon various sections of the Song of Songs: 1:3–4; 1:7; 1:13; 2:1; 2:9; 2:10–13; 4:6; 4:9; 5:1; 5:2; 5:10; 6:11–12; 7:1; 8:1. The weight of tradition is behind her famous commentary on the combined texts of Song of Songs 1:3 and John 17 in the second part of Manuscript C,[17] where she describes the indwelling effects of contemplation. Her letter to Céline on Song of Songs 6:10–12—"I went down into the garden of nuts, . . . my soul troubled me for the chariots of Aminadab"—shows that Thérèse is not afraid to be extremely allegorical. It is highly probable that her use of Zechariah 13:6, in a letter to a missionary, was gleaned from her reading, and the same is true of her traditional application of Tobit 12:7: "For it is good to hide the secret of a king . . . but honorable to reveal and confess the works of God" (Thérèse quotes these two parts of the verse in different places).

In considering these three classes of scriptural quotation, one is driven to a somewhat surprising yet inevitable conclusion: Thérèse had read the Scriptures most ardently and even knew sections by heart; but it was almost exclusively in the light of her own life and her personal mission that she allowed them to affect her. No matter how strange it may sound, it is true that Thérèse never acquired a genuine contemplation of the Scriptures. Contemplation, in the strict and essential sense, means losing oneself in the objectivity of God's revealed word, aban-

[17] SS 254–56.

doning all one's a priori categories of selection in order to feel
the full impact of God's word in all its breadth and depth of
meaning. In authentic contemplation, the word of God has to
be heard *as it is*, and not as I would like to hear it or as I imagine it is *in relation to me*. Strict contemplation is the school of
impersonality where the soul receives its extension from God
and the Church, from tradition and Scripture. Only a soul that
has received this extension is in a position to draw fruit from
its meditations, to apply them so that it is not the word that is
conformed to the self but the self to the word. Thérèse never
learned this strict form of contemplation—possibly because she
was so fixed beforehand upon her personal mission that it became a sort of absolute standard. Or it may have been because
her excessive self-awareness made it impossible for her to hear
the word except in relation to her life, her destiny and her mission. Or again—a factor that should not be lightly set aside—
she was never given any serious training during her novitiate
in the method of meditative prayer. People have praised her
manner of prayer for its "freedom" from restrictive methods.
But it is not a question of restrictions or freedom—a method
of contemplation can only become restrictive when it has not
been properly mastered; it is simply a question of what she
could and what she could not do.

As Abbé Combes has shown conclusively, Thérèse's "meditations" remain at a very modest level. Which does not mean
to say that her mystical graces were not authentic or that she
did not carry out the Rule with exemplary fidelity. Not only is
her meditation confined to one book—the *Imitation of Christ*
or the Sacred Scriptures—but her meditation consists simply
of prayerful, reverent reading, during which the poor child is
occasionally overcome by sleep.[18] The actual fruits of her meditations are granted to her in the form of brief—almost synthetic—illuminations, what are generally described as *lumina*,
which she receives most frequently outside the times of prayer:

[18] Co 223–36.

"At the very moment I need them, I see flashes of truth that were previously hidden from me. And it is not usually during the time of prayer but in the midst of my daily occupations that they are revealed to me."[19] Thérèse leaves us in no uncertainty about what kind of illuminations these are. They are all centered upon her mission. They guide her along her way and throw her "little teaching" into relief, giving it fullness and radiance. Thérèse has very few skills at her disposal, but she learns to develop them with ever-greater mastery. Apart from her biography and her letters, it is mainly from her poems that we learn what nourished her and was closest to her heart. Admittedly, they contain a great deal that is devised for her Sisters' tastes and omit many deep thoughts that she reserves for herself. But even here, Thérèse is attempting to give of her best. "These poor poems will show to you—not what I am—but what I would wish to be and ought to be. I have meant to express my feelings, or rather the feelings of a Carmelite, and so satisfy a wish of my Sisters."[20] Her compositions are not conventional, because she wishes to offer her "illuminations" to her Sisters. And the contents of her poems supplement the contents of her other writings so simply and naturally that the two together form a complete inventory of her spiritual world. The more one becomes absorbed in the poems, the more clearly they reflect the whole of Thérèse's experience and teaching— often amplified, more colored by emotion and more lyrical— but rarely enriched by fresh insights.

Among the poems, there are two in particular that are evidently inspired by Thérèse's scriptural meditations and contain their fruits: one, "Jésus, mon Bien-Aimé, rappelle-toi [Jesus, My Beloved, Remember]" written in 1895, is a poetic "Life of Jesus"; the other, "Pourquoi je t'aime, Marie [Why I Love You, Mary]", written in 1897, is a rhyming "Life of Mary". Both poems bring before us one scene after another, the stories of the infancy, the events of the public ministry, the Passion,

[19] SS 179.   [20] S 312 (GC II:1059).

the Resurrection, the life in the Eucharist and in heaven. Both afford us an intimate glimpse into Thérèse's method of meditation. The findings are the same: Thérèse sees all the gospel mysteries through the lens of her own teaching. Her choice of scenes and the standpoint from which she regards them and the application she gives them all bear the unmistakable Thérèsian imprint. The impression is even stronger in her little musical plays, "The Angels at the Crib" and "Jesus in Bethany", where Thérèse allows her inspiration free play, unhampered by the text of Scripture. These musical plays are a sort of mosaic of the favorite thoughts that are constantly recurring in her mind.

However, it would be quite perverse to doubt, on this account, whether Thérèse really did find the Scriptures a powerful stimulus. On the contrary, her fund of thought is tremendously enriched by her scriptural reading; horizons open up on all sides, tentative suggestions are transformed into shining certainties, and personal insights are confirmed as sure and universal doctrine. Scripture sets the seal on Thérèse's belief that her task is from God and that the form of life she has chosen is embedded in the objective deposit of revelation. For, although she reads the Scriptures without any previous study of theology or tradition and freely compares the objective revelation with her subjective, supernatural mission, setting one beside the other, nevertheless she reads in obedience, in the context of a daily round of self-denial and self-conquest. Never for a moment did she imagine that such reading might prove dangerous. And it is through being so thoroughly at ease within the framework of the Church that she differs widely from the Protestant or the Liberal enquirer. Luther, brought face to face with Scripture, came to conclusions that might be considered remotely parallel to those of Thérèse: the personal certainty of salvation, the stress upon trusting *fiducia* as opposed to ascetic practices and other good works, the clear-cut preference for New Testament mercy as against Old Testament justice. And, in this sense, all due reserves having been made, the "little way" can be regarded as the Catholic answer to the demands and questions raised by Luther. But, even though Thérèse does read Scripture without having been trained in it, she remains firmly rooted in tradition.

The danger in her case—if one can speak of danger at all —does not come from slipping into doctrinal subjectivity. It is rather the danger that she will start measuring God's love in terms of the love granted to her personally. She is prepared to abandon this standard once she is shown a higher one, but until then she firmly sticks to it: "O my Jesus, it seems to me as though you have never filled any soul with love as you have mine; so I dare to ask that you should love all those whom you have given to me as you have loved me. And if, on coming to heaven, I should discover that you love them more than me, then I will rejoice over it, because even here below I am aware that they are more worthy of your love. But, here in the world, I can imagine no greater measure of love than that you have bestowed upon me without my meriting it in the least."[21]

---

[21] SS 256.

SHADOWS

I N SPITE OF THE FACT that Thérèse's existential method is
considerably amplified through her reading of Scripture,
one cannot help feeling uneasy as one reads her writings and
sayings. Is it really necessary or possible to be talking about
oneself so constantly and setting oneself in the limelight so
much? Doing so even more persistently than either Paul or
Augustine? Is it sufficient justification to say that one has a
special mission? Is there not something more to it than just
that? In that case, what is it? Can it be found, as the psychological school maintains, in the very "littleness" of her mission and her love of analyzing herself? Or in the dark background of pride and a desire for approbation that she never
mastered?[1] And yet, does psychoanalysis not prove wanting
when it comes to understanding a divine mission? Because the
meaning of such a divinely approved life has to be interpreted
in terms of the mission, and so the shadows (which can often
be observed in the saints) have to be explained precisely in *the*

---

[1] G 54 (ET 45–46); cf. 77 (ET 61f.): Thérèse as a "nervous, hypersensitive
child"; 86 (ET 68): Thérèse "unknowingly on the dangerous path of an outsider
and eccentric"; 111 (ET 89): scrupulosity as "a highly dangerous state of the
soul"; 115 (ET 92ff.): her "thirst for glory"; 127 (ET 99, 100): "an unusually
strong drive for recognition", "the end of five years of alternation between the
abyss of bondage to false dreams of holiness and the abyss of despair"; 450 (ET
359): in the last months, sickness removes "the lovely balance of soul" that she
had found, "and the old, dangerous, dark nether regions of her soul" reappear,
"victorious again"; a "new wave of sick, compulsive images floods" her now
helpless mind. It seems that greatness of soul must of necessity involve danger
and risk. It all leads to the realization that: "at the bottom of nearly all her suffering there lies, like a hidden, ineradicable root, the deep, unhealed wound of
her being: that excessive egotism", the "typical note of the *really* 'little soul' "
(504 [ET 503ff.]). We will not simply reject this conclusion: Thérèse of Lisieux
certainly does not have the stature of an Augustine, Thomas or Teresa of Jesus.
The question—and it is a New Testament question—is whether a person's psychological "stature" is necessarily the same as his theological one. Perhaps our
interpretation will leave the impression that this question is a legitimate one.

light of the mission. Is this not especially true for the childlike soul of Thérèse, in which there is nothing dark or "demonic"? The shadows, which are undoubtedly there and need to be indicated if we are to gain a deeper understanding of her mission, are not to be found either in her mission or in the natural constitution of her soul. As is so often the case, they are the result of certain offenses against the ideal and integrity of the mission. Nothing is more delicate and fragile than a mission; it can be secretly, or even openly, spoiled and can occasionally become an irretrievable failure. Coarse hands may do great harm, no matter how well-intentioned their groping interventions. God does not place his messengers beneath glass cases but sets them straight down in the middle of the sinful world, in the midst of sinful Christianity.

There are two points in Thérèse's short life at which a slight and apparently trivial deviation led to grave and unsuspected consequences. She herself was the occasion of the first one. At the age of ten, she became extremely ill of a disease that brought her to the verge of madness, if not to the edge of the grave.[2] She became delirious and tossed about, unable to recognize her relatives any longer; her father had a novena of Masses offered for her in Paris; on the Sunday during the novena, her illness reached its climax. Marie, Léonie, Céline and Thérèse herself turned in despair to the statue of the Mother of God, storming her with prayers. The statue came to life before her eyes; it became beautiful, more beautiful than words could express, and the Mother of God smiled, moved toward Thérèse and cured her. It was the first "great miracle" within Thérèse's experience (the veiled face of her father in the garden had not

---

[2] On the subject of this illness, Father Rouquette is surely correct when he writes: "The strange illness that came upon Thérèse in her childhood, which she so honestly describes for us, escapes all diagnosis. It was undoubtedly a mystical trial, a physical reverberation caused by God's invasion of her soul; the illness as described by Thérèse is strikingly similar to the crises that Surin and Olier passed through; in Olier's case, it lasted a few months but in Surin's case for a large part of his life" (*Etudes* 80 [1947], 256 note).

registered in her mind as miraculous). It was her first direct and inexpressibly blessed encounter with the reality of heaven, her first entry into the world of the saints; now she had seen the opening of the secret door through which one can observe the innermost secrets of God. It was her first great vision (and anyone who tries to psychologize it away has to contradict the saint's own unambiguous testimony); and so it became the source from which her mission sprang. Her first reaction— Silence! Guard the secret! "Mary comes to me! She smiles at me! How happy I am. Yet I shall not mention it to anyone, *otherwise my happiness would vanish.*"[3] But then she recognized her sister Marie, who was looking at her full of Joy, as if suspecting the truth; had she already guessed it? The two were scarcely alone before Marie began to probe her. "I was unable to resist her loving, eager questions. Amazed that she had seen through my secret before I had even spoken one word, I entrusted it to her entirely."[4] Thérèse did not say whether she did so with a good conscience or with a bad conscience; but she traced the consequences for us; "Unfortunately I had not been mistaken; my happiness was to vanish and be turned into bitterness. *For many years the memory of this grace was to be a real torment to my soul.*" Why? Thérèse gives her account: "I have still to tell how my joy came to be turned into sadness. After I had told Marie quite openly and childishly about my 'grace', she asked me whether she might not also recount it to the Carmel. I could not refuse her permission."[5] At her very first visit, she had to endure the effects of her action:

> The Sisters questioned me about the grace I had received: whether the Blessed Virgin was carrying the infant Jesus in her arms, whether there was much light, and so on. These questions bewildered and pained me, and I was able to say only one thing: "The Blessed Virgin had seemed very beautiful to me, and I

[3] SS 66.
[4] At Thérèse's Process, Marie said that she had "immediately seen from her gaze and her rapturous attitude that she had beheld the Mother of God herself".
[5] SS 66.

had seen her smile at me." It was her countenance alone that had struck me, so when I noticed that the nuns had imagined something entirely different . . . I began to think that I had lied. Without any doubt, if I had kept my secret, I would also have kept my happiness . . . , whereas, humiliation becoming my lot, I was unable to look upon myself without a feeling of profound horror. Ah! what I suffered I shall not be able to say except in heaven![6]

And so, through Thérèse's talkativeness, her secret is betrayed and vulgarized. It is terribly humiliating for the child to see her secret sacrificed to the curiosity of these women, becoming the subject of misunderstanding and distress, casting suspicion upon her truthfulness and, as Thérèse herself points out, tempting her to vanity. Something heavy with consequences had happened, something on which Thérèse cannot quite put her finger but the effects of which she had to endure once she had put herself in this false position: from now on she is the miracle child. She is the one who had seen Mary. Which means that she is not like other people. Not entirely without blame herself, she is set upon a pedestal. And, even though the writers who say that her own book is an attempt to promote sugary Thérèsian piety are wrong, at the same time it is true that she did release that whole flood of misunderstanding of which sugary piety is but one instance. She did not do so consciously, but her slight infidelity toward her secret made it inevitable. For now that she has been cross-examined and her story believed, she becomes isolated, an actress learning to play the part of the little *miraculée* to give people joy. Until now everything had been in order. Even though she was her father's favorite, his "little queen", this was all naïve and uncomplicated, lightened by the clear family atmosphere. And Thérèse was not spoiled. Writing later for her sister Pauline, she says: "I sometimes ask myself how you managed to bring me up so lovingly without spoiling me; you never allowed a single

[6] SS 67.

fault to go unchecked."[7] And Pauline herself: "During your childhood, we made a point of training you in humility. We carefully avoided praising you. Someone went so far as to say that you were ugly."[8] Once on a trip to the seaside, they met some people who admired the charming little daughter. But her father immediately made a sign to them not to flatter her. "But I was very pleased about it because I did not imagine that I was pretty."[9] Then she adds that, being unused to special attentions, she quickly forgot their words of admiration. But the miracle changes all this. She can no longer conceal herself or slip into everyday obscurity. The searchlight of grace has been concentrated upon her; everyone knows it and behaves accordingly. Without her asking, she has to play the saint. Without her asking, but in response to an apparently legitimate demand, she has to turn her life into a proof that the vision was genuine. This may explain the sense of discomfort that she betrays during the years between the miracle and her entry into Carmel. She no longer enjoys the unselfconsciousness of childhood yet has not been granted the protective veil of the convent. Possibly, also, it explains her eagerness to enter Carmel with all speed and by any means, including her audience with the Pope. Perhaps her apostolate was meant to begin at the time of the vision and should have taken the form of speaking quite naturally among her companions, as friend to friend; however, this apostolate was postponed, because it was not warm humanity that was expected of her but supernatural counsels spoken from on high and for which she was still unprepared. At the end of her life, she rediscovers her strong, pure *novissima verba*; perhaps it was the fault of talkativeness that lost for her the *prima verba*. Which does not mean that Thérèse is not genuine in the meantime. It is simply that the plaster sanctity in which her companions encase her hampers the development of her real self. It will take a long time—until the beginning of her last illness, in fact—

[7] SS 44.   [8] 2 P 307 (G 73 [ET 59]).
[9] SS 48.

before she succeeds in tearing off this plaster mask, trampling it in pieces and becoming her true self again. For the irony of it all is that, after escaping from the gaze of the world and shutting the convent door behind her, as she had longed to do, she finds herself out of the frying pan into the fire. Here in the convent, she again meets those very Sisters who were first responsible for that false move on account of their curiosity and their embarrassing questions. It is true that she enjoys the protection of the veil, of the Rule and of the silence, as well as the still surer protection of the Mother Prioress' excessively strict training. She is also protected by the incomprehension and suspicion on the part of certain Sisters, by the fact that her real life is unknown and above all by the divine enclosure of the "little way". Yet the memory remains. And there are her own sisters, for whom she has to be an example and who are constantly observing her for signs of sanctity. At an incredibly early age, she becomes, in effect, novice mistress; as she puts it herself, she treads the perilous "path of admiration"[10] and hears nothing but expressions of praise. "Occasionally I am overcome with longing to hear something else but praise; my soul becomes sick of this sugary food."[11] "I shall be loved by you, Mother, and by all my other Sisters, and this affection is very dear to me; but that is precisely why I long for a different convent where I could be unknown, living among those whose hearts are foreign to my own."[12] Is it surprising that she would have been glad to go to Indochina? Her sickness over "sugary food" is really sickness at the sight of the model plaster saint who is always being set up before her eyes. She desires nothing more than to forget herself and be forgotten by everyone. But now she is placed under obedience to gaze upon herself. Pauline is Prioress and takes the opportunity to set her the task of writing—not a treatise on prayer or an exposition of Christian doctrine (which would have been truly wonder-

[10] SS 244.   [11] Ibid.
[12] SS 218.

ful)—but the reminiscences of her childhood. Overcoming her repugnance, Thérèse obeys her. And, since her book found favor with her superior, Marie also wishes to have a keepsake; Thérèse writes Manuscript B for her. Finally, when the former Mother Prioress is reelected, Pauline manages to persuade her to allow the composition of Manuscript C. Then, two months before her death, Thérèse can no longer even wield a pencil, she is so worn out; so Pauline now has every one of her dying sister's words taken down as if she were a sort of oracle.[13] Admittedly, Thérèse has in the meantime outstripped all threats to her interior truthfulness. Much too strong and sane to have succumbed in the face of this temptation, she devotes her remaining energies to fighting against that very counterfeit ideal of sanctity that people had tried to pin upon her. But the struggle to emerge as herself has left one mark upon her that she is unable to efface even at her mature period: the habit of using herself as an illustration. When she eventually comes to the Bible and everything now assumes divine proportions and the truth stretches before her into infinity, it is—humanly speaking —too late. She cannot straighten out the furrow in which she has been placed; being sick, she cannot even summon up the physical energy for it. And so she allows herself to be regarded as a faultless exhibit for the demonstration of Christianity. The Sisters force her, during her last years and months, to divulge "words of wisdom", which she again feels unable to refuse. Yet now such conversations do not exhaust her as they used to do. It is no longer harmful, and she simply speaks in order to give joy. She gives herself utterly so that all may share her. She has achieved the seemingly impossible by arriving at her goal after having set out on the wrong lines.

In her book, she describes how human beings can cooperate with the sanctifying grace of God in their souls. She likens them to a gardener whom God instructs with the necessary knowledge while reserving the question of its fruitfulness for him-

[13] N 142 (LC 152); G 460 (ET 367).

self to decide. But what if the cooperation is lacking? "What happens when an unskillful gardener does not prune his trees properly? If he is unable to distinguish the different species and tries, for example, to graft roses onto a peach tree?"[14] Thérèse leaves the question open until a curious association of ideas suddenly reminds her of a story from her younger days.

> I remember that there was once a finch among the little birds I kept that sang enchantingly. I also had a linnet that I used to look after with "motherly" care, because I had got it before it was able to enjoy the happiness of freedom. This poor little prisoner had had to grow up without any musical instruction from its parents and had to listen all day to the finch's joyous trills. One day it wished to imitate its companion—a difficult undertaking for a linnet! It was very touching to watch the poor little creature straining its tiny throat to equal the warbling noise of its teacher, yet to my amazement it finally succeeded. His song, though much softer, was absolutely the same as that of the finch.[15]

Her own destiny swings midway between the two of them. In the end, she learns how to speak authentic words from behind the mask fitted onto her.

This first fault, though a very small one, was to cast unsuspected shadows and troubles over Thérèse's life and was her own responsibility. The second, however, which is related to the first and had still further consequences, even more fateful than the first, was the fault of her confessor. A fault that the confessor committed unconsciously and with all the good will in the world, based on an ignorance of certain subtle yet fundamental Christian verities.

Father Almire Pichon, confessor to the Martin family, was perfectly honest and well intentioned. As we learn from his own deposition at the canonization process, he had a deep and

[14] SS 113. [15] SS 113–14.

benevolent admiration for the young girl.[16] When he committed himself to the fatal utterance, his intention was to make her a lovely present. It was about two months after Thérèse's entry into Carmel; she made a general confession to him, "after which he spoke the following sentences: 'In the presence of God, of the Blessed Virgin, the angels and the saints, I declare to you that you have never been guilty of a single grievous sin. Thank God for what he has done for you; had he abandoned you, instead of being a little angel, you would have become a little demon.' "[17] So the damage was done. The confessor had spoken, *the* authority in a nun's eyes; and with what solemnity! Nothing remained for Thérèse but to accept the judgment in obedience and to believe what had been said. "My heart was full of nothing but gratitude." And, as before, she did not realize what had been done to her. She did not understand what the consequences of such spiritual direction were to be. Thérèse

[16] Pichon's relationship to Thérèse is revealed in a letter to her that runs: "Your sisters may well envy you, and the elect in heaven are jealous. Jesus has given you his childhood and his Passion. How fortunate you are. . . . If you knew how my Canadian apostolate relies on you and cashes in your prayers, tears and sacrifices. I understand the silence of your soul, I see the far places of your heart. I can read and reread the thoughts you leave unuttered. You are blessed, dearest little lamb of God . . ." (S 149 [GC II:720]). Unfortunately Father Pichon's enthusiasm did not prevent him from being the only one of Thérèse's correspondents to destroy all the letters he received from her. These included the "Testament" in which she gave a commentary upon Psalm 22 and of which she said: "My whole soul was in it" (S 366 [GC II:1168]). "As Thérèse had chosen him to be her spiritual director, she must have confided more openly in him than in anyone else. Set in their context of the complete correspondence, these letters could have thrown light upon all the others. Their loss is irreplaceable" (Combes, p. xxv of his introduction to the French edition of her letters [Lisieux, 1948]). All that has been preserved is the rough draft of the letter in which Thérèse asks Pichon to be her director; it begins: "I thought, as you have concerned yourself with my sisters, that you would be kind enough to concern yourself with the youngest too. I wish I could tell you all about myself, but I am not like my sisters. I am not very good at expressing all I feel in a letter" (S 29 [GC I:297–98]). For more about Pichon, cf. Görres 46, 143f., 163, 180, 492 (ET 39, 111f., 128, 140, 157, 173, 396, 402f., 406).

[17] SS 149.

had never been guilty of grievous sin. Judging from Thérèse's own attitude afterward, one might even suspect that what Father Pichon actually said was: had never been guilty of sin. Since from now on, obedient soul that she is, she never speaks of her sins but only of "imperfections". Her sense of sin had been destroyed. The most fateful effect upon her mission was that, at a vital moment, she had been withdrawn from the community of sinners, divided off from them and banished into a lifelong exile of sanctity. She was to make superhuman efforts to escape from this cage but never completely succeeded, because she was fenced in by obedience.

Here again, the blame cannot be laid on her life at home. As a very small child, she possesses a most fine and delicate sense of sin, which her parents and sisters do nothing to blunt. At the same time, this sense of hers needs no sharpening whatsoever. Thérèse is acutely aware of her guilt; her repentance is immediate, and she confesses as soon as possible. Zélie, her mother, writes in a letter: "The child is a source of joy to us all, especially on account of her wonderful openness. It is charming to see her running after me when she has something to confess. . . . 'Mama, I have kicked Céline once and slapped her once. But I won't do it again.' (It's like this for everything she does.)" [18] "Without meaning to do so, she tore a little piece of wallpaper yesterday and right away she got herself into a pitiable state. She wanted to let her father know immediately. But he only came back four hours later when everybody else had forgotten about it. However, she ran over to Marie and cried, 'Tell Papa that I have torn the paper. . . .' She stood there like a criminal awaiting judgment." [19] There are other stories from which it is clear that the thought of her faults is unbearable to her. Once as she is settling down to sleep and her mother bends over her, she slips under the blankets—"I don't want anyone to look at me." But her mother is scarcely out of the room when she climbs out of her cot and, in her overlong

[18] SS 22.   [19] SS 18-19.

nightgown, runs barefoot down the stairs, bursting into tears as she throws herself into her mother's arms: "Mama, I was naughty, please forgive me."[20] Later, there is the incident with Victoire, the maid, at whom she suddenly stamps her foot in rage and shouts: "Victoire, you are a naughty thing." Victoire had been hiding two candle-ends beneath her apron as a surprise, and now she produces them. "At first I had cried with anger, but now I poured forth tears of bitter repentance. I was as much ashamed as distressed, and I firmly resolved never to lose my temper again."[21] Her intense sense of sin at this early age was God's way of introducing her to the severe trial of scrupulosity. Ignatius maintained that the school of scruples, which he himself had to live through in an extremely severe manner, is a great grace, because, as a result, one's awareness of sin grows supernaturally keener for the rest of one's life. God has trained many saints in this school.[22] This period of testing comes to an end in the events of Christmas 1886, which is incorrectly described as Thérèse's "conversion", or "second conversion". It is nothing of the sort but simply the end of a fixed period of testing, when God sets her upon her own feet and releases her again into normal living. God did not think it necessary to order his time of testing according to the sequence of Thérèse's own experience. He granted it to her as a special grace after the "miracle" had already driven her into the isolation of sanctity. It was an attempt on the part of providence to straighten out the slight crookedness that the vision had occasioned.

The combination of these two factors, her privileged position as a *miraculée* and her sinlessness, was sufficient to block the development of something that had played an important part in her childhood—a profound understanding of confession. All the faults that Thérèse speaks about date from her younger days. Later she does not commit any. She could not, in her con-

[20] Presumably placed in the *Story of a Soul* on the basis of something one of the Sisters remembered.
[21] SS 39. [22] *Spiritual Exercises*, nos. 149–51.

dition. Therefore certain of the central mysteries remain unacknowledged in her theology: the mystery of bearing sins and of solidarity in sin, the mystery of how love may be coupled with an awareness of sin, above all the mystery of confession. The urge to confession, which had previously been so powerful, ceases completely with the "miracle". Thérèse goes to confession regularly, like the other nuns, but confession is no longer an elementary need for her so much as a kind of blessing and confirmation of her way. Confession is far from being the elementary need for her that Holy Communion is. And yet, when one thinks of the early beginnings quoted above and compares the subsequent development of her mission, one can hardly say that her mission was not meant to enliven the meaning and deepen our existential understanding of confession.

Through the miracle that isolates her as well as through her less than apparent awareness of sinfulness, Thérèse is once again brought close to Saint Paul. He also has his miracles; on the road to Damascus, where he is stamped as the first "mystic" in the presence of witnesses; he is one set apart and regards himself as such all his life. Set apart from "ordinary" Christians and from the "regular" apostles, he is placed upon a special pedestal of his own to serve as a model for all the faithful; he does not have it in him now to sin or recognize his own sins. Even his earlier persecution of the Church and his part in the death of Stephen are not so much sinful as signs of ignorance and misdirected religious zeal. Although he does not consider himself justified, he was not truly responsible. His personal difficulties, like Thérèse's, are centered around the axis of grace and works, not grace and sin. In this respect, Thérèse's religious experience is much closer to Paul's than Luther's was. And, like Paul, though even more strongly, Thérèse is caught into the dialectic of sanctity expressed in Philippians 3:12–15, as the tension between perfection and imperfection.

Is she a saint? She has seen the Mother of God, but she has been robbed of the innocence of this meeting. She has been declared sinless. Even though Thérèse has not been thinking much about sanctity, yet the conviction is borne in upon her that life is somehow connected with sanctity. She does not ascribe personal sanctity to herself, yet she does belong in the "ranks" of the saints. After having spoken about the miracle, she writes two pages about her longing to imitate the heroines of French history, Joan of Arc above all. "Then I received a grace that I have always considered one of the greatest of my life."[23] That is, the Lord showed her that true fame does not necessarily demand striking deeds. "As I believed myself called to fame and was looking for the means to achieve it, it was revealed to me interiorly that my allotted fame was not to shine in the eyes of the world but consisted in becoming a great *saint*."[24] A curious revelation, which somehow presupposes that her mind had been deflowered of its innocence. It is as if she wishes to avoid being frozen into a conventional concept of sanctity, as if she is breaking through to the warm air and regaining her freedom of movement, when she says: "This desire might appear presumptuous when it is remembered how imperfect I was, and still am, even after so many years of life in the Order; nevertheless, I still cherish the same daring hope of becoming *a great saint*."[25] Between the saint and the great saint stretches a gulf of endless striving such as any great soul needs for breathing space. It was not ambition or thirst for "glory" that drove her to utter these words but the need to strive, quite simply the need to live. What was true at ten years remains true at seventeen, when she writes to Céline: "God heaps graces upon us as upon the greatest saints."[26] And even later, when telling the story of her childhood, she is to say of her illness that "a *miracle* was needed"[27] to heal her. She says this in praise of Mary, but she also says it because she belongs to the company of the saints.[28]

---

[23] SS 72.   [24] Ibid.
[25] Ibid.   [26] S 91 (GC I:542).
[27] SS 65.
[28] Compare also the following texts: "I want to be a saint" (S 47 [GC I:406]);

But the more she is taken at her word and "grows" in sanctity, the more she grasps her mission, the mission of the "little way", which is the only possible way: "He must increase, I must decrease." And so her progress means in a sense going backward, for once she is taken into the world of the saints, her only path leads from "great sanctity" to "little sanctity".[29] A month before her death, someone referred to her great sanctity. "No, I do not consider myself a great saint; I only think that the good God has planted seeds in me that are for my benefit and for the benefit of others." "No, I do not consider myself a great saint, I believe I am a *quite little saint*."[30] Or, in the paradoxical statement of her last months: "God is calling you to be a great saint without your ceasing to be little—in fact, to become less each day."[31] And the statement (which makes one ask whether it is really authentic): "You know well enough that you are nursing a little saint."[32] But what exactly is a "little saint"? What exactly is meant by "great" and "little" when it is God who bestows all grace and all sanctity? God is the Holy One; and does not all human sanctity consist in holding fast to the Holy One, nourishing oneself on him, clothing oneself in him and rejecting any description of oneself as holy? "Someone said to her, 'You are a saint.' 'No,' she replied, 'I am *not a saint*. I have never accomplished saintly deeds. I am quite a little soul on whom the good God has heaped graces. What I say is the truth. You shall see in heaven.' "[33] And now she says to her novices that one should "not labor to become a saint but to give joy to God".[34] Thus her path is finally cleared, and she

---

"Yes [my dearest little father], I shall always remain your little Queen, and I shall try to be your glory by becoming a great saint" (S 58 [GC I:433]; cf. S 72 [GC I:493]); "Ask the Lord that I may become a great saint" (S 88 [GC I:520]); and to Céline: "Jesus asks all, all, all of you, as he does of the greatest saints" (S 56 [GC I:450]).

[29] N 113 (LC 131).   [30] G 463 (ET 370).

[31] S 340–41 (GC II:1120).   [32] G 463 (ET 370); LC 263.

[33] N 133 (LC 143).   [34] 1 P ix, sec. 21 (G 132 [ET 103]).

escapes from the snare that threatened to entangle her in the notion of her own sanctity. Now that she has found her little way, the concept no longer troubles her. Call it whatever you wish, what matters is not the word but the thing.

Pauline is discussing the "degree of perfection" that she supposes her to have reached. Thérèse: "Sanctity does not consist in this or that practice, it consists in a disposition of the heart that makes us humble and little in God's arms, teaches us our weakness and inspires us with an almost presumptuous trust in his fatherly goodness."[35] Briefly, the word sanctity comes to include for her everything that is genuine and real to each one of us—because it is just so ordinary. In her most solemn pronouncement, that act of oblation that she was constantly performing and applying to herself, she writes: "O my God, O most blessed Trinity, I desire to love you and make you loved, to work for the glorification of Holy Church by saving souls on earth and delivering souls suffering in Purgatory. I desire to accomplish your will perfectly and attain the degree of glory you have prepared for me in your Kingdom. In a word, I desire to be a saint, but I feel my powerlessness, and I ask you, O my God, to be yourself my sanctity."[36] From this text, it is quite clear that the primary motive is no longer sanctity but the love of God, the glory of the Church, the salvation of souls and the fulfillment of the divine will. Sanctity is simply a name by which to summarize all these things and does not add anything essential to them. This is in line with the authentic teaching of the "little way", as I shall hope to show.

But Thérèse could have spared herself this long detour by way of "great sanctity". It did not lie in the substance of her mission but in its shadows. The coming of the shadows is to be traced to the lack of contact between her and the Church's ministry. If, instead of speaking to her sister about the miracle, she had spoken to a confessor (and obviously she had to tell someone), then the misfortune would have been averted. And

---

[35] N 112–13 (LC 129 note). [36] SS 276.

if her confessor had spoken to her quite objectively after her entry into Carmel, instead of in that indiscreet, personal fashion, the second derailment need not have occurred. Eventually, after heroic struggles, Thérèse managed to recover from these mishaps; this proves that she had a remarkably sound spiritual constitution and had received tremendous graces for her mission. But scars were left that remain visible until the very end; right until then, one observes a certain rigidity in her will that does not harmonize with her teachings. Ever since her childhood, she has known that her life is to be short, and yet she feels obliged to pack every moment of this short life with edification. This is expected of her by her companions and by the Church—it is inseparable from her mission. If she is to be a model, then she will not be a cause of disillusionment. And so, even to the end, her self-surrender and abandonment smack to some extent of a stage performance. How moving and shaking it is to watch her trembling the day before her death: "Mother, is this the death agony? How shall I manage to die? I shall never know how to die."[37] Death, the end of action, is sheer contemplation and passion. We do not manage to die; it is done for us. We do not surrender ourselves; we are taken. Thérèse regards even this extremity of life as a deed to be performed as well as possible. And her death is indeed harder than she imagined it would be. Time and again it is postponed; already four months before her death, she is comparing herself to Tantalus: "I know that I shall soon die. But when? It does not come. I am like a child who is constantly being promised a cake; he is shown it from a distance, but as soon as he reaches out for it, a hand withdraws it."[38] "I am like a child waiting at the station for its parents to come and put it on the train. They do not arrive, and the train departs . . . , but there are other trains, and I shall not miss them all."[39] But the waiting is so endless that by the time the day of her death comes she

---

[37] N 188 (LC 201).　　　　　　　　[38] N 12–13 (LC 47).
[39] N 33–34 (LC 62).

no longer believes in death: "Look how much strength I have today, Mother. No, I shall not die. It may go on for months. I do not believe in death for myself; I only believe in suffering. And tomorrow it will be still worse. If it is, so much the better." And a few moments later: "If this is the death agony, what then is death?"[40] Then, when she is finally plunged into the midst of death: "I can't breathe, I can't die."[41] And twenty minutes before the end: "Mother, is this still not the agony? Am I not going to die?"[42] But who, indeed "can" die? Perhaps it is hardest of all for someone whose consciousness is too intense, whose self-control has stretched to the remotest fibers of her soul.

But we owe a debt of justice to Thérèse—it is hard for a person to live in the knowledge that she is holy. In Thérèse's case, moreover, it is not only that certainty of salvation that God has always granted to individual souls (Denz. 805). Thérèse possessed this certainty in the highest degree, for as a child she had seen her name written in the stars and had never since suffered the least fear of being lost. She has no fear of evil: "Ought I in fact to be frightened of the devil? I do not think so, because I do everything out of obedience."[43] She knows how welcome she will be in heaven[44] and is already making arrangements here below for what she is going to do in the next world. She is so sure of her heaven that she really lives there more than here. But, as we said, there is more to her certainty of salvation than this. She even knows exactly what her mission is to be. She fixes upon her place within the Mystical Body[45] and penetrates into the central mystery of the universal economy of salvation, yet without losing sight of her personal role. She knows who she is; she knows how much she will be loved,[46] she makes arrangements for her cult and shares out

---

[40] N 191–92 (LC 204, 230, 243).   [41] N 195.
[42] N 196 (LC 206).   [43] N 177 (LC 188).
[44] N 83 (LC 257).   [45] SS 194.
[46] N 108 (LC 126 note).

her relics.[47] All this with the openness of a child, with that unconquerable, disarming smile that she never loses even in the midst of her breathtaking spiritual acrobatics. "A spectacle to the world and to angels and to men" (1 Cor 4:9), she does her conjuring before the gaze of everyone with all the simplicity in the world. Similarly, she takes over the legacy of her Order, when Mother Geneviève, the founder of the Lisieux Carmel, who had just died, appears to her in a dream; after she has distributed keepsakes to all the other Sisters, Mother Geneviève comes to Thérèse empty-handed; but, with a tender look, she repeats three times: "I am leaving you my heart."[48] In another dream, she meets Anne of Jesus, the adviser and companion of Teresa of Jesus who first brought the reformed Carmelite Rule to France; Thérèse asks her: "Mother, tell me please; does the good God not require anything more of me? Is he content with me?" and receives the radiant reply: "No, the good God requires nothing more of you; he is content, very content."[49]

[47] G 479-80 (ET 382-83).   [48] SS 171.
[49] SS 191.

II

VOCATION

VOCATION IN THE WORLD

T HE UNIVERSAL VOCATION of Christians to live within the Church may take one of two clearly distinct forms, both founded in revelation and both, therefore, sanctified by providence. There is the state of life that places a person in the world and in the framework of the family; and then there is a state of life that begins with a withdrawal from the family and takes God as its foundation. God alone is the end of this state: the religious life. The first state is the "fleshly" state, the only one known to the Old Testament, though at the same time it points forward to Christ. The Old Testament saint is married, because it is through the succession of generations that he receives his portion with the Messiah; in the relationship between man and woman, he produces in the flesh the relationship between God and his Bride, the Chosen People. The Messiah is born into this state of life to perfect it and to provide a starting point for the new, "spiritual" state of life where a person sells all he has and abandons everything to win the pearl of great price. Life in the world, marriage, the family are all sacramentally fulfilled by the Lord, because he came, not to destroy, but to fulfill; yet he fulfills them in such a way as to be the "fleshly image" (Eph 5) for those who utterly exemplify the mystery of Christ and the Church in the "state of perfection". The bond of the first state, marriage, is indissoluble for the space of life (Rom 7:2-3), because the bond of marriage is the symbol within time for something beyond time. The bond of the second state is both superior and more taut, because it is directly connected with the eternal link between Christ and the Church. The person in the first state remains "divided" (1 Cor 8:33), because he stands between the world and God, between promise and fulfillment. The person in the second state is "without care", because he lives for God and by God. Just as the salvation of man is accomplished in the play between the Old and New Testaments, between flesh and spirit, promise and fulfillment, and just as the Old Testament constantly provides the background to the New, with the New forever sanctifying and justifying the Old. And, just as the Christian lives by the constant passage from the Old to the New, eternally renewing his youth at the ancient springs, likewise the vital rhythm of the Church lies in the interplay between the secular and the religious states of life, the two forms bound in a fruitful interchange, in the strength of the family and the strength of the Rule, so that the secular state opens the way to the religious, which in its turn justifies and sanctifies the secular. For truly Catholic periods and people and countries, this is self-evident; it presents no special problem to them; a sort of equilibrium between life in the world and life in the cloister is established as the normal relationship; with modest pride, the family knows itself to be the seed-ground for vocations going beyond itself, and the monasteries, with the same modest pride, know that they are the chosen battlegrounds where sacrifices and prayers will be offered for the Christians living in the world.

The whole form and history of Thérèse's life are deeply stamped by this structure of states of life within the Church. In fact, her life, and the unquestioning way in which she understands the Church's teaching on the states of life, constitutes a clear justification for this traditional teaching. The society in which she was brought up, her family especially, regarded it as obvious that children are the primary end of marriage but that this natural end is itself ordered toward a supernatural end: the children are to be dedicated to God, so that they may be called, if he wills it, to the religious state. For people such as the Martins, it would be just as senseless and unchristian for a family to be shut in upon itself as for a believer in the Old Testament to reject its fulfillment in the New. But, if the secular state is open toward the religious state, it becomes radically transformed by it, as the example of Christ and Mary shows. Without in any way turning the family into a monastery, the truly Christian family will allow the light of God to permeate every natural event and attachment so that they all become symbolic of

Christ and the Church; thus the effect of the sacraments, their transforming power, is felt in the smallest, everyday incidents. The Christian family must be a reflection of the Holy Family, which is itself the type of the supernatural Christian family: "For whoever does the will of my Father who is in heaven, he is my brother and sister and mother" (Mt 12:50). So true is it that the Christian family has to be a form of sanctity that the child who is born into it and grows up there should be so impressed by the sacramental, symbolic reality of the family that it learns to pass naturally through fleshly images to the sanctity of God and the Church. At the same time, it is reminded that these images, no matter how wonderful, are no more than images whose molding lies in the hands of Christ.

No matter what people may say or think about the educational standards of the Martin family, their bourgeois mentality and tastes, it is certain that the narrowness of Louis and Zélie Martin in cultural matters did not color their religious ideas. Thérèse's parents were not "bourgeois Christians". They were deeply pious people whose piety was original and vital because they sought the will of God and strove to fulfill it in everything with complete sincerity. Neither tepidity nor formalism had any place in their household. The things that disturb us, their "petit bourgeois" mode of life and their bad taste, were simply the current fashion of that period; and, while they may have affected the external religious practices of the family, they never affected the heart of their genuine faith. The proof is that, in her later development, Thérèse never had to make the slightest effort to correct what she had learned or to shake herself free from dead formalism. She had never to face the crisis that so many people have to pass through when they are cutting through the shell of family traditions to reach the substantial truth of Christian life. Naturally Thérèse did not pass from life in her family to the religious state without feeling the pangs of sorrow; the sorrow inflicted by the twelve-year-old Jesus upon his parents, the sorrow of leaving Nazareth and, above all, the sorrow of turning aside from Mary and his relatives. All these are essential parts of the saving Passion. Yet Thérèse was not at all harmed or broken by this sorrow. Their tenderness, their unassuming faith and complete conviction of acting aright enabled Thérèse and her father to make this most Christian of separations all of a piece with the rest of their lives. Probably no chapter in the story of her theological development is so important as the way Thérèse managed this transition; her entry into Carmel was a perfect illustration of the Church's teaching on the states of life and the relationship between them. She presents this despised teaching to us in the concrete; all we have to do is to read off what we see in her.

Thérèse was born into a family that immediately served her as an image of heaven. Her family, with its customs and relationships, acted as a kind of picture book for her, in which she learned to spell out the reality of the Christian faith. Everything in this book was concrete, speaking directly and intelligibly, for it was composed in the simple language that God has devised for his children. There is no danger that the child will linger too long over the letters and miss their spirit and meaning. The picture is luminous, the letter significant, and the child absorbs the meaning directly from the picture it sees and the words it hears. Symbolic vision and grasp of wholeness precede the development of abstract thought and provide the surest guide for the awakening mind. The world is wholly sacramental, its appearance an effective symbol of the Spirit of God working through appearances and matter.

At the center of the family is the *Father*. Thérèse loved him, almost idolized him; at a glance she saw in him the unbreakable unity of love and authority. Never fearing him for a single moment, her relationship to him taught her that obedience and love are indivisible, because they are ultimately one. Through her father's authority, she came to understand what God's authority means. She looked toward her father; her father looked toward God, and so she learned to look to God. Thérèse was still quite small when her father took her to church; during the sermon, he bent over her and whispered: "Listen carefully, my little queen, he is talking about your patron saint." "I paid great attention, but I looked at my father more than at the preacher. His fine face was so eloquent to me. Many times his eyes filled with tears that he tried in vain to keep back. When he was listening to the eternal truths, it was as though he no longer belonged to this world, so much did his soul love to lose itself in the eternal truths."[1] And it was Thérèse who knelt beside her father during evening prayers; "I only needed to look at him to learn how the saints pray."[2] Throughout her life, Thérèse was convinced of her father's sanctity.[3] She told with delight how he was honored on the pilgrimage to Rome;[4] how he made wonderful "progress on the path of perfection" from the very beginning of his illness, overcoming his natural impetuosity to such an extent that "one could have thought him to have the most gentle nature in the world."[5] Is it not easy to understand how a daughter would see in such a father a direct reflection of God the Father? Indeed, the two were so intimately linked together in Thérèse's mind that she dared to write at the time of her father's death: "The good God has taken away the one whom we loved so tenderly. Did this not happen so that we might say in all truth, 'Our Father, who art in heaven'?"[6] And once, when speaking of God, she let slip the phrase: "Papa, le bon Dieu."[7] It is the biblical "Abba" Jesu. At the back of her mind was the image of her own father, "who, as dewdrops reflect the sun, himself mirrors the divine father-love from which all fatherhood takes its name".[8] "When I think of you, Papa, then I automatically think of the good God, for I cannot imagine anyone on earth more saintly than yourself."[9] But this father image did not become wholly transparent until the mystery of suffering began to overshadow this holy man. He had long been completely dedicated to God,

[1] SS 42.   [2] SS 43.
[3] S 85 (GC I:510).   [4] SS 124.
[5] SS 153.   [6] S 160 (GC II:724).
[7] N 28 (LC 57).   [8] G 310 (ET 249).
[9] S 57 (GC I:452).

so much so that he even accepted Léonie's leaving the Visitation as coming from God's hand.[10] Without a word, he offered his existence to God. But God, who hears our prayers before they are spoken, had long before revealed to Thérèse the form that her father's suffering was to take—in the prophetic vision of the figure in the garden, with his head veiled, the meaning of which neither she nor her sisters could unravel. Thérèse later gives voice to her awe as she remembers how Leo XIII at their audience had "laid his hand upon her father's venerable head as if wishing to set a *secret seal* upon him in the name of Jesus, whose venerable Vicar he is."[11] The children's sorrow as they watched the offering being fulfilled is heartrending; their father sank into darkness—he actually used to veil his head very often at the start of his illness;[12] he had to be taken into a nursing home, where he pined away during long years of desolation. Now it was not God the Father but the Son who became visible through the veil cast over the sorrowful face. Right into her period in Carmel, the image and destiny of her father remained with Thérèse as the shadowing forth of the divine mysteries. As one of the saint's sisters explains: "It was in Carmel, at the time when our father's serious illness was causing us such a severe trial, that Thérèse drew nearer to the mystery of the Passion. It was also during this period that she received permission to add the name 'of the Holy Face' to her own."[13] Her devotion to the hidden Face of Sorrows is later described by Thérèse as the very heart of her piety. Without any prompting, she took up the motif of the suffering servant of Isaiah, picking out the verse where it says "his face was hidden". And so the prophetic vision of her father in the garden was not an isolated or unintelligible event. We are indebted to Petitot for having shown us the profound connection between this seemingly chilling vision and the subsequent flowering of

[10] SS 153.
[11] SS 135.
[12] Pt 102–3.
[13] Pt 104.

Thérèse's *mystique* of the Hidden Face.[14] It is essential to notice that Thérèse's first sight of this did not come to her from the original, Christ, but from the reproduction, her father. This fact is a divine confirmation of the symbolism uniting the two orders. "As the adorable Face was veiled during the Passion, similarly the face of his faithful servant had to be veiled during the days of his humiliation so as to shine in the heavenly Fatherland near its Lord, the Eternal Word"[15] And Thérèse felt herself drawn into the drama that was being played out before her eyes: "I wished that my own face, like that of Jesus, might be hidden so that no one should know me. I thirsted to suffer and to be forgotten."[16] Two months before her death, she pays him her final tribute in the noble description she gives of him.[17] And, when making her Profession, she unites his sacrifice to her own by asking for the wreath she wore on that day to be placed on the desolate man's brow, along with the formula of profession.[18]

Of her *mother*, there is less to say, because she died when Thérèse was five. Yet the features of this beloved person were also graven in her heart and brought her to understand God's motherly love. Zélie herself tells us in a letter how Thérèse follows after her at every step and how she cries until she again reaches her mother's side. "Every time she climbs the stairs, she calls out at each step, 'Mama, Mama!' At each step a cry for Mama. And, if I forget even once to reply, 'Yes, my darling', she stands where she is and goes neither up nor down."[19] Thérèse's lively imagination, for which every scene was also a symbol, transformed such incidents into a charming tale for a disheartened novice:

> You remind me of a tiny child who is beginning to try to stand up; but it simply cannot manage to do so. More than anything

[14] Pt 100–106.
[15] SS 47.
[16] SS 152.
[17] S 363–64 (GC II:1165–66).
[18] S 141 (GC I:667).
[19] H 9 (SS 18 note 6).

else, it wants to get up the stairs to its mother and so lifts its little foot to climb the first step. Vain effort! Each time, it falls back. Look now, you be this tiny child, and go on lifting your little foot. . . . The good God only asks you for good intentions. He looks down lovingly upon you from the head of the stairs; and soon he will be disarmed by your vain efforts and will come down himself to take you up in his arms.[20]

There are subtle alterations in the second version of the story, yet the essential thing remains—the mother's love, the strength of which enables a person to climb, or at least to make the effort. Mama is the atmosphere of love and, above all, the atmosphere in which one prays. How significant is the little incident that Thérèse relates about the time of her mother's fatal illness: "Céline and I were like two little exiles! Every morning Mme. Leriche called for us, and we spent the day at her house. Once we had not had time to say our prayers before leaving home, and on the way Céline asked me, 'Should we mention that we have not said our prayers?' 'Yes', I agreed. At once she very shyly told Mme. Leriche, who said, 'Then you can do so now, little ones', and, leading us into a large room, left us there. Céline looked at me, and we said, 'Oh, it is not like that with Mama! She has always prayed with us'."[21] Only when their mother is no longer there do they realize that they have always prayed with her: one prays within one's mother as naturally as in the Church. Thérèse cannot pray in a vacuum. She prays with her parents, or her sisters, or the maid, but each time her prayer is a kind of festival, a festival in the communion of saints. Praying brings her into communion with her mother, her father and her sisters. For part of her experience in prayer is conditioned by the presence of beloved persons: the presence of human love is a sort of token for the hidden presence of God. How otherwise can a child be trained in prayer, in realizing the invisible presence, except by the sacrament of visible, tangible love? Thérèse is taken into their prayers and nestles there. She does not expect to receive a direct, personal answer from God, because the answer is already given in the praying community. She has never experienced the arid, unmediated prayer whose only answer is silence until she is staying with a stranger. Later, even before entering Carmel, she has to gain a deeper knowledge of it—especially through her illness, when she cannot even recognize her family. But dryness comes at the second stage in the development of prayer; it is the withdrawal of a presence that had first to be granted. And Thérèse's experience of this presence comes to her through the family.

Everything Thérèse achieves at the supernatural level is rooted in something she has experienced at the natural level. Nothing moved her more, perhaps, than the experience of being loved by her father and mother; consequently her picture of God is colored by a child's love. And it is to Louis and Zélie Martin that we owe the doctrine of the "little way" and of "spiritual childhood", for they allowed the God who is more than father and mother to find a dwelling in the heart of Thérèse of the Child Jesus. And, unlike the great Teresa, she was never stirred by a suitor. When she calls Jesus her Bridegroom, the expression sounds as flat and empty as the mouth of a child can make it; it is simply another sweet name for Jesus that she repeats, thankful to have found a new name for her Beloved. Compare her lack of feeling for the language of mystical marriage with the tears she sheds at the thought of God her Father. One day a novice entered her cell and stopped dead at the expression of heavenly radiance on Thérèse's face: "What are you thinking about?", asked the young Sister. "I am meditating on the 'Our Father'," she answered. "How wonderful it is to call the good God our Father!", and her eyes glistened with tears.[22] She discovers the key to the formulation of her teaching in the passage from Isaiah: "You shall be carried at the breasts, and upon the knees they shall caress you. As a mother caresses her son, so will I comfort you."[23] Or, as she puts it in her prayer:

[22] H 226 (T 213).　　　　[23] SS 208.

"O you who know how to mold the hearts of mothers . . . , your heart is more than motherly to me. At every moment you watch over me and protect me; when I call to you, you never hesitate. And, if at times you seem to be hiding, you are still the one who comes and helps me to find you."[24] Characteristic of Thérèse's realism, and of her need to realize her faith through family relationships, is her request for Céline to paint the Mother of God suckling the Christ Child. On it she wrote the lines: "Be so kind, my little Brother, as to invite me to the feast of love that your Mother provides for you." And, at her First Communion: "As I received Jesus, I received my mother as well."[25]

As a result of so Christian an upbringing, her whole relationship to God was always personal and never merely formal. Thus even when she is obeying, she is obeying out of love for a person, never out of compulsion or a bare concern for some "law". "To be good, in Thérèse's world, means only one thing: to do the will of the father, to give joy to her mother. Guilt means only one thing: having hurt her parents. Repentance and pardon blot out misbehavior entirely, instantly and without question. That is the first and basic ethical experience from which she never departs. Any suggestion of formalism has been wrenched out by the roots."[26] As her own reminiscences make clear: "Fear of punishment simply does not enter in. When her conscience begins to unfold, it starts, so to speak, in complete maturity: with an obedience that is free because it is love."[27] "Even when I was three years old, there was no need to scold me in order to make me better. One kind word was enough, and has been all my life, to show me my faults and cause me to repent."[28] And yet one wonders whether Thérèse really was an exception, or whether similar effects would not be produced in most children (who would love God in a personal

---

[24] Ged 406.
[26] G 56 (ET 46).
[28] N 17.

[25] SS 78.
[27] G 57 (ET 51).

way and without fear) if only parents showed children deeper
Christian love and humility. The fact that Thérèse, as a small
child, is not burdened with guilt feelings is accounted for by
the "sanctity" of the household. As she puts it herself: "Since
I have never had any but good examples before my eyes, it was
only natural that I should imitate them."[29] "The first memories
I have are stamped with smiles and the most tender caresses."[30]
Every command given by her parents is a command of love;
even when its purpose escapes her, she immediately grasps the
love that inspires it, and that is its complete justification. And,
when one sees such love, one immediately wishes to respond
to it and no longer feels the distinction between a command
and a wish. "Since the third year of my life, I have never refused the good God one single wish."[31] In this atmosphere, every moral and religious demand is graced by the uncalculating
love that flows out of the relationship between the parents and
their children. This miracle of love is renewed daily, so that it
imposes no strain on the children, who accept it naturally and
do whatever they can to live up to it.

All the more so when this relationship is complemented by
many similar ones between the siblings themselves. The more
children there are, the more completely they mirror the community and the Church. The love between the sisters so mov-
ingly described by Thérèse reflects the same atmosphere as the
love of the parents. When she later comes to love all her religious Sisters in Carmel with a tender and seemingly natural
affection, this represents the unfolding of her love for Pauline,
Marie, Céline and Léonie. And, when she later takes the two
chosen missionaries to her heart so unaffectedly, it is her memory of her three little brothers gone to God that enables her to
do so. How closely she would have been united to her three
beloved brothers and their work if only they had lived (Thérèse
takes it for granted that they would have been priests) with-

---

[29] SS 25.   [30] SS 17.
[31] G 64 (ET 52).

out letting them obscure the great concerns of the Church, "likewise I am spiritually united to the apostles whom Jesus has given me as brothers: all that is mine belongs to each of them."[32]

But this picture would be incomplete if we did not single out Thérèse's love for *Céline*, her favorite sister. Céline is both a sister and a friend, her heart's confidant, who introduces the young girl to all the enchanting secrets of human friendship in God. Although the letters to Céline do not start until after Thérèse's entry into Carmel, they reflect an almost passionate, entrancing love that suffers no break but finds yet more intense forms of expression. "Dearest sister, your Thérèse understands your whole mind; she has read even more of it than you wrote to her. I understood Sunday's sadness, I have felt it all, . . . it seemed to me, as I read, that the same soul animated us, that there is between us something so evident and so alike. Always we have been together, our joys, our griefs, have all been shared. Ah! I know that this will continue in Carmel; never, no never shall we be separated."[33] And, after pouring out her heart another time: "Forgive me. I felt I needed once more to have a conversation with you like those we used to have; but the time has not really passed, we are still just the SAME SOUL, and our thoughts are still the *same* as they were at the windows of the top room."[34] One year after she entered: "Céline!—the dear name echoes softly in the depths of my heart! . . . Surely our two hearts beat in perfect harmony."[35] "How easily I speak to you. . . . It is as though I were speaking to my soul. Céline, I feel that to you I can say all."[36] "Céline, all I have to tell you, you know, since you are I. . . ."[37] "We were ever but *one* soul. . . . Together we have grown up, together Jesus has instructed us in his secrets . . . , together too we suffered in Rome . . . , and Jesus, in separating us, united us in a fashion

---

[32] SS 254.

[34] S 67–68 (GC I:468).

[36] S 114 (GC I:588).

[33] S 54 (GC I:448–49).

[35] S 95 (GC I:546).

[37] S 132 (GC I:629).

till then unknown to my soul, for from that moment I have been able to desire nothing for myself alone but only for us both."[38] "Oh, Céline, let us love Jesus to infinity, and of our two hearts make but one, that it may be greater in love. . . . Do you know that we two together are forty already? It is not surprising that we have already experienced so much, don't you think?"[39] "I feel that these four years [of Carmel] have drawn still closer the bonds that already held us so close. The longer we live, the more we love Jesus, and, as it is in him that we love one another, you see why our affection grows so strong that between our souls there is *unity* rather than union!"[40] Soon afterward, Thérèse pictures this love under the image of one daisy with two stems,[41] both nourished by the same sap and ultimately enjoying the "same mission".[42] An inner voice tells her that, despite all opposition, Céline will eventually find her way into her Carmel. But beforehand, the complete oblation of this life is necessary: with her father already on his deathbed, Father Pichon writes to ask Céline to come out to Canada as an auxiliary on his mission. Thérèse writes:

> The good God wanted me to make my sacrifice. I made it, and then, like you, I felt serenity in the midst of suffering. But I felt something else, that often God only wants *our willingness*. He asks *all*, and, if we refuse him the least thing, he loves us too much to give way; but the moment our will is conformed to his, the moment he sees that we seek him alone, he behaves toward us as once toward Abraham. . . . I think that you are under *trial*, that the cutting-off of which you feel the need is taking place *now*. . . . It is *now* that Jesus is breaking your nature, giving you the Cross and tribulations. The more I go on, the more inner certainty I have that one day you will come here.[43]

And in the same letter, as if speaking to herself: "In the *present trial*, God is purging away anything in our affections that might

[38] S 159 (GC II:724).
[39] S 161 (GC II:725).
[40] S 167 (GC II:740).
[41] S 171-72 (GC II:747-48).
[42] S 174-75 (GC II:753).
[43] S 234-35 (GC II:870-71).

be too much of the senses, but the actual *foundation* of that affection is too pure to be broken. Listen closely to what I am going to tell you. Never, never, will Jesus separate us."[44]

Thérèse proved right, for soon afterward Céline was freed from her obligations by her father's death and entered Carmel; the sisters were united. But to understand all this properly, we need to remember that Thérèse, in all her letters, was guiding her elder sister; encouraging, warning, even scolding, but forever drawing her onward, almost by violence. It was to her that Thérèse told her loveliest parables; in her letters to her that she devised her most inspiring allegories. The stronger their love grew, the more objective and substantial Thérèse's letters became. Under no other conditions could this part of her life in the world and in her family be carried over without a break into the cloister. From the beginning, it was all built upon sacrifice and the hope of heaven. More than any of the others, her letters to Céline speak of death and the transitory quality of life. Their love is a love open to God's infinity.

Her love for the other sisters did not reach this pitch of passion and surrender. Her relationship toward Pauline is like that of a child toward its second mother. With Marie, she always remains a little distant, as with a not entirely congenial elder sister. And then there is "the poor Léonie", as Thérèse frequently calls her, the deviationist who follows a difficult, lonely path, twice leaves the Visitation convent and finally (quite certainly through Thérèse's prayers of intercession) does enter there. As last "outside", Léonie receives Thérèse's last and most mature letters; she also causes her sister a "veritable agony".[45] And, since Thérèse freely accords the quality of sanctity to her relatives (her father, her uncle, her aunt, her cousins[46] and even distant relatives whom she scarcely knows),[47] the same quality is exacted of Léonie: "If you want to be a saint, it will be easy,

---

[44] S 235 (GC II:871).   [45] S 253 (GC II:908).
[46] S 57 (GC I:452); S 59 (GC I:454); S 253 (GC II:908); S 254 (GC II:910).
[47] S 60 (GC I:455).

because in the depths of your heart the world means nothing to you . . . in heaven I shall ask him for all that is necessary for you to become a great saint."[48]

The eyes of the little Thérèse open onto a world of sanctity. She has an unbounded admiration for everything she encounters in her surroundings; she sees only what is beautiful. And she feels that this whole environment has been planned by the good God so as to nourish and preserve the "rare and sensitive plants"[49] that grow there. Everything is as it should be, everything has its place and is brought to fulfillment—though not on earth but in God. Everything is open toward God, speaks of God and leads toward God; for God is the mystery fulfilling the lives of these parents and their children. Everyone around her speaks of God and the saints and the Church with an unaffected certainty that God, even the ever-greater God, is wholly present even in their most childish activities. It is almost as though he makes the dolls and fine weather and bread, distributes sweets and presents the family with joyful feasts. At the point where her childish mind ceases to function, because it has reached the limits of her world, there begins an endless, *beautiful* mystery; and everything one sees or feels or grows aware of is a witness to the beautiful mystery behind it. Nothing that she knows but what God is behind it. The grown-ups know more and see more, and to be grown up means to grow in a deeper knowledge of God's mysteries. But she also has to grow, and so every fiber of her soul reaches out for any means that can give her more of God. When she is still too small to go to church, she boldly celebrates for herself at home. But as soon as she hears the front door opening, she flies to her sister: "O Céline, quick, give me some of the blessed bread!"[50] And one time, when there is none, she "arranges" some herself. She has a right to it, as she has a right to everything, this little queen —"la Reine de France et de Navarre"[51]—who had already re-

[48] S 356–57 (GC II:1149).
[49] Cf. SS 113.
[50] SS 26.
[51] S 53 (GC I:431).

alized in her cradle that "everything is there for the sake of the elect."[52] At that time she is still too young to realize the meaning of sacrifice. She must have everything; so when she is offered a choice she "chooses all".[53] She cannot have enough. Much later it even matters to her whether she receives half a Host or (what luck!) two instead of one. She loves to collect holy objects, no longer, as in her childish naïveté, for herself, but for the Church and for souls. But even now she cannot have enough. In her childhood, she had become so used to seeing all the trivial events of the day as God's gifts that later the very darkness of the night of faith, in which she cannot see to count graces, fails to obscure the visible signs of God's love. These signs act as tokens for her of the graces that are being poured onto the Church through her.

The family taught her to see the unity of grace and merit, gift and possession as self-evident. Everything that the "little queen" sees around her belongs to her; she knows that the love of her parents and her sisters makes it her property. Her own goodness is seen in the same light; the problem of where to fix the dividing line between grace and her own effort simply does not arise. The concepts of justice and love form no antithesis whatsoever in Thérèse's mind, for she sees that justice is finally integrated into love. It is this integration that she has in mind when she lists three anecdotes, one after another. First, how she was taught to overcome her natural timidity by being sent into a dark, distant room to fetch something—with no excuses allowed. "I regard it as a real *grace* that I have been accustomed since my childhood to overcome fear."[54] Thérèse learns that one can do things out of love and obedience that, *in themselves*, and apart from love, would fill one with fear. But "perfect love drives out fear"(1 Jn 4:18). This is coupled with the story of how Pauline filled several glasses of different sizes in order to explain how God completely fulfills the capacity of each of

<hr />

[52] SS 27.   [53] Ibid.
[54] SS 43.

the blessed without granting each the same amount of glory. Within the realm of grace, there is a rule of justice, but its fulfillment gives such bliss "that in heaven, the lowliest of the blessed cannot envy the happiness of the highest".[55] Finally, the story of the distribution of prizes: "With what joy I awaited the prize distribution each year! Justice was strictly observed here; I only received a reward if I had truly earned it. Alone, standing before the august assembly, I listened to my sentence being read by 'the King of France and Navarre'. My heart was beating rapidly as I received my prizes and my crown. For me, it was an image of the Day of Judgment! . . . Oh, how little I suspected what great trials were awaiting my dear King as I saw him then so radiant."[56] A judge radiant with happiness, the one to be judged awaiting sentence in an ecstasy of joy— and, in the midst of it all, the "beating heart" and "strictest justice"! Thérèse was never to form any other picture of the Last Judgment or of the relationship between love and justice. Her family and her apparently so simple life become reflections for her of the deepest Gospel mysteries. And her experience of this living likeness saves the child from all the false, abstract problems of an over-rationalized theology. The questions she puts are living and fruitful and just as relaxed; questions arise, and answers are as matter of fact as the rise and fall of breathing that sustain a life process.

Her part in the interplay of earthly and heavenly events is such a real and complete experience that the child cannot distinguish at times between faith and experience, between the sign that points beyond itself and the sign that contains its own meaning. Before her first confession, Pauline instructs her in the sacrament: "You know, Thérèse, you do not confess your sins to a man but to the good God himself." "I was very much convinced of this truth. I made my confession in a great spirit of faith, and I even asked you seriously whether I ought not to tell Father Ducellier that I loved him with my whole heart

[55] SS 45.   [56] Ibid.

since it was God I was going to speak to in his person."[57] And why not, indeed? Had not the bread that Thérèse took it upon herself to "bless" tasted "just like blessed bread"? And was she not quite right, when returning from her first confession, to stop by the street-lamp and take out the newly blessed Rosary in order to see "what a blessed Rosary looks like"?[58] Who would be so blind as to deny that a child would taste and see as Thérèse did? Again, during the Corpus Christi procession, Thérèse scatters flowers before the Lord and throws them high into the air so that they touch the monstrance as they come down; how obtuse one would be not to see that what she is doing then, in a symbol, is just as authentic as what she does later in naked truth!

The love that permeates the family is a completely pure love. Although it is an earthly and flesh-and-blood love, it is completely free from any trace of the disturbance, confusion and danger that concupiscence brings. Thérèse had the good fortune to have this completely human and incarnate family love beside her all the years of her life as the sure starting point for her venture into heavenly love. Consequently the difference between marriage and virginity never presented a problem to her. Married love within the framework of the Christian family was from the beginning *the* symbol and sacrament of the virgin love between Christ and the soul. "Is our family not a virginal family?"[59] No disillusionment ever descended like a spring frost upon the delicate blooms of love that this family had cultivated together. All her life, Thérèse remained uninhibited in her naïve and pure avowals of love. "*Tendresses*", "*caresses*" are the words that occur again and again to express her relations with God, the holy souls and her Carmelite Sisters. It might seem sugary, insipid and untrue; yet, coming from her, it is the very truth. Just because the shadow of concupiscence never fell upon her, she can gaily use bodily terms

[57] SS 40.   [58] H 27–28 (SS 41 note 38).
[59] S 124 (GC I:616).

for expressing her love, without any fear—and, indeed, with their full Christian meaning. When she first visits the Bishop of Bayeux, she accepts the affection heaped upon her with the same joy with which she slumbered in her father's lap. "He caressed me as no one (I was told) was ever caressed by him before."[60] Once again, on the day of her Clothing, the same prelate ". . . was very kind to me. . . . [He] told everyone I was 'his little girl'. . . . I remember especially his visit on the occasion of our Father Saint John of the Cross' centenary. He took my head into his hands and stroked my hair time and again; never was I so honored!"[61] It is characteristic that she immediately continues: "In that way God reminded me of the caresses he will bestow on me in the presence of the angels and saints, and now he was giving me only a faint image of that in this world; so I experienced great consolation."[62] In her eyes, all pure affection immediately puts her into contact with its source, the incarnate God. It also draws her close to the disciple of the Word-made-flesh:

Remember how the virgin Apostle
In holy ecstasy drew near to your heart!
Resting there, he knew your tenderness,
And entered into your secrets, Lord!
I am not jealous of your beloved disciple;
I know your secrets, because I am your bride . . .
O my divine Savior,
I rest upon your heart.
It is mine![63]

Far from being shut in upon itself, the Christian family is so completely open toward eternity that it suffers no break at the

[60] SS 117.   [61] SS 156.
[62] Ibid.
[63] Ged 391. Rappelle-toi qu'en une saint ivresse / l'Apôtre-vierge approcha de ton Coeur / En son repos il connut ta tendresse; / Et tes secrets il les comprit, Seigneur! / De ton disciple aimé je ne suis pas jalouse; / Je connais tes secrets, car je suis ton épouse . . .
O mon divin Sauveur, / Je m'endors sur ton Coeur. / Il est à moi!

hands of death. Heaven is so closely interwoven into their lives that the passing of one member to the next life, while emphasizing the transcendence of love, in no way weakens the family's love. The first to pass over are the four little angels, Thérèse's siblings, to whom she trustingly commends herself. "I talked to them with childish simplicity, reminding them that as I was the youngest in the family I had always been the most petted and loved by my parents and my sisters and that they also, if they had remained on earth, would doubtless have shown me the same love. Their going to heaven seemed to me no good reason for forgetting me; on the contrary, since they were in a position to delve into the divine treasures, they must take *peace* for me from these treasures and thus show me that in heaven they still knew how to love! The answer was not long in coming."[64] At the age of five, Thérèse lost her mother. Those were the days of the deepest sorrow for all of them, yet one cannot say that her "death destroyed the happy, sunlit family life at its roots".[65] Among those remaining, their love became gentler, full of longing, turned more than ever toward heaven. But there was no less motherliness in their love: "The ever-affectionate heart of our father seemed to be endowed with true motherly love, and I felt that you [she is addressing Pauline] as well as Marie became the tenderest and most selfless of mothers to me."[66] The family feasts now emphasized more than ever the earthly-heavenly interplay. Both aspects enter into Thérèse's descriptions of their Sundays: the radiant presence of God and the "melancholy haze" over this day. "My heart was sensitive to the exile of this earth, and I longed for the rest of heaven, for that *Sunday* that knows no evening, in our *abiding home*."[67] This melancholy in the young child's life is part of that nostalgia for beauty and perfection that every person of any depth feels in youth and that touches a far deeper chord than the subsequent melancholy of puberty. But there is no hint that this

[64] SS 93.   [65] G 68 (ET 55).
[66] SS 35.   [67] SS 42.

sensitiveness drove Thérèse into isolation or loneliness. Even the longing that used to seize her as she was accompanying her father on his fishing expeditions did not set a barrier between them; on the contrary, it drew them closer together, just as Pauline was drawn closer when the two of them saw the sun setting over the sea. No, the family is broad, pure and fine enough to cherish every one of God's mysteries in its midst, the mysteries of birth and death and the mystery of the beyond. It is strong enough to remain with Thérèse on her bed of sickness. The chaplain to the convent comments: "You have a great sacrifice to make in leaving your sisters." But Thérèse replies: "Father, I find I'm not leaving them. On the contrary, I shall be even nearer to them after I am dead."[68] And, at the time her father died: "Our Lord wishes to hold court on earth as well as in heaven; he desires angels who are martyrs and angels who are apostles." [69] Therefore, just as Thérèse's early days had been a sort of family paradise, similarly the paradise above takes on the features of a family celebration: "Soon we shall be dwelling in our Fatherland, soon the joys of childhood will be given back to us forever, the Sunday evenings together and our heart-to-heart talks."[70] That is how she writes to Céline. And to Léonie: "There we shall taste forever the joy of our family life . . . , and I believe that our joy will be still greater than if we had never been separated."[71] And once more to Céline: "Our dearly beloved father lets us feel his presence in a way that moves me most deeply. After the five long years of death, what bliss it will be to find him again just as he was!"[72] And, at an earlier date, when her sick father could not come to her Clothing: "Jesus wishes to take me as an orphan . . . , but the legitimate joys that Jesus has refused me in exile, he will grant to me anew in the Fatherland."[73]

We need to take to heart the fact that the family, as Thérèse

[68] N 46 (LC 74).
[69] S 160 (GC II:725).
[70] S 165 (GC II:732).
[71] S 201 (GC II:816).
[72] S 239 (GC II:881-82).
[73] S 145 (GC I:684).

knew and lived it, was something very different from the "flesh
and blood" that the gospel directs us to abandon, something
very different from that "flesh and blood" from which most
saints have had to break away with one sharp wrench. This
family does not stand in exactly the same position as the Holy
Family—*before* the threshold of the new order of the New
Testament (which cannot be established except by the Lord's
leaving them for this new state of life), Jesus' parents stand
disconcerted, bewildered in the face of this painful rupture of
customary bonds. Thérèse's family, on the other hand, bases
itself entirely upon New Testament foundations, already aware
that it is simply a stage in the ascent toward the ultimate state
of virginity. To surrender themselves entirely to the Lord in
the religious life had been the ambition of both parents; unable
to do so themselves, they had their longing fulfilled in their
children. Married love stands under the protective shield of the
absolute love between Christ and his Church, or, what is the
same thing, under the sign of virginity.[74] Thérèse knew this
well enough and so knew that there is no gulf to cross; the
picture transforms into life, the analogy fulfills itself in reality.
If only all Christian families were aware of this ultimate con-
tinuity between the two states of life, they could all say with
Thérèse: "I love my own people. I do not understand the saints
who do not love their own families!" And: "I love Théophane
Vénard, because he is a little saint. His life is quite everyday;
he loves the Immaculate Virgin very much and is very devoted
to his family."[75] And perhaps only those who have enjoyed a
similar childhood—really enjoyed it, and not simply projected
their paradisal joy onto it in retrospect—will completely understand her *mystique* of childhood. Such children feel themselves as near to God as to their mother's heart. They accept
love with the unquestioning candor peculiar to the world of
childhood, that world that the Lord had in mind when he called
the little ones to him and blessed them, not promising them

[74] S 124 (GC I:616).   [75] H 250 (T 235–36).

paradise but stating that it is theirs already. Here, without a doubt, Thérèse's family plays its part in her personal mission. In order for her task to be accomplished successfully, the family had to be what it was. Just as all missions assigned to great saints have something impersonal, matter-of-fact and paradigmatic about them, so this family life is lifted to a higher power by the mission given Thérèse. It has something "sacramental" about it; it is an effective sign—which must be interpreted in its entirety as a sign—of a reality dwelling within yet reaching beyond itself.

Which may explain why Thérèse behaves no differently in the great Catholic Church than she does at home. She takes her place in the great family of the Church just as unaffectedly as she claimed possession of all the goods and graces in her parents' home, without show or fuss. She was accustomed to going from one to the other without embarrassment. Every afternoon she went for a walk with her father: "We would make our visit to the Blessed Sacrament together, going to a different church each day."[76] And her father also showed her the Carmelite chapel, explaining to her what the Sisters behind the grille were doing. Thérèse was already used to feeling at home in these places by the time she set off on her pilgrimage to Rome. Naturally, when they arrived in Milan, she and Céline had to climb up to the Cathedral roof and, from the topmost tower, "enjoy seeing all of Milan at our feet".[77] In Loreto, she is enraptured by the lovely site chosen by the Mother of God for her house. Overwhelmed at the thought of being under the same roof as the Holy Family, she puts her Rosary into the bowl used by the Holy Child. Naturally she must make her Communion in the Holy House, and not simply in the great basilica—and naturally she succeeds through chance, cunning and providence. "You can imagine, Mother, the joy we both experienced at receiving Communion in that blessed house! It was a heavenly happiness that words cannot express. What then

[76] SS 36. [77] SS 126.

will it be like when we communicate eternally in the House
of the King of heaven . . . ; then we shall not have any need
to have some souvenir as we did, to scratch secretly upon the
walls that had been hallowed by the divine presence, for his
home will be ours for all eternity."[78] Children must touch everything and go looking in every corner. Thérèse does so and
is proud of it. She had to touch every relic in reach with her
crucifix—the one she was to bequeath to her priest-brother,
Bellière, shortly before her death.[79] She was not there to see the
Coliseum and listen to the guide's explanations. "One thought
only filled my mind—to go down to the arena! . . . We crossed
the barrier where there was an opening . . . , clambering over
ruins that crumbled beneath our feet; Papa stared at us, amazed
at our boldness. He was calling us back; but the two fugitives
heard nothing."[80] They must kiss the cross on the floor; in the
catacombs, Thérèse and Céline had to lie down in what had
been Saint Cecilia's tomb and take away some of the earth from
it. In the Church of Saint Agnes, they sought vainly for a relic;
they were refused when they asked at the monastery door,[81]
but God was on their side, for at their feet fell a fragment of
red marble, part of an ancient mosaic dating back to the time of
the gentle martyr; they picked it up so as to take it to Pauline,
who was by this time Mother Agnes of Jesus. Nor did she see
any reason why she should not clasp her hands on the knees of
Leo XIII in urging her wishes. She is at home in the Church.
Finally, the way in which Thérèse forces her way into Carmel
suggests that she regarded Carmel no less than the Church as
her property and inheritance. "I was determined to enter at
the very hour I had received 'my grace' the year before."[82] "I
begged Jesus to work the miracle I needed."[83] In fact, this child
seems to have made the transition from the world to the cloister
almost without a break; the cloister represents the fulfillment

[78] SS 129.   [79] S 367–68 (GC II:1173–74).
[80] SS 130.   [81] S 33 (GC I:335).
[82] SS 107.   [83] SS 109.

of everything for which her family had longed—certainly not
without the inevitable separation and sacrifices and suffering
—but even these were part of an organic, harmonious growth.
Their Christian family life unfolds easily into the life of the
cloister. For Thérèse, the two states of life are not mutually
opposed; they complement one another as man and woman
complement each other in the natural order. The family grows
in the shadow of the cloister, the children are accepted into the
religious state for which their parents had longed; the convent
that Thérèse enters already houses two of her sisters, she herself will draw the fourth one in after her, while the fifth finds
her home in a different Order. When Thérèse is four years old,
we hear the following account of her written by Pauline in a
letter:

> I want you to tell Sister Marie de Sales that in a few years she
> will have a future novice, guess who? . . . The new postulant is
> . . . is . . . Mademoiselle . . . Thérèse Martin. Yesterday evening
> she gave me her whole confidence, I could have died laughing.
> "I shall be a nun in a convent because Céline wants to go, and
> then, too, Pauline, people must be taught to read, don't you see?
> But I won't take the class, it would be too much of a nuisance,
> Céline will, I shall be the Mother; I shall walk around the con-
> vent all day, and then I'll go with Céline, we'll play in the sand
> and then with our dolls." . . . "Don't you know there has to be
> silence?" "Has there? . . . Ah well, so much the worse, I won't
> say a word." "What will you do, then?" "That's no great trou-
> ble, I shall pray to the dear Jesus; but then how I can pray to
> him without saying anything, I really don't know, and who will
> be there to show me, as I'll be the Mother?"[84]

When Pauline enters, Thérèse is nine years old, already prepared long since to go away with her "into a far-distant desert",[85] at a time when she still knows nothing very definite
about Carmel. Pauline consoles her for the grief of departure;
she understands that Carmel is the desert she dreams of and

[84] S 6 (GC I:108).   [85] SS 57.

suddenly feels "the certainty of a divine vocation". Next day she confides her secret to the Prioress; the latter believes in her vocation, "but told me that postulants are not received at the age of nine; I had to wait until I was sixteen. I resigned myself in spite of my intense desire to enter as soon as possible and to make my First Communion on the day Pauline received the Habit."[86]

This is all a matter of one day: Pauline's disclosure, Thérèse's vocation, her application and acceptance, and the decision is made. The six years of waiting do not count in her mind; the die is cast, and, as soon as she can manage it, she will follow Pauline and Marie, who enters four years after Pauline. In the face of opposition from ecclesiastical and Carmelite superiors, she simply storms the walls of the convent. She is called; she has responded; it is now up to God and men to smooth the path that providence has set for her.

Even in the convent, she remains the little queen. At the request of her sister, now Mother Prioress, she writes her first manuscript; this was supposed to deal only with childhood memories. Its conclusion is like a glorification of her inner childhood world from the convent.[87] "Our Lord has shown the same mercy to me as to King Solomon. He has not willed that I have one single desire that is unfulfilled. . . ."[88] And now, this twenty-two year old, in the evening of her life, looks back at the rich harvest. Looking down from the heights, she sees all her childhood wishes as paths that mount up to where she is. She has walked all these paths, and they have all led to fullness, to perfection. Everything is fulfilled—"not only my desire for perfection"—this, surprisingly enough, is the first thing she mentions, without any sense of her own audacity. But she is also including other wishes, childish wishes—perhaps even idle ones that the good God nevertheless condescends to satisfy for the sake of his little queen. At an early

[86] SS 59.   [87] SS 180ff.
[88] SS 174-75.

age, she had wanted to be good at painting and poetry but had to take a back place because other sisters were reckoned to be more gifted. Now, in the convent, her talents are discovered, and she is put to painting and composing verses. Again, "there are other desires of another kind that Jesus was pleased to grant me, childish desires, like the snow"[89] that she had longed to see covering the earth for the day of her Clothing, which does indeed fall, quite suddenly and contrary to all expectation. And the flowers that she treasured so much and found so hard to leave behind—these very flowers she now finds in abundance, and more besides; here in Carmel, their beauty shines more intensely even than before. Then came the last of her earthly wishes; to see her beloved Céline joining her. Her father, for whose sake Céline was remaining in the world, dies: a Sister who had been opposed to her entry now relents; the Bishop removes all other obstacles, and Céline can enter. Thérèse ends her hymn of thanksgiving: "Now I have no other desire except to love Jesus unto folly . . . , now abandonment is my sole guide . . . , and I have nothing more to ask except that the will of God shall be utterly accomplished in my soul."[90] And so she ends—with a short exposition of her special mission—for this is the greatest gift bestowed on her by God. What do they matter now, all those little wishes she had seen realized, those enchanting tokens of God's favor toward her? The birds that used to fly in through the open window to visit her; the relics for which she had sought and that she had, in fact, been given; the two missionary brothers through whom she had received a visible confirmation of her mission in the Church; what do these all matter now in comparison with the boundless grace of her mission? Yet this very mission, which asserts itself so unexpectedly in the last three years of her life, is nothing but her childhood world translated into supernatural terms. Her own childhood is lifted bodily onto the altars of the Church; the trivial little anecdotes of her early years are gathered up

[89] SS 175.   [90] SS 178.

like precious relics into the *Story of a Soul* and become bread for the thousands of souls hungering for eternal youth. Most of her predecessors among the saints, when describing their life in the world, had spoken with bitter regret at not having left the world earlier to love God alone. Thérèse regrets nothing. All was good. All was grace, leading directly to God and Carmel. The first state of life, that of the Christian in the world, with its many-colored moods and the rosy freshness of flesh and blood, becomes completely transparent to the truth of God. In the face of the gospel demand to be perfect, this state of life finds its most complete justification in the wordly life known to Thérèse.

IN RELIGION

W HEN WE DRAW ATTENTION to the new outlook on life
in the world that we owe to Thérèse, who shows us its
essential connection with the cloister, we need to remember
that this was only possible because the Martin family regarded
itself from the beginning as a "vestibule for the cloister". And
even that is not enough. The first part of her life is centered
upon the family and her remarkable childhood; and, while recognizing that her period in the Order constitutes a Carmelite
sublimation of her childhood, it can scarcely be overstressed
that the center of gravity during the second part of her life lies
quite certainly in the Order. Unless we emphasized this point,
we would fail to see the justification and goal of her development, since her previous life in the world simply provides
the basic, earthly material that she had to mold into heavenly
form. If this were not so, then her "doctrine of childhood"
would have to be described as a sort of infantilism, a flight
away from maturity, supernatural Romanticism. Thérèse is far
from all this. She is not a naïve child but what Navalis calls
a "synthetic child". She knows that earthly childhood is only
an image and reflection of true and actual childhood in God,
in which age is irrelevant. "Age does not count in the eyes of
God. Even if I were to live a long time, I would so arrange
it that I still remained a little child."[1] "In heaven, the Holy
Innocents are no longer little children, they simply retain the
indefinable charm of childhood. They are represented as children because we need such images in order to understand the
invisible world."[2] The eternal Child of the Father, the Son, is
not an image derived from fleshly childhood in this world; he
is the original form of all childhood. It is *fleshly* childhood, not
the supernatural, that is the reflection.

In choosing the cloister, Thérèse realizes quite clearly that

[1] N 20 (LC 51).   [2] N 15–16 (LC 48).

she is passing from the world of images into the world of truth. It is also a decisive parting of the ways: "Francis and Jeanne have chosen such a different path from ours that they cannot understand the sublimity of our vocation. But who laughs last laughs longest."[3] It is a choice, in the strictest Ignatian sense, not a natural drifting or attraction. The fact that this choice, and her vocation itself, was brought to light through the agency of other human beings is quite in accordance with the normal workings of Christian and ecclesial guidance and providence. The fact that it was Pauline, her little Mother, and not a priest who was chosen as the agent makes no real difference. How little her desire to be with her sisters decided her entry into Carmel becomes evident once she is inside: no one is more surprised than the Sisters to see how Thérèse immediately replaces the law of flesh and blood with the law of the Order. At the episcopal examination before pronouncing her vows, Thérèse answers the question of why she wishes to enter in the clearest terms possible: "I have come to save souls and, in particular, to pray for priests."[4] This "saving" and "praying", in concrete terms, means suffering. "She chose the Carmelite vocation", as Céline explains later, "in order to suffer more and so win more souls for Christ. It seemed to her harder for our natures to work without ever seeing the fruits of our labors. . . . Thérèse chose this life of dying for herself because it is more fruitful than any other in saving souls. In particular, she entered Carmel in order to pray for priests and to make sacrifices for the sake of the Church."[5] And Thérèse knows what she is letting herself in for. Completely conscious as she is (in this, the very opposite of childish), rational and with due calculation, she knows what she is doing. She does indeed conceal the acuteness of the choice by using friendly, disarming phrases; she garlands the trunk of the Cross with as many flowers as she can find. But her life speaks more eloquently. At

---

[3] S 239 (GC II:881).　　　　[4] SS 148.
[5] G 178 (ET 138).

the moment of her entry, she is entirely herself. The incredibly swift ascent toward perfection during her last years is the true, the sole, justification for her childhood in the world. It also makes sense of those dark and difficult years after Pauline's entry, when bodily and spiritual illnesses creep over her and Thérèse plays at being the odd one out among the family. All this was necessary in order to reach the true and real beginning of her life. Once she arrives there, after overcoming a thousand and one obstacles, she knows quite certainly that nothing has been achieved, that she is only just beginning. She might have credited herself with "merits" for the past; she does nothing of the sort. Real "meriting" can only begin when she is in the state to which God has called her. Until she is numbered among the "vanguard" to which she has been commissioned, until she grasps her weapons, all the sweat and rush is but part of the training. The nearer she approaches the cloister, the more impatient she becomes, like a sinner who cannot wait to get to confession. Thérèse is not fleeing from the world or her family but following the call to die and be born again. Only after this death and rebirth can one begin in earnest. And she knows no peace until the step has been taken. "It draws me on like a magnet."[6] She writes an urgent letter of entreaty to the Bishop, from whom nothing has been heard.[7] And to the Vicar General: "Monsieur l'Abbé, it is now only a week to Christmas. . . . Ah! Why should he call me so powerfully if I am to be made to languish far from him? Monsieur l'Abbé, I hope you have pleaded my cause with the Bishop, as you promised me."[8] The moment of her entry, blotting out the past, is from now on *the* starting point for Thérèse. Later she does not deny the longings and efforts and achievements of her early life, but all of them are related to the point at which she really begins. The point at which one has arrived is the point one begins from. There, perhaps, we have the shortest formula for the lit-

[6] S 38 (GC I:365).   [7] S 39–40 (GC I:387–88).
[8] S 42 (GC I:388).

tle way. It is both endlessly humiliating and endlessly encouraging; humiliating, because one is forever going through the same movements without ever reaching the goal—"Oh, I am still at exactly the same point as I was then"[9]—encouraging, because even one's tentative movements have not separated one from the source, one's growth has not been false, and one remains in communication with the eternal springs.

In order to start these tentative movements, Thérèse had to leave her family for the cloister. She fitted into her family, was protected by it, and everything was as it should be. The impulse to infinite movement was lacking. Her condition was fixed rather than dynamic, a status but not a *status nascendi*. Above all, it provided a firm background against which the personalities of her family showed up well. What Thérèse needs is that her *personality* should die and that she should be reborn as a *person* at a level where she has to draw upon all her latent potentialities. She is in a state of life where deeds and achievements can be measured. She seeks a state where human standards no longer apply, where every attempt to limit one's range or survey the horizons becomes vain. This zero-point, the intersection of the Absolute, is Christ's gift to the Church; it takes the form of utter poverty, consecrated virginity and the abdication of one's own will in favor of total obedience. "I choose all",[10] Thérèse had said as a child. And her choice of all means that henceforth she will never have to choose at all. "I choose all that you will",[11] she herself comments on her words as a child and later gives them their final form: "Were our Lord to offer me my choice, I would choose nothing. I only will what he wills."[12] Her choice of all while still in the world is simply the presupposition for choosing no more in the cloister, in the same way that her family serves as a mirror for her life in the Order.

Through entering this new state of life, Thérèse is given the

[9] N 45–46 (LC 74).   [10] SS 27.
[11] Ibid.   [12] H 237 (T 223).

opportunity to shed her personal limitations and acquire the stature that is hidden for her in God and is only to be revealed through her mission in the Church. We may conveniently distinguish three aspects of this new status and consider them separately: the Rule; her office within the Order and her mission in the Church.

The Rule

The strict and impersonal Rule of the Order enfolds the novice, as she enters, in a new and unaccustomed habit. This habit is not cut according to the measure of the person, for it has been designed beforehand and appears much too spacious. Far from being trimmed to the novice's shape, the habit requires her to grow to its shape. Moreover, in Carmel it is a rough habit, a habit of penance, and whoever wears it must learn to strip herself of all the things she had previously loved, all that seemed indispensable; she must strip herself of her own personality to enter the world of Christ and share his plans and answer his demands. His plan is the salvation of the world through love for the Father, a love unto death on the Cross—so absolutely does he put the will of the Father before his own will and plans. Although it reaches to every single soul, this salvation is not accomplished by an external action directed to each one of them singly; it springs from an interior deed of self-surrender by which the soul is expropriated in loving obedience "to the end", as John says. In his every word and deed, in all his miracles and suffering, the Son withdraws his "personality" to let the will of the Father become manifest; his own personality appears only as the personification of obedience to the Father. It is this rhythm of withdrawal and manifestation, returning to the Father and coming out from him, which gives the eternal Son his vitality as the revealing Word. Each withdrawal takes him toward death, each manifestation to the *Parousia*; each is a function of the one law in his life: to be an image and reflection and revelation of the Father. The Lord demands that each person whom he calls to his intimate service should conform to this law. Each of them is given a position in the society of the Church, a function within the Mystical Body, which requires the withdrawal of his own personality behind the veil of pure objectivity and obedience, so that he may be poured into the saving stream of sacrifice that redeems the world and its every inhabitant. In some cases, they will not appear again until they stand beside the Lord in the *Parousia*, when the world comes to judgment. In others, their following of Christ leads them to appear already in this world, as Christ appeared for forty days after the Resurrection; yet it is not in virtue of their personalities but in the service of some charisma and mission to the Church that they are reborn in the world. Whether they withdraw completely or withdraw to reappear, it is the will of the Lord.

In taking the veil, Thérèse knows full well what she is doing. She knows that conformity to the Rule means accepting the form of the Cross, a Cross, moreover, on which the subjective suffering of Good Friday is transformed by the Church's liturgy into the objective impersonality of Holy Saturday, in the pause between suffering and resurrection during which the old, this-worldly self is dead, while the new self has not yet been reborn into the divine, eternal form of its subjectivity. Life in the Order—a "life of death", as Thérèse describes it—inserts itself into this pause and its deep silence, welding a great link between earthly and heavenly existence, between suffering and resurrection.

Thérèse did not work out any novel theology of the religious state; but, as always with her, her own life is rich in suggestions that theologians only need to expand in order to bring out their lasting value. She finds religious life to be like a kind of dam that increases the potential of the soul for heaven. "In the religious life, the soul, like the young oak, is hemmed in on all sides by its Rule. All its movements are hampered, interfered with by the other trees. . . . But it has *light* when it looks toward heaven, there alone it can rest its gaze, never upon anything below; it need not be afraid of rising too high. . . ."[1] To be shut in on all sides is a form of defense, not to protect one against the world, however, but to arm one for God's battles: "I have put on the breastplate of the Almighty, and he has armed me with the strength of his arms. Henceforth no terror can wound me, for who now can divide me from his love? By his side, I advance to the battlefield, fearing neither fire nor steel; my enemies shall discover that I am a queen and the bride of a King."[2] Thérèse quotes the verse from the Song of Songs about the King's bride, who is "terrible as an army set in array", and the weapons that make her so terrible are poverty, virginity and obedience. Poverty, because the athlete wishing to gain the palm must be naked; virginity, because only those radiant as angels can win men's hearts; obedience, above all, because it is the virtue directly opposed to sin: "The proud angel, in the bosom of light, cried, 'I shall serve forever', and I feel the stirrings within me of a courage that is prepared to brave the fury of hell."[3]

It is most characteristic of Thérèse to interpret this "hemming-in" of souls by the Rule in both a social and a soteriological sense. She did not come into the convent in order to perfect her own soul—unless by "perfection" we mean a person's complete readiness to become the pure instrument in the hand of the Lord for his own designs. She came "to save souls and, in particular, to pray for priests". Of course she realizes that the religious life involves a battle with oneself, with the old self that tries a thousand-and-one ruses to secure its own comfort, rest, honor and will. Yet this battle never becomes an end in itself for Thérèse; it is nothing but the expression of the effort she makes afresh each day to station herself wherever God may need her, in the position of obedience, of complete availability to his will. Everything in the Rule that incites the

[1] S 209 (GC II:831). [2] Ged 414.
[3] Ged 414-15.

Carmelite to self-conquest is for her only a means toward the one important goal: readiness for God's service.

Everyone knows to what a hard school God called the young girl. She got what she was looking for—to see the last drop of her heart's blood and all the sap of her mind and body welling up in God's wine-press before pouring into the vats of the Church. But that was the way she wanted it: "A day in Carmel without suffering is a day lost."[4] Carmel is also a school in which human beings affect one another intensely. "Illusions: God granted me the grace not to have a single one when entering Carmel. I found the religious life just what I had imagined, and none of the sacrifices came as any surprise to me. Yet you know well, my dear Mother, that from the very outset my path was more strewn with thorns than with roses. . . . Our Mother [the Prioress, Marie de Gonzague], who was often sick, had little time to spend with me. I knew she liked me very much and said everything good about me possible, yet God permitted her, without knowing it, to be very severe with me. I couldn't meet her without having to kiss the floor."[5] She can do nothing right; she is no use at all. She regularly gets long scoldings without knowing what it is all about and what she is supposed to do differently. Yet she knows how to draw strength from it all. She is overflowing with gratitude: "How *visibly* God was acting within her who took his place! What would have become of me if, as people in the world believed, I had been the community pet?"[6] "Yes, suffering opened wide its arms to me, and I threw myself into them with love. . . . If one wishes to reach a goal, one must use the means to it. Jesus made me understand that he would grant me souls by means of the Cross, and my attraction for suffering grew in proportion to its increase. For five years, this was my path; nothing external revealed my suffering, which was all the more painful since I alone knew of it."[7] "From the bottom of my heart, I

[4] S 49 (GC I:423).   [5] SS 149–50.
[6] SS 150.   [7] SS 149.

want to thank you, Mother [this time she is addressing Marie de Gonzague], for not having spared me. Jesus knew that his little flower needed the life-giving waters of humiliation, being too weak to take root without their aid; and it is to you that she owes this blessing."[8] Thérèse's hardships have been described often enough and need not be dwelt upon here. More important is the charity with which Thérèse realizes her change of status and grasps the full implications of her new state of life. Although the youngest of them, it is she who decides upon the kind of relationship that is to be maintained between herself and her sisters. From the first, she knows them no longer according to the flesh, and she treats them as she treats any other nun. Which does not mean to say that she behaves stiffly but that she transforms natural love into spiritual love and so treats all the nuns as her sisters in the Lord. Thus she becomes more detached from Pauline and Marie than when the grille stood between them. With infinite delicacy, she deflects every attempt on their part to continue their natural intimacy; she remembers the Lord's words: "Whoever does the will of my heavenly Father is my brother and sister and mother." But it was hard for her to train herself in this new love, as we see in her note to Pauline just before her Clothing: "What is there in you that so draws my soul? You cannot imagine what a privation I feel it not to be able to speak to you."[9] The lax discipline in the convent, so often described by her biographers, is a source of constant suffering to her; but as she is not the superior and has no business to criticize, she uses the laxity as a means of redoubling her ardor and fidelity to the Rule. The slack and slovenly attitude toward the Rule helps her, in fact, to find even deeper solitude; for, when she finds no inspiring example among the Sisters to act as a subjective support, she is brought face to face with the purely objective Rule, written down in cold black and white. But have there not been great saints, Ignatius of Loyola for instance, who wished to enter a

[8] SS 206.   [9] S 80 (GC I:503).

lax Order because it would be harder there, lonelier and more testing than in the coziness of a "spiritual family"?

And this is where the miracle begins. Not only the miracle of Thérèse's shining example but the sheer miracle that makes life in religion possible at all: the strength of heart that the Lord bestows upon his chosen ones, enabling them to cast all their natural human sympathies and loves into the crucible of "living death", where they are transformed and born again on the spiritual plane. Thérèse is misunderstood, badly treated and scorned by the other nuns; it teaches her what the family could never have taught her, how to live through a running warfare of "pin-pricks".[10] "It is less bitter to be broken by a sinner than by one who is just; but, *in mercy for sinners*, to obtain their conversion, I ask you, O my God, to let me be broken for them by the just souls round about me."[11] Her answer to all rebuffs is a most charming smile, a loving glance and her attentive understanding. We possess a sort of documentary of this miracle at its every stage in the many anecdotes told either by herself or her Sisters. On the surface it seems to be a miraculous strength of character; Thérèse conquers her own feelings so successfully that even the laws of natural sympathy cannot prevent her from loving the least congenial nuns and giving herself to them *as though* she found them naturally sympathetic.[12] But Christian love is no *as-though*, for the Lord did not have to "conquer" himself in order to love us; his love for his enemies (and we were all his enemies when *he* first began to love us) was no artificial pretense. On the contrary, it was the unique original love of which natural sympathy is but a created likeness. And so the Christian should not start out from the likeness in order to understand the original and conform to it. He should not measure the latter in terms of the former but should go straight to the original, and, taking it as his model, should elevate and expand the likeness, using it as

---

[10] S 90 (GC I:530); S 97 (GC I:552).   [11] S 361 (GC II:1159).
[12] SS 222f.

a means for expressing Christian love. We find a very precise and concrete teaching on this relationship between natural and supernatural love in both parts of Manuscript C, which treat love of one's neighbor, which Thérèse wrote for her Prioress, Marie de Gonzague.

There is an admirable theological precision and deep psychological insight in the first part, where Thérèse describes the standard of love that should prevail within an Order. This standard is no other than the supernatural love of Christ; it is in, no way a mixture, according to the creature's capacity, of supernatural love with natural love—however authentic this may be. It may be necessary to combine the two and balance them outside religious life, in the family, for instance; there the laws of earthly love and blood relationships are meant to be transfigured, not eliminated. But, in the state of virginity, no account has to be taken of these laws of the flesh (which is ultimately subject to original sin); the one law to be regarded is the love of the Word-made-flesh, who sacrificed himself for his brethren and whose fleshly nature simply served as a means of expressing God's infinite love.

Thérèse says of herself that she did not learn the full meaning of this precept of love until "this year" (that is, 1897), the year she died. Until now, as she admits, she had never meditated closely upon the command to love our neighbors as ourselves; all her attention had been concentrated upon loving God. But now she grows aware of the mystery revealed in the sentence:

> "Not everyone who says Lord, Lord, shall enter the Kingdom of heaven: but those who do the will of my Father who is in Heaven." This will Jesus revealed several times, or I should say on almost every page of his Gospels. But at the Last Supper, when he knew the hearts of his disciples were burning with a more ardent love for him who had just given himself to them in the unspeakable mystery of his Eucharist, this sweet Savior wished to give them a new commandment. He said to them with inexpressible tenderness: "A new commandment I give you that you love one another: that as I have loved you, you also love one

another. By this will all men know that you are my disciples, if
you have love for one another." How did Jesus love his disciples,
and why did he love them? Ah! it was not their natural qualities
that could have attracted him, since between him and them there
was an infinite distance. He was knowledge, Eternal Wisdom,
while they were poor, ignorant fishermen, their minds full of
earthly concerns. Yet Jesus calls them his friends and brothers
and desires to see them reign with him in his Father's Kingdom;
and, in order to open this Kingdom to them, he wills to die upon
the Cross, for he said: "Greater love than this, no man has, that
a man lay down his life for his friends."[13]

It is not Thérèse's habit to break off a train of thought, once
it has taken hold of her, until she has carried it to its ultimate
conclusion. And she immediately detects a certain tension between the text in Matthew, "You shall love your neighbor as
yourself", and that in John, "Greater love than this no man
has, that a man lay down his life for his friends." She sees that
the latter represents an intensified love; it goes beyond the former, which completes the law of love in the Old Testament by
adding the specifically New Testament teaching. "When the
Lord told his people to love their neighbor as themselves, he
had not yet come down to earth, he knew full well how much
man loves himself and that he could not ask of his creatures a
greater love than this for one's neighbor."[14] So Thérèse regards
the Old Testament formula as a temporary concession to the
self-seeking of fallen human nature. "But when Jesus gives his
apostles a new commandment—his own commandment, as he
later calls it—he is not content that we should love our neighbor as ourselves but orders us to love him as he loves him and
as he will love him until the end of time."[15] And Thérèse goes
on to show how this superhuman and, therefore, apparently
impossible command may be accomplished. "O Lord, I know
you never command the impossible. You know better than I
how weak and imperfect I am; you know that I would never

[13] SS 219–20.   [14] SS 220.
[15] Ibid.

manage to love my Sisters as you love them unless you, O my Jesus, loved them *within me*. It is because you wished to grant me this grace that you made your *new* commandment. Oh, how I love this new commandment, since it makes me certain that it is your will to *love in me* all those whom you command me to love."[16] In the strength of this certainty, Thérèse's love is purely Christian with no other admixture. One can only love in this way by an act of pure faith and obedience; yet this obedient faith contains the evidence of its own truth, the witness of the Holy Spirit in the soul. Thérèse demonstrates as much when she continues: "Yes, I can feel it; when I am charitable, it is Jesus alone who is acting within me; the more I am united to him, the more I also love all my Sisters."[17]

The Lord does not love us "on account of our natural gifts"; that is the difference between his *caritas* and every form of human sympathy that, whether erotic or not, remains limited by nature. The first feature of Christ's love is, therefore, that it cannot be limited by human qualities, character, sins, weakness or boundaries but stretches beyond all limits and sins to the universality that is its own interior law. Whereas the family, therefore, takes Christ's love as an example to ennoble and deepen the natural love among its members, Christ's universal love is no mere example for those in the religious state; it is the one and only basis for the life of his Order.

As I meditated upon these words of Jesus, I saw how imperfect was my love for my Sisters, and I understood that I did not love them as Jesus loves them. Ah! now I can see that true charity consists in putting up with all my neighbors' faults, not being surprised by their weaknesses and being edified by their smallest acts of virtue. But, above all, I understood that charity must not remain hidden at the bottom of one's heart. Jesus has said: "No man lights a lamp and puts it under a bushel basket, but upon a lampstand so as to give light to all in the house." It seems to me that this lamp represents the love that should enlighten and

[16] SS 221.   [17] Ibid.

gladden not only those who are dearest to us but *all* who are in the house without distinction.[18]

In religion, therefore, love is entirely founded upon the universal love of Christ, which serves as the touchstone for everything else. This is the reason why a person in religion must be freed from all personal and earthly concerns: he needs to penetrate to the center of this universal love, unhindered by any ties. Thérèse did not unloose these ties as if to climb an impossible peak and live at an inhuman level, cut off from all earthly relationships. On the contrary, her earthly relationships, including those of the family, are drawn into this universal love; they form a part of it, a privileged part, even, but they can never come into conflict with it, because now they have themselves been secured by the vows. Love in the world means reaching to universality through sanctified relationships; in religion, it means stretching the universality of the vows to take in particular relationships.

Thérèse grasped this teaching with masterly assurance and applied it to her relations with her own sisters. Despite having clung so tightly to her family when she was in the world, once she crossed the threshold of the convent, she did not pay her own sisters any more attention than she paid to the other nuns. In fact, the presence of her own sisters "was an opportunity for the young postulant to exercise the greatest self-denial". She only saw Pauline and Marie during recreation, where she "preferred the company of the Sisters who were least congenial to her". And, when she was allotted the task of helping Pauline, this became another source of mortification for her; she knew that all unnecessary talk was forbidden and so did not permit herself the least exchange of confidences. Later she admitted: "O my dear Mother. How much I suffered then! I could not open my heart to you, and I thought you no longer knew me." Then, when Pauline was made Prioress, "God so disposed it that she saw her Mother Prioress less than any of

[18] SS 220.

the nuns." On her deathbed, she even declared herself "happy to die in the arms of another Prioress, so as to exercise all the more her spirit of faith in authority".[19] This was the Prioress to whom she wrote: "You know that Jesus has offered me more than one bitter chalice that he removed from my lips before I drank it, but not before making me taste its bitterness. How right the holy King David was when he sang, 'How good and pleasant it is for brothers to dwell together in unity.' It is true, I have felt this very often, but this unity can only take place on earth in the midst of sacrifices. No, it was not to live with my sisters that I came to Carmel, but to follow Jesus' call; on the contrary, I strongly anticipated that this living with one's own sisters had to be the cause of suffering, when one wishes to make no concessions to one's natural inclinations."[20] But Thérèse hastens to explain the true significance of this sacrifice.

> How can it be said that it is more perfect to separate ourselves from those who are bound to us by ties of blood? Have brothers ever been blamed for fighting on the same battlefield or for hastening together to win the palm of martyrdom? Surely it has been maintained, and quite rightly, that they encourage one another; but also that the martyrdom of each one becomes the martyrdom of all. And so it is in the religious life, which the theologians call a daily martyrdom. In giving oneself to God, one's heart does not lose its natural tenderness; on the contrary, this tenderness increases by becoming purer and more divine. It is with this tenderness that I love you, my Mother, and all my Sisters.[21]

Here the whole law of love within the Order becomes visible. The sacrifice does not consist in having to curb or even deaden her love for her sisters and relatives but in feeling this love grow more intense while at the same time subjecting it to a higher law of love and its universality. And so, for instance, she and Céline, in an attempt to help the community, finally

---

[19] H 225 (T 212); N 74 (LC 95–96). Further examples of her behavior toward the Sisters are to be found in Görres 225–29 (ET 180–83); 297–308 (ET 239–47).

[20] SS 215–16.   [21] SS 216.

cease pouring their hearts out to each other. "Don't send back a long letter to tell me of your soul, a single brief word will suffice. I should prefer you to write a *very amusing* letter for *everybody*."[22] To Léonie, however, she protests her "ever-increasing love",[23] as also to her cousin Marie. It is often supposed that the cloister only permits a poverty-stricken form of love, that it eliminates those vital personal relationships without which love fades, replacing them with a bare, abstract "Rule" that orders the religious to exercise an abstract love toward each and all, warming neither the giver nor the receiver. Far from it: "natural tenderness increases by becoming purer and more divine." The sacrifice to which Thérèse refers is both a sign of this intensified affection and its cause. Yet this "natural affection" itself provides no clues that might enable one to predict the forms it will take when it is transformed into an expression of heavenly love; only when the transformation has been felt can we know this. "I am happy to be fighting as a family for the glory of the King of heaven; but I am also ready to rush to some other battlefield if the divine General requests me to do so: an order would not be necessary, a mere glance, a simple sign would be enough."[24] And Thérèse informs us how she understood "that there might be separations even in Carmel". She was prepared for the transfer of both her sisters to Indochina, even though her heart broke at the thought; in the same way she herself longed to be sent there, despite the sorrow it would mean. "If one day I have to leave my dear Carmel, it will not be without pain, for Jesus has not given me an indifferent heart. And, precisely because it is capable of much suffering, I want it to give Jesus everything possible."[25]

The miracle by which love rooted in the supernatural and universal love of the Lord brings natural tenderness and affection to fruition is named *indifference*. Indifference does not

[22] S 231–32 (GC II:863).
[23] S 243 (GC II:889); S 256 (GC II:907).
[24] SS 216.   [25] SS 217.

mean that one's heart is unmoved whether one is separated
from one's friends or by their side, for the first brings sorrow
and the other joy; it means allowing one's natural ties and affections to be linked to supernatural ones that allow them to
swing freely wherever they are needed.

> I have long since ceased to belong to myself. I have surren-
> dered myself utterly to Jesus, so he is free to do with me as he
> pleases. . . . O my Mother, how much anxiety we are spared
> through taking the vow of obedience! How happy are the simple
> religious! Their sole compass being the will of their superiors,
> they are always certain of being on the right road; they have no
> fear of being mistaken even when it seems that their superiors
> are wrong. But, once they cease to be guided by this infallible
> compass, when under the pretext of doing God's will, unclear
> at times even to his representatives, then they stray into desert
> paths where the waters of grace quickly fail.[26]

Obedience, then, is the source of both certainty and love; this
source lies deeper than any natural evidence or love, since its
waters never fail to refresh one even in the direst need—that is,
when one's superiors seem to be mistaken. For Thérèse, obedience to the Rule is not abstract but the immediate expression
of the love of Christ. More precisely, in obeying, she loves the
Lord's love and the Lord himself; and therefore also loves, with
the Lord's love, the person who represents that love to her:
the Superior. She attends entirely and lovingly to the wishes of
the Prioress, whether this is her own dear sister Pauline or the
capricious Marie de Gonzague, whose moods were changeable
as the weather. In either case, she is quite ready to accept whatever they decide for her as coming from the Lord.

> Mother, you are the compass dear Jesus has provided to direct
> me safely to the eternal shore! How sweet it is for me to fix my
> gaze upon you and then carry out the will of our Lord! Since
> the time he permitted me to suffer temptations against faith, he
> has greatly increased the *spirit of faith* within me, which helps

[26] SS 218–19.

me to see in you not only a loving Mother but also Jesus living
in your soul and communicating his will to me through you.
I know well enough, dear Mother, that you are treating me as
a feeble soul, a spoiled child, and as a consequence I have no
trouble in carrying the burden of obedience. But it seems to me,
judging by my innermost feelings, that my attitude would not
change and that my filial affection would not grow less if you
chose to treat me with severity: because I would still see that it
was the will of Jesus that you were acting in this way for the
greater good of my soul.[27]

None of this is either artificial or highfaluting; it simply gives
a short formula for the law of love in religious life, which is
founded directly upon the love of Christ alone as the Rule of
the Order. The indifference to which it leads cannot be equated
with natural equanimity, for it is the result of a broader universalized love and affection that can take in every natural affection indifferently. Sometimes the transcendent claims of love
in the religious state do require ties of blood and the family
to be completely broken—in the violent way spoken of in the
Gospels and illustrated in the lives of almost all the great saints,
Francis of Assisi, Ignatius of Loyola, Frances de Chantal and
Margaret of Cortona. Yet even here the ties are broken, not
because they are unchristian and contemptible, but in order to
achieve that catholicity of love that both surpasses and includes
all "affection" of the world. Thérèse embraces the two priests
allocated to her under obedience with a warmth of supernatural affection. She desires to know the most important dates
in their lives so as to celebrate their feasts with them—nor is
she content with general information but wants to know all
the details.[28] "Since coming to Carmel, I have a much better
memory for dates."[29] "The grilles of Carmel are not made to
separate souls that love each other only in Jesus; they serve

[27] SS 219.
[28] S 281 (GC II:978); S 293–94 (GC II:1014); S 299 (GC II:1018); S 314 (GC
II:1061); S 327 (GC II:1085–86).
[29] S 103 (GC I:561).

rather to strengthen the bonds that unite them."[30] Thérèse is overjoyed at her privilege of keeping Father Roulland's photograph in her cell.[31] In the convent, her love becomes, not more abstract, but much more concrete. Through her delicate sensitiveness to the word of God, Thérèse tries to demonstrate this catholicity of love as simply and irrefutably as possible in her life and teaching. Quite unembarrassed, she tells her Mother what she understands by love and how she practices it, and her account ranges from the world-shaking miracle of Christ's love to the very tiniest stirrings of the heart that speak to her of love: "If the devil tries to point out to me the defects of such and such a Sister who is less attractive to me, I immediately hasten to discover her virtues and good motives; I say to myself that, if I have seen her fall once, she may well have gained many victories over herself that she is hiding out of humility; and that even what appears to me a fault may really be an act of virtue on account of its intention. I have no difficulty in persuading myself of this truth, because of a little experience I had that showed me we must never judge."[32] She then illustrates how this happened to her and continues: "Since my small acts of virtue can be mistaken for imperfections, it is just as possible for people to be mistaken in taking for virtue what is nothing but imperfection."[33] She adheres very strictly to the Lord's words, "Judge not and you shall not be judged",[34] and follows the Lord even farther, to say with him, "I am not come to judge but to save."[35] Thus the indifference recommended by religious obedience proves itself to be a means of arriving at the perfect indifference of the Father in heaven, who allows his sun to shine upon the good and the evil—as Thérèse is not slow to point out when she begins to discuss loving one's enemies. "Of course, one does not meet enemies in Carmel, but, after all, we have our feelings; and we feel attracted toward one

---

[30] S 220 (GC II:846).
[31] S 279 (GC II:977).
[32] SS 221.
[33] SS 222.
[34] Lk 6:37.
[35] Jn 12:47.

Sister, whereas another is enough to make you go out of your way to avoid meeting her. And so, without even knowing it, she becomes the subject of persecution. Very well, Jesus tells me that this Sister needs my love and my prayers, even though her behavior would lead me to believe that she does not love me. 'If you love those who love you, what reward will you have? For even sinners love those who love them' (Lk 6:32). Nor is it enough to love; we must prove it. Naturally, we are glad to give a gift to a friend; but that is not charity, for sinners do the same."[36]

Her behavior toward her own sisters draws them gently but firmly toward indifference; she convinces one of her fellow novices, who was passionately attached to the Prioress, that, "in loving Mother Prioress with natural affection, she was really loving herself".[37]—Natural affection, in Thérèse's eyes, is the same as self-love, and self-love the same as egotism. And all the while she is applying this principle in its farthest consequences to herself. The Lord tells us to give whatever is asked of us and, if someone takes what belongs to us, not to ask for it back. "To give to everyone who asks is less pleasant than to offer oneself following the movement of one's own heart; again, when they ask for something politely, it doesn't cost so much to give, but, if, unfortunately, they don't use very delicate words, the soul is immediately up in arms if she is not well-founded in charity. She finds a thousand reasons for refusing what has been asked, and it is only after having convinced the person asking of her rudeness that she will finally give what is asked, and then only *as a favor*."[38] This is to allow the legalism of the Old Testament to outweigh the pure principle of New Testament love. "If it is difficult for us to give to anyone who asks, it is even more difficult to allow what belongs to us to be taken without asking for it back."[39] Difficult for our natures, and yet "As soon as we accept the yoke of the Lord, we imme-

[36] SS 225.
[38] SS 225.

[37] SS 237.
[39] Ibid.

diately feel it to be sweet."[40] At this point, the commandment of love, which has already brought one to virginity, through freedom from all ties of flesh and blood, and to obedience, through freedom from one's own choice, now takes one to its ultimate consequence, perfect poverty.

Jesus does not want me to lay claim to what belongs to me. This ought to seem easy and natural to me, since nothing is mine. I have renounced the goods of this earth through the vow of poverty, and so I have no right to complain when something that is not mine is taken away. On the contrary, I ought then to rejoice when I happen to feel the pinch of poverty. Formerly, I used to think I was not attached to anything, but, ever since I understood the words of Jesus, I see how very imperfect I am. For example, if I start preparing to work and find the brushes and paints in disorder, or a ruler or a penknife is missing, patience begins to leave me, and I have to take my heart with both hands to reclaim the missing object without bitterness. No doubt we really have to ask for indispensable articles, but we are not failing to observe Jesus' command if we do so with humility; on the contrary, we are behaving like the poor, who stretch out their hands for the necessities of life and are not surprised when they are rebuffed, because no one owes them anything. Oh, what peace floods into the soul when one rises above natural feelings! No, there is no joy comparable to that tasted by the truly poor in spirit.[41]

True poverty is reached when we give something away without hoping for recompense, because we do not consider what we have given to be our own. We may give away some tangible object, but we can also give some spiritual good, on which we are the more likely to lay our grasping and possessive hands though doing it unconsciously. "Since earthly goods do not belong to me, I should find no difficulty in never reclaiming them when they are sometimes taken away from me. The goods of heaven don't belong to me either; they are lent to me by God, who can withdraw them from me without my having any right to complain."[42] In the realm of pure love, in the religious life, there is no "spiritual property". Not even "our inspirations of mind and heart, profound thoughts, form a treasury" that we may regard as our own property.[43] Thérèse acknowledges that it needed long practice to achieve this detachment. "Now I can say that Jesus has given me the grace of being no more attached to the goods of mind and heart than to those of the earth."[44] She is now simply a channel of grace, a tool, a paintbrush in the hand of the Holy Spirit.

Poverty, obedience and virginity, the contents of the Rule, are interpreted by Thérèse as so many functions of perfect love. Certainly, considered as "vows", they are also the means of reaching this perfection of love. But, for Thérèse, they are something more than the means, they are the pure, uncontaminated expression of true love itself. In the religious life, as in the life of Jesus, they are the indispensable proof of loving unto the end. Thérèse never regarded the vows as anything but functions and manifestations of the love that is its own source. Consequently the vows represent a desire to allow oneself to be guided and ruled by the love of the Lord alone, while including everything in the world that can truly claim to be called love. So, without in the least diluting the ideal of perfection under the Rule or, in the Protestants' manner, blurring the distinction between the state of religion and the lay state, Thérèse refuses to allow that there is any cleavage between the two states in respect to loving. She clings to the Lord's promise that whoever abandons all for his sake shall receive it back a hundredfold, even on earth. Her love, painfully lifting her beyond the "stirrings of nature", brings her to the most profound peace and to the sure possession of earthly loves. Never does she treat renunciation as something negative. Indeed, it is the only possible way to render love universal and catholic. The Rule had been provided by God to make the way smoother.

[42] SS 233.   [43] Ibid.
[44] Ibid.

I remember when I was a postulant I sometimes had such violent temptations to seek my own satisfaction and find some crumbs of consolation that I was obliged to hurry past your cell and cling to the banisters to prevent myself from turning back. My mind would become full of permissions that I might ask; in a word, Mother, a thousand pretexts for pleasing my nature. How happy I am now for having denied myself since the beginning of my religious life! I am already enjoying the reward promised to those who fight bravely. I no longer feel it necessary to refuse all human consolations, because my soul is strengthened by him whom I wanted to love uniquely. I can see with joy that, in loving him, the heart expands and can give to those dear to it an immeasurably deeper affection than if it had concentrated on selfish and barren affection.[45]

Thus the "restriction" by the Rule that she spoke of at first has finally been transformed into an undreamed of "expansion". This is in imitation of the infinite, eucharistic expansion of Christ's life, which takes place precisely through the restriction, humiliation—indeed, the "self-annihilation"—of his life in the Eucharist.

I wish to abase myself humbly and submit my will to that of my Sisters, without contradicting them about anything and without enquiring whether or not they have the right to give me orders. No one, O my Beloved, had that right over you, and yet you obeyed not only the Blessed Virgin and Saint Joseph but even your executioners. And now it is in the Host that I see you consummate your self-annihilation. O divine King of Glory, with what humility you submit yourself to all your priests, without making any distinction between those who love you and those who, alas, are lukewarm or cold in your service.[46]

Indifference and self-annihilation in the Eucharist, as in the religious life, are both functions of the one love and the source of Christian fruitfulness.

From a human standpoint, Thérèse's conduct appears to be based upon an *as-if*. Which makes it subject to the criticism of-

[45] SS 237.   [46] H 311–12 (T 453).

ten urged against the religious life, that it not only overreaches the limits of human beings but warps their hearts and teaches them hidden and subtle untruths. When people see only the good side of their fellow human beings and impute good motives to their actions, do they not lose their capacity for sound criticism and for seeing things as they are? A certain novice was described by Thérèse's sisters as "foolish, tactless and officious": in Thérèse's opinion, she is "open, innocent and of upright heart".[47] Who is right? Or are there, in fact, two standpoints, two standards—one of Justice and one of love? One should not dismiss off-hand the apparent dualism with which the truth often faces us; but this very dualism is grounded in the truth that God himself, by his creative love, known as *grace*, is constantly overcoming evil and bringing goodness out of evil, while at the same time fulfilling "all justice". But, in the Gospels, this manifestation of justice always remains a function of the love that casts a veil over evil before destroying it. And it may well be that God distributes his goods variously among his saints, one receiving more the gift of loving justice and another the gift of just love, and that this latter fell to Thérèse's lot. Which does not imply that she was spared the discernment of spirits, as the next chapter will show. But she knew that, despite all man's demands for justice, it is the loving eye that truly sees into the depths of another's soul; this love is also the most just.

There was once a nun in the community who "had a genius" for displeasing Thérèse in everything she did. "So I set about doing everything for this Sister that I would have done for the person I loved most. Each time I met her, I prayed to God for her, offering him all her virtues and merits. I felt that this was pleasing to Jesus, for there is no artist who does not like to receive praise for his works, and Jesus, Artist of souls, is happy when we do not stop at the exterior but penetrate to the inner sanctuary where he has chosen to dwell and admire

[47] G 258 (ET 208).

its beauty."[48] Deeper in the soul than all its murkiness and re-pulsiveness, Thérèse sees the hidden face of her Savior.

The person in whom Jesus dwells is like the veil bearing the marks of his face; the two aspects are inseparable, and whoever loves the one must, like Thérèse, love the whole person. "Ah! What attracted me was Jesus hidden in the depths of her soul. Jesus, who makes sweet even that which is most bitter."[49] All of which reveals the mystery of love's creative power. By this power, Christ recreates the sinner as the child of the Father, and the Christian shares in this power when he sees the counte-nance of the Lord and the seal of God's paternity in the depths of another's soul; in virtue of this creative act, comparable to an act of God's love, the Christian himself takes on the height and the breadth of Christ. "Remembering that *charity covers a mul-titude of sins*, I draw from this rich mine that Jesus has opened up before me. 'I have run in the way of your commandments, since you have enlarged my heart.' Only charity can expand my heart."[50]

We only appreciate how much all this costs when we con-sider how far from natural her heart found such love, what acts of naked faith and blind obedience she had to perform, day in, day out, in order that their fruit might appear in due time—the laughing smile and the love that seemed second nature. Not un-til the end, during the last two years, does the commandment to love her neighbor become sweet and light to her. "Previ-ously, almost her whole life long, it had been carried out un-der the sign of obedience."[51] The crown of perfection is not upon her work of obedience until she is in the cloister. Here the God whom she had loved so tenderly and happily in the midst of her family conceals himself beneath the veil of the strict, objective, strangely cold Rule. After the first glad days, the mists begin to lower, shrouding the landscape of her soul. It is the grey mist in which Thérèse was to be enveloped till

[48] SS 222.
[50] SS 224, 225–26.
[49] SS 223.
[51] G 297 (ET 239).

the end of her life; the melancholy prospect is only pierced by rare days of shining gaiety. God is still there but has become remote and strange; he is only accessible in pure faith, by making single acts of faith, each one of which could be numbered. God himself begins to take on the features of the Rule, the more so as time goes on. The more Thérèse's soul frees itself and dilates, the more she masters the art of making everything out of nothing, of changing the dead letter into the life of the spirit, bringing an all-embracing love out of a blank absence of sympathy; and the more God entrusts this art to her, the more hidden he becomes, leaving her room in which to exercise this magic art of love. With none of the soul's comforts, with the ground cut from beneath her feet, Thérèse is now in the van of battle, proving the training she had learned in her peaceful home. Every ounce of energy within her or about her—even the most hostile—is transformed (by violence if need be) into strong, shining love. She had proved beyond doubt that she understood what the "Holy Rule" means in the religious life: narrowness that points the way to infinite breadth; abstractness that pushes the very sap of life into each moment; mortification of the heart so that it may attain the crown of life.

The Office

Beside the Rule, and in some ways more important, it was her office in the Order that inspired Thérèse to grow out of that concern with herself, her perfections, virtues and progress that was so characteristic of her life in the world. When Pauline became Prioress in 1893, she handed over the office of Novice Mistress to her predecessor; she did so more for the sake of peace, really, than because she wanted to entrust the direction of the novices to Mother Marie de Gonzague. In fact, Sister Thérèse of the Child Jesus was to take over this direction. Which placed the latter in an extremely delicate situation; yet she acquitted herself so well in the office during the three years when Pauline was Prioress that Mother Gonzague reappointed Thérèse when she herself was again reelected Prioress in the spring of 1896.

There are other books where the reader may discover what inferior and discouraging material Sister Thérèse had to work upon and mold into shape;[1] how stubborn and undisciplined the young novices often proved; what strong resistance Thérèse had to face at first, so that she could not help being unpopular.[2] She bore it all with humor, was even glad of it, insofar as it protected her along the "dangerous path of honor" that her office compelled her to tread. But she was not long in winning their hearts, and Thérèse quickly became aware of her success. "In the eyes of creatures, I seem to succeed in everything. . . . Sometimes, however, I experience a great desire to hear something other than praise . . . , my soul wearies of this oversweet food."[3] Thérèse has to learn a completely new way—the way of humiliation through honor. "I cannot say that Jesus makes me openly walk along the way of humiliations; no, he is content to humiliate me in the depths of my soul."[4] She who would have been so glad to hide herself in the convent and draw a veil over her whole life has now—under obedience—to draw the veil aside. She has to play the role of teacher and model, while what she would most have liked others to see, her faults and imperfections, has now to be concealed. But this is essential, as Thérèse recognizes. "I understand that it is not for my sake but for that of others that I must walk this road that appears so dangerous. The fact is that, if I were looked upon by the other Sisters as a nun who was filled with faults, incapable, devoid of judgment and intelligence, then you would find it impossible, Mother, to have me helping you. That is why God has cast a veil over all my shortcomings, both exterior and interior."[5]

[1] G 401 (ET 321). [2] G 406 (ET 325).
[3] SS 244. [4] Ibid.
[5] Ibid.

That is also the reason why God picked her to receive the gift
of wisdom.

> You didn't fear, dear Mother, that I would lead your little lambs
> astray. My lack of experience and my youthfulness did not
> frighten you in the least. Perhaps you remembered that the Lord
> is pleased to grant wisdom to little ones. . . . I know it has long
> been the custom among men to measure experience by length
> of years, for the holy King David said to the Lord, "I am young
> and despised", yet in the same psalm he is not afraid to say, "I
> have had understanding above old men. . . ." You did not hesi-
> tate, dear Mother, to tell me one day that God was enlightening
> my soul and giving me the experience of years. I am too little
> now to be vain about it, I am too little still to coin well-turned
> phrases in order to give the impression of great humility. I prefer
> to admit quite simply that the Almighty has done great things in
> the soul of his divine Mother's child; and the greatest of all is to
> have shown me my littleness, my impotence.[6]

Before she could write such words, Thérèse had to become
detached from her own person in an entirely new way, through
the praise and even more the graces that her office brought with
it. Her period as novice mistress teaches her what every priest
learns in the exercise of his office: the complete discrepancy
between his office and his achievement. Indeed, this discrepancy represents the essence of every ecclesiastical office, since
the man occupying it has simply to be an instrument of the
divine will and a channel for divine authority. "When I was
given the office of entering the sanctuary of souls, I realized at
a glance that the task was beyond my strength."[7] Obviously,
an instrument can do nothing of itself, and the person who
wishes to serve as a divine instrument must rest completely
resigned to whatever use the divine hands make of it. And,
when someone resigns himself into God's hand, his own gifts
and experience are shown up for the puny things they are. At
one time they can be of use, and at another time they remain

[6] SS 209–10.   [7] SS 237–38.

unused or may even prove disturbing. And, the holder of an
office may only cite himself as an example when his office requires it. "From a distance, it seems easy and pleasant to do
good to souls, to make them love God more by molding them
according to one's own aims and ideas. Up close, it is quite the
contrary, the roses disappear; one feels it is as impossible to do
good without God's help as to make the sun shine at night.
One feels it is absolutely necessary to forget one's likings, one's
personal conceptions, and to guide souls along the road that
Jesus has traced out for them without trying to make them
walk one's own way."[8] This sentence contains Thérèse's own
judgment on herself and her existential method; clearly, her
tenure of office had taught her the limits of this method, and it
was only her ebbing strength that prevented her from explicitly revising it to bring it into line with her interior progress.
We may also detect here a certain weakness in the tradition
of Carmel that is traceable to those masters in psychology and
self-analysis, Teresa of Jesus and John of the Cross. This tendency to self-analysis has become part of the Order's tradition,
although it does not fit in absolutely with the Order's dominant motif, the hidden obligation before God. Thérèse of the
Child Jesus did at least learn to modify her method. Everything
purely personal is expunged, including even her fascinating experiences along the "little way" and the beautiful memories of
her pious childhood; there remains the one immovable land-
mark, the office manifesting the will of God. It is as though
she stands aside from herself and can then turn the light on
herself or away from herself, quote herself or leave herself out
of it, not as she feels but as her office demands. One remark
that she made to Pauline on her deathbed is evidence of the
objectivity to which Thérèse had attained when invoking her
own experience. "If we wish to receive illumination and help
from God in order to guide and comfort souls, then we should
not talk about our personal troubles in order to ease ourselves

[8] SS 238.

of the burden; apart from anything else, this does not give one real relief, one only becomes more disturbed instead of being at peace."[9] Everything personal only counts as material that can either be used or just as well left aside.

> From the first, I saw that all souls have more or less the same battles to fight; but they differ so much from each other in other aspects that I have no trouble understanding what Father Pichon was saying: "There are really more differences among souls than there are among faces." It is impossible to act with all in the same manner. With certain souls, I feel I must make myself little, not fearing to humble myself by admitting my struggles and defects; seeing I have the same weaknesses as they, my little Sisters in their turn admit their own faults and are glad that I understand them through experience. If I am to do any good with certain others, on the contrary, I have seen that I have to be firm and never go back on what I have said; to abase myself would not then be humility but weakness.[10]

The way in which all her personal experience is absorbed into her office represents the last stage in that process of self-forgetting that Thérèse began in her first days in the Order: "Oh how it [that is, the grain of sand with which she identifies herself] desires to be reduced to nothing, unknown by any creature; poor little thing, it desires nothing more, nothing but to be FORGOTTEN . . . , not contempt, not insults, that would be too much glory. . . . To be despised it would have to be seen, but it wants to be forgotten. Yes, I want to be forgotten, and not only by creatures but also by myself."[11] When she thus turns herself into an instrument, she excludes the possibility of judging the work she is doing; in the first place, the achievement is due to the artist, not to the brush; secondly, there is here no relationship between the quality of the instrument and the work it accomplishes: "If the canvas painted by an artist could think and talk, it would certainly not complain of con-

---

[9] N 181 (LC 191).   [10] SS 239–40.
[11] S 122–23 (GC I:612); cf. S 126 (GC I:580).

stantly being touched and retouched by the brush; nor would it envy the lot of that instrument, knowing that it owes the beauty in which it has been clothed to the artist, not to the brush. Nor could the brush, for its part, boast of the master-piece it had helped to produce, for it would not be unaware that artists are never at a loss, that they play with difficulties and sometimes amuse themselves by making use of the poorest and most defective instruments."[12] In her last thoughts, this image of humiliation through being put to any use whatever becomes more frequent, as, for instance, in the counsel she gave to an admiring novice:

> God does not love me the more just because he uses me as his interpreter among you. He makes me your little handmaid. It is for your sake and my sake that he has given me the charms and virtues you see. I often compare myself to a little bowl that God fills with all kinds of good things. All the *little kittens* come to take their share and sometimes quarrel about who shall have most. But the Child Jesus is there on watch. "I am very willing that you should drink from my little bowl," he says, "but take care lest you knock it over and break it." But to tell the truth, there is not much danger, because I am fixed firmly on the ground. The same is not true of prioresses; they are placed on high and incur much greater risks.[13]

More eloquent still than the image of the bowl, which, after all, simply *contains* the nourishment, is the image of fruit: "Think of a lovely peach so sweet that no confectioner could imagine so delicious a sweetness. Tell me, Céline, was it *for the peach* that the good God created that lovely red color, so velvety, so pleasant to see and to touch? Again, was it for the peach that he used up so much sugar? . . . No, it was for us, not for it. What belongs to it, what makes the *essence* of its life, is its kernel, we can rob it of all its beauty without robbing it of its *being*." As in the previous image, the kernel is something that, like the bowl, cannot be enjoyed but only provides the flesh of the peach as a

[12] SS 235.   [13] H 269 (T 300).

bowl contains milk; but the image is a richer one, because both kernel and flesh belong to the same peach. And, when Thérèse continues, her mind unconsciously moves beyond these similes to a yet more suggestive one: "Jesus delights to lavish his gifts upon some of his creatures, but very often he does it to draw other hearts to himself; and then, his end attained, he lets those exterior gifts disappear, despoils completely the souls dearest to him. Seeing themselves in such great poverty, these poor little souls are afraid, it seems to them that they are good for nothing . . . , but it is not so, the *essence* of their *being* works on in secret. *Jesus* is forming in them the seed that is to develop above, in the gardens of heaven."[14] So at first the kernel of fruit appears to be a hard thing, which may be a bearer of grace but is itself unusable; if this simile were maintained, it would result in a natural supernatural dualism, a division between the self and its graces, but later the hard kernel itself appears as grace from which precious fruits are grown. It is precisely the recognition that one's nature is not nourishing a profitless nothing that is the grace; grace draws fruit from this humble acknowledgment of nothingness. The way in which nature must glorify grace is not only by acknowledging its own impotence before the omnipotence of grace and seeing the gulf between them; its humility goes even deeper by seeing how even its own stony, barren heart is made to produce the fruits of grace.

The process of submitting her own subjective impressions to the claims of objectivity was completed when her office forced her to judge others, which meant that her every subjective judgment upon good and evil had to give way to the divine objectivity of the Rule. Once more this duty goes against the grain. "I regard the prophet Jonah as very excusable for having fled rather than announce the ruin of Nineveh. I would a thousand times rather receive reproofs than give them to others; but I feel it is very necessary that this task should cause me suffering, for, if one acts according to natural impulses, the soul being

[14] S 203 (GC II:814).

reproved cannot possibly understand its faults."[15] "When I am speaking to a novice, I am always careful to mortify myself. I avoid asking questions simply to satisfy my curiosity. If she begins to tell me something interesting and then passes on to something that bores me, without finishing what she was saying, I am very careful not to remind her of the subject she set aside, for it seems to me we can do no good when we seek ourself."[16] The pain of having to make official judgments, of being just as well as loving, is the surest way of killing a person's desire to make subjective judgments. Thérèse shrewdly puts her finger on "a great benefit I reaped from the mission you confided to me. Formerly, when I saw a Sister behaving in a way that displeased me and seemed contrary to the Rule, I said to myself, 'Ah, if only I could tell her what I think and show her she is wrong, how much good this would do me!' Ever since I have had a little practice at the task of correcting, I assure you, dear Mother, that I have entirely changed my attitude. When I happen to see a Sister perform an action that seems imperfect to me, I heave a sigh of relief, 'Thank God it is not a novice, and I don't have to correct her.' "[17] Her official post as watchman, to her great surprise, affords her a share in the incorruptibility of God's judgments. "I was going to say: Unfortunately for me—but no, that would be cowardice, so I say: Fortunately for my Sisters, since the time I took my place in the arms of Jesus, I am like the watchman spying out the enemy from the highest turret of a fortress. Nothing escapes my notice; often I am amazed at my clearsightedness. . . ."[18] But this very incorruptibility of her judgment remains a function of love. "I know, Mother, that your little lambs find me severe! . . . But, say what they will, they know deep down that I love them very, very much. . . . I am ready to lay down my life for them, and my love is so pure that I do not even want them to know this." Thus, in virtue of her office, Thérèse's love becomes selfless,

[15] SS 239.
[16] SS 252.
[17] SS 245.
[18] SS 239.

as selfless as the love of the divine Shepherd who tends the sheep, not for his own sake, but for the Father in heaven, who has entrusted them to him. "By the grace of God, I have never tried to attract their hearts to myself; I have realized that my task was to lead them to God and to make them understand that you, Mother, are the visible Jesus here below whom they must love and respect."[19] This attitude toward her neighbor is worlds apart from that which Thérèse had learned in the world, in her family circle. There, it was a direct love between person and person, a subjective attraction that took its form and color from the experience and strength of the person loved. Here, it is a completely objective, official love, into which persons certainly do pour all their energies and experience but which is subordinated to superpersonal laws and ends. It is as though love had acquired a new dimension; there, the dominant image is of the Son of Man's direct love for the heavenly Father; this love now falls under the law of the Holy Spirit—it becomes as if objective, ecclesial, seemingly utilitarian, but in fact it is expanded, made universal, a eucharistic outpouring. The first love is stationed before the Cross, gazing toward it; the second is born of the Cross, continually born again of the Cross. The soul expresses itself in that love; in this it is itself an expression of something higher, a medium for something beyond its own grasp. The first form of love and sanctity is the appropriate one for those living in the world; by it, the Christian commits his whole person to his tasks in the world, an example and encouragement to his brothers in the Church. The second form of love and sanctity is appropriate to the religious life —its starting point is the goal of the other form, the Cross, upon which subjective desires die and beyond which the official "charismatic" love of the Church begins.

Thérèse not only adopted this form of love when she entered the religious life, she deliberately sought after it. In the Order, both love and sanctity bear the sign of the Holy Spirit;

[19] Ibid.

here it is not so much that persons give their love as that love
shines through them. Thérèse makes this quite clear in reference to a remark made to her by old Mother Geneviève, the
foundress of the Lisieux Carmel; Thérèse's soul at the time
was shrouded in night, and the remark flashed before her like
a star of consolation: "The following Sunday, I wished to discover what revelation Mother Geneviève had received; she assured me that she had not received any. This only increased
my admiration, since it showed me in what high degree Jesus
dwelled in her soul, inspiring her words and actions. This kind
of sanctity seems to me the truest, the *saintliest*; that is what
I desire, for it contains no illusions."[20] What strikes Thérèse
about Mother Geneviève's sanctity is that the Lord dwells in
her soul and works through her without her being conscious
of it and without her receiving any "revelations" of her instrumentality. In her opinion, it is the absence of subjective coloring that guarantees the authenticity of this form of sanctity and
frees it from danger. Thérèse knows that she herself is not far
from the charisma of Mother Geneviève, a charisma that takes
her as an instrument of objective, hierarchical love and does
not lead her toward subjective mysticism. Some novices, she
tells us, "are even simple enough to believe that I read their
souls, because I have happened to anticipate them by saying
what they were thinking".[21] One novice undergoing a great
sorrow tried to hide it from Thérèse by behaving cheerfully;
but Thérèse immediately spoke to her about it when they met.
"If I had made the moon fall at her feet, she could not have
looked at me with greater surprise. Her astonishment was so
great that it even took hold of me, and for an instant I was
seized with a supernatural fright. I was really sure I didn't have
the gift of reading souls, and this surprised me all the more
because I had been so right. I felt that God was very close
and that, without realizing it, I had spoken words, as does a

[20] SS 169–70.   [21] SS 243.

child, that came, not from me, but from him."[22] Thérèse is not overcome by a "supernatural" feeling until *after* she has acted as a channel of truth. She did not speak the liberating words in virtue of some subjective, supernatural insight—a "reading of the soul"; only subsequently, as a kind of reaction, does she feel the force of the Spirit blowing through her. On another occasion, the novices express their astonishment at Thérèse's ability to guess their innermost thoughts. She replies: "Here is my secret. I never call your attention to anything you should do without first invoking our Blessed Lady; I ask her to show me what will be for your greatest good. I am often surprised myself at the things I teach you. All I feel, as I am saying them to you, is that I am not mistaken, and that Jesus is speaking through my mouth."[23] Some of the examples cited might be explained in terms of telepathy if it were not as clear as day that her gift of saying the right words is directed toward supernatural guidance and teaching. Even in writing her autobiography, Thérèse felt the effect of inspiration, but once again it is only subsequently: "My dear Mother, I am amazed at what I have just written; I didn't intend it."[24]

If only the soul does not seek its own but concerns itself entirely with God, then it presents no barrier to the outpouring of grace, and God works smoothly through it. "In spiritual direction," Thérèse says, "one must be very careful not to seek ourselves, for we can have our heart broken and then can truthfully say, 'the watchman took away my veil from me . . . , they wounded me. . . . When I had a little passed by them, I found him whom my soul loves . . .' (Song 5:7; 3:4). If the soul humbly asks the watchmen where to find her beloved, they will tell her; but if she tries to win admiration, she falls into confusion and loses the simplicity of her heart."[25] Thérèse fulfills her office solely out of her conviction of its usefulness; but for her, the usefulness of the office depends entirely on a mystery

---

[22] Ibid.   [23] H 244 (T 230).
[24] SS 256.   [25] N 92 (LC 111).

of love and dedication. There is a gap between what is subjective and what is objective, between the demand that cannot be fulfilled and what in the end is achieved. It is precisely this gap that demands that she place all her subjective power completely at the disposal of the objective office. "Mother, from the moment I understood that it was impossible for me to do anything by myself, the task you imposed on me no longer appeared difficult. I felt that the only thing necessary was to unite myself more and more to Jesus and that 'all these things will be given to you besides.' In fact, my hope was never mistaken, for God saw fit to fill my little hand as many times as it was necessary for nourishing the soul of my Sisters."[26] This inner dedication, on which all transmission depends, is a dedication free of all self-regard. It is a dedication of all one's personal strength, but a dedication so entire that the person doing the transmitting becomes almost invisible, as though extinguished and insignificant. "What difference does it make whether it is myself or another who reveals the little way? So long as it is revealed, the instrument is of no importance."[27]

It will be easily understood how authority and office within the convent acquire a sacramental significance for Thérèse. For they are the means of coming into direct contact with the divine will. She cannot put up with criticism of the Prioress: "For the moment, she possesses the sacrament of authority, and we must pay her reverence. If we behave in a spirit of faith toward her, the good God will never allow us to be deceived. Even without knowing it herself, she will at all times give us the divine answer."[28] So there is no essential difference for Thérèse between the case of the saintly Mother Geneviève, who transmits inspired messages unwittingly, and Mother Marie de Gonzague, who could do so only in virtue of her office. Though the preconditions are different and though the personal sanctity of the old foundress was far superior to the official, objective

[26] SS 238.   [27] N 88 (LC 105).
[28] 2 P 484 (G 290–91 [ET 233]).

sanctity of the new Prioress, the two forms of sanctity are sub-
stantially the same—at least in religious life—because they are
both forms of divine instrumentality. The objective instrumentality of the office is granted to the Church and the Order by
God so as to guarantee channels of grace even when the instruments are most imperfect subjects. It also means that absolute
obedience to God is always possible through the instruments,
the superiors. And subjective sanctity ultimately has no higher
ideal than that of complete transparency to God's light, which
God has formally bestowed upon his Church and her religious
Orders in the "sacrament of authority".

A person exercising office is brought to a peculiar point of
indifference; on the one hand, it means straining all one's energies in its service; on the other hand, it means being quite un-
worried, knowing that the issue rests with God. "In the work
of guiding souls, we should never just let things take their
course in order to save ourselves bother; let us fight without
slackening, even without hope, to win the battle! When we
encounter a stubborn soul, let us not say, 'We can do nothing
here! She understands nothing! We must give her up! I can do
no more!' How cowardly to speak like that! We must do our
duty to the end."[29] And yet: "I scatter the precious seed given
to me by the good God to right and left for the sake of my
little fledglings. And then it is no longer in my hands; I do not
trouble about it any longer. Many times it is as though I had
sowed nothing, and at other times good is produced. But the
good God says to me, 'Just give, and keep on giving, without
worrying about results'."[30] If these two statements are balanced
one against the other, it becomes obvious that indifference does
not mean carelessness or evading responsibility. The secret of
it lies in the "keep on giving". In the end, neither resignation
nor detachment but surrender alone justifies indifference.

And yet this work of sanctification would remain incomprehensible—indeed, would never have been achieved—if God

---

[29] Esprit 98 (G 408 [ET 326]).   [30] N 9 (LC 44).

had not at the same time thrust Thérèse into the trial of darkness. During this trial, which but for short breaks lasted the whole of her life in Carmel, a curtain of darkness cuts her off from the realm of subjective love. What she had most looked forward to in the convent was mental prayer and, after that, the Divine Office. But then she discovers a thousand and one things that have to be remembered; to watch for this genuflection and for that antiphon, and so on. Thérèse admits she found it very difficult to be at ease with this extremely objective, official manner of praying. The Divine Office weighs upon her like an imposition, hampering her free intercourse of prayer with God. And so this strangeness in prayer acts as her introduction to complete desolation. Concentration on external correctness extinguishes her spontaneous impulse to prayer. During these first few months, she suffers from a certain fear lest she may make a mistake; and even later, when she has mastered the technique, it seems to be at the expense of her subjective prayer. "I can say that the Office has been both a joy and a martyrdom, for I so much wished to recite it without mistakes. I gladly forgive the Sisters who make a slip or forget a verse. Often I have studied beforehand what I had to chant, marked it properly and taken every precaution, and then it would just happen that I went past the place without even opening my mouth because of a quite involuntary distraction. And yet I believe no one could be more anxious to pray the Office perfectly than I am."[31] But these distractions and fears only represent the beginning of a process that eventually eliminated her subjective prayer even during the time for personal meditation. Each day she looks forward to the hour for her personal meeting with God, but once it comes the mist descends relentlessly and blots out every prospect. Meanwhile the only effect of recreation seems to be to increase the strain of her mortification. This feeling of being tantalized is equivalent in her trial to the darkest night experienced by other mystics. "When one comes closer to grasp

[31] N 123–24 (LC 138).

it, a hand withdraws it."[32] Thus her contemplation becomes entirely intellectual. She receives many insights and illuminations, but all that is revealed to her is already labelled for the use of others rather than herself; it has to be passed on to them. It is a shower of grace that will become sap for other souls but scarcely moisten her. Even when she knows that she has been given something beautiful, something most useful for souls, the joy of it scarcely touches her, as though it cannot penetrate into the heart of her. Her own intimate self ought to have no share in it. But slowly she ceases to recognize her true self; she no longer knows who she is. Is she indeed that ideal that she tries to nourish with all the strength of her mortification and sacrifice? and that still refuses to exist in reality? Or is she really the self that has been supplying the nourishment, the self that she has given away so that it no longer belongs to her? While the one has passed away, the other has not come into being. Everything concerning her own self seems chaotic, cast into a world of dreams and shadows. How improbable it all seems! But at least she can use this doll for demonstrations and operate on it without danger. The overemphasis on herself in her writings is a compensation for passing herself over in her life. She is like a model sitting for an artist (and again she is the artist), but the perfection of the work is due more to the skill of the artist than to the model. All the saints have known what it is to be withdrawn from themselves, but, whereas it usually lasts only a limited time, in the case of Thérèse, it lasts till death. And this is the factor that puts the saints beyond the scope of ordinary psychology and, for all their attractiveness, often surrounds them with a chilling aura of strangeness. They prove especially disappointing to people who base their relations with others upon the laws of natural sympathy and fellow feeling. Paul must have had this effect, and the same is reported of Aloysius. And a novice, speaking about Thérèse, declares: "I observed her from every angle and could never find any flaw

[32] N 13 (LC 47).

in her. I felt no natural attraction toward her. Indeed, I kept away from her. Not because I did not appreciate her; on the contrary, I found her too perfect. It would have encouraged me if she had been a little less so."[33] When the saints' acquaintances judge them by natural standards, they experience a sense of alienation; it is an echo of the self-alienation that the saints have carried out for the sake of their missions. There is a very elevated point at which the different missions, vocations and offices within the Church run into one. The priest in his office accomplishes the *Opus operatum Dei* in the sacraments—above all, in the objective, sacramental representation of the sacrifice on Calvary; an Order is itself a sort of *Opus operatum Dei*, and its members have the office of subjective sacrifice, which is also a representation of Calvary. Thérèse grasps the similarity of the two and rejoices over it: "How proud I was when I was *Hebdomadarius* for the Office and had to stand in the middle of the choir reciting the prayers out loud! I used to think of how the priest recites the same prayers at Mass and that, like him, I had the right to speak out loud before the Blessed Sacrament, dispensing blessings and absolutions and, if I were First Chantress, reading the Gospel."[34]

The portrait of Thérèse in her office is completed by the sight of her behavior on Good Friday, 1896. She is standing in the choir after she has coughed up blood for the first time and received the blessed assurance that her sacrifice will soon be consummated. "Oh, my soul was filled with a great consolation; I was interiorly persuaded that Jesus, on the anniversary of his own death, wanted to have me hear his first call. It was like a sweet, distant murmur announcing the Bridegroom's arrival. I assisted at Prime and Chapter with great fervor. . . . I begged you, Mother, to give me nothing special. In fact, I had the consolation of spending Good Friday just as I desired."[35]

[33] Pt 97.   [34] N 123 (LC 137).
[35] SS 211.

The Church

If Thérèse's soul is unfolded in all its breadth by the Rule and her office in the Order, this is ultimately for the sake of the Church. The new dimension of one's being that one looks for through being born again in an Order has no other purpose for a Catholic than to make one wholly Catholic. Just as Mary's role, through the Cross, is extended to becoming Mother to all the faithful, becoming "the womb of the Church", so the Christian in an Order, through the cross of the vows, is enabled to share in all the concerns of Christ's Church. To be at the immediate disposition of the Church is the very essence and mystery of the religious life and the ultimate justification for the vows and the Rule; the fruitfulness promised to those who abandon all is meant for the benefit of the brethren.

Those entering an Order should be aware of this function within the Church that they are undertaking; they should also be aware of the new dimension of life that they are meant to acquire through the vows. If this tension between personal sanctification and the service of the Church is lacking in an Order and the narrow personal horizons of the cloister do not open outward onto the great objective horizons of the Church, then the whole purpose of the vows is likely to be frustrated. Thérèse not only had the good fortune to escape such frustration, she is an outstanding example of the fruitfulness that the vows can produce.

The horizons of the Church are thrown open to Thérèse's vision when she is allotted two priest-brothers. "For a long time I had harbored a desire that seemed beyond realization: to have a brother who is a priest. I often thought that, if my little brothers had not flown away to heaven, I should have had the happiness of seeing them at the altar; but since God chose to make little angels of them, I could not hope to see my dream realized. And yet, not only did Jesus grant me the favor I desired, he united me in the bonds of the spirit to two

of his apostles who became my brothers."[1] On the feast of
Saint Teresa of Jesus, 1895, Thérèse is busy at her work—it
is a washing day—when the Prioress takes her aside and reads
her a letter from a young seminarian, Father Adolphe Roulland,
who, "inspired as he said by Saint Teresa, was asking for a Sister
who would devote herself especially to the salvation of his soul
and aid him through her prayers and sacrifices when he was
a missionary so that he could save many souls. He promised
that when he was ordained he would remember each day at
the Holy Sacrifice the one chosen to become his sister. Mother
Agnes of Jesus told me she wanted me to become the sister
of this future missionary."[2] The way that Thérèse reacts to
this gift is both psychologically and theologically significant:
"Mother, I did not know how to express my happiness. Such
an unexpected fulfillment of my desires awoke a joy in my
heart that I can only describe as childlike. I have to carry my
mind back to the days of my childhood to recapture the memory of joys so great that one's soul is too small to contain them,
and not for years had I experienced this kind of happiness. I
felt my soul renewed; it was as if someone had struck for the
first time musical strings left forgotten until then."[3] Thus it
is more than a joy that bursts all the doors and windows of
the soul wide open; it is an experience that actually opens up
strange, new, unknown worlds. It is true that Thérèse had entered Carmel especially to pray for priests. And she knew why
she was doing so; on her Italian pilgrimage, she had had the
opportunity to observe bad priests. And two years later, when
a famous Carmelite preacher apostatized, she writes to Céline:
"Oh, my Céline, let us live for souls, let us be apostles, especially let us save the souls of priests, souls that should be more
transparent than crystal. . . . Alas! how many bad priests there
are. . . . Céline, do you understand the cry of my heart?"[4]

[1] SS 250–51. [2] SS 251.
[3] Ibid.
[4] S 112 (GC I:578); cf. G 358 (ET 288).

A novice says at the canonization process: "She taught us that the good God would hold a reckoning with us for the priests we ought to have saved through prayer and sacrifice but did not save because we were unfaithful and cowardly."[5] All of this becomes completely real to her in the moment when she is ordered to stake her life for a priest who is allotted to her. Eighteen months later, in the same manner, she receives her second brother, Maurice Bellière; and this step teaches her the law inspiring every action of the Church, the law of Catholic universality.

> I explained, dear Mother, that, having already offered my poor merits for one future apostle, I believed I could not do it for the intentions of another, and that, besides, there were many Sisters better than I who would be able to answer his request. All my objections were useless. You told me that one could have several brothers. Then I asked you whether obedience could double my merits. You answered that it could, and you told me several things that made me see that I had to accept a new brother without any scruples. In my heart of hearts, Mother, I was thinking the same as you; and, since the zeal of a Carmelite embraces the whole world, I even hope by God's grace to be useful to more than two missionaries, and I could not forget to pray for all. . . .[6]

And then she places herself at the very center of the Carmelite vocation: "In brief, like our holy Mother, Saint Teresa, I wish to be a daughter of the Church and to pray for all the intentions of our Holy Father, the Pope. That is the general purpose of my life."[7]

Thérèse had already had a vision of this universal scope of the religious life while she was still in the world. Unerringly, she recognized the danger of becoming narrow that threatens any weak soul in the confinement of the cloister and the Rule. On her Italian pilgrimage, she had deliberately allowed the beautiful scenery of God's wide world to impress itself upon her soul,

[5] 1 P VIII, sec. 105 (G 358 [ET 288]).
[6] SS 253.   [7] SS 253-54.

storing up reserves against the narrowness of the cloister. This is the sweep of her thoughts as she gazes on a Swiss landscape from a passing train:

> The religious life appeared to me as it really is, with its subjections and its small sacrifices offered up in secret. Then I understood how easy it would be to become turned in upon oneself and to forget entirely the sublime purpose of one's vocation. So I said to myself, "Later on, when I am a prisoner in Carmel and trials come my way and I have only a tiny bit of the starry heavens to contemplate, I shall remember what my eyes have seen today. This thought will give me courage. I shall easily forget my own little interests, recalling the power and grandeur of God, this God whom I want to love alone. I shall not have the misfortune of snatching after straws, now that 'my heart has an idea of what Jesus has reserved for those who love him'." [8]

The world's grandeur and majesty were to remain with her in the cloister, for that is where her dreams take her: "Usually I dream of such things as woods and flowers, of brooks and the sea. I nearly always see pretty little children or else catch butterflies and birds such as I have never seen before." [9] But this is all background, nothing but a symptom of her health of soul, which at a glance measures the heights to be climbed and aims directly at them. "O Mother, how beautiful is the vocation that has as its aim the preservation of the salt destined for souls! This is Carmel's vocation since the sole purpose of our prayers and sacrifices is to be the apostle of the apostles. We are to pray for them while they are preaching to souls through their words and especially their example. I must stop here, for were I to continue I would never come to an end." [10] In her vision of the Carmelite mission, the little Thérèse attains the stature of the great Teresa. [11]

---

[8] SS 125–26. [9] SS 170–71.

[10] SS 122.

[11] There is probably no better way of understanding the "little" Thérèse's relationship to the "great" Teresa than by collating the quotations that she makes

An apostle of apostles, that is how Thérèse sees her vocation; and the gift of priest-brothers thrills her to the marrow; her deepest longings are awakened, the tenderest fiber of her being is stirred. Everything else in her Carmelite life, her sacrifices and self-denial, her prayers and her silence, is woven around this deep, interior secret, the heart of her Carmelite mission. Thérèse formulated few parts of her teaching so clearly as this, her mission to the Church, which is primarily concerned with the relation between contemplation and action. In a word, the mystery of *contemplation as action*. It is in virtue of this mystery that Thérèse has become the contemplative patron of Catholic Action; she stands there warning us that this Action, now such a slogan in the Church, is but "wood, hay and stubble" (1 Cor 3:12) if it is not caught up and borne along by the groundswell of contemplation. She warns us that all the busyness of the ac-

---

from the latter's works. Some of these sentences she must have heard read out to her; others she had read for herself; in any case, the type of quotation she makes is significant of her attitude toward the foundress of her Order: "God alone suffices" (S 28 [GC I:289]); "Our life is a night spent in a bad inn" (S 51 [GC I:427]); "What a joy to be judged by him whom we have loved above all things" (S 105 [GC I:445]); "Souls are lost like snowflakes" (S 112 [GC I:578]); "We must feed the fire of love" (S 193 [GC II:801]); "My heart can be won by a sardine" (S 207 [GC II:830]); "Our holy Mother Teresa said jokingly to our Lord words that are very true: 'O my God, I am not surprised you have so few friends, you treat them so badly' " (S 212 [GC II:836]; S 254 [GC II:909]); "You know that a Carmelite who was not an apostle would be losing sight of the goal of her vocation and would cease to be a daughter of the seraphic Saint Teresa, who would have given a thousand lives to save a single soul" (S 292 [GC II:1011]); "Saint Teresa, who said to her daughters, 'I want you in nothing to be women but in everything to equal strong men' " (S 297 [GC II:1016]). She cites Saint Teresa's description of the devil as "that loveless wretch" (S 298 [GC II:1017]). "Saint Teresa said to her daughters, when they wanted to pray for themselves: 'What care I if I stay in Purgatory till the end of the world, if I save a single soul by my prayers' " (S 319 [GC II:1072]). "As our holy Mother Saint Teresa says, 'God is not—as we think—rigorous over trifles; we should never burden our souls with them' " (G 376 [ET 302–3]). Only once does she make a critical observation: "No one will ever be able to say of me what our Mother Teresa said of herself, 'I die because I do not die' " (N 109 [LC 128]).

tive apostle, and especially of the priest, depends for its power upon the immovable contemplative Orders. Here, in prayer and suffering, rises the source of all Catholic Action; consequently, a primary task for this Action is to found centers of contemplation. In some ways, Thérèse develops her teaching about contemplative action along traditional lines, presupposing the medieval formula *explenitudine contemplationis activus* and amplifying it. But, in other respects, the construction she puts upon the usual formula opens up entirely new possibilities of welding contemplation and action together.

As a child, Thérèse's inclination toward contemplation was quite marked. When she was very small, accompanying her father on his fishing expeditions, she used to sit on a beautiful, blossoming meadow a little apart from him. "Then my thoughts would become very deep; and, without knowing what meditation meant, my soul became absorbed in true prayer. I would listen to distant sounds, the murmur of the wind, and so forth. Sometimes indistinct notes of military music reached me where I was and filled my heart with gentle melancholy. The earth seemed to be a place of exile, and I dreamed only of heaven."[12] Once the two of them are caught in a thunderstorm; Thérèse is thrilled with the thunder and lightning that make "the good God seem very near to me".[13] In her seventh year, she sees the sea, and the sight of it overpowers her; the whole drama of it speaks to her of God. Along with her cousin Marie, she plays at "hermits" in the garden, "who had nothing but a poor hut, a little corn and a garden in which to grow other vegetables. Their life was spent in continual contemplation; that is to say, one hermit would take the other's place at prayer whenever either was called to the active life. All this was done in harmony and silence, so religiously that it was just perfect."[14] About two years later, she asks her older sister, Marie, who had now become her second mother in succession to Pauline, if she

[12] SS 37.   [13] SS 38.
[14] SS 54.

may be allowed to practice half an hour of mental prayer each day. Marie refuses. She then bargains for a quarter of an hour, which is likewise turned down. Marie's comment was: "She seemed to me so pious that I was anxious for her. I feared that the good God might take her to himself too quickly."[15] But the nine-year-old child does not allow herself to be discouraged. At the Abbey School, she approaches the headmistress with the request to be instructed in contemplation. The headmistress is amazed and not a little embarrassed; clearly she found this a most difficult subject to teach.[16] About this time, on the days when there were no lessons, Thérèse used to go into a corner of her room and pull the bed-curtains, so as to make a little cell where she could meditate. When a mistress asked her what she used to do there, she told her truthfully. "But what do you think about?" asked the good nun, laughing. "I think about the good God, about life, about eternity; well, *I think*." Thérèse adds: "Now I realize that I was actually practicing mental prayer and that God was already instructing me in secret."[17] This adventure in contemplation reaches its climax when she makes her Communion; at this point, Thérèse's finite being is assumed into God's hands: "They were no longer two. Thérèse had disappeared, like a drop of water loses itself in the immensity of the sea. Only Jesus remained. He was the Master, the King! Had Thérèse not asked him to take away her freedom?"[18] Like all the other pupils at the Abbey School, Thérèse was taught to follow the Mass by reading the prayers in her missal. "But the dear child did not stick to it. When someone showed her which parts she was to read, she used to thank them with a gracious smile and fix her gaze upon the book for a few seconds; then she would raise her head again as if the book were a distraction."[19]

The cloister does not alter her ways in this respect. "Apart

---

[15] Pt 62–63.   [16] Pt 63.

[17] SS 74–75.   [18] SS 77.

[19] Pt 66. These are the words of Canon Domin.

from the Divine Office, which I am very unworthy to recite, I have not the courage to set myself searching in books for beautiful prayers: there are so many, it gives me a headache! Besides, each is more beautiful than the next! Since I cannot say them all and do not know which to choose, I do the same as children who do not know how to read. I simply say whatever I wish to the good God, without composing beautiful sentences, and he always understands me."[20] It is as though contemplation is her center of gravity to which she is constantly being pulled back. "Whenever the kind of work she was engaged in did not necessarily absorb her whole attention, her mind turned quite naturally to God."[21] That was in accordance with her own teaching: she insists that in the midst of activity one should still remain detached, in contemplation: "You worry yourselves too much about your tasks, as if you alone were responsible for them. Are you concerned at this moment about what is happening in other Carmels? whether the nuns there are busy or not? Does their work prevent you from praying or meditating? Well, in the same way you should banish yourself from personal tasks. Conscientiously spend the prescribed time at them, but with detachment of spirit."[22] "I once read that the Israelites, when building the walls of Jerusalem, worked with one hand and held a sword in the other. That is what we should do; never lose ourselves completely in action. . . ."[23] These illustrations allow us to glimpse the attraction that contemplation exercised upon the soul of Thérèse; and yet one cannot say that Thérèse was by nature predestined for a contemplative life. One witness says of her: "Sister Thérèse of the Child Jesus had an extremely active and energetic soul beneath her gentle and friendly appearance; her actions at all times bore the marks of a very strong character and a manly spirit."[24] She feels herself strongly drawn toward action; she would gladly have become

---

[20] SS 242.
[21] H 226 (T 212–13).
[22] H 283–84 (T 313).
[23] N 75 (LC 96).
[24] Pt 125.

a Vincentian in order to nurse and educate orphans. Her sister Léonie declares that no amount of dirt or poverty could put her off minding children. Once, at the age of fourteen, with her heart already set on Carmel, she happens to start reading a missionary periodical. Suddenly she shuts it and explains: "I will not read it. Even as it is, I have such a burning desire to go on the Missions that I must not even flick through the illustrations of this apostolate. I will enter Carmel."[25]

Céline tells us that Thérèse followed the contemplative vocation on no other grounds but that she regarded it as the most powerful and far-reaching action.

> The religious life seemed to her primarily a means of saving souls. She even thought at one time of becoming a nun in the foreign missions; but the hope of being able to save more souls by penance and sacrifice was responsible for her decision to enclose herself in Carmel. She confided the reason for her decision to me: to win more souls for Jesus by suffering. She was of the opinion that it is much harder for our natures to work without seeing the fruits of our labor, without encouragement or distraction of any kind . . . ; she wished to embrace this life of death, so much more profitable than others for the salvation of souls, in order, as she herself put it, to become a prisoner as soon as possible and so transmit to souls the beauty of heaven. Her very special aim in entering Carmel was to pray for priests and sacrifice herself for the needs of the Church. She called this form of the apostolate "dealing with the chief", meaning that one reached the members through the Head.[26]

Thérèse thinks of contemplation as the ultimate source of fruitfulness, the most powerful active force in the Church and the most helpful for sinners; yet this does not mean that she allows a sort of activism to pervert the traditional view of contemplation.

Thérèse's contemplation has all the marks of authenticity; it involves complete surrender and openness to the Word of the Lord, reaching beyond all active prayer into a state of being

[25] Pt 126.   [26] Pt 126–27.

held, of simply receiving and, finally, of necessity, passing on to suffering and to passion. It is not the essence of her contemplation that is different but the insight into its effects, the thoroughly ecclesiastical and soteriological vision, which has perhaps never before in the history of spirituality manifested itself so radically and with such purity. The Fathers, for instance, had a predominantly individualistic conception of contemplation—influenced, no doubt, by the Platonic, Aristotelian, Stoic and Neoplatonic contemplative ideals. And, while the medieval mystics certainly do lay great stress on the fruitfulness of contemplation, they never free themselves entirely from the categories handed down to them. Spanish mysticism, on account of its psychological, self-analytical attitude, also remains largely centered upon the condition of the contemplative, however apostolic-minded it may become in practice. The little Thérèse is the first to rid contemplation of its Neoplatonic relics; this fact alone is sufficient to guarantee her place in the history of theology. In fact, though not in so many words, she has substituted the notion of fruitfulness for that of effectiveness. She is the first to see quite clearly that action is not simply an effect of overflowing contemplation (in the sense that anyone filled with wisdom can then pass over without danger into a period of action) but that contemplation in itself is a dynamic force and is indeed the source of all fruitfulness, the first impulse in all change. This is the sense in which contemplation is more active than action, if the latter is taken to mean external deeds.

Once Thérèse is wondering what a person can do best in order to save souls; a simple sentence from the Gospels presents the key to her problem: "Lift up your eyes and see the countries, for they are already white for harvest."[27] And the gloss on it: "The harvest indeed is great, but the laborers are few. Pray, therefore, to the Lord of the harvest that he send forth laborers."[28] Why, Thérèse asks, does the Lord humble himself so as to attend to our prayers? "Because he harbors such an

[27] Jn 4:35.   [28] Mt 9:37–38.

incomprehensible love for us that he wishes us to share in the salvation of souls. He wishes to do nothing without us." But what form should this cooperation take?

> Our vocation, yours and mine, is not to go harvesting in the fields of ripe corn; Jesus does not say to us, "Lower your eyes, look at the fields, and go and reap them. . . ." Our mission is still loftier. Here are Jesus' words, "Lift up your eyes, and see. . . ." See how in my heaven there are places empty; it is for you to fill them . . . , each one of you is my Moses praying on the mountain; ask me for laborers and I shall send them, I await only a prayer, a sigh from your heart! Is not the apostolate of prayer lifted higher, so to speak, than the apostolate of preaching? Our mission as Carmelites, is to form those gospel laborers, they will save millions of souls whose mothers we shall be. . . . What have priests that we need envy![29]

Here we have a doctrine of contemplation, explicitly formulated, such as the medievals never worked out clearly. Contemplation is not superior to action because it allows a person leisure and tranquility, as the ancients thought who despised work as illiberal. Nor even, as Saint Thomas argued in stating the traditional doctrine, because contemplation is directly concerned with God, whereas action deals "only" with one's neighbor. It is solely because, of all the Church's manifestations of love, contemplation bears the most abundant fruit, so abundant that Thérèse does not hesitate to compare the contemplative vocation to that of the priesthood. She believes that her vocation quite literally makes her the mother of souls, an office no less dignified than that of the priest, who also fulfills a family role. ("To be your spouse, O Jesus!, to be a Carmelite and, in union with you, the mother of souls.")[30] How typical of her witty, playful mind is the image of herself as the "little zero" that she hits upon to express her relationship to her priest-brother: "Let us work together for the salvation of souls; I of course can do very little, absolutely nothing, in fact,

[29] S 174–75 (GC II:753).   [30] SS 192.

alone; what encourages me is the thought that by your side I
can be of *some* use; after all, zero by itself has no value, but, put
alongside *one*, it becomes potent, always provided it is put on
the *proper side*, after and not before! . . . So please, Brother, be
good enough to send your blessing to the *little zero* the good
God has put beside you."[31]

This fructifying contemplation is the greatest task that can
be set to a Christian and makes the highest demands. The fact
that contemplation is superior to action means that it must integrate into itself the whole pathos and strength of action. What
Thérèse calls contemplation is the very opposite of Quietism:
it is the fruit of an endeavor into which one throws all one's
energies. And it has to be applied to the smallest details of everyday life if the truth of God's word is to be brought down to
earth. "Many souls say, 'I have not the strength to make this
or that sacrifice.' But they should try! The good God never
refuses the first grace that gives one courage to act, and, if that
is grasped, then one can take heart and march from victory to
victory."[32] But this initial action is focused into a central act
of contemplation that does not waver but firmly directs the
energies that are bent toward external action. Here Thérèse
touches upon the second formula governing action and contemplation, not Thomas' formula but that of Ignatius: *in actione
contemplativus*. Except that it is better reversed in the case of the
Carmelite Thérèse: *in contemplatione activus*. When Thérèse is
entrusted with the office of novice mistress and recognizes that
it is far beyond her own powers, she does not sit down to work
out a scheme for dividing her time between prayer and action.
"I quickly threw myself into God's arms and behaved like one
of those children who bury their fair heads on their father's
shoulder when they are frightened; I said, 'Lord, you see that
I am too small to feed your little ones; if you wish me to be
the means of giving each what she needs, then fill my little
hand; and, without leaving your arms, without even turning

[31] S 333–34 (GC II:1095).   [32] N 132 (LC 142).

my head, I shall distribute your precious gifts to the souls who come asking for food'."[33] After making this prayer, she finds her task much simpler: "I felt that the only thing necessary was to unite myself more and more to Jesus and that 'all these things will be given to you besides'."[34] Consequently Thérèse acquires an attitude that cannot be described exactly in terms of either contemplation or action; she is beyond them both in the all-embracing law of love, which governs both receptivity and fruitfulness, both Mary and Martha. This transcendent point of unity is the ultimate knowledge granted to Thérèse; her account of it concludes Manuscript C:

> For simple souls, there must be no complicated ways; as I am of their number, one morning during my thanksgiving, Jesus gave me a simple means of accomplishing my mission. He made me understand these words of the Song of Songs: "Draw me: we shall run after you in the odor of your ointments." O Jesus, there is no need, then, to say, "In drawing me, draw also the souls I love." The simple words, "Draw me", are enough. I understand, Lord, that when a soul allows itself to be captured by the intoxicating odor of your perfumes, she cannot run alone, all the souls she loves are drawn in her train; this is done without constraint, without effort, it is a natural consequence of her attraction toward you. Just as a torrent, throwing itself with impetuosity into the ocean, carries after it whatever it meets on the way, in the same way, O Jesus, the soul who plunges into the boundless ocean of your love draws all her treasures after her! Lord, you know it, I have no other treasures than the souls it has pleased you to unite to mine; you have entrusted them to me. . . .[35]

Thérèse then proceeds to comment on the longest scriptural quotation to be found in her writings, the prayer of Christ the High Priest. It is a prayer of pure contemplation, since it is completely concerned with the Father's will, but also of pure action, since it expresses completely the Son's will in regard to the Father. The two wills coincide; their object is that men should be

---

[33] SS 238.   [34] Ibid.
[35] SS 254.

one as the Son is one with the Father, that they should be drawn
to where the Son returns after accomplishing the will of the
Father. Thérèse is aware of having discovered the Archimedean
point beyond which passivity and activity no longer produce
a dualism. "A scholar has said, 'Give me a fulcrum and a lever,
and I will lift the world.' What Archimedes could not obtain,
for his request was not directed by God and was only made
from a material viewpoint, has been fully granted to the saints.
The Almighty has given them a fulcrum—*Himself alone!* And
for a lever, prayer that burns with the fire of love; that is how
they have lifted the world, that is how the saints still fighting
on earth lift it and will continue to lift it till the end of time."[36]
She is beyond the dualism of passivity and activity, at the point
where they meet in Christian love. "Jesus has said, 'No man
can come to me unless the Father who sent me draw him.'
Then, through beautiful parables, and often even without using this means so well known to the people, he teaches us that
it is enough to knock and it will be opened, to seek in order to
find and to stretch out one's hand humbly in order to receive
what is asked for."[37] Ultimately, in fact, the two aspects, the
seeking and the finding, coincide; the moment we knock is the
moment we are given entry, and the more openly and passively
we surrender to God's operations, the more actively he works
in us and we in him. "I ask Jesus to draw me into the flames
of his love, to unite me so closely to himself that he lives and
acts within me. I feel that the more the fire of love inflames
my heart, the more I shall say, 'Draw me', and the more also
will those souls around me (poor little piece of iron, useless
if I withdraw from the divine furnace), the more these souls
will *run swiftly in the odor of the ointments of their Beloved.*"[38]
And now we come to the crucial point:

For a soul that is burning with love can never remain inactive.
Certainly, like Saint Mary Magdalen, she will sit at the feet of

[36] SS 258.   [37] SS 257.
[38] Ibid.

Jesus, listening to his sweet and burning words. She seems to give nothing and so in fact gives much more than Martha, who torments herself *about many things* and wants her sister to imitate her. It is not Martha's works that Jesus finds fault with; his divine Mother submitted humbly to these works all through her life, since she had to prepare the meals of the Holy Family. It is only the *restlessness* of his ardent hostess that he willed to correct. All the saints have understood this, most of all those who filled the world with the light of the gospel teaching. Was it not in prayer that Saint Paul, Saint Augustine, Saint John of the Cross, Saint Thomas Aquinas, Saint Francis, Saint Dominic, and many other friends of God, acquired the wonderful knowledge that has enthralled the finest minds?[39]

In these modest words, Thérèse succeeds perfectly in restoring both contemplation and action to their true value. She justifies contemplation by basing the superiority of contemplation on its fullness and fruitfulness, not on the fact that it empties the mind of externals: "She seems to give nothing and so in fact gives much more."[40] Action is also given its due, because it is not made subject to contemplation. Although the Lord blames Martha, Mary the Mother of God is the standing proof that it is not for her activity; furthermore, the Lazarus episode completely justifies both sisters, showing that they loved equally and are equally sanctified. Once again, Thérèse is in the right as against the traditional patristic and Scholastic interpretation of the Mary–Martha antithesis, which was all too strongly influenced by the prejudices of the ancient world. Thomas Aquinas, whether consciously or unconsciously, interpreted the gospel view of action and contemplation in Aristotelian terms; the grounds he gave for the superiority of contemplation were all derived from the "philosopher", and so he gave currency to the ancient conceptions of action and contemplation (*S. Th.* II–II, q. 192, a. 1, c). In order to grasp the gospel message on this subject, one is well advised to ignore Aristotle and con-

[39] SS 257–58.   [40] SS 258.

centrate on the interpretation given to it by the Lord in his
own words and deeds and in his saints.

The ideal for Thérèse did not consist in alternating from one
to the other, or in balancing them, but in perfecting the two
attitudes simultaneously. Whereas Augustine loved to separate
action and contemplation, Martha and Mary, Peter and John,
as types of earthly and heavenly life, Thérèse cannot imagine
heaven except in terms of their unity. Unlike any previous
saint, she regards heaven as the scene for her most intense missionary activity—"It is not happiness that attracts me . . . but
Love alone! To love, to be loved and to return to earth to
make Love loved."[41] "I wish to spend my heaven in doing
good upon earth. . . . No, I shall not be able to take any rest
until the end of the world."[42] "I feel that my mission is soon
to begin, my mission of making God loved as I love him . . . ,
to give my little way to souls."[43] Thérèse bases this possibility
on the example of the angels: "That is not impossible, because
the angels keep watch over us from the heart of the Beatific
Vision."[44] They proceed from God as his messengers and yet
never leave him. Thérèse might equally well have referred to
the Son of God, who leaves his Father in heaven and yet retains
the vision of his Father in the midst of his earthly activity—
for his earthly activity is shaped at every moment by his vision
of the Father. The ancients show no traces of this ideal that the
Christian is called upon to live. One can easily understand now
why the Carmelite Thérèse felt a closer kinship and union with
the saint of action, Joan of Arc, than with any other saint. Their
two missions are united in the Lord's saying: "At all times I
do the will of the Father."

But we have still not described the precise content of Thérèse's mission, which places her beyond the action-contempla-
tion antithesis. In order to do this, we must first outline her
own conception of her mission and her place in the Church,

[41] H 245 (T 231).   [42] G 478 (ET 381).
[43] N 81–82 (LC 102).   [44] H 245 (T 231).

which involves an inquiry into her doctrine of the Church. It is typical of Thérèse's existentialism that she knows no way of envisaging the Church other than from the standpoint of her own membership.

Thérèse presents her doctrine of the Church in the course of an exposition of 1 Corinthians 12–13. She penetrates deep into the meaning of this passage through her boundless longing to do everything for God that can be done. "To be your spouse, O Jesus!, to be a Carmelite and, in union with you, the mother of souls, should this not be enough for me? And yet it is not so. No doubt, these three privileges sum up my true vocation: Carmelite, spouse, mother. Yet I feel other vocations within me; I feel within the vocation of warrior, of priest, of apostle, doctor and martyr. . . ."[45] Then she begins to depict the unique quality of each of these missions and then the uniqueness of the personal vocations within each type of mission. For instance, she lists the various types of martyrdom—which are clearly mutually exclusive: "I would wish to be flayed like Saint Bartholomew; to be plunged into boiling oil like Saint John; I would undergo all the tortures inflicted upon the martyrs. With Saint Agnes and Saint Cecilia, I would present my neck to the sword, and, like Joan of Arc, my dear sister, I would whisper your name at the stake. . . ."[46] She even regrets not having been born at the time of the Antichrist. "Jesus, Jesus, if I wanted to write all my desires, I would have to borrow your Book of Life, for in it are reported all the actions of all the saints, and I would accomplish all of them for you."[47] In this torment, itself a magnificent preparation, she opens the Letter to the Corinthians and immediately comes upon the doctrine about the different members of the one Body, which supplement each other and by their diversity make up the unity of the Body. "The answer was clear, but it did not satisfy my longings nor give me peace."[48] Indeed, she refuses to let herself be listed

[45] SS 192.
[47] Ibid.
[46] SS 193.
[48] SS 194.

in any of these diverse offices and tasks. "In considering the Mystical Body of the Church, I had not recognized myself in any of the members described by Saint Paul, or rather I wished to recognize myself in them all."[49] So, hesitatingly but hopefully, she moves on from the twelfth to the thirteenth chapter, which opens up the supreme way of love. "The Apostle explains that even the most perfect gifts are nothing without *Love*. . . . At last I had found rest. . . . Love gave me the key to my vocation."[50] Love is the central organ of the Mystical Body, the heart. Therefore it is much more than a single organ, it is the source of life for all the others: "I understood it was Love alone that made the Church's members act and that, if love were ever to die out, then apostles would cease to proclaim the gospel and martyrs would not shed their blood."[51] Just as a watch or a machine with dancing dolls or a music box will stop if the spring is broken, so the whole action of the Church would come to a standstill if the contemplative love at the heart of it all were to cease. And so love increases in the life of each and every vocation, because it is essentially universal: "I realized that love includes every vocation, that love is all, that it embraces all times and all places. . . . In a word, it is eternal!" "Then, in the excess of my delirious joy, I cried out: O Jesus, my love! at last I have found my vocation! My final vocation is love. Yes, I have found my place in the Church, and it is you, O my God, who have given me this place—in the heart of my Mother, the Church, *I shall be love*! Thus I shall be all. . . ."[52]

We have already learned how this love was to become universal: in this "life of death"; in wiping out all individual subjectivity by the vows, the Rule and authority; in hollowing out her own personality until she became simply a "bowl" from which others might be fed, simply the kernel for others' fruit, the "zero" rounding off all unity. It is precisely through be-

---

[49] Ibid. [50] Ibid.
[51] Ibid. [52] Ibid.

ing zero, through accepting her complete unimportance, that
the miraculous, total fulfillment of grace is accomplished. "I
am nothing but a weak and helpless child; but it is my very
weakness that gives me the courage to offer myself as a victim of your love, O Jesus. . . . And love has chosen me as a
holocaust, poor and imperfect creature that I am! Is this choice
not worthy of love? Certainly, for in order to be completely
satisfied, love must stoop even to nothingness and transform
this nothingness into fire."[53] But into a fire that must burn
other things, elsewhere and for something else. Through the
all and nothing of her own mission, Thérèse has to discover
the communion of saints in love.

The communion of saints is the community of grace and,
therefore, of love; because all love is fruitful, each member is
indebted to the love of the others: "In heaven, we shall never
be greeted with stares of indifference; for all the elect will recognize how they owe each other the graces that have brought
them glory."[54]

There, each will be proud of the others, whereas no one will
claim any merit for himself. "As a mother is proud of her children, so we will be proud of each other, without the slightest
trace of jealousy." "But how clearly we shall see that everything comes from the good God. The glory that I shall possess
will be an unmerited grace, which does not even belong to me
—and everyone will see this clearly."[55] But, since love is the
root of all merit, as well as its fruit, and never seeks its own,
Thérèse lives more for others and in others than for herself.
She who had been promised universal love now expounds one
of her most remarkable ideas.

"Use the riches that make men unjust in order to make friends
who will receive you into everlasting dwellings." . . . As a child
of light, I understood that my desires to be everything and embrace every vocation were riches that could well make me un-

<hr />

[53] SS 195.   [54] N 78 (LC 100).
[55] N 60 (LC 88).

just; so I used them to make friends. Remembering the prayer of Eliseus to his Father Elias when he dared to ask him for his double spirit, I presented myself before the angels and saints, and I said to them, "I am the least of creatures, I know my own misery and feebleness, but I also know how much noble and generous hearts love to do good; therefore I beg you, blessed inhabitants of heaven, to adopt me as your child; all the glory you help me to merit will be yours alone; deign to hear my prayer. It is bold, I know; but I dare to ask you to obtain for me your *double portion of love!*"[56]

So Thérèse wishes to add the love of the other saints to her own love. Besides her own spirit she wishes to possess the spirit of the martyr, of the doctor of the Church, and so on; nor will this double spirit be a divided one—it will be entirely her own, as the spirit of Eliseus was his own, and just as the spirit of John the Baptist was his own yet still the spirit of Elias. However, this concentration of the spirit of all the saints in Thérèse is simply the necessary counterpart to the outpouring of her own spirit upon the spirits of the saints. "I realized that love includes every vocation, that it is all in all . . . , thus I shall be all, *thus* will my dream be fulfilled."[57] The result is complete communism in all goods and graces, which at the same time preserves the uniqueness of persons and their special missions. It is Thérèse's special mission to insist upon this communism, which is like the circulation of blood, making them all blood relations. "All those above are my blood relations! With the virgins we also shall be virgins, and doctors with the doctors, martyrs with the martyrs, because all the saints are our relations."[58] Henceforth communism of merits is the rule: "When we are suffering through knowing that we are incapable of doing good, our only remedy is to offer the good works of others. That is the benefit of the communion of saints."[59] This form of community became a very real personal experience for Thérèse when she resolved to renounce possession even of

[56] SS 195–96.
[57] SS 194.
[58] N 67 (LC 93–94).
[59] H 271 (T 302).

her private thoughts and insights. "However, the goods that come directly from God, inspirations of the mind and heart, profound thoughts, constitute a treasure to which we are attached as to a good that no one has a right to touch. . . . Jesus has given me the grace of being no more attached to the goods of mind and heart than to earthly goods. If I happen to say or think anything that pleases my Sisters, I find it perfectly natural for them to take it as a good that belongs to them; this thought belongs to the Holy Spirit, not to me."[60] Thérèse develops this thought, after saying: "God has granted me the grace to understand what charity is. . . ."[61] At this depth, not only do the divisions between one person and another vanish, but the laws of nature no longer apply—difficult and easy, great and little, important and unimportant lose their usual meaning.

> Sister Marie of the Eucharist wished to light the candles for a procession. She had no matches with her, and, when her gaze fell upon the little lamp burning in front of the relics, she went toward it; but there was nothing but a weak glimmer at the end of the charred wick. Nevertheless, she managed to get her candle burning and use it to light all the community's candles. So it was a little, flickering lamp that produced these beautiful lights, which in their turn could light innumerable others, indeed could set the whole world ablaze. And yet that little lamp remains the cause of this burst of fire. . . . And often the graces and illuminations we receive are to be attributed to some hidden soul. For the good God wishes the saints to communicate grace to each other, by their prayers, so that they shall love each other in heaven with greater love, love much greater than love within a family, even the most ideal family on earth.[62]

It will be "love of gratefulness" but also the love that finds in the beloved the fruit of its own love. "Who knows whether the joy we shall experience at the sight of the glory of the great saints, through being aware that we have contributed to it under God's providence, who knows whether this joy will

---

[60] SS 233–34.   [61] SS 219.
[62] N 77 (LC 99).

not be as intense as—perhaps even sweeter than—the bliss that they themselves enjoy?"[63] Once more Thérèse is confronting us with that "double spirit" that transcends the limits of persons.

We have finally come to the point where all our preconceptions as to great and small in the kingdom of God fail us. The differences between great and small are not overcome, however, by levelling out but by fulfillment. To level out personal differences and gifts would be an empty caricature of the true community of the saints. In her childhood, Thérèse had already been worried about "why the good God does not give all the Elect in heaven the same glory".[64] At that time, Pauline had filled two vessels with water, one large and one small, and explained that in heaven everyone is filled to the brim "so that the last have nothing to envy in the first".[65] Yet this answer, which forestalls all subsequent questions, remains fundamentally individualistic; for the time being, it might set the child at rest, but in the long run it could not satisfy her thirst for souls. The next step was to transfer the locus of sanctity away from the subject into the will of God: "In the lives of the saints, we see how many of them did not want to leave anything behind after their deaths—not the least souvenir, not the least bit of writing. But others again, such as our holy Mother Teresa, have enriched the Church with their sublime revelations, having no fears of revealing the secrets of the King. . . . Which of these two types of saints is more pleasing to God? It seems to me, Mother, that they are equally pleasing to him."[66] Even more incisively: "I understood that the Lord's love reveals itself just as perfectly in a simple soul, which in no way resists his graces, as in the sublimest soul. Indeed, since it is the essence of love to abase itself, if all souls were to resemble those holy Doctors who have enlightened the Church with the clarity of their teachings, it would give the impression that God did not stoop

[63] H 270 (T 301–2).   [64] SS 44–45.
[65] SS 45.   [66] SS 207.

so low in coming to their heart. But he has also created the little child who knows only how to make his feeble cries heard; he has created the poor savage whose only guide is the natural law; and it is to their hearts that God deigns to stoop."[67]

Once more the fact that standards of great and small no longer apply exactly in heaven has nothing to do with "making everyone equal", not even "levelling upward".[68] It is God's marvelous doing, as Paul showed long ago: "God has tempered the body together, giving to that which wanted the more abundant honor, that there might be no schism in the body: but the members might be mutually one for another" (1 Cor 12:24-25). Thérèse has given us a charming picture of this mutual care between great and small: "And do you not think that when the great saints see what they owe to little souls they will love them with an incomparable love? There, I am sure, will be delightful and surprising friendships. The favorite of an apostle or a great doctor may be a little shepherd boy; and the intimate friend of a patriarch, a simple little child. Oh, how I long to be in that kingdom of love!"[69] And the whole of this mutual care, in Thérèse's teaching, is based upon "gratitude", loving and serving one another and being fruitful. Without fruitfulness, which means cooperating in the work of redemption, there is no community of saints.

Consequently Thérèse immediately puts these truths into practice; she offers vicarious penance for her brothers, for Christians, indeed for all men. As always, she brings it straight down to earth, into concrete detail. When she is already seriously ill she goes for a daily walk in the garden, despite the intense strain, because the infirmarian had recommended it. Another Sister remarks that she would be better resting in her cell. "That is very true," she replies, "but do you know what gives me the strength? I offer each step for a missionary; I am thinking that there may be one over there, far away, tired

[67] SS 14.   [68] G 426 (ET 341).
[69] H 271 (T 302).

out by his apostolic labors; and to lessen his fatigue, I offer mine to God."[70] The doctor ordered her tonics: "I am convinced that these expensive medicines are useless for curing me. But I have made an arrangement with the good God by which he will bestow their benefits upon the poor missionaries who have neither the time nor the means to look after themselves."[71] And again: "I feel that the good God wishes me to suffer. The remedies, which ought to do me good, and do alleviate other patients' sufferings, only make me worse."[72] One hot July day, just before her death: "Around one o'clock, I said to myself, 'Just now the Sisters in the laundry must be very tired.' I besought the good God to console you so that the work might go peacefully and in love. And since I was feeling so ill, I rejoiced at having to suffer like you."[73] And even during her hidden wrestling with the dark powers of death: "Something is taking place within me; I am suffering, not for myself, but for another soul . . . , and the devil is angry."[74]

Throughout all this, until the very last, it is the mystery of the "double spirit". Her soul is disposed so that, not only does the Lord suffer and love with her and in her, but she also suffers and loves with her brothers, in their place. In her suffering, she relieves their suffering, in her loving, she bestows love upon them. Truly the spirit of contemplation makes her present everywhere—"So I shall become everything." And the same spirit that leads her to sink down into sheer powerlessness so that God may arise in all his power, that spirit gives her a share in his power over all things. The thought is so high-flown that only a child can insist on it. "Jesus, I cannot fathom the depths of my request [for the twofold spirit]. I should fear to be overwhelmed beneath the weight of my bold desires! My excuse is that I am a *child*; and children do not reflect on the meaning of their words."[75] And yet this child knows precisely what it

---

[70] H 228 (T 215).
[71] H 248 (T 234).
[72] N 141 (LC 151).
[73] N 93 (LC 113); G 476 (ET 380).
[74] H 238 (T 224).
[75] SS 196.

wants. It wishes to overstep not only the bounds of nature but even the bounds of grace that fix the diversity of gifts within the Church. The other saints, who are each granted particular charisma, together constitute the Body of the Church. Not so Thérèse. Thérèse is not to be localized. She will be everywhere and nowhere. She wishes to make herself felt throughout the whole house, like the aroma of Christ; she will be—and this is perhaps her shrewdest description of herself—a light, a ray issuing from the brow of her Mother, the Church:

> Now, then, I am a child of the Church, and the Church is a Queen, since she is your Bride, O divine King of Kings! The heart of a little child does not seek riches and glory (not even the glory of heaven). She understands that this glory belongs by right to her brothers, the angels and saints. Her own glory will be the reflected glory shining from her Mother's forehead.[76]

[76] Ibid.

TIME AND ETERNITY

THE CONCEPT OF ONE'S STATE OF LIFE answers the question of where one is, spatially or spiritually; it presupposes a position or point of view. But for each Christian, whatever his state of life, this position can only be that of the Lord: "If any man serves me, let him follow me; and where I am, there also shall my servant be" (Jn 12:26). "Father, I will that where I am they also whom you have given me may be with me" (Jn 17:24). For those in the world, that means placing themselves in the world at the place where Christ stood in the world and in the manner of his coming in the flesh from the Father. For those in religion, it means going out from the world by way of the Cross back to the Father; going out from the "abiding city" into the beyond—"Jesus suffered beyond the city gate . . . , let us, too, go out to him away from the camp, bearing the ignominy he bore" (Heb 13:12–13). "I am no more in the world. . . . I am coming to you." "They do not belong to the world, as I, too, do not belong to the world" (Jn 17:11, 16). But neither can those stationed in the world exempt themselves from this continual withdrawal from the world on the part of God; nor can those in religion so withdraw themselves from the world that they do not also remain in the world and follow God on his mission into the world —"I am not asking that you take them out of the world but that you keep them clear of what is evil" (Jn 17:15); "The utterance fills every land, the message reaches the end of the world" (Rom 10:18). The Christian needs to be "crucified to the world" (Gal 6:14) with the Lord, to undergo death and be buried with him (Col 3:3; 2:12), and then be sent back to the world as the leaven in the mass. If he is to fulfill these demands and realize the mystery of his station, he needs also a veil of protection. United with Christ's death and burial, the Christian now shares in his Resurrection, is even enthroned with him above the heavens (Eph 2:6; Col 2:12, 3:1); he has entered "the heavenly Jerusalem, the city of the living God", where there are "gathered thousands upon thousands of angels . . . , those first-born sons whose names are written in heaven . . . , the spirits of just men, now made perfect" (Heb 12:22–24). In truth he lives in heaven and is a stranger here below. But so as to be able to bear this heavenly life without dying, without losing his earthly mission in the abyss of God's mystery, his own life has, so to speak, to be withdrawn from him until his earthly mission is complete: "You have undergone death, and your life is hidden away now with Christ in God" (Col 3:3). The true saints are those whose ardor in their earthly mission is fed solely by the eternal, heavenly life that they have tasted but that has been so painfully withdrawn. They do not turn their backs on the world in order to enjoy the rest of heaven in advance. Rather, they live a life of intense longing and move the world by the strength of that heaven that has first been granted to them and then closed to them. They hang crucified between this world and the beyond; exiles from earth but not yet in their heavenly home, their position serves as a kind of pulpit, and their whole life is a sermon. It does not matter whether the preaching takes the form of action or of contemplation—this decision is left to God; in both cases, their position is the same, stretched between earth and heaven. And the longer they hang there, the more intimate the presence of heaven within them, for nothing brings a person nearer to God than hanging there. Therefore the veil must be drawn closer across the face, because one fraction of light too much would kill them. But they themselves understand the fruitfulness of their position; they know that they are, by grace, conformed to Christ upon the Cross; and so the more they feel the light overwhelming them, the more they long for the darkness of night. The paradox of their situation is unveiled: whereas God hangs there in pure desolation, they share obscurely the resurrection in heaven and know that they must turn again from the light of heaven to the darkness of the Cross. That is existentially the status of saints.

Since her childhood, Thérèse had known how delicate is the

veil that separates time and eternity. So thin that there glistens through each moment of time the gold of eternity, and the rushing noise of time is hushed to a low murmur in the face of eternity. Her first letters scarcely speak of anything else except the transparency of time and of every earthly event. When the little lamb that her father had given her dies quickly: "You don't know, my dear Godmother, what food for reflection the death of the little creature gave me. Oh! truly on earth we must be attached to nothing, not even to the most innocent things, for they fail you just when you least expect it. Only the things that are eternal can content us."[1] "How great a thing is our soul! Let us lift ourselves above all that passes, not stay close to earth; higher, the air is pure! Jesus is hidden, but one senses him. . . ."[2] This is just what the child Thérèse meant by "meditation": to sense the eternal through the veil of passing things. "The earth seemed to me a place of exile, and I dreamed only of heaven."[3] And, at the end of the feast of Sunday: "My heart felt the exile of this earth, I longed for the everlasting repose of heaven, the endless Sunday of our true home."[4] On the way home at night, she used to run along beside her father, holding his hand: "Then, wishing to look no longer upon this dull earth, I asked him to lead me; and, without looking where I put my feet, I threw back my head, giving myself over completely to the contemplation of the starry heavens."[5] And, writing from Venice: "In the beautiful churches we visit, I do not forget you. I have thought of you also in the presence of the wonders of nature, amid those Swiss mountains we crossed; one prays so well there; one feels that God is near."[6]

At the beginning of her religious life, the thought of how quickly time streams away almost became a real obsession with her: "Time passes rapidly, I see it slipping away from me at frightening speed."[7] "Life passes . . . , eternity comes to meet

---

[1] S 44 (GC I:396).   [2] S 56 (GC I:450).
[3] SS 37.   [4] SS 42.
[5] SS 43.   [6] S 32 (GC I:317).
[7] S 63 (GC I:459).

us with great strides. Soon we shall be living with the very life of Jesus. 'The fashion of this world passes away' . . . , soon we shall see 'new heavens' . . . , a 'sun more radiant shall lighten with its splendor ethereal seas, horizons infinite. . . .' " Thérèse is very fond of this sentence from Lamartine and quotes it often: "Immensity will be our abode . . . , we shall no more be prisoners on this earth of our exile, all will have *passed away!* The infinite has neither bed nor bounds nor shore. . . ."[8] "We must see life in its true light. . . . It is an instant between two *eternities*." "A thousand years in your sight, Lord, are as yesterday; which is *past*."[9] "One more year gone by! Céline, it is gone, gone, it will never come back. As this year has gone from us, our life also will go, and soon we shall say, 'It is gone.' We must not waste our time, soon eternity will shine for us!"[10] "Everything passes, the journey to Rome with its harrowing experience has *passed* . . . , the life we used to live has passed . . . , death will pass too, and then we shall enjoy life —not for centuries, but millions of years will pass for us like one day . . . , and other millions of years will come after them, filled with repose and felicity . . . Céline."[11] "Time passes like a shadow, soon we shall be together again above."[12] The young girl is almost sent giddy as she is struck by the breathtaking speed of this journey; she can no longer discover any fixed point for measuring yesterday, today and tomorrow: "When I remember that in a week I shall have been four months in Carmel, I can't get over it! I feel as if I had always been here, and in another way I feel as if I had only entered yesterday. How everything passes!"[13] "When I remember, dearest Aunt, that your little girl will soon have been in Carmel nine months, I can't get over it, it seems to me only yesterday that I was still with you. How quickly life passes, already I am sixteen years on earth, oh! soon we shall all be together in heaven. I greatly

[8] S 95 (GC I:546).   [9] S 98 (GC I:553).
[10] S 120 (GC I:602).   [11] S 152 (GC II:709).
[12] S 225 (GC II:851).   [13] S 57 (GC I:452).

love this phrase from the Psalms, 'A thousand years in the sight
of the Lord are as yesterday that is past.' What speed, oh! I mean
to work hard while it is still the daylight of life, for then comes
the night when I shall be able to do nothing."[14] "Céline, my
heart is filled with memories. . . . I feel as if I had been loving
you for centuries, and it is not twenty-one years after all. But
now, I have eternity before me."[15]

Never for a moment can Thérèse forget the flow of time,
which sounds in her ears like a torrent in spate, drumming
two certainties into her mind; the towering closeness of eternity and the unique treasure of each moment. "A day will
come when the shadows will vanish away; then there will remain only joy, ecstasy. . . . Let us turn our single moment of
suffering to profit, let us see each instant as if there were no
other. An instant is a treasure."[16]

Even when she outgrows this youthful form of world-rejec-
tion and conceives a desire to pass her heaven on earth, she
retains this deep sense that time is but a reflection of eternity.
"What will this old age be for me? It seems this could be right
now, for: two thousand years are no more in the eyes of the
Lord than twenty years . . . than a single day!"[17] The changing foreground, time, is unimportant; for Thérèse keeps her
"gaze" fixed[18] upon that point in the background where true
life persists unchanged, half-veiled by the shimmering spray
of time. "Life is not sad! On the contrary, it is very gay. If
you were to say, 'This exile is very sad', I should understand
you. It is a mistake to give the name of life to something that
must end. One should only give that beautiful name to the
things of heaven, to that which knows not death; and since
we enjoy them even in this world, life is not sad but gay, very
gay!"[19] Already eternal joys are accessible, because in secret she
is growing strong wings for eternity. Thérèse feels the tension

[14] S 75 (GC I:491).   [15] S 121 (GC I:611).
[16] S 102 (GC I:558).   [17] SS 208.
[18] SS 200.   [19] H 300 (T 326).

of earthly suffering stretching her interior life into new dimensions, into the breadth of eternity. "He wills to set no limit to the SANCTITY of his little lily. . . . Her limit is to have no limit! Why should she? . . . We are greater than the whole universe. One day we shall have, even *we*, a divine existence."[20] "Life is very mysterious! It is a desert and an exile . . . , but in the depths of the soul one feels that there will be one day infinite DISTANCES, DISTANCES that will make us forget forever the sadness of desert and exile."[21] The groundswell of eternity beneath the passage of time becomes ever more visible and the eternal presence of God more tangible; at the same time, creatures begin to display his presence. The presence of God makes itself felt everywhere—God alone, as the Carmelites have it. "Life . . . ah! It is true that for us it has no more charm . . . , but I am wrong, it is true that the charms of this world have vanished for us, yet it is a mist . . . , and the reality remains to us, yes, life is a treasure . . . , each instant is an *eternity*, an eternity of joy for heaven, an eternity . . . to see God *face to face* . . . to be simply one with him . . . , only Jesus *is*; everything else *is not*. . . ."[22] "There is no one to lean upon save Jesus, for he only is *immutable*."[23] For Thérèse, "there are no joys left but those of heaven . . . , joys in which the whole of creation, which is naught, gives place to the uncreated, which is reality. . . ."[24] "Jesus is *all*, so you must lose your little nothing in his infinite all. . . ."[25] So the creature becomes the "shadow" of God.[26] Nor does Thérèse hesitate to pursue the theme of our "deification". "One day we shall have, even *we*, a divine existence",[27] "having drunk deep at the source of all bitterness, we shall be deified in the very source of all joys, of all delights . . .",[28] and "God will say, 'On earth you gave me the *one refuge* no human heart wants to renounce—yourself—

[20] S 91 (GC I:542).
[21] S 137 (GC I:662–63).
[22] S 113 (GC I:587).
[23] S 124 (GC I:616).
[24] S 143 (GC I:671).
[25] S 130 (GC I:641).
[26] S 97 (GC I:552).
[27] S 91 (GC I:542).
[28] S 95 (GC I:546).

and now I give you my eternal substance—myself—and that
is your home for eternity.' "[29]

Yet this heightened sense of God's presence does not mean
that he blots out the world; on the contrary, the world and creatures take on firm new outlines in the radiance of God. Certainly "there is no evil in enjoying *the pure pleasures of life*, but
Jesus is jealous of our souls . . . , they can lead to the Beloved,
but by a detour, like a disc or mirror that reflects the sun but
is not the sun."[30] But later, in her maturity, she adopts a more
positive view: "*Blessed is the man whose help is from me. In his
heart, he has disposed steps* (Ps 83:6) to ascend to heaven. Note
well, little lamb, I did not say to separate oneself completely
from creatures, to despise their love, their kind thoughtfulness,
but on the contrary to *accept* them to give me pleasure, to *use
them as so many steps*; for to go aside from creatures would have
only one result, that one would walk and lose one's way in
the pathways of the world. . . . To ascend, one must *place one's
foot* upon the steps of creatures and attach oneself to none but
me."[31] When a person reaches these heights, all things become
transparent to God's light: " 'Blessed are the pure of heart, for
they shall see God' (Mt 5:8). Yes, they shall see him even upon
earth, where nothing is but where all creatures grow limpid
when we can look at them with the face of the loveliest and
whitest of lilies between!"[32] Yet here below we are kept until
the end in twilight: "The darkness is luminous, but nonetheless it is darkness",[33] a hidden participation in eternal life. It
is this longing for eternal truth, for living on the substance of
God, that urged Thérèse toward frequent Communion, a later
practice of the Church that owes so much to her championship.
But her wrestling with God's hidden truth did not stop at the
sacramental level. Thérèse is acquainted with the theology of
the word: "To keep Jesus' *word*, that is the sole condition of

[29] S 220 (GC II:841).   [30] S 205 (GC II:827).
[31] S 273 (GC II:961).   [32] S 125 (GC I:618).
[33] S 86 (GC I:511).

our happiness, the proof of our love for him. But what *is* this word? It seems to me that Jesus' *word* is *himself, Jesus,* the *word of God*! . . . He says so in the Gospel of Saint John. Praying to his Father for his disciples, he expresses himself thus: 'Sanctify them by your *word*, your word is *truth*.' In another place, Jesus tells us that he is the *Way* and the *Truth* and the *Life.* We know then what the *Word* is that we must keep . . . , we possess *Truth*, we *keep* Jesus in our *hearts*! . . ."[34]

Since we are already granted this experience not only in hope but also in truth (for is not hope itself, like faith and love, the truth of eternal life dwelling in us?), it means that the Christian can, so to speak, dispense with time—under providence. So the Christian can have the uncanny experience of having to decide things in time that have already been decided by God from eternity. God's providence so disposes human events that time is beneath his sway.[35] Furthermore, there is no necessary connection between temporal succession and the creative effects of eternity in time. God is eternally free, free to fill the empty succession of time with eternity. "In the evening of this life, I shall appear before you empty-handed . . . , but in your sight, time is nothing. A single day is as a thousand years, so that in an instant you can prepare me to appear before you."[36] "If the greatest sinner in the world repents at the moment of death and dies in an act of love, immediately our Lord . . . will see nothing else, will take nothing into account except his last prayer and will immediately receive him into his merciful arms."[37] "It seems to me that the good God does not require years to perfect his work of love in a soul; one ray from his heart can in an instant cause his flower to blossom for eternity. . . ."[38] And, when one old Sister in Carmel maintained that a long life of faithful service to God was more meritorious than a short one: "Oh no! I don't think so. Remember

[34] S 229–30 (GC II:862).　　[35] S 294 (GC II:1015).
[36] SS 277.　　[37] H 280 (T 309).
[38] H 322, cf. S 100 (GC I:557); S 136 (GC I:662); S 155 (GC II:714); S 326 (GC II:1085).

the reading in the refectory, where the letter to Saint Aloysius'
mother said that he had no more to learn and that he could
not have become holier even if he had lived to the same age as
Noah."[39] The mystery behind this dispensing of time does not
lie in time itself but in the glance cast upon time by the eternal
God: "It seems to me that love can substitute for a long life.
Jesus takes no account of time, since there is none in heaven.
He must take account only of love."[40]

In this flight of thought, Thérèse ascends still higher, to the
most beautiful and daring vision of time she could offer us: "I
ask myself what time is? Time is only a mirage, a dream; already
God *sees us in glory*, he *is enjoying* our *eternal beatitude*! Ah! what
good the realization of this does to my soul! I understand why
he does not bargain with us. . . ."[41] God the eternal does not
bargain with time; he does not see time in us, nor us in time.
He sees that life that is "hidden for us in God with Christ"; it is
not hidden from him, for it is his own eternal life of bliss. And,
because this is *our* true life, it does not cost him so much to let
us wander into the dream of time and suffering. It is as though
Thérèse, with this vision, is excusing God, showing him that
in the light of eternity he is loving men rightly by expecting
temporal suffering from them. The more a person takes this
suffering to heart, the darker the veil that he draws across his
eternal love and bliss. And so Thérèse's progress leads her into
an overwhelming paradox: she, for whom the veil of time was
so thin in her childhood, finds that the farther she advances,
the emptier her life becomes, as time is rapidly vanishing with
no prospect of eternity. Each new stage at which she arrives
only proves to be a still darker place of waiting. She waits like
a child at a railway station; the trains draw away, but none takes
her with it.[42] "I think that I shall have to wait in patience for
my death, as for the other great events of my life. You see, I
was young when I entered Carmel, but, after everything was

[39] N 18 (LC 51).   [40] S 136 (GC I:662).
[41] S 132 (GC I:630).   [42] N 33–34 (LC 62).

finally arranged, I still had to wait three months, the same with my Clothing, and the same with my Profession. Very well, it will be the same with death; it will come soon, but first I shall have to wait."[43] "Yesterday my side was hurting me, but it has gone today. Ah! when shall I eventually go to be with the good God? How gladly I would go to heaven! . . . My soul feels so exiled; heaven is closed to me, and even on earth it's a trial."[44]

And yet, in another way, the veil is only thickening because it is fraying, fraying so quickly that it might easily tear. And at moments streaks of unbearable, overpowering light break through, so searing that the veil must be drawn in again lest her earthly life should be consumed. Gratefully, Thérèse draws around her the mantle of night, the night of faith that prevents her faith from being transformed into vision like a piece of paper going up in flames. "Had I not these trials of soul, these temptations against faith, which are impossible to understand, I believe I should die from happiness at the thought of leaving this world."[45] "Oh, how good it is of God to veil my eyes and only rarely to show me the works of his mercy, as if through a lattice."[46] This intensity is only bearable in sudden "transports of love",[47] lasting no more than a minute: "It would have taken only one minute more, one second more, and I wouldn't have been able to sustain this ardor without dying."[48] The thought of certain scriptural phrases makes her break into tears. "No one knows whether he is worthy of love or hate."[49] A short while before her death, she is saying her breviary in the infirmary; suddenly she is overcome, and her eyes fill with tears. She motions to one of the novices to come nearer and, with an indescribable expression on her face, shows her this text from Saint John: "Little children, the purpose of this letter is to keep you clear of sin. Meanwhile, if any of us does fall into

---

[43] N 47 (LC 74–75).　　　　[44] N 38 (LC 68).
[45] N 16 (LC 48).　　　　　　[46] N 31 (GC II:1101).
[47] N 52 (LC 77).　　　　　　[48] Ibid.
[49] G 315 (ET 253).

sin, we have an advocate to plead our cause before the Father in the Just One, Jesus Christ."[50] Another time she was walking in the garden, supported by one of her sisters, when she saw a little white hen sheltering its chickens under its wing. Her eyes filled with tears, and, turning toward her sister, she said: "I cannot stay here any longer, let us go back. . . ." And, in her cell, she wept for a long time without being able to utter a word. Finally: "I was thinking of our Lord and the lovely comparison he chose in order to convince us of his tenderness. All my life that is exactly what he has done for me—he has hidden me entirely beneath his wings!"[51] She is overcome in just the same way when she meditates on the divine Fatherhood of God. She is ringed around on all sides by fire; only a tiny zone is left to her, and she never knows when the next burst of flame will come licking up at her. She lives in a thunderstorm in which flashes of lightning alternate with a darkness all the darker because of them. She does not count upon the light's dawning gradually, knowing that it will only come in fierce bursts. " 'Tear the veil of this sweet encounter' [Saint John of the Cross]. . . . I have always applied this phrase to the loving death that I wish to die. Love will not slowly wear out the veil of my life but will tear it suddenly."[52]

This all fits in with that image that she placed at the center of her entire devotion: the face of the Lord suffering, with his eyelids closed. Her whole life in Christ is concentrated into her *devotion to the Holy Face*; unwaveringly, she gazes upon God in the extremity of his love, gazing on his face, where the eternal light seems to have been extinguished and yet is most transparent, streaming irresistibly from beneath the closed lids. Pauline gave an account of this devotion.

Devotion to the suffering Face was the special way along which God drew her. Touching as her devotion to the Child Jesus may have been, it cannot be compared to that which she paid to the

[50] Pl 65. [51] H 239–40 (T 225).
[52] N 94 (LC 113).

Holy Face. During her religious life, at the time of the great trial
caused by her father's mental illness, she clung ever closer to the
mystery of the Passion. It was then also that she received permission to add the name "of the Holy Face" to her own . . . ; in
her most important poems, what scope she gives to her favorite
devotion! She dedicates a hymn to it; she paints the Holy Face
on Mass vestments and pictures; for the sake of her novices, she
composes a form of consecration to the Holy Face as well as a
prayer for her own use. . . .[53]

"The Holy Face was the mirror in which Sister Thérèse beheld the soul and heart of her Beloved. It was her book of
meditation . . . , she always had the picture before her in her
breviary and at her place in choir during meditation. It hung
on the curtain of her bed during her illness."[54] The Holy Face
assumes exactly the same place in her life as the Heart of Jesus
does in the lives of Margaret Mary Alacoque and her followers. Once, in fact, Thérèse sets the two side by side: "I possess
your heart, your adorable Face, and your arrow has wounded
me";[55] though the arrow here is not the same as pierced the
heart of the great Teresa, it is the glance from the suffering
Lord. The traditional devotion to the Sacred Heart left her almost unmoved; in the one and only poem she devotes to the
Heart of Jesus, she speaks nearly as much about the divine Face
revealed to Mary Magdalen as about the Heart of Jesus.[56] And,
when she does mention it, it is always as another term for the
incarnation of God's love. The Holy Face, on the contrary, is
for her the direct revelation and vision of the divine countenance. She searched in each feature of the Holy Veil for the
silent depths of eternal truth and precisely the silence of the
divine Word, which, though visible, is no longer audible and
yet speaks more insistently to her than any human word. It
seems almost incredible—but shows how irresistibly Thérèse
was drawn toward the Holy Face—that she used to make the
sixth of August, the feast of the Transfiguration, into a day

[53] Pt 75.   [54] Pt 76.
[55] Ged 509.   [56] Ged 395.

of special devotion to the Sorrowful Face. And not only as a
"compensation" but precisely because she saw perfect glory in
this Face. "O adorable Face of Jesus . . . , we seem to hear
you say, 'Open to me, my sisters, my spouses, for my face is
wet with dew, and my locks with the drops of the night' [Song
5:2]. Our souls understand your language of love; we desire
to wipe your sweet face and to console you for the forgetfulness of the wicked. In their eyes you are still: 'as it were, hidden . . . , they esteem you an object of reproach' [Is 53:3]. O Face
more beautiful than the lilies and roses of spring, you are not
hidden from our eyes!"[57] "Remember how your divine countenance remained forever unknown to your own. But for me
you have left behind your sweet picture; and you know that I
have recognized you! Yes, I recognize you, even through tears,
Face of the Eternal, I recognize your beauty."[58] The shrouding
is, in fact, a revelation: "Your beauty, which you know how
to shroud, reveals a whole mystery to me."[59] The fascination
and love penetrate through the veil: "Often your love unveils
itself, and as through a veil I glimpse your hands in the shadows."[60] Revelation through a veil; that is the form that revelation takes if we on earth are to bear it without dying; it is God
gazing at us through lowered eyelids. "How good of our Lord
to lower his eyes when he left us his picture! For the eyes are
the mirror of the soul, and, if we had seen his soul, we should
have died through happiness."[61] Our Lord, then, lowered his
eyelids to soften the light, but so that enough streams through
to light the way of those souls who have to journey through
"subterranean tunnels; . . . a tunnel where I see nothing but
a brightness half-veiled, the glow from the downcast eyes in
the Face of my Spouse."[62] This light not only suffices—it is
all she asks; she "wishes to look upon the face of her Beloved
only for a sudden glimpse of the tears flowing from eyes that

[57] H 308 (T 450).
[58] Ged 392.
[59] Ged 383.
[60] Ged 509.
[61] N 118 (LC 134).
[62] S 139 (GC I:652).

have enchanted her with their hidden charms".[63] Thérèse is
never tired of returning to the "eyes that fascinate her",[64] this
view in his "glazed and sunken eyes",[65] in his "half-veiled,
downcast",[66] his "closed eyes [of the Child Jesus] . . . that he
will deign to open [in eternity]",[67] "in his luminous face",
from which a "hidden light" radiates,[68] his "look veiled with
tears",[69] his "veiled", "unknown countenance",[70] from which
the "visor" will be "raised" on the "Day of Eternity".[71] She
gazes entranced upon those downcast eyes; everything is centered there. "The words of Isaiah, 'There is no beauty in him
nor comeliness, and we have seen him, and there was no sight-
liness . . . , despised and the most abject of men, a man of
sorrows and acquainted with infirmity: and his look was, as it
were, hidden and despised, whereupon we esteemed him not'
[Is 53:2–3]—My devotion to the Holy Face, or rather, my entire piety, has been based upon these words of Isaiah."[72] And,
since love seeks likeness, Thérèse continues: "I also desired
to be without comeliness and beauty, 'to tread the winepress
alone' [Is 63:3], unknown to all creatures."[73] "Oh, I wished
that my face, like the Face of Jesus, might be hidden from
all glances, that no one on earth might know me any more.
I thirsted to suffer and to be forgotten."[74] Even more profoundly: "Jesus is a hidden treasure, a good beyond price that
few souls can find, for it is *hidden*. . . . *To find a thing hidden, we
must be hidden ourselves*; so our life must be a mystery."[75] Our
life, which is hidden with Christ in God (Col 3:3), participates
in this same play of hiding and revealing, like the divine Face;
it is revealed in the same measure as it is hidden, sunk in the
divine mysteries. The soul is no longer set *before* the veil of the

[63] S 141 (GC I:667).   [64] S 286 (SS 200).

[65] S 98 (GC I:553).   [66] S 139 (GC I:652).

[67] S 223 (GC II:849).   [68] S 127 (GC I:580); S 113 (GC I:588).

[69] S 159 (GC II:724); S 183–84 (GC II:781); S 144 (GC I:675).

[70] S 146, 147 (GC I:684, 685).   [71] S 263 (GC II:933).

[72] N 119 (LC 135).   [73] Ibid.

[74] Pt 105.   [75] S 197 (GC II:809).

Lord but behind it, in the hidden-togetherness of the nuptial mystery: "Tomorrow she will be the bride of him whose face was hidden so that men knew him not! What an alliance and what a future!"[76] "Let me hide myself beneath the veil that withdraws me from the gaze of mortals."[77] Yes, his face itself will be the veil, for the Psalmist has already spoken of hiding oneself in God's countenance. "Your face is my only treasure, I long for nothing more; I will always hide myself in it, O Jesus, to be like unto you."[78]

And so there begins this marvelous play of gazing and turning away, of raising one's gaze and then lowering it again. For it is precisely the downcast eyes of the Lord that Thérèse unwearyingly looks toward, fascinated—she can spend whole nights looking at a picture of the sorrowful face;[79] and she can only answer by lowering her eyes. The following is a prayer she composed for a novice to use in the refectory:

> O Jesus, your two little spouses resolve to keep their eyes cast down during refectory so as to honor and imitate the example that you gave them at the house of Herod. When that godless prince mocked you, O infinite Beauty, your lips uttered no complaint, you did not even deign to fix your adorable eyes upon him. O, it is certain, divine Jesus, that Herod did not deserve to be looked at by you; but we who are your brides, we wish to draw your divine gaze upon ourselves. We ask you to reward us with this glance of love every time that we refrain from raising our eyes. . . .[80]

But the point of this external Rule is that it corresponds to an interior law; to the law of wishing to pass unregarded—not even to see oneself. And the less one sees, the more one draws the divine gaze upon oneself. "O beloved Face of Jesus! While waiting for the eternal day when we shall contemplate your eternal glory, our sole desire is to attract your divine gaze

---

[76] S 143 (GC I:671–72).　　[77] Ged 421.
[78] Ged 384.　　[79] N 120 (LC 135).
[80] H 267 (T 298).

by hiding our faces also, so that no one here below may recognize us. . . . Your veiled face, O Jesus, that is our heaven."[81] To hide one's face is the same as renouncing the sight of God's face, renouncing all sight, sound or feeling, everything, in fact, that makes him present to us. And that is where the bride is most like the Bridegroom, whose face was in darkness during the Passion, itself an expression of the Father revealing his countenance to the Son and withdrawing again. "O adorable Face of Jesus, the only beauty that ravishes my heart, deign to impress on me your divine likeness, so that you cannot look upon the soul of your little bride without beholding yourself. O my Beloved, for the love of you I am content not to see here below the sweetness of your gaze, not to feel the ineffable kiss of your mouth, but I implore you to inflame me with your love so that it may consume me rapidly and bring me soon to appear before you: Thérèse of the Holy Face."[82] It is as though the two of them, Thérèse and Jesus, could not both raise their eyes at the same time; as though Thérèse has to lower her eyes if the gaze of God is to rest upon her, as though the Lord has to lower his eyes so that Thérèse may gaze unwaveringly upon him. All the same, this game of veiling and unveiling is the most exquisite play that love could invent—the play of indirect communication that conveys more than any direct statement could express. For there are things so deeply hidden that they can only be revealed through hiddenness. There are, as Thérèse herself says, "things that lose their fragrance when exposed to the air; and there are thoughts so intimate that they cannot be translated into earthly language without losing their heavenly meaning".[83] Consequently Thérèse wishes to wrap her life in mystery, wishes to make the mystery an essential part of her existence. In no other way can she experience God's mystery and be "alone with the Alone".[84] Never does she beseech the Lord to open his eyes so that Thérèse may look into them; she

[81] H 309 (T 451).   [82] H 310 (T 451–52).
[83] SS 77.   [84] S 145 (GC I:684).

knows that one glance would kill her—it would be eternal life. For it means, in Augustine's words, *videntem videre*, to behold the Beholder. But she does pray to be seen by the Lord. As Paul knew: Being seen is more than seeing. "Tell Jesus to look upon me."[85] "The little *grain of sand* . . . desires to be *seen* by Jesus. The gaze of creatures cannot sink low enough to reach it, but at least let the bleeding Face of Jesus be turned toward it. It desires but one look, only one look. . . ."[86] Nor does she want this look to awaken her self-consciousness: "Jesus wants his dewdrops not even to be aware of themselves; he delights to contemplate them, but only he regards them; and they, not realizing their worth, think themselves below other creatures. . . ."[87] Thérèse relies entirely upon this creative regard; it is that which impresses the image of God upon the creature. "When Jesus has looked upon a soul, in that act he gives it his divine likeness, but the soul must not cease to keep its gaze fixed upon *him alone*."[88] And it is this also that, better than any words, expresses the way that God and creatures communicate with each other. "But one day in heaven, in our beautiful homeland, I shall *look* at you, and in my *look* you will see all I want to say, for *silence* is the language of the blissful inhabitants of heaven."[89] But even now Thérèse feels this look "concentrated" upon her,[90] and already the secret exchange of glances[91] between herself and Jesus has begun. Thérèse, however, unlike certain of the Greek Fathers, does not prolong the indirectness of faith and love into eternity. "When I am in heaven," she declares, "I shall not imitate the seraphim in God's presence. They cover themselves with their wings. I will take care not to cover myself with my wings. . . ."[92] And, as her face will be uncovered, the eyes of God will open to her in all their splendor: "O ineffable bliss, when I am caught

[85] S 123 (GC I:613).
[86] S 127 (GC I:580).
[87] S 188 (GC II:785).
[88] S 172 (GC II:748).
[89] S 226–27 (GC II:853).
[90] S 219 (GC II:841).
[91] S 160 (GC II:725).
[92] N 185 (LC 198).

for the first time in the divine brightness of your adorable Face."[93]

> These eyes veiled in tears and blood
> Will blaze with ineffable light.
> We shall behold this adorable Face
> In the splendor of its radiance![94]

Thérèse knows full well that the most beautiful mysteries of time will not be superseded or eliminated in eternity. Eternity also will be mystery, hidden in the abyss, in the womb of the uncreated Godhead. But these will only be mysteries of love; when all the lovers rest in childlike simplicity. Thérèse pictures the innocent children in heaven, for whom nothing is forbidden, playing with the treasures of the great ones, their victory palms and their crowns, the confidants of God's most marvelous secrets. To them, she daringly promises:

> You dare to caress his adorable Face.[95]

And she herself requests the same favor. "Like them, in heaven I wish to kiss the dear Face." Nothing could be purer, more transparent or more childlike than the tones in which Thérèse speaks of kisses. Never perhaps in the history of mysticism has this word been so free from overtones, almost as if the child did not know what she was talking about. Her intercourse with the Holy Face should not be seen as separate from the devotion that inspired her first title of the Child Jesus. If the depth of her childishness is only revealed to those who also take into account her adoration of the Head covered with blood, the boldness of this later devotion needs to be seen in terms of her childishness if it is to be properly understood. She is a child, with nothing to hide; without embarrassment, she can write a

---

[93] Ged 402.

[94] Ged 482. Ils brilleront d'un éclat ineffable, / Ces yeux voilés de larmes et de sang. / Nous la verrons cette Face adorable, / Dans la splendeur de son rayonnement!

[95] Ged 437. Vous osez caresser son adorable Face.

poem about the virginal milk of Mary, comparing the Son in her arms—his throne and cradle—to the rising sun receiving the dew of heaven from the breasts of his mother. But in the Child's eyes, she already sees the future, seeing in the bud the blossoming flower, seeing the milk of the Virgin transformed into the deep red blood of the Cross.[96] The Cross conceals a mystery of Mary, just as all Mary's mysteries for their part are christological mysteries. And so Christ's secrets, veiled in suffering, unfold into the womanly mysteries of silence and hiddenness: "When the good Joseph is ignorant of the miracle, which you humbly conceal from him, you allow him to keep close beside the tabernacle that encloses the divine Beauty. O how I treasure your eloquent silence!"[97] It is the same silence that the Gospels spread ever farther over the life of Mary and is consequently "so deep" because "the eternal word itself refrains from singing the mysteries of Mary's life."[98] Mary's mysteries are found in Christ, mysteries of contemplation in action, of childhood in maturity, of the Child's countenance in the Face of Sorrows.

> Divine Jesus, in the dawn of your life
> Your beautiful countenance is bathed in tears.
> Until sorrows fade, there will be tears of love
> Streaming across your blessed Face. . . .
>
> On this bloody veil I recognize
> All the beauties of your divine countenance.
> In this imprint, O Jesus, I recognize
> The pure radiance of your childhood's Face.[99]

It is the same countenance, in heaven, in the crib, on the Cross —naked and veiled, completely hidden or else, as eventually in

---

[96] Ged 422.   [97] Ged 427.

[98] Ged 431.

[99] Ged 480. Divin Jésus, au matin de ta vie / Ton beau Visage est tout baigné de pleurs! / Larmes d'amour, sur la Face bénie / Vous coulerez jusqu'au soir des douleurs. . . .

Je reconnais, de ton divin Visage / Tous les attraits, sur ce voile sanglant / Je reconnais, Jésus, en cette image / L'éclat si pur de ta Face d'enfant.

the Resurrection, shining openly—"O hidden God beneath the features of a child; I already see you radiant and triumphant."[100] All these various manifestations reflect one another, explain one another and depend upon each other. The darkness over the Head that is wounded and bloody never grows too thick for Thérèse to see a glorious ray of eternal childhood streaming through the lowered eyelids. Nor do the mists of time ever envelop her so completely that she does not know where the path to eternity lies; though cut off from the sight of eternity, she continues to live on the strength of it. The eyelids of God are transparent and so is her own veiled life. She wishes to become like those angels of whom she says "their countenance appears to be like a transparent picture, sheer effulgence of the divine beauty."[101] For in her every feeling and action, she aims at being a tiny mirror for the Child:

> Every child likes to have
> A mirror placed before it,
> And to smile graciously at the other child
> It imagines it can see there.
> Oh! come into this poor shed;
> Your soul is a glistening jewel;
> Reflect the adorable Word,
> The charms of the God become a child. . . .
> Yes, be the living image,
> The *pure mirror* of your Bridegroom;
> He wishes to behold the divine radiance of his Countenance,
> He wishes to contemplate it in you![102]

---

[100] Ged 481.   [101] Ged 439.

[102] Ged 473. Tout enfant aime qu'on le place / Devant un fidèle miroir, / Alors il sourit avec grâce / A l'autre petit qu'il croit voir. / Ah! venez dans le pauvre étable: / Votre âme est un cristal brillant; / Reflétez le Verbe adorable, / Les charmes de Dieu fait enfant. . . . / Oui, soyez la vivante image, / Le *pur miroir* de votre Epoux / L'éclat divin de son Visage / Il veut le contempler en vous!

III

DOCTRINE

THE LITTLE WAY

E VERY CHRISTIAN—and, much more, every saint—lives a
theological existence; his life is an expression of the gospel
teaching whose kernel is found in the unity of word and life.
Thérèse's mission goes beyond this; it is, in the Pope's words, an
explicitly doctrinal mission. It was God's purpose for Thérèse
to light up certain aspects of revelation afresh for the benefit
of contemporary Christendom, to make certain accepted but
neglected truths astonishingly clear. She herself was aware of
this doctrinal mission, and she does not hesitate to underline
its significance.

When she was still a child at the Abbey School, the Abbé
called her "my little Church doctor",[1] because she was always
ready with a good answer. Her intensely conscious mind inevitably led her to it. Yet it was not on her own initiative that
she formulated her own teaching in the convent. This teaching
took form later, and almost by chance; its dominant themes do
not appear before 1893, five years after her entrance.[2] But then
she quickly realizes that she has a mission to teach. Marie had
expressed a desire to get to know Thérèse's "little doctrine",[3]
and Thérèse adopts the expression and seeks to satisfy her desire. But Manuscript B, which she addresses to Marie, is not
the first one containing her teaching; there are elements of it in
the childhood reminiscences written for Pauline, where she is
not only describing and entertaining but above all instructing.
And, when Pius XI acknowledges that she had received the
gift of wisdom to a rare degree, he is simply repeating what
Thérèse said of herself: "How is it, Mother, that my youth and

[1] G 82 (ET 65).
[2] On the question of her doctrinal development, the essential work is André
Combes, *Introduction à la spiritualité de Sainte Thérèse de l'Enfant Jésus* (1946);
English translation: *The Spirituality of St. Thérèse: An Introduction* (New York:
P. J. Kenedy, 1950).
[3] SS 189.

my inexperience did not scare you? How was it that you did not fear that I might let your lambs stray? In acting as you did, perhaps you remembered that the Lord often likes to give wisdom to the little ones. . . . Everyone is ready to admit of exceptions here below; only the good God is not allowed this right!" And Thérèse then applies to herself the Psalmist's statement: "I have understanding above old men." "You did not even deem it imprudent, Mother, to tell me one day that the divine Master was enlightening my soul and granting me the experience of years. O Mother, I am too little now to fall into vanity, I am also too little still to start coining beautiful phrases to give the impression that I have a great deal of humility. I would rather acknowledge simply that the Almighty has done great things in the soul of his divine Mother's child. . . ."[4] Therefore, Marie de Gonzague, to whom these lines are addressed, has played a part in quickening Thérèse's appreciation of this point. She has no cause for surprise when she finds Thérèse giving her lessons as well. "What I am saying to you now, Mother, is very important."[5] Indeed, we even find her writing a long and very understanding letter to her own Prioress, instructing her as to how she may achieve indifference of heart.[6] She deliberately undertakes spiritual direction, advises her relatives and clarifies the vocations of Léonie and Marie Guérin; she smooths the path for Céline, step by step, and refers to her *petite direction*.[7] Even her letters to her priest-brothers make it "clear that, with all her respect for the preeminent dignity of the priesthood, Thérèse assumes the office of teacher and director in both their cases. It is she who consoles and warns, encourages and praises, answers their questions, confirms their opinions and lays down her little way."[8] "When I am come into harbor, I shall *instruct* you, dear little Brother of my soul, how you must navigate on the tempestuous sea of the world;

[4] SS 210.   [5] G 233 (ET 189).
[6] S 270–74 (GC II:958–62).   [7] S 252 (GC II:903).
[8] G 231 (ET 187).

with the love and utter trustfulness of a child."[9] When she reads over her manuscript, she becomes even more convinced of its importance than when she was actually composing it: "What I find written in this notebook, Mother, that is really my soul. Mother, these lines will do much good. . . . I know that everyone will love me." "After my death, you should not discuss my manuscript with anyone until it is published; you must speak about it only to Mother Prioress. If you do anything else, the devil will set more than one trap for you to hinder and destroy the work of the good God, and a most important work."[10] She is sure of herself. Her "little way" is derived straight from the Gospels as God had interpreted them for her. Even before reading Surin and John of the Cross, all the elements of her doctrine are there and need only to be brought into the brighter light of consciousness. Father Alexis, by confirming that her views were fundamentally sound, had given her the Church's official approval. Anne of Jesus, in her eyes the authentic representative of Carmelite tradition, said she was "most content" with her. That is enough. She does not need to know that her doctrine also stands firmly in the lines of the best theological and spiritual traditions.[11] If one takes her sentences materially, one can say that "in itself the doctrine of our saint is neither new nor original";[12] but frequently one has to go back centuries before finding teachers who have been so bold and have laid such emphasis on certain elementary truths of Christ's teaching. Thérèse is by no means inclined, therefore, to see her teaching minimized. Just as she herself placed the doctrine of the Mystical Body at the center of her doctrine, similarly she treats her doctrine as the heart of theology. The way she is indicating is not one way among others. It is the only way: "I know no other means of arriving at perfection save love. . . ."[13] "The science of love. Oh . . .

[9] S 358 (GC II:1152).

[10] N 107–8 (LC 126).

[11] G 429f. (ET 344ff.).

[12] G 429 (ET 344).

[13] S 130–31 (GC I:641).

I desire that science alone . . . , love is the sole treasure that I covet. Jesus condescends to show me the only way that leads to this divine furnace. It is the surrender of a small child who sleeps without fear in its father's arms. 'Whoever is a little one, let him come to me', was what the Holy Spirit said through the mouth of Solomon."[14] The only way—not because it is Thérèse's way, as opposed to the ways of other theologians and ascetics, but because it is the way of love that surpasses and includes all others. "That is everything that Jesus asks of us."[15] In this sense, her teaching is just as new and unique as her mission. "She feels herself to be the bearer of something quite new."[16] And a privileged position is given to this new teaching: "Our Lord once answered the mother of the sons of Zebedee, 'To sit at my right or left hand is not mine to give to you, but to them for whom it is prepared by my Father.' I imagine that these privileged places that were denied to the great saints and martyrs will be granted to the little children. Did not David prophesy it when he said, 'The little Benjamin shall preside amid the assemblies [of the saints]'?"[17] There is even a sense in which Thérèse uses her little way as her measure of the saints. "Théophane Vénard is *a little saint*, his life is quite ordinary."[18] "As soon as God sees us convinced of our own nothingness—he stretches out his hand to us; but if we wish to attempt great things, even under the pretext of zeal, he leaves us alone. It is sufficient therefore to humble oneself and to bear our imperfections meekly: that is *true sanctity*."[19] The correctness of her doctrine is self-evident for Thérèse. "Not a single book, and no theology, guided me, and yet I know in the depths of my heart that I am within the truth."[20] And her conviction urges her, toward the end of her life, to communicate these truths to everyone; continually we hear her: "You must tell souls. . . ." And she leads those whom God has sent

[14] SS 187–88.
[15] SS 189.
[16] G 432 (ET 345).
[17] H 262 (T 294).
[18] H 250 (T 235).
[19] H 272 (T 303).
[20] G 432 (ET 345–46).

to her along *her* way; to the hesitant Bellière, she writes: "I feel that we must go to heaven by the same road."[21] "I see, even more clearly than in your other letters, that you are *barred* from going to heaven by any other way than your poor little sister's."[22] Her teaching is not a theological system of propositions held together by inferences; it is an immediate, total vision and, on that account, requires many different forms for its exposition. And, however important it may be to understand the exposition, it is even more vital to grasp the original power of the vision. It is a primitive Christian power following the primitive Christian system of dying and rebirth, of death and resurrection, of pulling down and building up. It is the power of God, who has command over the living and the dead. We find it in the Sermon on the Mount, which in a series of lightning flashes annihilates every tenet that contradicts divine truth —the Pharisee with his religion of good works brushed aside in favor of the poor and the abandoned. And again, in Paul's gospel, the life that flowed from the death of Damascus. It is the power of the Augustinian either/or: *caritas* or *cupiditas*. It is the power of unconditional surrender in Carmel. And this is the rhythm that must be at the back of our minds as we listen to Thérèse's teaching.

Demolition

By going directly to the Gospel sources, Thérèse joins with all her force in the Lord's initial movement: the demolition of religious façades. The blazing passion with which John the Baptist in the Jordan, in the spirit of Elias, clears the ground to give the approaching Messiah room and air is itself only a preparation for the absolute passion with which the Son flattens every obstacle to the Father's glory. "Whoever draws near me draws near to fire", runs one of Christ's apocryphal sayings,

---

[21] S 358 (GC II:1152).   [22] S 362–63 (GC II:1164).

and each of his words, his actions and his miracles is fire—a fire all the more consuming since it is not the fire of justice but of love. And once God has cast this fire upon earth, he sends his saints to fan it into flame so that it cannot be damped down in the hearths of a "bourgeois" Christianity.

Thérèse of Lisieux also cleanses the Temple with a whip. She is fearless and aggressive. She loves *war*. She is a fighter by nature. "God wanted to make me conquer the fortress of Carmel at the sword's point."[1] "God has granted me the grace of being totally unafraid of war; I must do my duty, whatever the cost."[2] "Let us always grasp the sword of the spirit . . . , let us never simply allow matters to take their course for the sake of our own peace; let us fight without ceasing, even without hope of winning the battle. What does success matter! Let us keep going, however exhausting the struggle may be. . . . One must do one's duty to the end."[3] "This morning I read a passage in the Gospels where it is said, 'I come not to bring peace but a sword.' All that remains for us then is to fight. When we have not the strength, it is then that Jesus fights for us. Together let us put the axe to the root of the tree. . . ."[4] "Sanctity! It has to be won at the point of the sword."[5] She speaks of "the way to *force* Jesus to come to your help";[6] and asserts that victory will not come cheaply: "It does not come in a day."[7] But for all her failings, there is one quality she never lacks: "I am not always faithful, but I am never discouraged."[8] "During meditation, I fell asleep for a moment. I dreamed that soldiers were needed for a war. You said, we must send Thérèse of the Child Jesus. I replied, I would prefer a holy war. But I went all the same. O Mother, how gladly I would have fought in the Crusades or later against the heretics. Certainly I should not have feared the fire. . . . Is it possible that I shall have to

[1] S 298 (GC II:1017).   [2] SS 240.
[3] H 298 (T 324–25).   [4] S 56 (GC I:450).
[5] S 101 (GC I:558).   [6] S 245 (GC II:1117).
[7] S 359 (GC II:1152–53).   [8] S 193 (GC II:801).

die in bed?"[9] "I am not a warrior who has fought with earthly weapons but 'with the sword of the spirit that is the word of God'. Consequently not even my sickness has laid me low, and only yesterday evening I used my sword on a novice. I said, I shall die weapon in hand."[10] And she teaches the novices to do likewise. "I always want to see you behaving like a brave soldier who does not complain about his own suffering but takes his comrades' wounds seriously and treats his own as nothing but scratches."[11] And that is how she herself behaves, on her deathbed, when she is burdened with visitors. "I thought that I ought not to want more rest than the Lord. When he fled into the desert after preaching, the people came and disturbed his solitude. Come to me as often as you like. I must die with my weapons *in my hand, in my mouth the sword of the spirit that is the word of God*."[12] Thérèse is convinced of the connection between holiness and energy. "In order to be holy, the most essential virtue is energy. With energy one can easily reach the height of perfection."[13] "Jesus said that 'the Kingdom of heaven suffers violence, and the violent take it by storm.' "[14] "You cannot be half a saint, you must be a whole saint or no saint at all. I felt that you must have a soul of great energy, and I was happy to become your sister."[15] This feature of Thérèse's make-up explains her admiration for Judith. "I have always been struck by the praise addressed to Judith, 'You have done manfully, and your heart has been strengthened.' At the beginning we must act courageously; then one's heart becomes bolder, and one marches to victory after victory."[16]

Above all, it explains the love and friendship for Joan of Arc that permeate all her writing. In her early days, she used to read chivalrous stories with great enthusiasm, "When reading the accounts of the patriotic deeds of French heroines, those of the venerable Joan of Arc in particular, I felt a great desire to

[9] N 115 (LC 132).   [10] N 113 (LC 237).
[11] H 272 (T 303).   [12] H 295 (G 322).
[13] S 254 (GC II:909).   [14] S 297 (GC II:1017).
[15] S 347 (GC II:1133).   [16] H 267 (T 298).

imitate them." [17] And her attitude toward Joan of Arc remains absolutely unchanged even later, when she had come to realize that her glory would not lie in external deeds.

> When I began to learn the history of France, the story of Joan of Arc's exploits entranced me; I felt in my heart the desire and the courage to imitate her; it seemed to me that the Lord meant me for great things too. I was not mistaken, but, in place of voices from heaven calling me to war, I heard in the depths of my soul a voice sweeter, more powerful still, the voice of the Spouse of Virgins calling me to other exploits, conquests more glorious, and, in the solitude of Carmel, I realized that my mission was not to get a mortal king crowned but to get the King of heaven loved, to bring the realm of hearts under his sway. [18]

Her numerous poems and hymns in honor of Joan always celebrate her sanctity, which forms the heart of her mission on the battlefield. In the "Shepherdess of Domrémy", [19] the vocation to burning love and suffering is the theme; in the "Victory Hymn for Joan of Arc", [20] it is her firm will to fight for Jesus in saving souls; in "Joan of Arc's Prayer in Jail", [21] it is her memory of her free life in the world and her longing for martyrdom. In "Joan's Voices during Martyrdom", [22] she describes the promised salvation of France through her vicarious suffering; in the "Triumphant Song", [23] she pictures her storming heaven. At every turn, Joan walks beside Thérèse. She wishes, like Joan of Arc, to whisper the name of Jesus "at the stake". [24] She compares her mission to Joan's—on seeing a picture of her in prison, she exclaims: "Your saints also encourage me in my prison. They say to me, 'As long as you are in chains, you cannot fulfill your mission; later, after your death, your hour of victory will strike.' " [25] "My mission will be accomplished according to God's will, like Joan of Arc's, in spite of the envy

[17] SS 72.

[19] Ged 447–51.

[21] Ged 454.

[23] Ged 457.

[25] N 134 (LC 144).

[18] S 327 (GC II:1085).

[20] Ged 453.

[22] Ged 455.

[24] SS 193.

of men."[26] "I am plagued with questions; it reminds me of Joan of Arc before the Inquisitors. I believe I am answering with the same sincerity."[27] Her "Prayer Inspired by a Picture of Joan of Arc" draws their two missions together in the bonds of sisterly love:

> O Lord of Hosts, you have said in your Gospels, "*I am not come to bring peace but a sword*"; arm me for the battle. I long to fight for your glory; but I beg you to uphold my courage—O my Beloved. I know what struggles you have prepared for me; it is not on the battlefield that I shall fight. . . . I am the prisoner of your love, I have freely riveted the fetters that bind me to you and cut me off forever from the world. My sword is LOVE! With it, *I shall drive strangers from the land and shall have you proclaimed King over souls*. It is true, Lord, that you do not need such a weak instrument as myself; but Joan, your virginal and valiant spouse, has said, "We must do battle before God gives the victory." O my Jesus, I shall fight for love of you until the evening of my life.[28]

Thérèse is a warrior even though her battles are fought for love by means of love, for peace by means of peace. Her warlike qualities simply bring out new aspects of her action in the midst of contemplation. And, just as no action can be more effective than that contemplation by which she inspires all forms of action in the Church, similarly no battle can be fiercer and more final than the battle of love that she conducts with the sword of the Spirit.

Her battle is to wipe out the hard core of Pharisaism that persists in the midst of Christianity; that human will-to-power disguised in the mantle of religion that drives one to assert one's own greatness instead of acknowledging that God alone is great. "With the utmost severity and unsparing clarity, Thérèse directs her attack against every ascetical practice that aims, not at God, but at one's own 'perfection', which is nothing more

---

[26] N 94–95 (LC 113).   [27] N 87 (LC 104).
[28] H 310–11 (T 452).

than a spiritual beauty treatment."[29] "Jesus does not demand great deeds but only gratitude and self-surrender. '*I will not*', he says, '*take the he-goats from out of your flocks, for all the beasts of the forest are mine. . . . Shall I eat the flesh of bullocks, or shall I drink the blood of goats? Offer to God the sacrifice of praise and thanksgiving*.' See, then, all that Jesus lays claim to from us; he has no need of our works but only of our love."[30] It is generally recognized that "cosmetics for the soul", "that overwrought, incessant measuring, counting, calculating, touching and examining one's own 'perfection', that most dangerous distraction of attention from God to the ego under the pretext of tender conscience, and even humility",[31] constitute a special danger for those living the monastic life and, particularly for contemplatives, constitute the universal "temptation to perfection". This danger of Pharisaism would not have been depicted in such detail by the Lord if its significance had only been restricted to one small caste. The enemy toward whom the Lord shows himself so relentless is the one who remains the enemy for all time. Whenever Thérèse meets this enemy, she is as hard and cutting as the gospel itself. "One feast day, as a special treat, dessert was served, but one of the novices was accidentally passed over; her neighbor having failed to notice it, this novice pointed out to her the 'mortification' that she had borne in silence. Thérèse ordered her to go immediately to the kitchen Sister and ask for the portion she had missed. Covered with confusion, the novice defended herself; but Thérèse was immovable. 'Let that be your penance. You are not worthy of the little sacrifices God asks of you.' " "The same novice tells of how she once boasted during direction of an 'act of virtue' she had performed. 'What a pity', the saint answered, 'that you behave like that. Considering all the graces and illuminations that Jesus grants you, you would have been most blameworthy to have done anything else. What is that in comparison with

[29] G 415–16 (ET 332).   [30] SS 188–89.
[31] G 416 (ET 333).

what he has a right to expect of you on account of your vows! Humble yourself, rather, at the thought of the many opportunities of exercising virtue that you have let slip.' "[32] It is the everlasting misunderstanding that was to cling to her throughout all her years in the cloister and which she never managed to destroy; it is ever more firmly fastened upon her the nearer death approaches. Pauline says to her: "How you must have striven in order to have reached the degree of perfection at which we see you now!" And Thérèse, with indescribable emphasis: "Oh, that's nothing." Or again, later: "Sanctity does not consist in performing such and such acts; it means being ready at heart to become small and humble in the arms of God, acknowledging our own weaknesses and trusting in his fatherly goodness to the point of audacity."[33] It is a hopeless struggle, for the more Thérèse defends herself and tries to prevent herself from being regarded as a saint, the more the others wonder at her "humility" and her "perfection".[34] There is only a shade of difference between true and false, but it is just that shade of difference that makes all the difference. There are two ways in which a Christian can regard "virtue"; either he can treat it as a quality inherent in himself, a *habitus* that he has some justification for attributing to himself (after all, he sees that he has initiated these "acts of virtue", rejected temptation and acquired skill in doing good); or else he can realize that it depends entirely upon the grace of God working within him—in spite of him! If he chooses the first way, then he can collect "merit" and store it up, in which case he can stand back and survey his treasure. If he chooses the second, then the matter is no longer in his hands; it all remains in the hands of God, his possession.

As a child, Thérèse was trained to "collect" merit; Marie taught her to do so: "I can still hear you saying to me, 'Look at the shopkeepers, how much trouble they give themselves to

---

[32] 2 P 710 (G 409 [ET 327]).   [33] N 112–13 (LC 129 note).
[34] Cf. G 460–61 (ET 369–70).

make money, whereas we can amass treasure for heaven without giving ourselves so much trouble; all we have to do is to
gather diamonds with a RAKE'. And off I went, my heart filled
with joy, overflowing with good resolutions."[35] And, in her
early letters, we see the child busy at this work of collecting:
"Every day I try to do all the 'practices' I can, and I do my
best not to let any opportunity pass. From the bottom of my
heart, and as often as possible, I say the little prayers: they are
sweet-scented like roses . . . , my thanks to Sister Thérèse of
Saint Augustine for her dear little rosary of practices. . . ."[36]
But gradually, without its being noticed, the meaning of the
word changes and surrenders its kernel of Christian truth; the
treasure is love, but love is the prodigality that knows neither
to count nor reckon. "It's very simple. Hold nothing back;
distribute your goods as soon as you get them. As for myself,
if I live to be eighty years old, I shall still be as poor. I do not
know how to make economies; everything I have I give away
immediately to buy souls."[37] And so she devises a joyous new
version of the old fable: "I have been almost *nine years* in the
house of the Lord. So I ought by now to be far advanced in the
ways of perfection, but I am still only at the foot of the ladder;
it does not discourage me, and I am as merry as a grasshopper;
singing away all day and hoping at the end of my life to share
in the riches of my Sisters, who are much more generous than
the ant."[38] And even during her last few days: "I know that
my Sisters have told you of my cheerfulness, and it is true that
I am like a finch, except when I have a temperature, luckily it
usually comes only at night, at the hour when finches sleep,
their heads beneath their wings."[39] Because love "seeks not its
own", she always thinks first of others, and the more she loves,
the less it occurs to her to think of herself. "If I had been rich,
I could not have seen a poor person hungry without giving

[35] S 106 (GC I:563).   [36] S 15 (GC I:190).
[37] H 281 (T 310).   [38] S 300 (GC II:1021–22).
[39] S 356 (GC II:1146).

him something to eat. That is what I do in my spiritual life: as soon as I acquire something, knowing that there are souls on the point of falling into hell, I give them my treasures, and I have not yet had a minute to say, 'Now I am going to work for myself.' "[40] "I do not know whether I shall go to Purgatory. Nor am I worried. If I have to go there, then I shall not regret having done nothing to avoid it. . . . I am happy to know that our holy Mother Teresa did not think differently."[41] "If I do go to Purgatory, then I shall be very content to do so; I shall do like the three young men, sing the song of love as I am being transformed in the furnace. How happy I should be if by these means I could save other souls and suffer in their place. . . ."[42] "I would not have picked up a single straw in order to avoid Purgatory. Everything I have done was in order to give joy to the good God and to save souls."[43]

Progress does not come through acquisitions but through losing everything; it does not mean climbing, it means descending. A novice sighs: "When I think of everything I still have to acquire!" "You mean, to lose! Jesus takes it upon himself to fill your soul in the measure that you rid it of its imperfections. I see that you have taken the wrong road; you will never arrive at the end of your journey. You are wanting to climb a great mountain, and the good God is trying to make you descend it; he is waiting for you at the bottom in the fertile valley of humility."[44] As we have seen from her teaching about time and eternity, one does not achieve sanctity by piling up "acts": Aloysius could have learned no more if he had lived to Noah's age.[45] We have also seen how Thérèse as a child was trained to make her particular examen; and no one had been more eager to finger the pearls of sacrifice and acts of virtue on the thread of her life. Pauline even gave her a little notebook in which she might enter her daily progress.[46] The mature Thérèse grew out

[40] H 297 (T 323).
[41] N 26-27 (LC 56).
[42] N 55-56 (LC 81).
[43] N 99 (LC 118).
[44] G 423 (ET 338).
[45] N 18 (LC 51).
[46] G 60, 104 (ET 49, 83).

of these habits. "I know that certain spiritual directors advise us to count our virtuous acts in order to advance in perfection. But my spiritual director, Jesus, does not teach me to count my acts. He teaches me to do it all for love."[47] If a person can no longer reckon, then that person approaches God in a condition of complete poverty, the poverty spoken of by the Gospels, without which the vision of grace is impossible.

> I cannot rely upon anything, not on one single work of mine, for security. . . . But this poverty is a real light and a grace for me. I thought of how I could not pay God for even one of the faults I had committed in the whole of my life, and that precisely this could be my richness and strength if I wished. And so I prayed, O my God, I beg you yourself to pay the debt I have contracted toward the souls in Purgatory, but do it as God, so that it will be infinitely more successful than if I had said my Offices for the Dead. And I took great comfort in the thought expressed by Saint John of the Cross in his canticle: "Pay all debts." I have always related this to love. I feel that one can never repay this grace . . . , it is a source of such peace to be utterly poor, to count on nothing but God.[48]

Because she attaches such tremendous importance to poverty, Thérèse mistrusts every form of penance and asceticism that is easily liable to become an occasion for showing-off. In regard to works of penance, she says:

> One has to be very prudent in such practices, for they quickly become the work of nature rather than of virtue. A passage from the life of Blessed Henry Suso about penitential practices has stuck in my mind. He had performed the most terrible penitential practices, which had ruined his health, when an angel appeared and told him to stop it. And the angel added, "So far you have fought as a simple soldier. Now I will dub you a knight"; his meaning was to show the saint how spiritual combat is superior to corporal mortifications. Now, little Mother, the good God no longer wishes me to remain a simple soldier; he has just dubbed

[47] G 424 (ET 339).   [48] N 121–22 (LC 137).

me a knight. . . . In this hidden combat, which lies beyond the reach of nature, I have found peace and humility.[49]

Admittedly Thérèse, like all the saints who have spoken similarly, had already gone through a great deal of penance. At the start of her religious life, she experienced "a strong inclination to works of penance". "I had taken too much pleasure in them", she confesses, "and so the good God let me realize that the strictest penances can be mingled with natural satisfaction."[50] She once tried wearing a little iron crucifix with a sharp point upon it on her breast, but the point pressed into her flesh and caused a slight inflammation. "I would not have abandoned it for such a trifling reason if the good God had not wished me to realize that the mortifications of the saints are not meant for me nor for the little souls who will also walk in the way of childhood."[51] Nor was it only a question of bodily harm. She tells Pauline that her previous mortifications at mealtimes had been the occasion of disagreeable thoughts: "Later I found it simpler to offer to the good God whatever pleased my taste."[52] "It was well that the Lord warned us, '*In my Father's house there are many mansions, if not I would have told you.*' Yes, if every soul called to perfection were obliged to perform these mortifications in order to enter heaven, he would have told us, and we should have undertaken them with willing hearts. But he explains to us that '*there are many mansions in his house.*' If some are for great souls, those of the desert Fathers and penitential martyrs, there must also be some for the little children."[53]

Nevertheless, Thérèse's whole life is one long hymn of penance. And not only in the general sense that to live under vows means having a penitential status but in minute application to the details of penance. Yet the aim of this penance is not to perform great feats or achieve personal perfection but to ex-

[49] N 110-11 (LC 130).   [50] G 368-69 (ET 296-97).
[51] H 231 (T 218).   [52] N 168 (LC 178).
[53] H 278 (T 308).

ploit every single opportunity for gratitude that God offers.
Thérèse never refuses, but neither does she snatch. She realizes that everything in the religious life, down to its least ac-
cidentals, is providential. The rattling of rosary beads in choir
nearly drives her to distraction; but she does not turn around
and fix the guilty Sister with a withering glance. Nor does
she try to shut the noise out of her mind; instead, she transforms it into part of her prayer. At the washtub, an energetic
neighbor splashes the dirty water over her face; she does not
turn her face away; and when washday comes around again,
she takes up the same position. According to her own testimony, she suffered terribly from the cold, especially since her
cell was never heated. One word and she could have had more
blankets; but she remains silent. "One should not betray the
fact that one is cold", she says, "by hunching oneself up or
shivering or rubbing one's hands."[54] In the refectory, it is impossible to work out which dishes she likes or dislikes. The
result is that she is invariably served with what has been left
over; not until her last illness was she made to say, under obedience, which dishes disagreed with her.[55] There is something
Franciscan—and yet typical of Thérèse—in the story of the
flies that plagued her during her last months but that she was
glad to have there. "They are my only enemies, and since the
good God has urged us to love our enemies, I am glad to have
this opportunity. Let them be."[56] She scolds a novice who was
warming her slippers at the stove: "If I had done that, except
under obedience, I should have accused myself of a great lack
of mortification."[57] It is quite in keeping that she endured the
inhuman tortures of the last weeks without morphium at the
request of the Prioress. Accepting anything, never flinching,
and exploiting every opportunity: with this attitude, Thérèse
performs much harder and more persistent penance than by

---

[54] LC 258, cf. H 231–32 (T 218); 1 P xiii, sec. 44 (G 372 [ET 297–98]).
[55] H 230 (T 217).   [56] N 99 (LC 119).
[57] Pt 50.

making sporadic "heroic" acts, where there always lurks self-glorification. On the other hand, Thérèse never comes near to Quietism, which is the danger when penance is neglected. Her will to penance is an active one, driving her to accept every opportunity and to note the least failure.[58]

Here she does not cut out the notion of merits.[59] "So you want to acquire merits?" "Yes, but not for myself. For souls, and for the needs of the whole Church. . . ."[60] And she robs the notion of its sting. "Merit does not arise from performing great deeds or giving much but in receiving and loving."[61] She keeps her eye on the intention and the results, not on the act of self-conquest. In the matter of loving her neighbor, she is almost excruciatingly sensitive; yet no one could tell what it cost her to conquer her emotions. In fact, she not only hides her self-conquest from others; she conceals it from God and, whenever possible, from herself. She lays the emphasis entirely on the love that has to be achieved, not on the achievement itself—even, going one step farther, on the objective sacrifice, in which she herself remains as if anonymous. She fulfills the command not to let the left hand know what the right is doing, even when left and right signify part of the same soul. This is the point at which God intervenes to ensure that her achievement should be unconscious, and he does so by allowing all feeling to be withdrawn. Her achievement remains, and is infinitely greater, but separate from her, as if it had gone dead in her hands. "Ah! that is indeed a great love, to love Jesus without feeling the sweetness of that love, there you have martyrdom. . . . All right! *let us die martyrs!* . . . Martyrdom unrealized by men, known to God alone, undiscoverable by the eye of any creature, martyrdom without honor, without triumph. . . ."[62]

Even in this martyrdom, the point is not the record of suf-

---

[58] N 152.

[59] Cf. S 292 (GC II:1011).

[60] N 143 (LC 153).

[61] S 189 (GC II: 794–95).

[62] S 111–12 (GC I:577).

fering but the intensity of love. Every penance that increases true love is good; any penance that narrows and preoccupies the soul is harmful. "Certainly every penance is laudable and meritorious if one is convinced that the good God requires it of one. Even if one errs in doing it, [God] is touched by the intention. But I could never bind myself to anything if it became a constant preoccupation . . . ; as our mother Saint Teresa says: God is not concerned with a heap of trifles, as we too easily believe; and we should never let anything narrow our souls."[63] "Love is the one thing at which we should aim, consequently we should always prefer that deed into which we can crush most love, whether it is 'harder' or 'easier'; it is better to do something that is in itself indifferent than something 'worthwhile' in itself if we can do the first more lovingly than the second."[64] Thus love becomes the measure of penance, and therewith the measure of pleasures and enjoyment as well. "She is very fond of fingering fruit, such as the peach, and admiring its velvety skin, or distinguishing the scents of individual flowers. For her, it would have been an offense against simplicity not to derive enjoyment when it was an occasion of love and thankfulness toward God for the beauty of nature and music." "Out of love, I will suffer and, out of love, rejoice."[65]

Not penance, but the reckoning of it, is demolished with her. Not the deed, but the aspiring for merit. By eliminating all human reckoning, Thérèse makes room for grace. In the religion of the Old Law, one deed was set against another, God's deeds and human deeds. And, on account of human weakness, it was almost inevitable that this religion should terminate in Pharisaism. The grace of the New Law eliminates every reckoning. It is not only that God takes the initiative by the totally unmerited gift of grace but that subsequently the relations between God and the soul are not governed by any law of reckoning within human grasp. As far as Thérèse is concerned,

[63] G 376 (ET 302–3).   [64] 2 P 290 (G 276 [ET 303]).
[65] Pt 52 and SS 196.

the real purpose in demolishing the whole ethic of works is
to allow the shining miracle of divine grace to light up the
life of every Christian. Here, the best known of all Thérèse's
metaphors and images begin to crowd in; they are images of
the incomprehensibility of divine grace. If men ought not to
reckon, that is because God does not reckon, indeed, cannot
reckon, because it would be contrary to his innermost essence,
which is overflowing love. "There is one science that he does
not know—arithmetic."[66] (Even at school, Thérèse had shown
a distaste for arithmetic.)[67] Whereas the very quickest calculation proceeds on the assumption of a continuous gradation of
numbers, grace is in no way limited to such gradations. The
image that occurs to Thérèse to express this vision is that of
an elevator.

> Alas, I have always noticed, in comparing myself with the saints,
> the same difference between them and myself as we see between
> a mountain whose summit is lost in the clouds and an obscure
> little grain of sand trampled underfoot by passers-by. . . . It is
> impossible for me to grow great. . . . But we live in an age of
> inventions: today there is no need to go to the trouble of climb-
> ing stairs; among rich people, an elevator has replaced the stairs.
> I also wished to discover an elevator to take me up to Jesus; be-
> cause I am too little to climb the steep stairway of perfection.[68]

In this enchanting picture, the elevator is nothing else but the
love that destroys all distances and eliminates all calculable con-
tinuity. She writes to Abbé Bellière: "More than ever I realized
the degree to which your love is sister to mine, since it is called
to go up to God by the elevator of love, not to climb the rough
stairway of fear."[69] And, if the picture simply seems to replace
the slow methodical climb by a sudden jerk, which remains
equally bound to the imagery of ascending, it can be supplemented by a picture of grace descending in power. She pictures
a mother standing at the head of the stairs, who sees her child

[66] H 280 (T 309).   [67] Pt 65.
[68] SS 207–8.   [69] S 358–59 (GC II:1152).

vainly trying to mount the stairs; the mother comes down to lift the child up into her arms.[70] She pictures the divine eagle swooping down to the little bird helplessly fluttering on the ground and then soaring with it on its pinions into the abyss of light.[71] The pattern is always the same: the human beginning, faltering, scarcely perceptible, and then the completion of the work by a lightning-flash of divine intervention. When the Father Superior visits her to encourage her, he exclaims: "What? You wish to go to heaven soon? But your crown is not yet perfect. You have scarcely begun!" Thérèse replies: "Oh, Father, how right you are! I have not made my crown, but the good God has made it."[72]

At this point, grace seems to be something magical; more precisely, it is something creative. God calls that which is not into existence. Powers are bestowed upon the creature that are far beyond its own reach, beyond its dreams even. Vistas are opened up that it could never attain of itself and aims that it could never have set itself. Yet nature is not eliminated by the magic of grace. Nature is there, not even neglected or concealed, but multiplied, intensified and broken into a richer existence. Thérèse tells us of a kaleidoscope that she possessed in her childhood. "A sort of little telescope at the far end of which one could see pretty patterns of different colors; if one turns the instrument, it produces infinite variations on these patterns." She takes the magical tube to pieces to see how the miracle happens; she discovers "some little bits of paper and cloth scattered inside and three mirrors on the inside of the tube". And this becomes an image for her of a great mystery. "So long as our actions, no matter how trivial, remain within the focus of love, the Blessed Trinity . . . gives them a wonderful brilliance and beauty. When Jesus looks at us through the little lens, which is to say himself, he finds all our doings beautiful. But, if we abandon the ineffable center of love, what does

---

[70] T 293.   [71] SS 199.
[72] N 57 (LC 276).

he see? A few straws . . . besmirched and worthless deeds."[73]
Rarely has anyone hit upon such a striking and theologically
exact image of grace, provided that God's vision through the
lens is taken as the true and creative vision and the natural
materials as no more than the presupposition on which the
truth works. The magic of grace is not something subjective, a
form of mystification. In fact, the vision of the three-personed
God, the loving vision, is the one objective, truth-revealing
vision. Thérèse realizes this, and that is why she begs the three-
personed God "to look at me only with the Face of Jesus between, and in his Heart burning with *Love*".[74] For God sees
us as we really are, in our eternal reality and not in time's deceptive mirror.[75] To the same end, she invokes "imagination"
(that is, hypnotism) as an illustration: "Oh, how I should like
to be hypnotized by our Lord! . . . With what meekness I have
surrendered my will to him! Yes, I want him to take over all
my faculties so that I no longer perform human and personal
actions but utterly divine ones, inspired and directed by the
spirit of love!"[76] In this instance, a spiritual nature is treated
as the stuff that has to be taken over, controlled and reformed
—though the image is obviously incomplete, since hypnotism
eliminates the subject's personal freedom, whereas grace preserves and intensifies it. The point is that man cannot be "hypnotized" by grace apart from his own will and self-surrender
but that, once he is in the power of this higher will, then he
carries it out without knowing its laws and purposes. One final picture, in which she expresses our inability to penetrate
into God's schemes: "At this moment, your Thérèse does not
find herself on the heights, but Jesus is teaching her. . . . He is
teaching her to play at love's bank, or rather, he plays for her,
not telling her just how he goes about it—for that is his business and not Thérèse's; her part is to abandon herself, to give
herself over, keeping nothing for herself, not even the joy of

[73] H 290 (T 317-18).   [74] SS 276.
[75] S 132 (GC I:630).   [76] H 290 (T 318).

knowing how his bank is paying."[77] She depicts the "magic" of grace so perfectly that it appears to act without laws. Winnings come out of it that no one, with all the science in the world, could have predicted. There is only one condition for winning: to stake all and, in the same act, stake all one's winnings as well as the knowledge of them. Just as the lover does not belong to himself, so also his winnings are not his to keep. God will use them as he wishes, sharing them or keeping them or investing them where he thinks best. The lover's stake in God's play is himself; he throws himself into it for God's sake. He does not care to know whether he will be multiplied a hundredfold, sixtyfold or thirtyfold, for the sum of his winnings no more belongs to him than the ear of wheat belongs to the seed that died. The original sum no longer exists; it has vanished into the sum of the winnings. Therefore love, in a sense, is magic: it produces what was not there and spirits away what was there. "The principal plenary indulgence, and one that everyone may obtain without the customary conditions, is the indulgence of *charity that covers a multitude of sins* [Prov 10:12]."[78]

By eliminating all reckoning, she at the same time demolishes the structure of "merit" or "reward" in the human sense. Reckonings and rewards are both Old Testament metaphors for New Testament realities. But we may also plunge directly into the interior law of love, and then we discover the limits of the Old Testament concepts, which are all based upon one-to-one reckoning. But not only is there no comparison between the sufferings of the present time and the glory of eternity (Rom 8:18); even the blessed enjoying eternal happiness will see it —lovers that they are—as pure unmerited grace, not a reward for services rendered. Perhaps they will appreciate God's joy in rewarding good service; they may even discern some proportion between the rewards and merits of others; in their own case, these notions simply do not apply. And so heaven is a "stolen heaven": "My protectors in heaven, my favorites, are

[77] S 189-90 (GC II:795).   [78] H 288 (T 316).

those who stole it, such as the Holy Innocents and the Good Thief. The great saints have won it by their works: for myself, I wish to imitate the thieves, to take it by a trick, a trick of love that will give me entry, me and other poor sinners."[79] In one's dealings with God, one should never allow grace to be twisted into a matter of obligation, for that is to treat a child as an adult, subject to reward and punishment. "To be little means recognizing one's nothingness, expecting everything from the good God, *as a little child expects everything from its Father. . . .* Even among the poor, a little child is given everything it needs so long as it is little; but, as soon as it grows up, its father will no longer feed it and says, 'Work now, you can look after yourself.' Well now, it is because I did not want to hear those words that I have not wanted to grow up, because I feel incapable of *earning my living, the eternal living of heaven.*"[80] There was nothing Thérèse feared more than to find herself settling debts with God. And, since it is only grown-ups who settle debts, she intends at all costs to preserve that relationship that one finds among children when they are dealing with each other. She simply *will* not grow old, and so will not be obliged to earn heaven. She wants no reward: "At Sext a verse occurs in the Divine Office that I recite each day with reluctance; it is this: '*I have inclined my heart to do your justifications forever, because of the reward*'. I hasten to add in my heart, 'O my Jesus, you know well that I do not serve you for reward but solely because I love you and in order to save souls.' "[81] Therefore, at the end of her life, she desires to appear empty-handed before God and rejoices at the thought.[82] When Pauline says, "Oh, when I die I shall have nothing to show to the good God, I shall arrive empty-handed, and that makes me very sad", Thérèse answers: "You are not like me, then, though we are both in the same position. Even if I had performed all the deeds of Saint Paul, I would still consider myself an unprofitable servant; I would

---

[79] H 263 (T 294–95).   [80] H 263 (T 295).
[81] H 289 (T 317).   [82] T 448.

find that my hands were empty. But that is precisely the cause of my joy; since I have nothing, I shall receive everything from the good God."[83] It is easily seen that Thérèse does not sit in judgment on anyone's works or labors, but the one thing she cannot abide is that human beings should boast of their works in the face of God. To do so would be to insult grace, since "Jesus wants to grant us the same graces, wants to give us his heaven *as a free gift*."[84] The fact that there is no relation between earthly labor and heavenly reward was already her greatest incentive for throwing all her energies into the love and service of God when she was no more than fourteen: "I already had an experience of what God has prepared for those who love him . . . and, seeing the lack of proportion between these eternal rewards and the petty sacrifices of this life, I desired to love, to love Jesus passionately, to offer him countless tokens of my love while I could still do so."[85] This lack of proportion cannot be identified with the empty dialectic between sin and grace characteristic of Protestantism; it is the Catholic truth that the relation between grace received and grace to be received is infinitely increasing. It is this that touches Thérèse so deeply in the Lord's words to Saint Mechtild: "I am telling you the truth, that it gives me great joy when men expect mighty things of me. However great their faith and boldness may be, I shall bestow on them far more than their merits."[86] And so Thérèse entrusts herself to this "far more" promised by God's grace. "I know well that I shall never be worthy of what I am hoping for; but I put my hand out like a begging child, and I know that you will grant me so much more than I ask, because you are so good."[87] And we are now shown the reverse side of Thérèse, the thief of heaven. Previously it was Thérèse who stole heaven; now it is God, the great eagle, who steals her and carries his booty off to heaven. "I see him from

[83] N 37 (LC 67).
[85] SS 102.
[87] 2 P 361.

[84] S 290 (GC II:1000).
[86] 2 P 253 (G 346 [ET 279]).

afar and take care not to shout, '*There goes the thief!*' On the contrary. I call to him, '*This way! This way!*' "[88] In the Gospels, we are told that God will come like a thief. Soon he will come to steal me. And how I'd like to help the Thief!"[89]

✤

We have been led unawares into the very heart of Thérèse's mission. What Thérèse goes on to say, as she acknowledges, is the secret source of her doctrinal message. By demolishing the religion of works for the sake of pure love (which in itself is more effective than all justification by works), she places herself at the very center of the gospel, at the very point where the joyous message of redemption marks the decisive step from the Old Testament to the New. The mentality that confronts Thérèse so frequently in the Catholic asceticism of her day, and that she feels more and more obliged to reject, is the Old Testament mentality of justification by works expressed in its most extreme form in Pharisaism. Since this attitude assumes that man's relations with God are based entirely upon justice, and this limited conception of justice is the limit of these relations, it can imagine only one ideal—to step up one's own achievements so as to produce a corresponding increase in God's favors. But this ideal overlooks what Paul showed to be the very basis and *raison d'être* of God's testament with the chosen people: Abraham's faith, which implicitly includes hope and love as well. The people forgot that the law and its works are prophetic in character, pointing toward the Messiah; they are meant to express faith in the promised Christ, who would fulfill the law and its works. The people attributed a significance to the law in itself that obscured and sometimes even destroyed its true significance. Yet how easy it was under the Old Law to fall into a religion of justification by works! God first revealed himself as the God of justice, not as the God of love. And, besides

<hr>

[88] H 301 (T 327).   [89] N 33 (LC 61).

wishing to prepare humanity for love by means of the law, God also wished the failure of the law and its works to demonstrate what happens when men rely upon their own achievements apart from the Cross of Christ. "Now the law entered in, that sin might abound"(Rom 5:20).

Thérèse inserts her New Testament theology and asceticism at the exact point where the transition takes place. Her "little way" to "little sanctity" at first appears quite innocently as one way among many others, and she contrasts it particularly with the "great ways" of the "great saints" (to start with, these include her big sisters Pauline and Marie, both of whom she describes as "eagles"[90] in comparison with herself, the "little bird"). These great saints have done mighty deeds for God, but they are so superior as to discourage Thérèse, who does not dare to set out on their highway. But the more she gets to know the little way, the more she realizes, to her genuine surprise, that it is the only way. So we need not ourselves be impressed when we notice an ironical, scolding twinkle in her eye as she gazes reverently toward the "great saints". The twinkle becomes more obvious as time goes on and she assumes the role of David, armed with a sling and venturing into the open to attack the Goliath of "great sanctity". "The great saints have gained heaven by their works; myself, I wish to imitate the thieves, I wish to take it by a trick, a trick of love that will give me entry, me and other poor sinners."[91] And what is this trick? "It is quite simple. Hold nothing back. Distribute your goods as soon as you get them. . . . If, at the moment of death, I were to present my little coins to have them estimated at their true worth, our Lord would not fail to discover dross in them that I should certainly go and deposit in Purgatory. Are we not told that, although the great saints appear before God's judgment seat with their hands full of merits, yet they sometimes go to that place of expiation because no justice is without blemish

[90] S 51 (GC I:427); cf. S 54–55 (GC I:449).
[91] T 294–95.

in the eyes of the Lord."[92] And now she transfers her amused gaze away from men toward God, as it were, teasing the God of justice: "When I think of the good God's statement: 'I shall come soon and bring my reward with me, repaying everyone according to his works', then I say to myself that he will find himself very much embarrassed with me, because I have no works! So he will not be able to repay me according to my works. Very well, then, I trust that he will repay me according to his works."[93]

Thérèse here is preaching a lesson straight from the gospel of Paul: "Now to him that works, the reward is not reckoned according to grace but according to debt. But to him who works not yet believes in him who justifies the ungodly, his faith is reputed to justice, according to the purpose of the grace of God" (Rom 4:4–5). Thérèse is well aware of her kinship with Paul, since she heads her "Song of the Innocent Children" with this very text, joined to Romans 3:24: " 'Being justified freely by his grace through the redemption that is in Christ Jesus'—for the reward will not be reckoned as grace for those who perform works but as a debt. Therefore those who do not perform works will be justified freely through grace by the redemption worked by Jesus Christ."[94] Just as fundamentally Pauline is the thought that those stripped of justice (which means everyone) will by God's grace be clothed in his justice. Thérèse follows her master exactly: "In the evening of this life I shall appear before you empty-handed, for I do not ask you, Lord, to count my works. All our justices have stains in your sight. So I want to be clad in your own *Justice* and receive from your *Love* the possession of *yourself*. I want no other *Throne* or other *Crown* than *you*, O my *Beloved*."[95] Thérèse does not reject works out of hand; there is nothing even remotely Protestant about her interpretation of Saint Paul. But she knows that everything good and virtuous in man is grace, the gift of God's justice. "To be

---

[92] H 281 (T 310).   [93] N 6–7 (LC 43).
[94] Ged 435.   [95] SS 277.

little means not attributing the virtues we practice to ourselves in the belief that we are capable of them; but recognizing that the good God places this treasure in the hands of his little child for him to use when necessary; but the treasure remains God's always."[96]

Once more the need to remain a child is clear. The child cannot do as he pleases with the treasure entrusted to him; he can only hold it in his hand. A grown-up, however, is faced with the temptation to use the treasure on his own initiative. His maturity obviously throws a responsibility upon his shoulders that the child does not have to bear. And so Thérèse is impelled along her little way into another of Paul's secrets: "Thérèse is weak, very weak; every day she experiences it afresh, but Jesus delights to teach her . . . the science of glorying in one's infirmities. . . . Seeing yourself so worthless, you wish no longer to look at yourself, you look only at the sole Beloved. . . ."[97] Thérèse stands therefore in the true Augustinian tradition of *non parum, sed nihil*: "Maybe, if Peter had caught a few *small fish*, Jesus would not have worked a miracle, but he had *nothing*, so Jesus soon filled his net so that it almost broke."[98] From all this, it is clear that for Thérèse the idea of a perfection resulting from one's own efforts was an Old Testament concept; that is where she relegates the "great achievements" of the "great saints" whenever they are really the results of personal effort rather than of God's grace. She herself allots the "great" asceticism of perfection to the Old Testament and the "little" asceticism of love to the New: "I am but a weak and powerless child; yet it is my very weakness that makes me dare to offer myself as a victim of your love, O Jesus! In earlier times, only pure and spotless victims were acceptable to the strong and mighty God: perfect victims were needed to satisfy divine justice; but the law of love has replaced the law of fear, and love has chosen me for a holocaust, weak

---

[96] H 264 (T 295–96).   [97] S 130 (GC I:641).
[98] S 225 (GC II:851).

and imperfect creature as I am! Is this choice not worthy of love?"[99]

The change in the holocaust is not carried out in an arbitrary fashion but in response to a change in God's demands. Previously God himself demanded complete justice; now he asks for love. God himself has transformed the justice of the Old Testament into the mercy of the New. Whereas, in the Old Testament, justice ranks first among God's attributes, in a way restricting and limiting love and mercy, in the New Testament, it is so outshone by love that justice ranks as one quality of God's love. Love is the revelation of God's innermost being: "God is love" (1 Jn 4:8), we are told—never "God is justice." Consequently, justice can only be eternal and infinite insofar as it is one with the boundless love of God; if it ever seems to impose limits on love (as in the economy of the Old Law), then it can only be a temporal and finite revelation of God's being. By demolishing the limits that the old conception of justice imposes on love, Thérèse reaches the peak of her theological audacity. She refuses to acknowledge that there is the same tension in God between justice and love as there is between the Old and New Testament, or between fear and love. She refuses to relegate God's justice to the Old Testament and, therefore, to the law of fear. "Fear brings us only to Justice . . . , to *strict* Justice as it is shown to sinners, but that is not the *Justice* Jesus will have for those who love him."[100] She insists that we should take the Pauline gospel of the *Dikaiosyne Theou* seriously; it is a gift of God's grace and has to be treasured as an essential part of the New Testament. At the end of the first draft of her manuscript, she lets us into the inner chamber of her theology.

---

[99] SS 195.

[100] S 290 (GC II:1000). Thérèse had first written: "It is trust, and trust alone, that brings us to Love—Fear, doesn't fear bring us only to Justice?" But then she crossed out the words "to Justice" and substituted "to *strict* justice as it is shown to sinners, but that is not the *Justice* Jesus will have for those who love him."

It seems to me that if all creatures had received the same graces as I, God would be feared by no one but loved to the point of folly; no longer would any soul consent to cause him any pain, refraining out of love and not out of fear. At the same time, I realize that all souls cannot be alike; there must be different families of them, so that all the divine perfections may be particularly honored. To me, he has allotted his INFINITE MERCY, and only through it do I contemplate and adore the other divine perfections. They all appear to be radiant with love—*justice*, in fact, perhaps more than any other, seems to be clothed in love. What a sweet joy it is to think that the Lord is just, which means that he takes our weaknesses into account and is perfectly aware of the frailty of our nature! What, then, need I fear? Ah, must not the God who is infinitely just and deigns in his great mercy to pardon the faults of the prodigal son, be *just* to me also, *who am always with him?*[101]

Thus Thérèse sees it as her special mission to view all God's attributes in the light of his merciful love; his love is not simply connected with the other attributes, it embraces them. Even his justice is manifested and comprehensible through love. And Thérèse attaches the greatest importance to having her teaching on this point properly understood. Not many months before her death, on July 16, 1897, she says to Pauline: "In my manuscript, I have only said a word or two on the good God's justice. But if you wish, you can discover my whole mind on this matter in a letter to Father Roulland, where I have explained it at length."[102] This letter, however, though very valuable, does not really take us beyond the point in the *Story of a Soul* that I have quoted above: Thérèse writes to her missionary brother, Father Roulland, as follows: "I know one must be most pure to appear before the God of all holiness, but I know, too, that the Lord is infinitely just; and it is this justice, which terrifies so many souls, that is the basis of my joy and trust. To be just means not only to exercise severity in punishing the guilty but also to recognize right intentions and to reward virtue. I hope

[101] SS 180.   [102] N 80–81.

as much from the good God's justice as from his mercy—
because he is 'compassionate and merciful, long-suffering and
rich in mercy'." [103] Once again, she rejects the parallel between
fear and hope, on one side, and justice and mercy on the other.
The New Testament hope is equally directed toward each of
these attributes. The novelty in this text is that here Thérèse
is pointing toward God's justice as the source of his mercy,
whereas in the other text she describes justice more as a quality immanent in God's love. However one may interpret the
mutual inherence of justice and mercy, one thing is certain:
the rewards of virtue on which she sets her heart in this letter
should not be seen, in the Old Testament sense, as repayment
for good deeds. This would mean that Thérèse was now questioning everything she had said earlier and casting doubt on
the whole of her mission. What she is saying, in fact, is that
in the New Testament God distributes rewards in virtue of his
grace; the reward is one factor within his uncovenanted mercy.
God is so merciful that he *even* rewards virtue. Thérèse has now
arrived at the classical formula of Catholic teaching on merit:
Saint Thomas Aquinas, on the one hand, bases the correspondence between merit and reward upon the free disposition of
divine love and, on the other hand, takes supernatural love in
man as the principle of all merit (*S. Th.* I–II, q. 114, a. 4, c).

Thérèse takes one final step farther when she quotes Psalm
35:5 as her justification for confining God's primitive justice to
the temporal, finite economy of salvation, whereas she regards
the realm of merciful love (in which God's justice is immanent)
as eternal and ultimate. "If your justice loves to release itself,
this justice that extends only over this earth, how much more
your merciful love desires to inflame souls, since your mercy
reaches to the heavens." [104] That is why Thérèse will offer herself as host and sacrificial victim to God's mercy rather than to
God's justice. In doing so, she has deliberately placed herself
at the point of which John wrote, where love casts out fear:

[103] S 331 (GC II:1093).   [104] SS 181.

"He who abides in love abides in God and God in him. In this is the love of God made perfect in us, that we may have confidence in the Day of Judgment; because, as he is, we also are in this world. Fear is not in love: but perfect love casts out fear, because fear has to do with punishment. And he who fears is not perfected in love" (1 Jn 4:16–18). From now on, true to the spirit of Saint John, Thérèse is beyond fear, making room within herself for the fullness of love to dwell. From now on, she places her life beneath the law of complete love and considers that the fire of love is more effective in purifying her than the fear of Purgatory. "Oh, since that happy day, it seems to me that love surrounds and penetrates me; at every moment this *merciful love* renews me, purifying my soul and leaving no trace of sin within it, and I need have no fear of Purgatory. I know that of myself I would not merit even to enter that place of expiation, since only holy souls can have entrance there, but I also know that the fire of love is more sanctifying than that of Purgatory. I know that Jesus cannot desire useless suffering for us and that he would not inspire me with the desires I feel if he did not wish to grant them. . . ."[105] "How can he possibly let himself be outdone in generosity? How can he purify in the flames of Purgatory souls consumed in the fires of divine love?"[106] Whoever places himself beneath the law of divine love for good and all is in truth beyond judgment and no longer needs to fear it. One novice was "extraordinarily frightened of God's judgment; and, in spite of everything, she [Thérèse] said to me that nothing could drive away my fear." Thérèse shows her the only way to escape the judgment, which is "to appear before God empty-handed" and so deprive him of any matter for judgment. We should not hold on to any good that we do but should pass it on immediately. " 'But', I broke in, 'if God does not judge our good actions, he will judge our bad ones, and then?' 'What is it that you are saying? The Lord is justice itself. If he does not judge our good deeds, neither

---

[105] Ibid.   [106] S 331 (GC II:1093).

will he judge our bad ones. It seems to me that there will be no judgment for the victims of love; rather the good God will hasten to bestow eternal bliss upon them, rewarding his own love that he sees burning in their hearts.' "[107] Once more it is not merely in virtue of his mercy, restraining his justice, that God does not pronounce judgment but in virtue of his very justice, insofar as it is one with his love. Within love, divine justice discerns a certain correspondence and proportion between love as it is in God and love as it is in the believer who has accepted and preserved the love of God through grace. The property of perceiving this proportion *is* the justice of God's love and automatically dispenses eternal rewards. Consequently, the person in whom grace dwells must order all his thoughts according to the law of love and must abandon all judgments: " 'It is the Lord who judges me!' And, in order to secure a favorable judgment, or rather so as not to be judged at all, I wish to be charitable in my thoughts toward others always, since Jesus says, 'Judge not, and you shall not be judged.' "[108] And, with the judgment almost in sight: "If you only knew how mild my judgment will be! For, even if the good God scolds me a little, I shall still find it mild."[109] "When will the Last Judgment take place? Oh, I wish it were at this very moment!"[110] " 'As for little ones, they will be judged with great gentleness' [Wis 6–7]. And it is possible to stay little even when one is entrusted with responsible positions and lives a long life. . . . It is written that 'in the end, the Lord will rise up to save the lowly and meek of the earth.' It does not say 'to judge', but 'to save'."[111]

This whole process of demolishing the "great way", the way of justification by works, has shown the little way of love to be the only way. It is the way of grace and of the New Dispensation, but it is not on that account the easier way. Although Thérèse depicts the great way as involving extraor-

---

[107] H 281 (T 310–11).   [108] SS 222.
[109] N 55 (LC 81).   [110] N 49 (LC 76).
[111] N 185–86 (LC 199).

dinary penances and heroic deeds—the vocation of the few
—and contrasts it with the little way, along which all little
souls have to follow her, she herself knew from hard experience how much determination it requires. Isolated acts are not
enough; it demands one's whole being. What matters is not
the act but the condition of the soul from which it proceeds.
Not the deed but the attitude. It stands in the same relation
to the other way as does the knight to the soldier in Suso's
vision.[112] Nor does Thérèse hesitate to describe the "way of
weakness" as the more meritorious: "What merit would you
earn if you had to feel full of courage before you would fight?
What does it matter if you feel like it or not so long as you
behave as if you did? If you find yourself too tired to pick up a
bit of thread but do so nevertheless for the love of Jesus, you
gain more merit than if you were to perform a much more
remarkable deed in a moment of fervor."[113] It requires more
spiritual courage to make light of one's sufferings, or to say
nothing about them, than to attract other people's admiration
and pity.[114] On one occasion, when a novice deemed herself to
have performed an "heroic act of virtue", Thérèse, not without a certain sarcasm, relegates her to the ranks of the begin-
ners: "What is that little act of virtue in comparison with what
the Lord might legitimately demand of you? You ought rather
to feel humble at having neglected so many opportunities of
proving your love."[115] Céline regrets that the enthusiasm she
felt on first entering the convent has evaporated. "That was
simply youthfulness. Real courage does not consist of that momentary flush in which one longs to go out and capture souls
in the face of every danger, which only lends a delicious attraction to this beautiful dream. To be really brave means asking
for the Cross when one's heart is full of fear, and withstanding
this fear, like the Lord in the Garden of Olives."[116] This is the

[112] N III (LC 130 note)   [113] H 279 (T 309).
[114] T 303.   [115] H 274 (T 305).
[116] 2 P 395 (G 411 [ET 329]).

most difficult of all, to go on suffering when one is weak, and it is precisely because she can manage it that Thérèse seems hard, almost Nietzschean. A Sister had remarked: "I do not like to see people suffering, especially holy people." Thérèse took her up straight away: "Oh! I am not a bit like you! Holy people suffering never rouse my pity. I know that they have the strength to bear their sufferings and that it enables them to give God great glory; but those who are not holy, who do not know how to profit from their sufferings, oh, how sorry I am for them! How much pity I feel for *them*! I would move heaven and earth to console and relieve them!"[117] She sugars the bitter pill with humor sometimes, as in the anecdote from her childhood, when a horse was blocking the garden gate and the grown-ups did not know how to get past; in a twinkling Thérèse scrambled through between its legs. "Why do you always try to fly above temptations? Just *pass underneath*. It is all very well for the great saints to fly over the clouds when the storm is raging; we simply have to put up with the showers. So much the worse if we get a little damp! We can dry ourselves afterward in the sun of love."[118] There is something military about the way she makes light of difficulties and suppresses her complaints. In military service, we take many troubles in stride that would have made us grumble for hours in civilian life! That is the "ethos" of the little way. There is much sound, Gallic irony in Thérèse of Lisieux's make-up. Typical of her attitude is the image in which she manages to combine motifs from the first Psalm and Saint Paul, Pascal's famous *roseau pensant* and La Fontaine's fable of the oak and the reed. "What does it matter to the *little reed* if it bends? It is in no fear of breaking, for it has been planted on the edge of the waters. Instead of touching the earth when it bends, it meets only a pleasant wave that gives it new strength and makes it long for another storm to break over its frail head. It is its weakness that gives it all its confidence. It could not possibly break,

[117] H 285 (T 314).   [118] H 262 (T 294).

since, whatever happens to it, it sees only the gentle hand of Jesus."[119]

To demolish the ethic of good works produces the very opposite of Quietism. In fact, it empties the soul of all its own perfections, which are always "full of blemish before God", in order to free it for the service of Christ, which far exceeds its own strength: to be perfect as the Father in heaven is perfect. Thérèse well knows what this command with its tremendous promise demands of her. "Céline, do you think that Saint Teresa received more graces than you? . . . For my part, I do not tell you to aim at *seraphic* sanctity but simply 'to be perfect as your heavenly Father is perfect'. . . . Ah! Céline, our *infinite desires* are, after all, not dreams or fantasies, since Jesus himself gave us this *commandment*."[120] Bypassing the fruitless discussions as to whether the Sermon on the Mount is "practicable"—a discussion only indulged in by the fainthearted and the theorists—Thérèse simply takes the Lord's statement as a command. And she sets about putting it into practice at the very point that Christ indicates—"Be perfect, therefore, as your heavenly Father is perfect . . . who makes his sun rise upon the good and the bad and rains upon the just and the unjust. For, if you love those who love you, what reward will you have?" (Mt 5:48, 45–47). Thérèse strives to make love of her neighbor and her enemy an all-embracing law reaching to the smallest details of life. By doing so, she allows the will of the heavenly Father, as manifest in the Son, to do its work in her. "Judge not, then you yourselves will not be judged." "To try to convince our Sisters that they are in the wrong is not fair play—even if it is true—because we are not responsible for their conduct. We must not be *judges of peace* but only *angels of peace*."[121] In her chapters on loving our neighbor, Thérèse herself took good care to illustrate her every theoretical observation with some practical anecdote.[122] And the more

---

[119] S 104 (GC I:442).
[120] S 129 (GC I:621–22).
[121] H 283 (T 312–13).
[122] Cf. G 295–308 (ET 327–47).

one studies the picture that emerges, the more its supernatural pattern stands out. Thérèse's masterpiece is not the result of strenuous human application—if it were nothing but that, it would belong to the Old Law that Thérèse had rejected. It is so light and transparent, so sunny and smiling, so seemingly ordinary, that it can be regarded as the clearest sign of the grace welling up within her. It is a miracle of divine grace for which Thérèse had prepared the way, clearing aside every obstacle to God's perfect love. Humanly speaking, the whole drama seems to be one great "as if", a straining and perversion of human nature. "One must behave like everyone else, not leaving the ranks either for weal or for woe, not pushing oneself forward or becoming the center of attention; one must behave as if there were nothing lacking. . . . No! One should not behave *as if* one were of no importance; one must know that it is, in fact, true and that whatever one does, thinks or feels is really not worth talking about or calling attention to."[123] One of her Sisters later testified that Thérèse was certainly good and conscientious but nothing outstanding. She had nothing to suffer and was rather insignificant . . . , virtuous, certainly —but that is no tremendous feat when one is blessed with a happy disposition and has no need to struggle through suffering to virtue, as "we others" have to. . . .[124] Another Sister, during recreation, remarks: "I cannot understand why people speak of Sister Thérèse of the Child Jesus as if she were a saint. She never does anything notable. One never sees her practicing virtue, and so one cannot even maintain that she is a good nun."[125] Or, according to another version: "She did indeed practice virtue, but her virtue was not acquired through humiliations and suffering."[126] Thérèse is as light as a feather— "By the grace of God, I try hard not to burden others with the trials that God deems good for me."[127] She had demolished

---

[123] G 379 (ET 305).   [124] G 379–80 (ET 305–6).
[125] G 380 (ET 306).   [126] N 96 (LC 115–16).
[127] G 383 (ET 308).

herself so completely that she personally weighs nothing; her only weight is the weight of love.

Construction

In its negative aspect, the little way means demolishing the structure of "great deeds". If this were its only result, it might just as well be described as the way of mediocrity or feckless-ness. But, in fact, it is the way of New Testament love, a way therefore that leads "unto the end" (Jn 13:1). Yet Thérèse does insist that it is a quite ordinary way[1] and is for everyone: "In my little way, there are only very ordinary things; *it is essential that little souls should be able to do everything I do.*"[2] It is a *way*, however, not a standing still. Furthermore, it is a Christian way, a way that follows Christ, which means that it permits neither indecisiveness, nor hesitation, nor mediocrity, for it is a way of perfection. Naturally, this way draws the whole person into its service—otherwise it would not be a Christian way. It wants to teach us God's love lived with all our heart, with all our soul and with all our strength. Anyone who does not accept this goal as the universal Christian aim should not hope for anything from Thérèse's particular way.

Thérèse had emptied her soul of all her own perfections and deeds to create room for the love of God within her. She did not even clear aside the "moral virtues" so as to make room for virtue, but for God. What matters is not her love or even her love for God; all that matters now is that God wishes to be loved and must be loved. Not until her last years does the whole depth of this mystery open up before her. She explains this herself in the concluding pages of her original manuscript: "This year, on June 9, the feast of the Holy Trinity, I received the grace of understanding better than ever before how much Jesus desires to be loved."[3] In her earlier writings, her po-

---

[1] T 316. [2] H 246 (T 232).
[3] SS 180.

ems and letters, we find scarcely a trace of this insight.[4] Until now her vision had stretched no farther than the need to love God. Her love was an urge and a longing to surrender herself utterly. Now she sees farther: God wishes to be loved. God urgently needs the creature to demonstrate his love and pour upon him the free stream of his love. God wishes to redeem; he wishes to show mercy. But he can do so only when his love is free to overflow into the world, into the hearts of men. But that is just what is prevented everywhere; everywhere his love is misunderstood and rejected. ". . . The hearts on whom you wish to lavish it turn toward creatures, seeking happiness from them in the miserable satisfaction of the moment instead of throwing themselves into your arms and accepting your infinite love. O my God, must your despised love remain shut in your heart forever? It seems to me that if you were to find souls offering themselves as SACRIFICIAL VICTIMS OF YOUR LOVE, you would consume them rapidly and be glad not to hold back the waves of infinite tenderness within you."[5]

In the same year, Thérèse composes two little mystery plays dealing with the same thought. In "The Divine Child Begging at Christmas",[6] the Christ Child is depicted as subject to all human needs, all of which are equally love's needs and may be satisfied by love in its different forms. This same thought constantly recurs as the *leitmotif* of "Jesus in Bethany": "Yes, it is your heart that I desire", says Jesus, "I came down to it from heaven, leaving infinite glory for the sake of it."[7] "You have understood the mystery that brought me down to earth: the interior soul is much more precious to me, much more

---

[4] It is, however, already evident in May 1890: "Ah! let us refuse him nothing. He has so great a need of love. He is so parched that he awaits a drop of water from us to refresh him" (S 129 [GC I:622]). And July 1893: "Jesus is and will be our ocean . . . , but great is our consolation to be, in our turn, an ocean for Jesus" (S 191 [GC II:796]).

[5] SS 180–81. [6] Ged 466–77.

[7] Ged 496.

precious than the glory of heaven."[8] God is the beggar of love. It means that love of man is transformed into the *pure service* of God's love, and this service extinguishes the last remnants of self-seeking in human love, in Christian love even. Faith, hope and charity become what Christ wills them to be: a living representation of the Father, which means the pure service of the Father's will.

The "little way" that Thérèse now constructs comes from renouncing everything in Christian love that seems to lend it greatness, power and glory. Love is brought to a state of weakness in which it learns the power of divine love, of littleness and darkness in which the greatness and glory of divine love are displayed. The basis of the little way, therefore, is one series of renunciations after another.

The first renunciation is of the pleasure and joy that accompany love. At a very early date, we find her writing: "I need to forget the earth; here below everything wearies me, everything is an effort, I find only one joy, to suffer for Jesus. . . . But this *unfelt joy* is above every joy. . . . I hit upon the secret of suffering in peace. The word *peace* does not mean *joy*, at least not *felt* joy; to suffer in peace, it is enough to will whatever Jesus wills."[9] Unfelt joy; peace, not joy; a first formula in which to express the mysterious transcendence of Christian love. For that is the purpose of it all: to transfer the impulse toward acts of faith, hope and charity, away from the subject into God himself. One year later: "If you knew how great is my joy at having no joy, to give pleasure to Jesus! . . . It is the essence of joy (but wholly unfelt)."[10] Once more we perceive the subtlety of her psychological reflections, the joy of *unfelt* joy; but the purpose is plain enough: "To give pleasure to Jesus." In this way, faith itself is drawn out of its own center: "If you are willing to bear serenely the trial of being

[8] Ged 498; S 55–56 (GC I:450); S 113 (GC I:587–88); S 197 (GC II:808); S 244 (GC II:894); S 276 (GC II:966).

[9] S 95 (GC I:546).   [10] S 87 (GC I:511).

displeasing to yourself, you will be to Jesus a pleasant place of shelter; you will suffer, of course, for you will be outside the door of your own home; but have no fear, the poorer you are, the more Jesus will love you."[11] And, since faith seizes upon the whole of a person, the whole person is drawn out from himself into the transcendence of the act of faith. Certainly he still commits acts and feels their stress, but now they are centered outside his own experience. For instance he suffers and is at the same time beyond suffering. "He is not here, for he is risen. . . . Come and see the place where the Lord was laid": commenting on this text, Thérèse says: "That is, I am no longer susceptible, as I was in my childhood, to every sorrow. I am, so to speak, risen. I am no longer in the place people believe. Mother, do not worry about me; I cannot suffer any more, because all suffering has become sweet to me."[12] To be placed outside the door of one's own home is God's grace, for it gently compels us to stop living unto ourselves. "When we are brought to misery, we have no desire to gaze at ourselves, and we turn our gaze toward the One beloved."[13] "Alone with ourselves, oh, how wearisome is company when Jesus is not there!"[14] Thérèse is taken at her word when she renounces all desire for feelings or visions in her faith. The more she offers, the more God takes, until all her feelings are hidden in God, and she is left in the darkness of naked faith. "I have no wish to see the good God while I am on earth. And yet I love him! I also love the Mother of God and the saints very dearly, but I do not wish to see them either. I would rather live by faith."[15] Naked faith for her is not, as with Saint John of the Cross, a transition stage toward a later condition in which the soul can gaze upon itself without danger. They quoted to her a sentence from Saint John of the Cross and applied it to her: "The souls that have arrived at perfect love can contemplate their own su-

---

[11] S 303 (GC II:1038).   [12] N 20-21 (LC 52).

[13] S 130 (GC I:641).   [14] S 55 (GC I:449).

[15] N 177 (LC 188).

pernatural beauty without danger." Thérèse answered: "What sort of beauty? I cannot see my beauty at all. I see only the graces I have received from God."[16]

Renunciation of one's feelings in love and faith includes renouncing the sight of their fruit; and the specific fruitfulness of the supernatural virtues is derived from the latter renunciation. During her retreat before Profession, during which her Spouse seeks to detach her from all but himself, he does indeed "lead her by fertile and magnificent countrysides, but the *night* prevents her from admiring anything and, what is worse, from enjoying all these marvels."[17] "Nor must you desire to see the fruits of your efforts", she writes to Marie Guérin. "Jesus likes to keep for himself alone these little nothings that console him."[18] And to the novices: "Offer to the good God the sacrifice of never collecting your own fruits. If it is his will that all your life long you feel repugnance at having to suffer and being humiliated and seeing all the flowers of your desires and good will fall to the ground without bearing fruit—do not be disturbed."[19] Thérèse on her sickbed is like a tree that lets its fruit fall unregarded and therefore does not worry about it.

> I cannot bring myself to say, "Dear God, this one is for the Church; this other, dear God, for France", and so on. The good God knows already what use he will make of my little merits; I have given him everything to do with as he pleases, and in any case it would make me tired to be saying at every moment, "Give this to Peter and that to Paul." I do it quite automatically when a Sister asks me for some special purpose, but after that I never think of it. When I am praying for my missionary brothers, I do not offer up my sufferings. I say simply, "Dear God, give them everything I wish for myself."[20]

When the fruit vanishes from sight, however, it takes away the consciousness of achievement and leaves one feeling in-

[16] N 134 (LC 144).
[17] S 140 (GC I:654).
[18] Esprit 140 (G 412 [ET 330]).
[19] H 268 (T 299).
[20] N 115–16 (LC 133).

capable of anything more. Quite early she writes to Céline: "What unutterable joy to bear our crosses FEEBLY! . . . The *grain of sand* would set herself to the task without *joy*, without *courage*, without *strength*, and all these *conditions* will make the enterprise easier, it wants to work for love."[21] "Here are we wanting to suffer generously, greatly. . . . What folly! . . . We want never to fall? What does it matter, my Jesus, if I fall at every instant, for thereby I *see* my weakness, and that for me is great gain."[22] Not until we are suffering without display, but suffering in weakness, are we really suffering with the Lord: "It is very consoling to remember that Jesus, the *God of Might*, knew our weaknesses, that he shuddered at the sight of the bitter cup, the cup that earlier he had so ardently desired to drink."[23] The desire for martyrdom may prove to be one of those spiritual treasures that "*make* us *unjust* [Lk 16:9]"—

> when we rest in them complacently and think they are something great. These desires are a consolation that Jesus sometimes grants to weak souls like mine (and such souls are numerous), but, when he does not give this *consolation*, it is a grace of *privilege*. Remember the words of the Father [the Jesuit, Pichon], "Martyrs have suffered with joy, and the King of Martyrs suffered with sorrow". . . . Are you not ready to suffer whatever the good God wants? I know well that you are; then if you want to feel joy in suffering, to be drawn to it, what you seek is your own consolation, for when one loves a thing, the pain vanishes— one must consent to stay always poor and without strength, and that's the difficulty, for where are we to find the man truly poor in spirit? . . . Ah! Do let us stay *very far* from all that is brilliant, let us love our littleness, love to feel nothing, then we shall be poor in spirit.[24]

"*Please* understand that to love Jesus, to *be* his *victim of love*, the weaker one is, without desires or virtues, the more apt one is for the operations of that consuming and transforming Love."[25]

[21] S 93 (GC I:537).   [22] S 101 (GC I:557).
[23] S 306 (GC II:1042).   [24] S 288–89 (GC II:999).
[25] S 289 (GC II:999).

And Thérèse is again relentlessly taken at her word, as the end of her life brings her nearer at each step to sheer impotence —for the first time, perhaps, in the history of mysticism, we find a privileged soul who has passed through the Passion but whose resurrection is put off into the next world. She hangs there suspended unto death: "I shall never know how to die! . . . I cannot go on! . . . I can't breathe, I can't die!"[26]

More important even than the renunciation of her strength is her renunciation of progress. Not that life in God means standing still and accepting a condition where nothing happens. On the contrary, God asks us to step out, one foot after the other. But these steps do not mark any progress. When one's vision is obscured and one loses all sense of what has been achieved, it becomes impossible to measure distances. That is why Thérèse invokes the eloquent image of the underground journey. The Lord asks her where she wishes to travel; as a good Carmelite, she chooses the ascent to the summits of love. And immediately she is confronted with many different paths; she feels incapable of basing her choice on her own survey; she leaves the way to the divine Leader.

> Then Jesus took me by the hand and brought me into a subterranean way, where it is neither hot nor cold, where the sun does not shine and rain and wind do not come; a tunnel where I see nothing but a brightness half-veiled. . . . My Spouse says nothing to me nor do I say anything to him either, save that *I love him* more than *myself*, and, in the depth of my heart, I feel that this is true, for I am more his than my own! . . . I do not see that we are advancing toward the mountain that is our goal, because our journey is under the earth. . . . I shall consent, if it is his will, to walk all my life the dark road upon which I am, provided that one day I arrive at the goal of the mountain of love, but I think it will not be here below.[27]

This also is something new in the history of mysticism and of tremendous significance. Every means of measurement is

---

[26] N 188, 189, 195 (LC 201, 202, 205, 243, 267).
[27] S 139 (GC I:651–52); S 141 (GC I:667).

abandoned, and the measure rests with God alone. Nor is this
just an episode, a dark but temporary night of the senses or
the spirit; it is lasting, to the end. The difference from John
of the Cross—and particularly from Teresa of Jesus—is more
marked than ever; they faced the road, walked it and put it
behind them, whereas she goes on striding endlessly in the
darkness, below the earth, without bearings. Instead of the satisfaction of climbing higher, she puts one foot in front of the
other along a road whose direction God alone knows. That is
the message in her metaphor of the little bird vainly fluttering
its wings: "I wish to fly, I wish to imitate the eagles; but the
most I can do is to flutter my little wings; it is not within my
poor power to fly off. . . . But if you should remain deaf to the
plaintive chirpings of your pitiful creature, if you remain in obscurity. . . . Very well! Then I am content to remain drenched,
numb with cold, and I shall even rejoice at this suffering, which
is so well merited."[28] We are reminded again of the child trying in vain to climb the stairway: "You be that child, keep on
lifting your little foot . . . , but do not imagine that you will
ever be able to reach even the first step."[29] Taken as a whole,
the three images, of the subterranean way, the little bird and
the tiny child, give a precise concept of the *inchoate* nature of
all Christian effort. From man's point of view, which cannot
see what progress there is, it means placing all one's effort into
the realm of purely quantitative, and thus empty, time in order
to leave all the qualitative formation and use of effort in God's
hands. Thérèse stands by this teaching right to the end: "I will
be tormented by a foolish thing I said or did. Then I turn to
myself and say, 'Ah, still standing at the same spot as at the
beginning!' But I say it to myself very peacefully and without
sadness. It is so good to feel one's weakness and littleness."[30]

This quotation shows that the renunciation of progress is
only complete when a person realizes that falls are inevitable.

[28] SS 198–99.   [29] H 261 (T 293).
[30] N 45–46 (LC 73–74).

The natural man wishes to climb or at least to stand. But Jesus, who descended from heaven, chooses to fall. "Why should it frighten you that you cannot bear his Cross without weakening? On the way to Calvary, Jesus fell three times; and you, poor little child, would not be like your *Spouse*, would not fall a hundred times, if need be, to prove him your love by rising up again. . . ."[31] "He would rather see you striking your foot against the stones of the way by night than walking in broad daylight along a road gemmed with flowers that could easily slow your advance."[32] "You are wanting to climb a mountain, whereas the good God wishes you to climb down. He is waiting for you in the fertile valley of humility."[33] Once more it is the trick of slipping underneath: "Pass underneath . . . , that is the advantage of keeping little."[34] But there is a finality about this decision to "slip underneath", for the person doing it knows there will be no standing upright again, only the ultimate fall into the hands of God. A week before her death: "This afternoon I heard someone say to one of the Sisters who asked how I was, 'She is terribly tired.' And I thought to myself, that is very true. I am like a tired, harassed traveler who arrives at the end of the journey and falls over. . . . Yes, but it is into the arms of the good God that I am falling."[35] And again, this falling shows the advantages of being a little person; children do not fall far. "Children often fall, but they are too little to do themselves serious harm."[36]

We must also, however, renounce any heroics in our falls. If the Lord deigns to share his falls with us, that is no reason for us to start comparing our own with his. Children's falls are usually the result of faults or silly mistakes. And it is not until *these* falls are taken at their true worth, until these falls may be included in the great renunciation of one's own perfection, that

[31] S 89 (GC I:529).   [32] S 303 (GC II:1038).
[33] H 266 (T 297); cf. S 178–79 (GC II:761); S 190 (GC II:795); S 199 (GC II:811).
[34] H 262 (T 294).   [35] N 180–81 (LC 191).
[36] N 126 (LC 139).

Thérèse is completely sure that her little way is valid. During her younger days, this had proved the tender point at which her scruples and anxiety had festered. This was also the point where the flow of healing began when she was assured that there are faults that do not offend the good God. This assurance was given to her during a conversation with Father Alexis; she was confirmed in her belief that there is a narrow but vital area between sin that can never be permitted and a faultlessness that cannot be attained—and ought not to be sought, on account of the danger of Pharisaism. Thérèse has again introduced something original into the tradition of Christian spirituality, which had previously drawn a straight line from mortal sins to venial sins through imperfection to the point where perfection is reached in an immaculate condition of sinlessness. For Thérèse, there is no such simple diagram. There are faults that do not offend God. There are even faults that it is better to have committed if one would otherwise have missed the grace and tears of repentance through not falling. "Many sins are forgiven her because she has loved much. But to whom less is forgiven, he loves less" (Lk 7:47). "Look at little children: they are always breaking things, tearing things, falling down, while loving their parents very much."[37] Father Alexis told her that her little faults were of no concern to God.[38] But two years before that, she had written to Pauline: "It seems to me that Jesus could very well give one the grace never to offend him again, or rather to commit only faults that do not OFFEND him but merely have the effect of humbling oneself and making love stronger."[39] It is true, then, when she writes: "I felt at the bottom of my heart that this was really so, for God is more tender than a mother. . . ."[40] The discovery originates in her own experience and could only have been made in connection with her doctrine of childhood, which does not propose any abstract norm of perfection but is adapted to every stage of

---

[37] N 128 (LC 140).   [38] SS 174.
[39] S 136 (GC I:662).   [40] SS 174.

human development with all its vicissitudes. Taken in the abstract, the notion of a fall is inseparable from that of defeat and disgrace. But the same is not true in the realm of love, where a man's fall is incorporated into the law of Christ's fall, which is itself one moment in the downward movement of Christ from the Father to the world, to the Cross, to hell. For this is the realm where God or his angels quickly set everything right. "At the moment of Communion, I liken my soul to a little baby of three or four whose hair is all tangled and his clothes all dirty as a result of playing—these accidents have happened to me through struggling with souls—but soon the Virgin Mary takes me in hand. She quickly takes off *my dirty little pinafore*, straightens my hair and adorns it with a pretty ribbon or simply with a little flower . . . , and that is enough to make me presentable so that I can take my place at the feast of angels without blushing."[41] There are certain conditions that make these falls and faults permissible, and Thérèse adheres to them most faithfully: one must stand up again immediately after falling and return to the way of perfect love. "For those who love him and, after each discourteous act, cast themselves into his arms and ask pardon, Jesus is vibrant with joy. . . . We must humble ourselves, see our own nothingness, which is what many souls will not do."[42] This immediate conversion is not called forth by the shame a person feels that such a thing could happen to *him*. If that were its basis, it would still be dominated by the Old Testament ideal of perfection. Its only adequate basis is the need to have God's light streaming over the whole of one's soul. "If we meekly accept the humiliation of being imperfect, then God's grace returns to the soul immediately."[43] Neither the desire for perfection nor its renunciation acts as her standard. The one standard is love, the love of God and the loving response to it of the soul that puts herself entirely at the disposition of God's love.

[41] H 295 (T 322).   [42] S 363 (GC II:1164–65).
[43] N 171 (LC 181).

By this time, it has become clear what this way of renunciation involves and what a surprise it holds in store for those accustomed to traditional spirituality: Thérèse's demand that we must even love our own imperfection and not long to escape from it. First the joy of being treated as weak and imperfect. "What you need, what is most profitable for you, is that you should be found imperfect. When creatures realize that you are without virtue, that deprives you of nothing and does not make you any the poorer; it is they who lose inner joy! For there is nothing sweeter than to think well of our neighbor. . . . For myself, it is a great joy not only when others find me imperfect but, above all, when I feel I am."[44] The first thought was traditional. The originality comes in the conclusion. "Now I have reconciled myself to seeing myself imperfect always and even to finding my joy in it"—and this knowledge is connected with another one, which clarifies it: "At the beginning of my spiritual life, at the age of about thirteen or fourteen, I asked myself what I would have to strive for later on, because I then thought it impossible for me to understand perfection better; but I learned very quickly that the farther one advances along this road, the farther from the goal one believes oneself to be."[45] It is indeed the case that the feeling of getting nowhere is a sort of indirect guarantee of being on the right road. Yet Thérèse's joy has an even deeper foundation —a genuine love of her imperfection. "How fortunate I am to see my imperfection, to need God's mercy so greatly at the hour of my death."[46] Mercy can only be fully accepted with the whole soul by a person who feels a deep need for it. Faults are welcomed as occasions of humility toward God: "Whenever I have been guilty of a fault that causes me sorrow, then I know that this sadness is a result of my infidelity. But I do not let it rest at that. . . . I say to the good God, 'I know that I have deserved this feeling of sorrow; nevertheless, let me offer it to

<hr/>

[44] H 268 (T 299–300).   [45] SS 158.
[46] N 97 (LC 116).

you as a trial bestowed on me by your love. It grieves me that
I have done it, but I am glad to have this suffering to offer
to you.' "[47] They are also occasions of humility toward one's
neighbor. When she was seriously ill, one of the Sisters asked
her to perform some superfluous service: Thérèse, betraying
her momentary annoyance, then stood there silently blushing.
"That evening she wrote me a little note, 'This evening I have
again shown you my "virtue", my "store" of patience. I, who
am so good at preaching to others! I am glad that you were
present to observe my failure. You did not correct me, and yet I
deserved to be. . . . Oh, how it does me good to have behaved
badly; I prefer to have failed rather than to have appeared, by
God's grace, a model of gentleness. It helps me beyond measure to find that Jesus is just as gentle and loving toward me
as ever.' "[48] It is better to feel humbled through remembering one's faults than to be self-satisfied at the thought of one's
conquests. "The remembrance of my faults humbles me and
prevents me from ever relying upon my own strength, which is
only weakness; it just tells me more and more of God's mercy
and love."[49]

Not that Thérèse loves her weakness for its own sake. But
she prefers to be in a condition where she is naked to the grace
of God. Weakness, not only physical but moral weakness, also
brings with it a marked sensitivity to grace that she would not
have apart from her failures. Thérèse's Christian view of time
as a constant encounter with eternity demands this refinement
of her soul if her whole being is to be bared to the whole stress
of God's love. In this fallen world, that is only possible through
constant humiliations. Without them, the soul would soon re-
lapse into contentment and transform the uniqueness of eternity into a long extent of time. And, since this encounter with
eternity in faith, hope and charity is not a measurable "experi-

[47] N 43 (LC 71).
[48] I P xvii, sec. 8 (G 466 [ET 372]); S 336–37 (GC II:1100–1101).
[49] Esprit 135 (G 415 [ET 331–32]).

ence", the refinement of soul is not directed toward exquisite feelings but toward a more intense fidelity, which the New Testament prefers to describe as patience and which often appears as the lived embodiment of the attitude of faith, hope and love. Infidelity, according to Thérèse, stands very close to unbelief:

> Mother, if I were to be unfaithful, if I were to commit the very least infidelity, I feel that I would pay for it with the most frightful troubles, and it would leave me incapable of facing death. I always pray to the good God, "O God, preserve me from the misfortune of infidelity." From any voluntary thoughts of my own superiority, such as imagining that I have acquired some virtue that I am certain I can practice. For then I should be relying on my own strength, and whoever does that is in danger of plunging into the abyss. . . . If I were to say, "O God, you know I love you too much to be disturbed by thoughts against faith", this would so increase my temptations that I should undoubtedly succumb to them.[50]

One would have to be blind not to see that Thérèse's doctrine of the little way answers point by point the program outlined by the Reformers and that she presents the Church's bold, irrefutable answer to Protestant spirituality. One can find innumerable points of contact between Thérèse and the Reformers: the rejection of Old Testament justification by works; the demolition of one's own ideal of perfection to leave room for God's perfection in man; the transcendent note in the act of faith, the center of which remains in God; the existential fulfillment of the act of faith, which means more than a mere intellectual assent to the content of faith and involves utter personal fidelity toward the personal truth of God; and, finally, disregard for one's own failings—even for that joy over them that says *felix culpa*. But the contrasts between Thérèse and the Reformers are equally striking. Thérèse's little way is a way to perfection, a way for those who have courageously resolved to

[50] N 126–27 (LC 140).

love and to do nothing else but love. And the faults of which she speaks are not the sins that Luther had in mind; they are "faults that do not offend God". What divides Thérèse from Luther is that the drama of sin never entwines itself round her soul. She recognizes the drama of God's descending into the nothingness of the creature and the flame of love with which the Absolute, God, unites himself to his creature's nothingness. But she is only acquainted with this drama within the framework of her experience in the cloister. It is Luther's error to have profaned mystical truths, which presuppose an intimate exchange of love between God and man, by treating them as general formulae for the sinner's relation to God. Thérèse's mistake is to have restricted the whole drama between God and the soul to what happened in her own exceptional case. But more of that later.

⚜

The whole succession of renunciations demanded by Thérèse has been entitled "Construction" because they represent the steps leading directly to the state where each new call of God's love finds its response in faith. These renunciations form the entrance to the realm of ultimate love, a love so delicate as to require special laws for its workings. Here every obligation is simply the external expression of one's deepest desires; the most exacting commands are simply preparations for that free response to love that for the lover is far more compelling than the sternest command. Because the Son of God is perfect love, the Father's wish is a command to him, which he freely fulfills —he can do no other, for "at all times I do what is pleasing to the Father." All lovers love freely and freely take upon themselves the command of the beloved. They treat his wishes as commands and subject themselves to him as servants; to those standing outside this relationship, it is all incomprehensible, they cannot grasp its laws. An inner, secret realm with a far-ranging geography is formed. For the lover, it is delightful to roam there, but, for one who does not love, it is just a white spot on the map that represents his image of the world. Few theologians have shown the same skill as Thérèse in mapping out the realm of love; she has sketched a sort of map of the spirit on which certain hills and rivers are noted for the first time. But how much even then she has left to be discovered!

Thérèse begins, as is the custom among saints, at the point where most Christians leave off—where what God commands shades off into what he "merely" wishes. But again, like all the saints, she realizes that this shading is deceptive, because the supreme commandment of love includes every one of God's wishes. Only a person who is neither saint nor lover would dream of separating the obligation *ex justitia* from the free gift *ex caritate* in this commandment that requires one's whole heart, whole soul, whole mind and strength. For the saint, *caritas* becomes *justitia*; if he were ever to make the distinction in his own case, he would know that he was not obeying the law of perfect love.

We have Thérèse's own word for it that she had never refused any of God's wishes since the age of three. As was pointed out earlier, since reaching the age of reason, her relationship toward God had never been legal but always personal. When fulfilling God's commands and wishes, she never thinks about herself: how easy or how hard it will be for her to fulfill them, how much she likes or dislikes doing something, nor does she consider the harm it will bring her or what her reward will be. She thinks only about God, whom she loves—whether this or that is the way to give him joy, or how she must act in order to come into line with his will. The care she expends will appear exaggerated to the average Christian; the unbeliever will treat it as crude anthropomorphism. Thérèse knows better. For her, there is nothing more tender than God and his love, nothing more delicate and precious, requiring to be handled with the utmost care. And if it seems that the eternal Godhead of inaccessible light and absolute power has no need of such attentions, still she knows that the Son of Man, tender of heart, whose face is hidden in sorrow, is the true revelation of God's being. Thérèse wishes all her life long to be doing what Veronica did once: to console the Lord and lighten his burden by her boundless self-surrender. Here, more than ever, we must allow her to speak for herself.

"Ah! I feel it more than ever, Jesus thirsts. He meets only the ungrateful and indifferent among his disciples in the world, and, among his own disciples, he finds few hearts who surrender to him without reservation, who understand the real tenderness of his infinite love. Dear Sister, how fortunate we are to understand the intimate secrets of our Spouse."[51] "When I was a postulant, it cost me a great deal to perform certain exterior penances customary in our Order; but I never gave way to my repugnance, for it seemed to me that the Crucifix in the courtyard was looking at me with imploring eyes and begging these sacrifices of me."[52] As soon as she catches God's eye, she finds it impossible to deny him anything. "O Jesus, we seem to hear you say, 'Open to me, my sisters, my spouses, for my face is wet with the dew, and my locks with the drops of the night' [Song 5]. Our souls understand the language of your love; we long to wipe your sweet face and console you for the neglect of the wicked. In their eyes, you are still, 'as it were, hidden. . . . They esteem you as an object of reproach'. . . . Knowing that the thirst that consumes you is a thirst for love, we desire infinite love in order to quench your thirst."[53] "Then all *shall* be for him, all! Even when I feel nothing that can be offered to him, I shall (as tonight) give him that nothing!"[54] "Let us, let us suffer for them [that is, bad priests], and on the last day Jesus will be *grateful*."[55]

> I am sending you a lovely picture of the Holy Face that our Mother gave me some time ago. I find that it goes so well with Marie of the Holy Face [Céline's first name in Carmel] that I

[51] SS 189.
[52] H 231 (T 217).
[53] H 308 (T 450).
[54] S 81 (GC I:504).
[55] S 112 (GC I:578).

cannot keep it for myself; for a long time now, I have been thinking of giving it to my Céline, *my* Céline. Let Marie of the Holy Face be another Veronica, wiping away all the blood and tears of Jesus, her *sole* Beloved. Let her win him souls, especially the souls she *loves*. . . . Let her boldly face the soldiers, that is to say, the world, to come to him. . . . Oh! how happy she will be when one day she gazes in glory upon the *mysterious* draught with which she has slaked the thirst of her heavenly Spouse, when she sees his lips, once parched, open to utter for her the *unique* and *eternal* word of *love!*[56]

"His look was, as it were, hidden! . . . It is still hidden today. . . , for who comprehends the tears of Jesus? . . . *Forgetfulness*—I feel that that is what causes him most pain."[57] "He makes himself poor so that we may be able to do him charity; he stretches out his hand to us like a *beggar*, that upon the sunlit day of Judgment, when he appears in his glory, he may be able to utter, and we to hear, the loving words, 'Come, blessed of my Father. . . .' " "Let us rejoice in our lot, it is very lovely! Let us give, give to Jesus, let us be misers to others but spendthrifts to him!"[58] So this very descent, this emptying of the soul, is simply a spontaneous gesture of love, an automatic movement to catch him as he falls, so that he lights gently on the ground without being hurt.

"Make haste, and come down" was what our Lord said to Zacchaeus. Jesus tells us to come down! But where must we come down? Céline, you know better than I. . . . "The birds of the air have their nests, but I have nowhere to lay my head." That is where we must come down, if we are to serve as a dwelling for Jesus; we must be *so poor that we have nowhere to lay our heads.* . . . Jesus wants us to receive him in our hearts; by now, doubtless, they are empty of creatures; but alas! I feel that mine is not wholly empty of me, which is why Jesus tells me to come down. And I too want to hide my face, I want my Beloved alone to be able

[56] S 115–16 (GC I:591).   [57] S 133 (GC I:630).
[58] S 197 (GC II:808).

to see it . . . , that in my heart at least he may lay down his dear head and feel that there he is recognized and understood.[59]

This care for our Lord eventually becomes the essential mark of sanctity. She writes to Léonie (who had left the cloister for the second time): "If you want to be a saint, it will be easy. . . . You have but *one* goal: to give pleasure to Jesus."[60]

In order to please those who are suffering, one has to tread lightly not to disturb them. A novice imagined she was doing a great work when she promised that in future she would not cry anywhere except in the presence of God. Thérèse answered vigorously: "Cry in the presence of the good God! Do nothing of the sort. You ought to be less sad in his presence than in the face of creatures. Goodness! Our dear Master has only his monasteries to gladden his heart; he comes to us to rest, to forget the ceaseless complaints of his friends in the world; because generally people on earth moan and groan instead of appreciating the value of the Cross; and you intend to be just the same as other mortals? Really, that is not selfless love. *It is up to us to console Jesus, not up to him to console us.*"[61] It is less from her words than from the uncompromising way she unmasks any hidden self-pity that we see how in earnest she is; and she assumes that anyone with the least inkling of Christianity must share her attitude. Thus she manages to smile during the prescribed scourging, "so that the good God does not notice how it hurts me".[62] "Let us make our heart a little garden of delight where Jesus may come to find rest."[63] "When I am suffering a great deal, instead of adopting an air of sadness, I answer with a smile. At first I never used to manage it, but now it is a habit that I am very glad to have contracted."[64] "It hurts the good God enough to have to test us on earth without having to listen to us complaining of how hardly we are being used. So we should not let anyone notice how we are being hurt.

[59] S 178–79 (GC I:761–62).   [60] S 356–57 (GC II:1149).
[61] H 273–74 (T 304).   [62] G 384 (ET 309).
[63] S 152 (GC II:708).   [64] H 247 (T 233).

It is really a question of delicacy and tact not to complain of the heat and cold or wipe away sweat or rub our frozen hands together—or, if we do, to do it secretly, so as not to reproach the good God."[65] The sufferings that God sends us are tokens of his love and favor. How boorish it would be to accept them with a gloomy countenance and so burden him with our ingratitude! "He is here, close, looking at us, begging us to offer him this grief, this agony. . . . Alas, it is great pain to him thus to fill our cup with sorrows, but he knows that it is the only way to prepare us 'to know him as he knows himself'."[66] He must not have to be the least embarrassed with us. In one of her poems, Thérèse asks the Mother of God: "Tell him never to be embarrassed with me."[67] Nor must he be allowed to think that our sole concern has been for the reward. "If the good God did not see my good deeds, I would not be the least disturbed by it. I love him so much that I would like to give him pleasure with my love and my little sacrifices without his needing to know that they come from me. By knowing about them and seeing them, he is, so to speak, obliged to reward me, and I want to spare him the trouble."[68] One must constantly smile at him even when he hides himself or sends us suffering: "My smile shall shine upon him whom I love, even when he conceals himself in order to try me."[69] "Comfort this child, dear Sister, who stretches his arms toward you. To comfort him, I beseech you to smile without ceasing."[70] And, when he is weary, the Christian should be ready to fight in his place. When getting up in the morning, Thérèse used to kiss the crucifix, lay it on her pillow and then say: "My Jesus, you labored and wept enough during the thirty-three years of your life on this poor earth! This day, take your rest. . . . It is my turn to fight and suffer."[71] One must not only smile upon him, one must also do everything to bring a smile to his lips. "I wish

[65] G 383 (ET 308).
[66] S 55–56 (GC I:450).
[67] Ged 429.
[68] N 7 (LC 43).
[69] Ged 401.
[70] Ged 471.
[71] H 278 (T 308).

for no other joy but that of making you smile."[72] "The great saints have labored for the glory of God. I, who am but a little soul, labor only for his pleasure, and I would be happy to bear the very greatest suffering if that would make him smile just once."[73] Yet all this is not an "achievement", an expression of her own "tender heart", but an attempt to respond to the untold, overwhelming tenderness that God showers upon us. The first essential is to see God's attentions toward us for what they are. "I am very glad that you feel no natural sense of pleasure in coming to Carmel. That is Jesus' *delicacy*, he wants to receive a *present* from you. He knows that 'it is much more blessed to give than to receive.' "[74] And, when Thérèse feels herself to be a castaway, she interprets this as a sign of how the divine Shepherd trusts her, for he lets the faithful sheep wander off to bring back those that are lost. "How I am touched by this trust." And, as if to assure her, during the night of temptation, that it is he who is testing her, he sends external tokens of it—little favors. He sends her flowers; a robin redbreast hops onto her bed, looks at her knowingly and then performs lots of amusing antics. "Mother, I am terribly moved by these favors that the good God is showing me; to all appearances, I am loaded with them . . . , and yet I remain in the deepest darkness. . . ."[75] And, when the infirmarian renders her an unexpected service: "I looked at her without being able to speak, and, as soon as I was alone, I burst into tears. How good our Lord is! How tender and loving! How easily his heart is touched."[76]

Here Thérèse truly lives up to her name, "of the Child Jesus". Although the substance of her piety is more fittingly described by her title "of the Holy Face", she conceals the pain of it in the imagery of childhood. It makes all her movements light and quick, unhampered by care. Childish imagery is the reflection of a much wider reality—of the all-embracing universe of

[72] H 309 (T 451).
[73] N 81 (LC 102).
[74] S 240 (GC II:882).
[75] H 249 (T 234).
[76] H 249 (T 235).

love—the universe of play. While the adult groans under the curse of original sin, the child abandons himself to play, which originates in Paradise and is the creaturely reflection of God's creative act. God is at play with men; that is, he handles them in a divine fashion, according to his own laws—for there are none higher. Quite early (perhaps through contact with the Italian people?), Thérèse entered into the spirit of divine play:

> For some time past, I had offered myself to the Child Jesus to be his *little plaything*. I told him to treat me, not like a precious toy such as children only look at and dare not touch, but like a little ball of no value that he could throw on the ground, kick, *pierce*, leave in a corner or press to his heart, just as he pleased. In a word, *I wished to amuse the little Jesus and abandon myself to his childish whims*. And he has granted my prayer. In Rome, Jesus *pierced* his little toy . . . , *no doubt he wished to see what was inside* . . . , and then, satisfied at his discovery, he dropped his little ball and went to sleep.[77]

"Do you wish to give him pleasure? Then stay in his hand. May the darling Child stroke you and draw you to his breast, and occasionally throw you aside—let it all be your joy. Let his divine glance fascinate you so that you may respond to his every whim. Henceforth all your joy will be found in his childish desires."[78] In the same spirit, she composes the prayer: "O little Child Jesus! My own treasure, I abandon myself to your divine whims, I wish for no other joy but that of making you smile."[79] "I am willing to suffer all that Jesus pleases, to let him do as he likes with his *little ball*."[80]

> He RIDDLES me with *pin-pricks*, the poor *little ball* can take no more; all over it are tiny holes that cause it more suffering than if it had but one great gash! . . . Nothing from Jesus. Dryness! . . . Sleep! But at least there is silence! Silence does good to the soul. . . . But creatures, *creatures*! . . . The *little ball* shudders at

---

[77] SS 136; cf. S 172 (GC II:748); S 251 (GC II:903).
[78] Ged 471–72. [79] H 109–10 (T 451).
[80] S 87 (GC I:514).

the thought of them. . . . Realize that it is Jesus' *toy*. When it is that loving Friend who pierces his *ball* himself, suffering is only sweetness, his hand is *so sweet*! But creatures. . . . Those who surround me are good, of course, but there is a touch of something in them that repels me! . . . I can't explain it to you. . . . All the same I am VERY *happy*, happy at suffering what Jesus wants me to suffer. If he does not himself pierce his *little ball*, it is he who guides the hand that pierces it! . . . Jesus chooses to sleep, why should I keep him from sleep? I am only too happy that he does not put himself to any trouble about me.[81]

"But *Jesus' toy* is weakness itself; if Jesus does not carry it, or throw his *little ball*, it stays there, inert, on the one spot."[82]

Besides the little ball, Thérèse invokes skittles and tops in order to illustrate aspects of the spiritual life. These similes, harsh, almost crude, become laughing and joyous in Thérèse's hands, as when she describes the lashes needed to keep the top turning. "Let your Sisters perform this service for you, and be particularly grateful toward those who are most bent upon keeping you going. . . ."[83] And, finally, everything likely to gladden the Child and turn into a toy in his hands is tipped into the crib: birds, stars, roses, grapes, pillows, flowers, bread, milk, mirrors, cakes, honey, a little lamb, sweets and everything else that might fill a child with gladness.[84]

But a child cannot always be praying, it must also sleep. This childish sleep is Thérèse's wonderfully sweet version of the dark night. "What did he do during his gentle sleep, and what became of the little abandoned ball? Jesus dreamed that he was still playing with his toy, that he keep picking the ball up and putting it down, that he sent it skimming away and finally pressed it to his heart, never to let it go out of his little hand again. You will realize the little ball's sadness, dear Mother, at finding itself on the floor! However, I never ceased hoping against hope."[85]

[81] S 82–83 (GC I:499–500).   [82] S 87 (GC I:514).
[83] H 293 (T 320).   [84] Ged 475.
[85] SS 136.

And she sings a little cradle-song—with no echo from the mysterious night of darkness and abandonment in the background.

> If you wish to rest
> While the storm is raging,
> Deign to place your little golden head
> Upon my heart.
>
> How entrancing is your smile
> As you sleep!
> Lovely Child,
> I long forever to rock you gently
> As I sing my cradle-song.[86]

Then again, the confession: "Jesus, the tiny child of Bethlehem whom Mary bore as 'a light burden', grows heavy, so heavy that Saint Christopher marvels. . . ."[87]

"Most people on earth are only willing to serve the King of Glory; if Jesus goes to sleep, they stop serving him or believing him. But the Child Jesus loves to go to sleep in safety, without fear of being wakened."[88] Why not serve beside the crib? Since entering Carmel, it had become normal for Thérèse to find Jesus sleeping. "As usual, Jesus was asleep in my little skiff. Ah! I see very well how rarely souls allow him to sleep peacefully within them. Jesus is so fatigued with always having to take the initiative and to attend to others that he gladly accepts the rest I offer him. Doubtless he will not wake up before my great retreat into eternity."[89] But it needs two to play at this sleeping game. During the time of prayer, when she would have loved to sing her comforting cradle-song to the sleeping Lord, she too sleeps. "I should be desolate for having

---

[86] Ged 411 (G 309 [ET 248]). Si tu veux te reposer, / Alors que l'orage gronde, / Sur mon coeur daigne poser, / Ta petite tête blonde.

Que ton sourire est ravissant / Lorsque tu sommeilles! / Toujours avec mon plus doux chant / Je veux te bercer tendrement, / Bel Enfant!

[87] S 195 (GC II:804).   [88] Ged 475.

[89] SS 165.

fallen asleep (for seven years) during meditation and thanks-giving. . . ."[90] "During meditation, without wishing to, I shut my eyes and go to sleep and believe all the time I am look-ing on my Beloved. . . ."[91] "All this, however, does not keep both distractions and sleepiness from visiting me, but at the end of thanksgiving, when I see I've made it so badly, I make a resolution to be thankful all through the rest of the day."[92] What a distressing contrast between the exalted desires of the nun and the modest, almost shameful, reality. In fact, Thérèse had never been able to meditate in the manner of the "great saints". And, when she is nearly dropping through fatigue, she has to use a book as a crutch to help her through the period of meditation. "In my helplessness, the Holy Scriptures and the Imitation come to my aid; in them, I discover a solid and very *pure* nourishment. But it is the Gospels more than anything else that hold my attention during meditation."[93] "Thérèse's medi-tation never went farther than a meditative reading of Scripture, and of the Gospels in particular, on which she nourished her spirit and devotion whenever sleep was threatening her fidelity to the Rule."[94] Moreover, even this humiliation is woven into her mystique of childhood. "I should be desolate for having fallen asleep (for seven years) during meditation and thanksgiv-ing. Well, I am not desolate! I think of how little children are as charming to their parents when they are sleeping as when they are awake. I also think of how doctors put their patients to sleep before operating on them. Lastly, I think of how 'Our Lord sees our weakness and knows that we are but dust.' "[95] The first comparison is in line with her usual teaching: she is God's child and can sleep without offense; this is also true of the third comparison, where she relies on God's knowing our human frailty. But what strikes one about the second is that she shifts the responsibility onto God; he puts her to sleep,

[90] Ibid.　　　　　　　　　　　　[91] Co 219.
[92] SS 172–73.　　　　　　　　　[93] SS 179.
[94] Co 226.　　　　　　　　　　　[95] SS 165.

because he is obviously using this sleep for some special purpose, and, through knowing this, Thérèse has little cause to worry. She treats this petty weakness as a fulfillment of God's will, to which she is abandoned. We scarcely need to stress that Thérèse can only take this line in virtue of her scrupulous, heroic fidelity to the Rule and her fervent desire to stay awake and pray as long as possible. Her "taking it lightly" has nothing in common with everyday carelessness; it is entirely derived from supernatural love. This lightness has its own center of gravity, at the point where utter weakness is transformed into a strength that appears effortless. "What does it matter whether you have courage or not, so long as you behave as if you had!"[96]

Having trained herself to regard only her Beloved's reactions ("I do not desire love that I feel, only love that Jesus feels"),[97] she lives outside herself all the time, yet without enjoying mystical ecstasies. She experiences the one essential ecstasy, to be drawn by love into the Beloved. When her Beloved is happy, she cannot help being happy, whether her natural self is suffering or joyful. "If only he is satisfied with me, then I am more than happy."[98] "Nothing makes me happy except doing the will of God."[99] "I have come to the point where I cannot suffer, because all suffering has become sweet to me."[100] The fact that she lives in a region beyond herself in no way implies that she wanders around in a rapturous condition. On the contrary, she is as natural as could be, living in the sort of familiarity with God that God intended when he placed man in the garden of Eden. She writes to her cousin Marie: "You seem to me like a little village girl to whom a mighty king proposes marriage and who dares not accept because she is not rich enough nor trained enough in the usages of the court; she does not reflect that her royal suitor knows her quality and her

[96] H 279 (T 309).   [97] S 136 (GC I:662).
[98] Ph 89.   [99] N 167 (LC 175).
[100] H 235 (T 222).

weakness much better than she knows it herself. . . . Marie, if you are nothing, you must not forget Jesus is *all*."[101] True love is without affectation, is perfectly natural. There is a touch of irritation in one of her last letters, a reply to Abbé Bellière, who had begun to feel rather depressed and inferior in the face of Thérèse's greatness and had tearfully described his own sinfulness.

> Please, Brother, do not follow the example of the Hebrews, who looked back with longing to "the onions of Egypt". For long I have served you too many of those raw vegetables that make you *weep* when you bring them, raw, too near to your eyes. . . . You must know me very imperfectly to fear that a detailed account of your faults would lessen my affection for your soul. . . . Jesus has long forgotten your infidelities. . . . Please, I beg you, never again "*drag* yourself to his *feet*"; follow the "first impulse that would draw you into his arms". . . . I would have you be simple with the good God—and with me too.[102]

Just as she wishes God not to be embarrassed with her, similarly she refuses to be embarrassed by him. The way she speaks of him often seems to us bordering on irreverence. But she is a child, at home with him. And Thérèse possesses a quality that we seldom find in the realm of sanctity (though Thomas More, and occasionally Saint Teresa of Jesus and Saint Ignatius of Loyola, had it), a quality that must be reckoned as one of God's good gifts—a sense of humor.

> Personally I find perfection quite easy to practice because I have realized that all one has to do is *take Jesus by the heart*. Consider a small child who has displeased his mother by flying into a rage or perhaps disobeying her; if he sulks in a corner and screams in fear of punishment, his mother will certainly not forgive his fault; but if he comes to her with his little arms outstretched, smiling and saying: "Kiss me, *I won't do it again*", surely his mother will immediately press him tenderly to her heart, forgetting all that he has done. . . . Of course she knows quite well that her dear

[101] S 130 (GC I:640–41).   [102] S 362–63 (GC II:1164–65).

little boy *will do it again* at the first opportunity, but that does not matter; if he takes her by the heart, he will never be punished. . . .[103]

And the more daring sentence: "If he seems to forget me, very well, he is free to, since I am no longer mine but his. . . . He will weary of keeping me waiting sooner than I of waiting for him."[104]

⚜

The way of childhood offers no recipe for sanctity: Christianity does not dole out recipes. It is an attitude that colors everything and can therefore be displayed in ever-varied aspects, although its each aspect is quite clear and unique. Thérèse herself attempted many times to give a brief synthesis of her little way, using aphorisms that were usually unprepared answers to sudden questions.

"The little way . . . is *the way of spiritual childhood, the way of trust and total surrender.* I wish to point out [to people] the little methods that have served me with perfect success; to tell them that there is only one thing to do here below—to strew before Jesus the flowers of little sacrifices and win him with caresses."[105]

> To remain little means recognizing one's nothingness, expecting everything from the good God, *as a little child expects everything from his father.* It means not worrying about anything or being on the lookout for favors. . . . I have always remained little, having no other ambition but to collect flowers of love and sacrifice and offer them to the good God for his pleasure. Again, to stay little means not attributing the virtues we practice to ourselves, under the impression that we are capable of such things, but to recognize that the good God places this treasure of virtue in the hand of his little child for him to use as he needs it; and that it remains God's treasure.[106]

---

[103] S 275 (GC II:965-66).   [104] S 123 (GC I:612).
[105] H 245-46 (T 232).   [106] H 264 (T 295-96).

And, finally, she expresses it in theological terms that knit together the themes of Saint Paul and the Gospel:

> We must do everything that is within us: give without counting the cost, practice the virtues at every opportunity, conquer ourselves all the time and prove our love by every sort of tenderness and loving attention. In a word, we must carry out all the good works that lie within our powers—out of love for God. But it is truly essential to put our whole trust in him who alone can sanctify our work, who can indeed sanctify us without works, since he may even bring forth children of Abraham from the very stones. It is necessary for us, when we have done all we can, to confess that we are unprofitable servants, while hoping that God in his grace will give us all that we need. That is the way of childhood.[107]

The little way is *one* way, yet it is also *the* way. It is *one* way in the sense that it differs from other ways, above all, from those of the "great souls" who go in for extraordinary penances and receive extraordinary mystical graces. But, since neither the gospel nor the great saints themselves reckon these latter as essential to Christian love but recognize that love of God and one's neighbor contains the whole of the law, and all mysticism and asceticism, Thérèse's way, which makes this love absolutely central, can be described as *the* way.

There are many reasons for this epithet "little". In the first place, because it bypasses extraordinary methods with a warning against them and, like the gospel itself, presupposes everyday life as its field of application. Again, because it can find no better picture to express the soul's eagerness to receive God's love than that of a little child aware of its littleness before God. Lastly, because it is a short way: it eliminates all measurable distances and, if it is really followed, keeps one in immediate contact with one's goal. But it is not at all little in the sense that, as opposed to the way of the "great souls", it is for the "imperfect", who hesitate and compromise. Otherwise it would not

[107] G 348 (ET 281–82).

be a Christian way, for Christ's way leads without compromise to perfect love. What, then, are the hosts of the imperfect and the sinners to do? Is there no way for them? Of course; they are just the people for whom the little way has been prepared. They only need to enter upon it and expose themselves to the rays of divine love, and this fire will certainly not fail to purify them. The objection that Thérèse's little way makes it all too easy is far less justified than the suspicion that it begins too high and presupposes too much. For, even though Thérèse tries her hardest to encourage the sinner, turning around all the time to show him just how closely he may follow her footsteps and proclaiming her own solidarity with sinners, it is still true that her basic presupposition is that of a saint: that life has no meaning unless it is the service of God. In fact, once a person has grasped this, everything else follows automatically. And such a person will find in Thérèse the most delightful guide to love. But, if he does not grasp this, or tries to add other possible meanings to life, then it will be useless for him to try to adopt any part of Thérèse's system. This system is indivisible, like the love of God and the gospel. "Who is not for me is against me." "No man can serve two masters." Thérèse cannot make the way any smoother than Christ himself made it. And, insofar as she presupposes that the first step, that of total surrender to God's love and service, has already been made, her little way is meant especially for religious, who have already "abandoned all things". Primarily Thérèse is writing for her Carmelite Sisters; only after finishing the manuscript does it dawn on her that the effect of her writings might extend beyond the walls of the Carmel. In her letters, moreover, she tries to lead everyone to the religious life who shows a real desire for absolute surrender to God. In this sense, too, her way is *the way*, the continuation of the gospel and the age-old tradition of the Church.

This summary of the little way cannot be concluded without a reference to how infrequently a central Christian doctrine is mentioned in it: the doctrine of the Trinity. Obviously Thérèse is not ignorant of this doctrine, and she invokes it decisively in places. Her act of oblation to the merciful love of God is drawn up on the feast of the Most Holy Trinity, 1895, and accordingly she addresses God: "O my God, Most Blessed Trinity, I desire to *love* you and make you *loved*. . . ."[108] She also makes a striking comparison between the Trinity and the kaleidoscope with the three mirrors in its tube, through which one can see creatures as they are meant to be. And, at the end of Manuscript B, she prays to the Lord, the divine Eagle, to carry all souls away and plunge them into the "eternal fire of the Blessed Trinity".[109] However, only two aspects of the Blessed Trinity are concretely manifest in her teaching: the Son incarnate, the suffering Savior, who invites man to cooperate in his work and to whom we can offer all our love; and then the Father, but not so much the Father in his trinitarian relations with the Son and the Holy Spirit as the Father who represents divine goodness and mercy and in whose arms we can nestle. He is also the heavenly realization of all the goodness she found in her earthly father. The fact that Thérèse did not see farther into the interior life of the Trinity and its reflection in the economy of salvation is characteristic of her "existential theology". Her teaching is far too narrowly conditioned by her own life: she has to demonstrate it all in her own person, and even her life cannot demonstrate such an objective, massive doctrine as that of the Trinity. Consider the way in which her visions (infrequent though they are) all refer specifically to herself: she sees the devil who flees *before her*; she sees the Mother of God, who smiles at *her* and approaches *her*, and the whole vision is directly related to *her* cure. Thus her teaching cannot be explicitly trinitarian; for this, she would have needed a quite different, almost antithetical, basis of experience. Elizabeth of the Trinity is able to develop an explicitly trinitarian doctrine because her mind goes out toward its object so completely, leaving only the very slightest scope for her own personality and history—just sufficient to remain a subject for the oper-

[108] SS 276.   [109] SS 199.

ations of the Trinity. If she has barely sufficient personality, Thérèse has too much. Another possible explanation of why Thérèse does not emphasize the doctrine of the Trinity, and especially the operations of the Holy Spirit, is that she never establishes any vital relation with the Church's ministry. After her father, her only confidants were her sisters; she never had a discussion with a confessor that went beyond subjective considerations and dealt with objective hierarchical relations. Through the power of the Holy Spirit, a saintly confessor is in a position to detect the work of the Holy Spirit in a soul; once this atmosphere of confidence is established, it leads to objective exchanges free from personal overtones yet calculated to call forth the deepest truths about a person. It is by means of this sober relationship, grounded in obedience, that the confessor can lead a soul to understand objective dogmatic truths about God. Thérèse had opened herself up to these truths, but the recipients of her confidences were her sisters, not a confessor. They had not the capacity to lead her farther, and so her doctrine is confined to the little way. Here, she is both original and masterly. She knows it inside out, because she has experienced it and tested it on herself. Her childish delicacy leaves the inner mystery of God untouched. It is enough for her to know about love, how to love and to be loved. Yet she even understands divine love in terms of human love, which reaches its summit in the love of the God-man. She surrenders herself to this love and lets it master her, without going into its distinctions. And so, to the end, she remains the child trying to lift its foot, unable to get its foot onto the first step up the stairway.

INDIFFERENCE

THE TWO MOVEMENTS within Thérèse's doctrine, demolishing one's own perfection and making room for God's to be built in, clearly demonstrate the paradox of all Christian asceticism. On the one hand, it means resolute action, the determination to do one's utmost—"when you have done everything you can": it is the very opposite of moral or dogmatic Quietism, which "leaves it all to grace" and drowns works in a flood of faith. On the other hand, all this action simply means making room for God; it is a preparation for contemplation, for God to "increase" and the self to "decrease". This paradoxical feature of Christian spirituality is valid in every age but becomes sharper in those exponents of spirituality whose vision of God is distinctly voluntaristic or, more exactly, personalistic. Patristic and even mediaeval spirituality (influenced by classical conceptions) takes eternal happiness, the contemplation of God, as man's goal; consequently, the supernatural end of human nature can serve, under the elevating influence of grace, as man's sure compass throughout his spiritual journey. For example, man only needs to gaze upon his own "restless heart" in order to realize where his path lies to "eternal rest in God". The emphasis shifts as soon as Ignatius, in his "Principle and Foundation", fixes on the "praise, reverence and service of God" as man's end and subordinates everything else, the contemplation of God and one's own happiness, to this end. Once this is accepted, human nature, even when it is elevated by grace, cannot act as the guide for man in his praise, reverence and service of God; ultimately such guidance can only come from God and the revelation of his will. Therefore Ignatius builds his whole spirituality upon the concept of choice; that is, upon God's choice, accomplished in eternal freedom, which is offered to man to choose for himself. This new "identity" and "fusion" between the Creator's choice and that of his creature begins ever more surely to replace the classical ideal of identifying their essences, the ideal of "deification". If this identity is to be achieved, man must strain every nerve to clear aside all obstacles and, by means of the "spiritual exercises", become entirely "disposed" to receive God's will. When he has been trained to indifference in respect of his own will, it is God alone who makes the difference. But, though each individual has to discover through personal contemplation what God wills for him personally, the general revelation of God's will is to be found in the Old and New Testaments. So this general revelation acts as the framework within which man must become generally disposed to receive God's will—Ignatius interprets this general framework as "three stages of humility"[1] that a man has to pass through, each of them a fresh renunciation of his own will. The first stage represents the Old Testament world of the "law" and demands readiness "to be in all things obedient to the law of the Lord, our God", indifferent to all else but the choice "for or against God". The second represents the threshold between the Old and the New Testament, where God appears in person, with a personal will and plans; but before he exposes his plan, he must be assured that his disciple will follow him absolutely. This is the specific point of indifference, because at this stage the demand is that I should "stand at the point [and there is, in fact, only *one* point!] where I no longer prefer either riches or poverty, glory or contempt, a long life or a short one, where the service of God and the salvation of my soul are one". And, by following this law of indifference, I am preserved against the slightest deviation from God's will, preserved, that is, from venial sin. The third stage exposes the New Testament of salvation, and the difference is made by God's choice in Christ, which is the poverty, contempt and folly of the Cross. But Ignatius does not immediately regard this choice as the automatic one for every individual; the individual must first of all be in a state of complete indifference,

[1] *Spiritual Exercises*, nos. 165–68.

brought about by passing through the Old Testament to the threshold of the New. If an individual chooses the Cross, there is a twofold precondition: "The first and second stages are pre-requisites." The person must have not only a general training in obeying commandments but also a particular training in in-difference. "Praise and honor of God's majesty would be the same." Thus no individual shall make the choice of the Cross through personal preference or momentary enthusiasm but in the sober, objective knowledge that one has been chosen by God for this.

All this has to be borne in mind if we are to understand Thérèse's subsequent development. Her way bears an amazing resemblance to that of Ignatius, especially since both stress the intense paradox underlying human actions and dispositions and connecting human and divine choice. Thérèse's originality is not diminished if we point out her Ignatian touch in bracket-ing her whole existence within the choice of God. Already as a child she had "chosen all", and this total choice is but the reverse side of God's grip upon her; he had chosen her all. At the age of two, she confesses to Pauline her intention of enter-ing Carmel: "I, too, will be a nun."[2] "In spite of all contrary impressions, this must be clearly stated: the thought that God was calling her did not originate from Thérèse's own reflec-tions on life and love. It originated before all these reflections. Before any theological conception of a spiritual vocation had entered Thérèse's soul, there came an absolute decision in the form of a personal and irrevocable choice."[3] She chooses early, but not until she has been chosen.

If, during the time before entering Carmel, Thérèse seems obstinately set upon having her own way, this is ultimately a sign of her obedience to the will of God, her determination that nothing shall thwart it. It comes to a climax in her audience with Leo XIII; and Thérèse knows this, as her letters at the time show: "Since Monseigneur is opposed, the last resource

I have left is to speak to the Pope; so that has to be possible."[4]
"I don't know how I shall get to speak to the Pope. . . . It
seems that to speak to everyone, the Holy Father passes before
the faithful, but I don't think he stops; in spite of all, I am
fully resolved on speaking to him: before Pauline wrote to me,
I was thinking of it."[5] "It is tomorrow, Sunday, that I shall
speak to the Pope. O my dearest little sister, if you knew how
hard my heart beats when I think of tomorrow!"[6] The Pope
is obviously disturbed by the girl's insistence and the urgent
look in her eyes—he was to gaze after her a long time when
the guards forcibly removed her—but he cannot gauge the authenticity of her request at a moment's notice. As a prudent
successor to Saint Peter, he can only refer her to the regular ecclesiastical channels through which the will of God is normally
manifest. "Holy Father," she had pleaded, "in honor of your
Jubilee, allow me to enter Carmel at the age of fifteen." The
Vicar General was displeased because he had expressly forbidden her to say anything to the Pope; he cut in; "Holy Father,
this is a child who wishes to become a Carmelite; but the superiors are considering the matter at the moment!" "Well, my
child," said the Pope, "do whatever the superiors may decide."
Thérèse cannot accept this; her call is absolute, more powerful
than her own will, more powerful than her own self; it is the
very source of her being. She has been chosen and cannot pay
more heed to human arrangements than to God's will. And,
even if it means getting churned up between the wheels of ecclesiastical clockwork, she must still go on. So, contrary to all
"ecclesiastical obedience", she tries again: "Resting my hands
on his knee, I made one last effort, saying in a suppliant voice:
'Oh! Holy Father, if you say *Yes*, everyone else will agree!'
He looked fixedly at me and clearly emphasized each syllable
as he said, 'Come, come . . . you will enter if the good God
wills it.' "[7] That is quite true, and at the moment there was no

---

[4] S 33 (GC I:335).   [5] S 34–35 (GC I:332).
[6] S 35 (GC I:342).   [7] SS 134–35.

more for the Pope to say. Only Thérèse can know that God does, in fact, will it: and she alone now can prove to everyone, against all the appearances, that her fussiness and seeming lack of indifference is actually the height of indifference. But still Thérèse is without a foothold, suspended between the will of God and the Church's decision. "In the bottom of my heart, I felt a great peace, since I had done everything in my power to answer the call of the good God. All the same, this peace dwelt only in the depths, and my soul was full to overflowing with bitterness. And Jesus kept silent. He seemed to be absent, there was nothing to reveal his presence."[8] It is important to notice that Thérèse had done "everything in her power" to clear away all obstacles but that her success is not the fruit of her efforts, at least not directly. The result of her own efforts is a plain failure. And the solution comes suddenly, as if by chance, quite unexpectedly and without connection apparently with what had happened previously. Thérèse puts her finger on this discrepancy:

> He whose heart is watching even when he sleeps taught me that, for the person whose faith is as a grain of mustard seed, he grants miracles and moves mountains in order to strengthen this faith that is still small; but, for his intimate friends, for his Mother, he works no miracles until he has tested their faith. Did he not let Lazarus die, although Martha and Mary had sent word that he was ill? And, at Cana, when the Blessed Virgin asked him to help the master of the house, did he not reply that his hour had not yet come? But after the trial, what a reward! The water was changed into wine, Lazarus was raised again. . . . That is how Jesus treats his little Thérèse.[9]

The examples are striking; the relation between human action and divine action in man, or the relation between human choosing and divine choice, is the same as that of water and wine in the miracle. Between each there is the same gulf of death and resurrection, the abyss of indifference into which

[8] SS 135–36. [9] SS 142.

every human work and plan has to be cast before emerging afresh as a clean-cut act of God's will in man. That is the drama of indifference in the first period of Thérèse's life. Yet it is only a prologue to the intensity and subtlety of the second period, a drama that presents us with new vistas almost without parallel in previous spirituality. Thérèse knows that she has been chosen for the religious life, for Carmel in particular, and she has recognized it as a call to suffer with Christ for the sake of souls. The humility that Ignatius places at the third stage, the consequence of poverty, contempt and folly, could never be the result of a long "ascent" in Thérèse's case: it is included in the original act of choosing, it is the presupposition from which she begins. And, just as she had pressed forward through thick and thin into the cloister, so now she presses on, looking neither to left nor right, into the heart of *suffering*. In her view, suffering is the summit of a creature's attainments, the most precious gift of God and the most precious offering that a creature can give back to him. Suffering, for a person who loves God, is the height of existence. "You know, dear Mother, my first steps met with more thorns than roses! Yes, suffering stretched out its arms toward me, and I threw myself into them with love. . . . In order to attain a goal, one must adopt the means of fulfilling it; and, since Jesus had taught me that he would give me souls by means of suffering, the more I encountered suffering, the more I was attracted to it."[10] How deeply Thérèse was to drink of the cup of suffering needs no elaboration, since the works of Father Ubald, Maxence van der Mersch and I. F. Görres [as well as John Beevers and Guy Gaucher] have made the conditions prevailing in the convent generally known. Yet they can only describe what has been recorded; of her hidden sufferings, Thérèse says that "many pages could be written, but these pages will never be read on earth. . . ."[11] "These memories are too deeply engraved in the bottom of our hearts to require any mention in

---

[10] SS 149.   [11] SS 160.

writing."[12] "I wished that my face, like Jesus', might be, *as it were, hidden so that no one on earth should know me*; I thirsted to suffer and be forgotten."[13] The Lord hears her request and grants her every form of suffering so that she clings ever closer to the Cross, becoming conformed to the death of Christ in the night of abandonment: "Do not be troubled, Mother, if I suffer a great deal and if I show no sign of happiness at the last moment. Did our Lord not die as the Victim of Love, and see what agony he had! . . ."[14] Again Thérèse's wishes were heard. Her death was to be a terrible one: "The air of this earth is failing me, when shall I breathe the air of heaven?" It is the naked agony of death, with no glimmer of consolation. . . . "Mother, the chalice is full to overflowing! Oh, I would never have believed it possible to suffer so much. . . . I cannot explain it except through my longing to save souls. . . . I would not wish to suffer less."[15] It is the opposite of those mystical theories about saintly deaths being ecstasies of love; but it fits in with the teaching on death that Thérèse herself had worked out from her training in the hard truth of the gospel: "The death of love that I long for is that of Jesus on the Cross."[16] She thirsts for "the spring where after drinking one thirsts still . . . , that spring is suffering."[17]

Thus she regards suffering as the highest potentiality of human nature. Which is why God has clothed this nature in earthly habits to provide an expression for his love that he could not have given to that nature if it belonged purely to heaven. But at this point, we have to stand back a little and take our bearings. Man, through suffering, is capable of more than heavenly creatures. Man, the earthly creature, possesses a greater treasure through suffering and humiliation than the treasure of the angels. The burdensome, anxious life of man on earth is more significant, glorious and fruitful than the light,

---

[12] SS 154.
[13] SS 152.
[14] H 253 (T 238).
[15] H 254-55 (T 238-39).
[16] H 255 (T 240).
[17] S 84 (GC I:501).

untroubled existence of heavenly creatures who know only light and love. Where does this notion take us? To the edge of the latest philosophy? Into the company of the existentialists, and especially Rilke in his Duino Elegies, where he conducts his proud dialogue with the angel: the angel who has all the privileges of heaven but lacks one thing—the glorious, irreplaceable burdens of earth, the humble subjection to time and death? Does time, then, count more than eternity and man more than the angels, who in wonder bow before the mystery of suffering and death in the Person of Christ? The fact is that Thérèse does join in this chorus. There are few more persistent themes running through her teaching: the angels are inferior to man. It is like an echo of Rilke: "Let us not fancy we can love without suffering, without suffering deeply. Our *poor nature* is there, and it is not there for nothing! It is our wealth, our livelihood!"[18] Three days before her death, she exclaims: "No, I am no angel! The angels cannot suffer, they are not so fortunate as I."[19] Even the angels cannot deny it:

> I absorb myself in God and gaze upon his charms.
> But I cannot sacrifice myself and suffer for him.
> I can give him neither my blood nor my tears;
> Nor can I die to show him my love.
> Purity is the shining destiny of the Angel,
> And there is no end to his wonderful happiness;
> But the advantage you have over the Seraphim
> Is that you can both suffer and be pure.[20]

Thérèse sees Mary in a poor manger holding the whimpering Christ Child in her arms. "Mary, how could I at this moment envy the angels? Your adorable Lord has become my

---

[18] S 101 (GC I:557).   [19] N 187–88 (LC 150).

[20] Ged 440. Je m'abîme en mon Dieu, je contemple ses charmes, / Mais je ne puis pour lui m'immoler et souffrir, / Je ne puis lui donner ni mon sang, ni mes larmes; / Pour dire mon amour, je ne saurais mourir. / La pureté de l'Ange est le brillant partage, / Son immense bonheur ne doit jamais finir; / Mais sur le Séraphin vous avez l'avantage: / Vous pouvez être purs et vous pouvez souffrir!

Brother."[21] It is rather the angels who "envy our good fortune",[22] as they see the hidden favor we have received, which outweighs the favors of heaven:

> The Seraph feeds upon glory,
> On pure love and perfect happiness;
> Weak child that I am, I see nothing in the ciborium
> But the color and appearance of milk.
> But milk is what is fit for children.[23]

Thérèse goes farther. She does not accept any sharp division between heavenly life and earthly life. From revelation and tradition, she knows that virginity is a form of heavenly existence. She also quotes the opinions of the theologians that the religious life is a form of martyrdom. Should she not, then, be able to achieve a synthesis of heaven and earth that is beyond the capacity of angels? The thought is intoxicating—perhaps too intoxicating—and she has no desire to be raised too high above the angels. She invents an "Angel of the Holy Face" who is devoted to the Lord's Passion and mirrors his suffering. And this leads her to ascribe complementary roles to man and angel, each reflecting the other. The Divine Child instructs the angel of suffering:

> O you who on earth desired
> To know my cross and sorrow;
> Beautiful Angel, listen to this mystery:
> Each suffering soul is your sister.
>
> In heaven, the glory of its suffering
> Will be reflected from your brow;
> And the rays of your angelic nature
> Will radiate its martyrdom.[24]

[21] Ged 428.   [22] Ged 423.

[23] Ged 422. Le Séraphin se nourrit de la gloire, / Du pur amour et du bonheur parfait; / Moi, faible enfant, je ne vois au ciboire / Que la couleur, la figure du lait. / Mais c'est le lait qui convient à l'enfance.

[24] Ged 485. O toi qui voulus sur la terre / Honorer ma croix, ma douleur; / Bel Ange, écoute ce mystère: / Toute âme qui souffre est ta soeur.

But this balance is not maintained; it is soon tipped in man's favor, because man can truly unite the two roles. "Dearest Céline, you asked me so many questions when we were little, I wonder how it happened that you never asked me this one: 'But why did the good God not create me an angel?' Ah, Céline, I shall tell you what I think; if Jesus did not create you an angel in heaven, it is because he wants you to be an angel on earth, yes, Jesus wants to have his heavenly court here below as well as above! He wants angel-martyrs, he wants angel-apostles." [25] And it is prophesied of the sinner Mary Magdalen: "You shall ascend beyond the choirs of angels; we shall sing your hymn of praise and envy your love." [26] Finally, all the angels bow before the God-man:

> Sweet child, the Cherub bows before you:
> Lost in wonder at your boundless love,
> He longs, like you, to die one day
> Upon the bleak hillside.
>
> What wonderful happiness for the humble creature!
> Rapt in admiration, the Seraph,
> O Jesus, longs to quit his angelic nature,
> *and become a child. . . .* [27]

And Thérèse's last poem, her great "Life of Mary", is entirely woven around this theme: the hidden things are superior to what is manifest, suffering is better than freedom from suffering, ordinary fidelity than the extraordinary graces of "raptures, miracles and ecstasies". It is all summed up in the astonished

---

Au ciel, l'éclat de sa souffrance / Sur ton front viendra rejaillir; / Et le rayon de ton essence / Illuminera le martyr.

[25] S 160 (GC II:724–25).   [26] Ged 494.

[27] Ged 487.

Devant toi, doux Enfant, le Chérubin s'incline: / Il admire, éperdu, ton ineffable amour, / Il voudrait, comme toi, sur la sombre colline / Pouvoir mourir un jour!

Qu'il est grand le bonheur de l'humble créature! / Le Séraphin voudrait, dans son ravissement, / Délaisser, ô Jesus, l'angélique nature, / *Et devenir enfant. . . .*

cry, "Then it is good to suffer on earth?" and the answer,
"There is no purer bliss than to suffer with love."[28]

One may seriously wonder whether Thérèse does not go too
far with this line of thought and actually fall into the excesses
of "existentialism". If so, it arises out of her need to bring all
her life into the clear light of consciousness so as to reflect
upon it. It is her desire to be constantly reviewing her position
(on the assumption that she is called to sanctity and apparently
is a saint), which ensnares her in these comparisons between
earthly existence and that of heaven. This precise point is made
clear in her beautiful "Life of Mary", where Mary's gaze rests
upon the Son alone and where she regards whatever he wills
for her as the best. Thérèse, on the contrary, is always gazing at herself, and her contemplation bears the mark of her
personality as clearly as a pious picture bears the marks of its
designer. Since her lot, moreover, is the best *for her*, she automatically transforms it into the best possible, the objectively
best. But here lies the danger: that by preferring the "third stage
of humility", she is rather losing sight of the essential presupposition, that indifference that Ignatius secures by means of the
first two stages. She is meant to suffer; doubtless she is right.
But she seizes upon it so eagerly that there is no room left for
God to propose any other destiny. It is, as it were, on her own
initiative that she compresses suffering and happiness into a
synthesis. "It is the little crosses that constitute our good fortune."[29] "I desire the Cross, I love sacrifice; oh, call me, I am
ready to suffer. To suffer for your love, Master, is bliss; Jesus,
my Beloved, I will die for you."[30] "If bitterness should ever
invade your heart, then take your pleasure in it; what sweetness to suffer for God!"[31] "I will hymn the ineffable grace of
suffering and bearing the Cross. I have learned that suffering
has its charms."[32] "Lord, suffering becomes enjoyment if love

[28] Ged 429.

[29] Co (*Dieu vivant*, 9).

[30] Ged 452.

[31] Ged 464.

[32] Co (*Dieu vivant*, 9).

throws itself into your arms."[33] "In the wine-press of pain, I will give proof of my love. I desire no other joy but to offer myself up each day."[34] All this certainly sounds "heroic"— and occasionally that is the word used ("There you have love pushed even to heroism"),[35] but it needs to be refined before it can become indifference. Thérèse has gone a step too far. She has overstepped the point of indifference that Ignatius situates between the first and third stages. She has to be pulled back into a serene, mature recognition that her mission of suffering must be united to indifference. "That is the only grace I desire —one must not be more royalist than the King. . . ."[36] This movement backward takes place gradually, imperceptibly, in proportion as the distinctions between joy and suffering vanish. At the beginning, ever since her First Communion, "I had a perpetual desire to suffer."[37] But the longing changes as she comes, near the end of her life, to grasp the unique meaning of suffering (and of joy), which is love. "Now I have no other desire but to love Jesus unto folly! . . . It is LOVE alone that attracts me. . . . For a long time I desired suffering and death; I possessed suffering and believed I had touched the shores of heaven. . . . Now abandonment is my only guide, I have no other compass! I no longer beg ardently for anything except that the will of God shall be accomplished perfectly in my soul."[38] This is a sudden and surprising about-turn. One minute a stormy longing for the Cross, and the next minute serene composure. "How sweet is the way of love. . . . It leaves a profound and humble peace in the depths of one's heart."[39] Her swirling desire to suffer has been smashed against the wall of indifference. She is not borne along any farther. She will no longer ask for suffering. Just in time she remembers the whole point of her own little way: to leave the choice to God. She embraces the sacrifice that God asks of her. "I could never ask

[33] Ged 397.
[34] Ged 405.
[35] S 112 (GC I:577).
[36] S 319 (GC II:1072).
[37] N 103 (LC 123).
[38] SS 178.
[39] SS 179.

him to send me greater sufferings, because I am too small."[40] "I shall never pray God to withdraw consolations, only the illusions and joys that might lead me astray from the good God."[41] Especially here, one is not allowed to insist on having one's own way. "I don't know the trade",[42] namely, how to get one's own way. It has become clear that the supreme renunciation is to renounce even one's renunciation. "I desire nothing but to be FORGOTTEN, . . . not contempt, not insults, such things would be too much glory for a *grain of sand.*"[43] Yet it is not his "dark night" that she wishes to have in common with her father John of the Cross but that ordinariness that allowed him to pass unnoticed. "One thing that struck me when reading the life of Saint John of the Cross was how people said of him, 'Brother John of the Cross is a religious who is less than ordinary.' "[44] In a letter to Céline, she instances the dewdrop that for a short time is a tiny miniature of the sun and then "changes into a light vapor"; it evaporates and becomes invisible as it is drawn into the sun, the one true light.[45]

How was this change brought about in Thérèse? One can hardly doubt that it was the purifying effect of that "half-night" into which she had been drawn and which gently detached her from all her preferences and dislikes. Light and shadow were not banished from her life, but the twilight softened their edges. She still found some tasks burdensome and others light, but none now broke through her indifference. Ignatius had reached the same indifference by means of purely rational considerations, by meditating on the purpose of man's creation, the means necessary to achieve it and the attitude required in order to make proper use of those means. Thérèse, by contrast, was brought to indifference by another route that was not at all rational; everything that seemed to make any difference was taken from her, all life's coloring transformed into

---

[40] H 247 (T 233).

[42] N 57 (LC 83).

[44] N 122 (LC 128).

[41] N 88.

[43] S 126 (GC I:580).

[45] S 185–88 (GC II:783–86).

uniform greyness. God placed a ban on everything that would have passionately attracted or revolted her fiery nature. Hers is the subterranean way that she described, where it is neither hot nor cold, where there is neither wind nor rain but a half-gloom enveloping everything. This is the means whereby God eliminates every trace of her preference for suffering. It had been necessary to excise oversensitive fibers of her soul, to slacken certain of her tensions and give her weary soul room for a more profound serenity. She emerges beyond the third stage of humility—or, if one is to stick to Ignatian terms, the second and third stages are integrated within her. The word used by Thérèse at the end to describe her condition was *abandon.*

Now she chooses no more. She does not even choose to suffer. God chooses; indeed, God had been choosing all the time, but now her choice is whatever he chooses. "I desire neither to live nor to die; if our Lord offered me the choice I would choose neither; I want nothing except what he wants; *whatever he decides, that is what I prefer.*"[46] Over and over again, Thérèse repeats this maxim during her last months. Did she not wish to know beforehand the hour of her death? "Oh, no! I wouldn't be at all happier. Nothing makes me happy except doing the will of the good God."[47] Would she not rather die than live? "Oh, Mother, I repeat, I don't love one thing more than the other. . . . Whatever the good God prefers and chooses for me is what pleases me best."[48] Would she be frightened of dying at this very minute? "Not at all. With what happiness I would go from this world." What a disappointment, then, if she had to go on living! "Not in the least. . . . I would say, 'I am very glad to be cured so as to go on serving the good God on earth since that is his will.' "[49] And, if she had to die without the sacrament? "It is truly a great grace to receive the sacrament. But if the good God does not permit it, it is good, just the

[46] H 237 (T 223).   [47] N 167 (LC 175).
[48] N 173 (LC 183).   [49] N 173-74 (LC 184).

same. All is grace!"[50] Was she not weary of suffering so long?
"Of suffering? but I am glad of it." Why? "Because it pleases
the good God."[51] "The reason why I rejoice at the thought
of death is because death is an expression of God's will for
me."[52] On the other hand, God gives her his will so that she
may love it: "The good God always led me to desire whatever
he wanted to give me."[53] "If he changes his mind, we shall
change ours too, that's all!"[54] "He makes us desire, then grants
our desires. . . ."[55] "And, if he did not wish it, would he have
put into the heart of his poor little brides a desire he could
not fulfill?"[56] Now she is no longer convinced that suffering
is the only source of fruitfulness. That comes from fulfilling
God's will and may just as well spring from joy. "It seems to
me that if our *sacrifices* are hairs to hold Jesus prisoner so are
our *joys*; to make them so, it is enough that we are not concentrated in a selfish happiness but that we offer our Spouse
the *small joys* he sows in life's path to win our souls and *raise*
them to him. . . ."[57] In the end, she has no room in her heart
for anything but the will of God: "My heart is filled with the
will of the good God; if someone pours anything else over
it, it does not seep inside but slips off as if it were nothing—
like oil that will not mix with water. Fundamentally, I retain a
profound peace that nothing can disturb."[58] The person who
never tries to impose his own will upon God can be certain of
doing God's will. "I have never prayed to the good God for
an early death. So I am certain that it is his will that is now
being accomplished."[59] Which is Thérèse's aim at all times—
that God should heed no one but himself. Someone prays that
her pain should be eased. "I have prayed to the good God not
to listen to any prayers that might get in the way of his plans

[50] N 28 (LC 57).
[51] N 35 (LC 65).
[52] N 95 (LC 114).
[53] N 67 (LC 94); S 351 (GC II:1140).
[54] S 283 (GC II:1035).
[55] S 294 (GC II:1015).
[56] S 162 (GC II:728).
[57] S 276 (GC II:966).
[58] N 70 (LC 97).
[59] N 95 (LC 115).

for me."[60] Her indifference is of the kind that allows her to chuckle about the good God's embarrassment; someone has mentioned that she must be very content today because she has spat blood, a sign that the "divine Thief" is drawing nigh. "Ah, even without such a sign, I love him so much that I should always be content with what he does. I should love him no less even if he were not to come and steal me away; quite the contrary. When he seems to be deceiving me, then I pay him all sorts of compliments, and he doesn't know what to do with me."[61] "I myself am never disappointed, because I am always content with what he does. I desire his will alone."[62] "I love the night as well as the day."[63] And so Thérèse can risk the paradox: "Truly I am fortunate, I always have my own way" —because her way is the way of Jesus.[64] "The only happiness on earth is to train oneself always to find the lot Jesus gives us delightful."[65]

She knows that none of it is her own work, that all is grace; for it is God who inspires her longing for what he will give her. Yet she is also convinced that one must strive for it. And it is significant that the little Thérèse should criticize the great Teresa for constantly harping on her desire for death. "No one shall ever be able to say of me what our Holy Mother, Saint Teresa, says of herself: She died because she could not die. As for my nature, yes: heaven! But grace has won great power over my nature, and so I can only say over and over to the good God:

> Lord, if you desire it,
> I wish to go on living for a long time,
> But I would gladly come straight to heaven
> If that would please you.
> The love that burns at the heart of our Homeland
> Never ceases to consume me.

[60] N 135 (LC 240).

[61] N 47–48 (LC 75).

[62] Co 287.

[63] Ged 412.

[64] Ibid.

[65] S 356 (GC II:1148–49).

> What does life or death matter to me
> Whose sole happiness is loving you?"[66]

And, when someone proposes to ask the Mother of God to lighten her suffering: "No, we must leave them alone up there."[67] Her attitude toward prayers of petition remains the same: "When we have asked the Mother of God for something that she does not grant, then we must resign ourselves and not keep on insisting and making a fuss."[68] Thérèse regards the Mother of God as the protector of indifference: "To petition the Mother of God is not the same as petitioning God. She already knows what to make of my little wishes. Whether to say yes or no. In fact, it is her business to deal with them, so that the good God is not forced to answer me, to allow him to do everything as he pleases."[69] "Often I have asked the Mother of God to tell the good God not to trouble over me. It is to her that I address my requests. I do not understand this illness at all—here I am getting better! But I abandon myself and so am happy. What would become of me if I were hoping to die soon! What disappointments! But I do not have them, because I am content with everything the good God arranges."[70]

As always, once Thérèse has discovered this form of indifference, she fully exploits its paradoxes. She has a certain desire—and how not, unless she were inhuman? She expresses her desire. And, for a moment, with one part of her soul, she expects it to be fulfilled (otherwise, again, she would be inhuman). But, knowing that God's love for her is so much more sensitive than hers for him, she assumes that it must pain God to have to refuse her requests for some reason or another. So, when she is delivering her request, she puts bias on it at the last minute so that, if it is not on the mark, at least it may swing

---

[66] N 109 (LC 128). Longtemps encore je veux bien vivre, / Seigneur, si c'est là ton désir, / Dans le ciel je voudrais te suivre, / Si cela te faisait plaisir. / L'Amour, ce feu de la Patrie, / Ne cesse de me consumer. / Que me fait la mort ou la vie, / Mon seul bonheur, c'est de t'aimer.

[67] N 142 (LC 151).   [68] N 158 (LC 166).

[69] N 26 (LC 55).   [70] N 34 (LC 63).

over into God's will. Which has the paradoxical result that the less her requests are heard, the deeper her love grows. "Often I pray to the saints without being heard. But, the more they seem deaf to my requests, the more I love them." Why is that? "Because I have a stronger desire to remain in the night of faith and not see God and his saints than others have to see and grasp everything."[71] "Yesterday evening I prayed to the Mother of God that I might stop coughing so as to give Sister Geneviève more sleep. But I added: If you do not grant this, I shall love you all the more."[72] After prayers to relieve her suffering had been offered without avail: "In spite of what I felt at the first moment, I repeated to God that I loved him even more, and all his saints, too."[73] This typifies her wonderful skill at using her suffering as an argument for the goodness of God: "I have never had such a terrible night. O how good God must be to give me strength to suffer as I do!"[74]

If such an attitude is not to become abstract and inhuman, this state of indifference must preserve human desires and hopes in all their vitality. Thérèse's indifference certainly does so. It is obvious that she, like Paul, would rather die. "My good Blessed Virgin, here is what gives me the desire to leave: I am tiring the infirmarian out and giving pain to my Sisters, through being so ill. Yes I would gladly go."[75] "When shall I go to the good God? How gladly I would go to heaven!"[76] "I find resignation necessary only for living. For dying, it's only joy I experience."[77] And one can just sense the effort it takes to accept living. "I have surrendered myself completely, whether to life or death. I wish even to be well again, so as to go to Indochina, if that is what the good God wants of me."[78] On August 18, some of the Sisters said how hard she would find it if she got better. "On the contrary, if it were the will of the good God, I should be most happy to make that *sacrifice*. But I

[71] N 136 (LC 146).   [72] N 140 (LC 149).
[73] N 161 (LC 169).   [74] N 152 (LC 164).
[75] N 165 (LC 174).   [76] N 38 (LC 68).
[77] N 29 (LC 58).   [78] G 484 (ET 386).

can also say that it would be no small matter to have gone so far and then to come back again."[79] Thérèse also harbors desires about the manner of her death. Thus she wishes not to die on a feast, as this would not be in accordance with her little way. "Let us hope that nothing will go wrong with me tomorrow morning."[80] Nor does she wish to die in the night. "Believe me, I shall not die during the night, I have had the desire not to die at night, and I have prayed to the Mother of God about it."[81] There is no trace in Thérèse of the Quietism that simply allows a person to drown his own will in the will of God. The mystery of indifference is much more a mystery of personal love and the exchange of wills, one that requires explanation in terms of the Trinity. Though she was not conscious of this trinitarian explanation, she actually describes it in an observation that she threw out. "The good God will have to carry out my will in heaven, because I have never done my own will on earth."[82] Are we not told in the Psalms: "He will do the will of them who fear him" (Ps 144:19)? And her observation needs to be read in conjunction with another. "I have never given the good God anything but love, and he will repay me with love."[83]

Nevertheless, even when a creature's will is free and creative, not slavishly cringing before the decrees of the Absolute, it must still remain subject to the divine will. So long as God's will is the decisive factor, then he also assumes responsibility for bringing our actions to a successful conclusion. But, whenever a creature sets up his own will as autonomous over against God's will, immediately he has to find the strength for his schemes from within himself; and the result is catastrophic. That is her final warning to those who seek for suffering and the Cross without the necessary indifference. "I should never ask the good God for greater suffering, because then they would

[79] N 143 (LC 153).   [80] N 75 (LC 98).
[81] N 97 (LC 116).   [82] N 66 (LC 91).
[83] N 89 (LC 106).

be my sufferings. I would have to bear them entirely alone, and I have never yet managed anything on my own."[84] "The good God inspires me with courage in exact proportion to my suffering. At the moment, I feel as though I cannot hold out any longer; but I am not anxious, because, if my suffering increases, God will at the same time increase my courage."[85] "I am not in the least unhappy. The good God gives me just as much as I can bear."[86] "I am glad of never having asked the good God for suffering; it means he has to supply me with courage."[87] At this point, her teaching on indifference reverts once more to the theme of spiritual childhood. The same spirit that makes us indifferent and places us at God's disposition also prevents us from tearing ourselves out of God's fatherly arms so as to stand alone and achieve heroic deeds. "Sanctity consists in a disposition of the heart that leaves us little and humble in God's arms, aware of our weakness and trusting unto folly in his fatherly goodness."[88]

[84] N 136 (LC 145).
[85] N 140–41 (LC 149).
[86] N 160 (LC 168).
[87] N 162 (LC 169).
[88] N 112–13.

THE PLUNGE

H ER INDIFFERENCE LED THÉRÈSE to take a step backward. She had taken her love of suffering so far that it almost became self-willed. She had to go back to the point at which suffering and joy are equally acceptable so long as they come from the hand of God. Far from turning back to an inferior goal, she returns enriched with the experience of suffering and without losing any of the *élan* that had driven her on to the Cross. The result is something far removed from passivity that slackly waits on the turn of events or resignation that bows its head in advance to whatever is to come. Her attitude remains intensely active; she is ready to plunge into the fray. Eagerly she seizes upon a quotation from Madame Swetschin with which she agrees heartily: "Resignation is still distinct from surrender to the will of God, there is the same difference as between union and unity; in union, we are still two, in unity, we are but one."[1] Surrender, *abandon*, is a human act, the highest of human acts, since it passes over into the omnipotence of God. It means abandoning one's own ground in order to hang upon the will of God. "No one knows whether he himself is just or sinful, but, Céline, Jesus gives us the grace to feel in the very depth of our heart that we would rather die than offend him. And, in any event, it is not our merits but those of our Spouse, which are *ours*, that we offer to our Father who is in heaven. . . ."[2] " 'We know not what we should pray for as we ought: but the Spirit himself asks for us with unspeakable groanings' (Rom 8:26). We have nothing to do, then, except surrender our souls to the care of almighty God."[3] Give up all securities and guarantees, because God will look after them. "People say to me: You will be frightened of death. That is quite possible. If they only knew how unsure of myself I am. I

[1] S 67 (GC I:468).   [2] S 163 (GC II:729).
[3] S 231 (GC II:863).

never rely on my own thoughts; I know how weak I am. . . ."[4]
"Why should I be more immune from the fear of death than
others? Unlike Peter, I do not say: I shall never deny you."[5]
"I am not frightened of the last struggle or the suffering of
the illness, however terrible they may be. The good God has
helped me and led me by the hand ever since my childhood; I
count on him. I am sure that he will continue to help me till
the end."[6]

Trust is the first word that she gives to this active indifference. Trust is an act, but not a "work" on whose merits one
can rely. The greatness of a person who trusts is that he goes
on trusting even when he knows that his task is beyond him.
"With daring abandon, [the little bird] wishes to remain gazing
upon its Divine Sun. Nothing will frighten it, neither wind nor
rain, and if dark clouds come and hide the Star of Love . . .
and it seems it should believe there is nothing but the clouds
surrounding it, this is the moment of *perfect joy*. . . ."[7] She has
to stop planning and reviewing her position, to give up every
assurance about what lies on the other side. "What anyone says
to me about my imminent death no longer penetrates. . . . It
is clear that the good God does not want me to think of it as I
used to before my illness. Such thoughts then were necessary
and useful; now the opposite is true. He wishes me to surrender myself like a little child and not concern myself over what
is to happen to me."[8] "Since we wish to be *little children*, little
children do not know what is best, they find everything good;
let us copy them. Besides, there is no merit in doing what is
reasonable."[9]

How vital this all is to Thérèse is shown by the frequency
with which she cites the example of Saint Cecilia. After Joan of
Arc, the saint who inspires her most and whom she wishes to
resemble is Saint Cecilia ("*Saint* of ABANDONMENT").[10] When

---

[4] N 12 (LC 46).   [5] N 58 (LC 83).
[6] N 17–18 (LC 50).   [7] SS 198.
[8] N 35 (LC 65).   [9] H 263 (T 294).
[10] S 224 (GC II:850).

visiting the Roman catacombs, she had lain in the saint's sar-
cophagus and brought away some of the earth sanctified by
her remains.[11] Thérèse wished to be like her not only in her
martyrdom but above all in her abandonment. Cecilia knows
that she is to remain a virgin of God. And yet she cannot escape being betrothed to a heathen. The conflict is beyond human solution. But Cecilia does not run away; she does not try
to skirt the darkness but plunges into it. "I love those saints
who triumphed over all difficulties by surrendering themselves
to God; Saint Cecilia, for instance, who allowed herself to be
taken in marriage yet was not afraid."[12] "What a model! In
the midst of the world, with every sort of danger ringing her
round, on the point of being married to a young pagan who
dreamed only of earthly love, Cecilia might well have trembled
and wept . . . , but no, 'Leaving the instruments sounding for
her wedding, Cecilia was singing in her heart'. . . . What total
trust! . . . She was not afraid . . . , she knew that Jesus was
under obligation to guard her and protect her virginity, and
she knew the reward."[13] Thérèse is attracted to Saint Cecilia
by her rare combination of courage and gentleness, by her lyrical womanly abandonment even when the tide of battle threatens to overwhelm her. "Saint Cecilia is like the Bride in the
Canticles; I see her as *a choir in an armed camp.* Her life was
one melodious song in the midst of terrible trials; which does
not amaze me, because *the Holy Gospel rested upon her heart* and
in her heart the Spouse of Virgins."[14] And, in the hymn that
she dedicates to the saint, Thérèse sings of her "complete surrender, the sweet fruit of love",[15] the "unspeakable abandonment, the love that knows no fear but goes to sleep and forgets, like a little child in the bosom of God."[16] Standing in the
foreground, Cecilia is meant to draw our gaze toward Mary in
the background; her abandonment is a pale reflection of that

[11] SS 131.   [12] N 39 (LC 69).
[13] S 206 (GC II:827–28).   [14] G 198 (ET 154).
[15] Ged 441.
[16] Ged 438–39; see also the poem "Abandon", p. 419.

abandonment in which Mary unites virginity and fruitfulness, the married state and the religious, betrothal to Joseph with marriage to God.

But, in poising herself to make the final surrender, she is not faced with a completely unintelligible mystery. She stands by the abyss of inconceivable love that grows deeper at each moment. Early in life, Thérèse had encountered the abyss, and the longer she lives, the more she is drawn toward it. She is unable to take her eyes away from it; she stands breathless with excitement, overpowered by the blissful mystery of love. This love is not based upon "truth" or "being"—such love is itself the source of truth and being, the explanation of all things and therefore beyond explanation itself. "O my God, you know that I have never wanted anything but to love you alone; I desire no other glory. Your love opened up before me in my very childhood; it has grown with me, and now it is an abyss whose depths I cannot sound."[17] This abyss of light is beyond our conception,[18] and so we have to be stripped of every notion as we approach it, ready to abandon ourselves to the infinite. We must offer to be dissolved, "as a drop of water loses itself in the boundless ocean".[19] Or, to use another comparison, "The divine call was so insistent that, had I been forced to pass through flames, I would have done it to be true to Jesus."[20] The experience she is trying to relate by means of these different comparisons is expressed most perfectly in the image of *the rose shedding its petals*. Everyone knows how much this image meant to Thérèse—how as a novice she used to scatter roses before the crucifix in the cloister courtyard and how she maintained this practice upon her deathbed. As a child, during the Corpus Christi procession, she used to walk right in front of the Blessed Sacrament carrying a basketful of sweet-smelling flowers with which she strewed the good God's pathway; and she was "never so happy" as when she saw her "rose petals

[17] SS 256.
[19] SS 256.

[18] Cf. N 93 (LC 239).
[20] SS 106.

touch the sacred monstrance".[21] This same picture leads us to the most lyrical passage in her book, where she describes the very essence of her mission: "I have no other way of showing you my love except to strew flowers; which means not letting slip any little sacrifice, any glance or any word, but turning the least action to profit for the sake of love. For love I will suffer and for love rejoice. Thus shall I strew flowers before your throne. None that I see but what I shall *unpetal* it for you."[22] And she also knows that these worthless petals will be gathered by the heavenly Church and pass through the hands of the Lord, who will imprint an infinite value on them for the sake of the suffering Church. "Then Jesus will take the flowers and, conferring an infinite value upon them, will strew them in his turn."[23]

> This plucked rose is the faithful image of the heart that at every moment wishes to sacrifice itself to you. O divine Child, Lord, there are many fresh roses that love to blossom on your altars. They do so for your sake. But I want something different: to shed my petals for you. These blooming roses can adorn your feasts. But the plucked ones are forgotten and thrown to the winds and are no more. They are trodden on unnoticed, yet the remnants of them provide a natural adornment that requires no skillful dressing. I have understood. Lord, for love of you I have squandered my life and my future; in the eyes of mortals I must die a faded rose. For you I must die, Jesus most beautiful. In shedding my petals, I will prove that I love you with all my heart. Here below I wish to live in darkness beneath your feet; and on your path to Calvary I shall soften your last steps.[24]

When the Sister for whom Thérèse had written this poem read it, she thought it beautiful but wished for another stanza, in which the good God would collect all the scattered rose petals together again and make a complete rose that would bloom to all eternity. But Thérèse answered: "Our good Mother herself

---

[21] SS 41.   [22] SS 196.
[23] S 323 (GC II:989).   [24] Ged 417–18.

may compose this stanza, if she wishes; as far as I am concerned, I do not feel inspired to go farther. It is my wish to be plucked for the joy of God."[25] No. When she surrenders herself and entrusts herself to the abyss, it is not so as to find herself again in the depths. Her plunge into God is not calculated and conditional but absolute and unconditional. It is her mission to take this plunge so that others may follow.

And, since it was her mission to see all God's attributes in terms of his mercy, her plunge into God is especially a plunge into his mercy, an offer as a victim of mercy. In this respect, she herself is conscious of her originality; she knows that she is making an unprecedented discovery. Previously all souls who placed themselves wholly at God's disposition had been dominated by the thought of his justice. They give the impression that man can turn aside God's avenging, Old Testament justice. Thérèse does not despise this attitude, since there may well be other missions, meant to display God's actions in the light of justice. She simply recognizes that this is not her mission. "One day I was thinking of the souls who offer themselves as victims of God's justice in order to turn away the punishments due to sinners, drawing them upon themselves. I considered their sacrifice great and generous but was far from feeling attracted to making it."[26] Thérèse had never met the God of Justice; she knew nothing about him; so as far as she is concerned, he does not exist. For her, such a God is a purely theoretical possibility, a concept that means nothing—because no concept comes alive for her until she has tested it in her conduct as a Christian. From the first, she had known only the God of mercy; she begins the story of her life by "singing what I must sing eternally: *the mercies of the Lord*".[27] *This* love is what she offers to serve. " 'O my God,' I cried from the depths of my heart, 'is it only your justice that will find souls willing to immolate themselves as victims? Does not *your merciful love* need them as

[25] Co 75.   [26] SS 180.
[27] SS 13.

well? On every side this love is misunderstood, rejected. . . . It seems to me that if you were to find souls offering themselves as SACRIFICIAL VICTIMS TO YOUR LOVE, you would quickly consume them and be glad not to hold back the waves of infinite tenderness within you.' ''[28] Since it is true that God's love is deeper and more comprehensive than his justice (it is written, "God is love", but never, "God is justice"), then it is God's love rather than his justice that calls for our response and service. And, "because the problem of sin, if we go to the root of it, is not a problem of justice, punishment and giving each his due but is a problem of love, the fundamental question does not run, 'O God, is your justice to remain unsatisfied through the hardness of sinners?', but rather, 'O God, is your despised love to remain sealed in your heart?' ''[29] "Why not offer oneself to justice? Because, as brought to bear upon a sinner, justice is of limited application and is not in accordance either with the original aim of divine love or its deepest longings. But, in contrast, to surrender oneself to love means giving oneself to God as he *is* and as he will be eternally on earth, as in heaven." No sooner said than done. By a sort of liturgical deed, Thérèse asks for permission to consecrate herself as a victim of divine mercy. On the feast of the Holy Trinity, June 9, 1895, she pronounces the consecration that she has so carefully formulated. She has composed it with an earnestness and desire to leave nothing out that is typical of a schoolgirl essay. She refers to all the models whom she has learned to admire from reading holy lives, from her prayerbooks and from her own memories, and yet she puts them together so as to leave her personal preferences in no doubt. And, after promising everything that she has— herself and, even more, the merits of the saints and the treasure of the Church—she then goes on to state three wishes, just as they do in fairy stories. These three wishes are: that the Lord should dwell in her as he does in the Host; that he should take away her freedom to do wrong; and that in heaven he should

---

[28] SS 180–81.   [29] Co 142–43.

bestow his sacred wounds upon her. They are uneven wishes; the second is vital, the third childish and rash, while the first is extremely curious if taken literally, as it was no doubt intended. But there is a stream of love flowing through every sentence. There were other requests that she could have voiced; and, if she had seen better, she would have wished better.[30] Yet, fundamentally, the act of oblation is meant to express only one thing —the plunge into the abyss of love, into which she throws herself without reserve or guarantee. She just has "*blind hope in his mercy*".[31] She sums up at the end: "I OFFER MYSELF AS A BURNT OFFERING TO YOUR MERCIFUL LOVE, calling upon you to consume me at every instant, while you let the floods of *infinite tenderness* pent up within you flow into my soul, so that I may become a *Martyr* to your *Love*, O my God! . . ." Nor is God long in responding.[32] "A few days after I had offered myself to *merciful love*, I began to make the Stations of the Cross in choir, when I suddenly felt myself wounded by such a burning shaft of fire that I thought I would die. . . . It seemed as though an invisible power was plunging me whole into fire. But what fire! And what sweetness!"[33] Henceforth—even after returning into the darkness of this life—she feels herself "burning with this *merciful* love" that purifies her and removes all trace of sin from her heart.[34] And from now on it is the image of fire that recurs again and again. "Lured by its light, the insect casts itself into the fire; I have the same hope of your light; I will fly into it and be consumed. . . ."[35] "I beg that your *divine gaze* may purify my soul instantly, consuming all my imperfections, as fire transforms everything into itself."[36] "Ask Jesus that all the prayers being offered for my cure may serve to fan the flames that must consume me."[37] "Your little bird . . . wants to become the prey of your love. One day I hope that you, the Adorable Eagle, will come to fetch me, your little bird; and,

[30] Co 145.   [31] S 289 (GC II:999).
[32] SS 277.   [33] H 226 (T 213).
[34] Cf. SS 181.   [35] Ged 509.
[36] SS 276.   [37] H 294 (T 322).

ascending with it to the Furnace of Love, you will plunge it for all eternity into that burning abyss of this Love to which it has offered itself as victim."[38] "For love to be completely satisfied, it must sink itself into nothingness and transform this nothingness into fire."[39] "Burning dart, consume me without ceasing." And Thérèse is convinced that the flame in her heart is sufficient to set the world alight.[40]

It is the climax of surrender when a person plunges into the abyss of mercy, plunging ever deeper into its mystery. Nor (since the abyss is boundless on every side) can anyone's trust be too great. In Thérèse's case, trust increases trust, and she plunges ever onward. "I believe", she said, referring to God and the saints, "that *they want to know how far I will push my trust*. . . . But these words of Job have not entered my heart in vain: 'Even if God should kill me, I would still trust him.' "[41] "Believe in the truth of what I am saying: we can never place too much trust in the good God, who is so powerful and merciful! We receive from him just as much as we hope from him."[42] But that is the minimum, for Thérèse also remembers the Lord's saying to Saint Mechtild: "In truth, I tell you, it gives me great joy when men expect wonderful things of me. No matter how great their faith and daring, I shall reward them far beyond their merits. It is impossible, indeed, that a man should not receive what his faith has led him to hope from my power and mercy."[43] And this thought is with Thérèse right until the end. "We can never place too much trust in the good God, who is so powerful and merciful! We receive from him just as much as we hope from him." And, with a forward glance toward her mission in heaven: "All my expectations will be fulfilled beyond measure, and the Lord will do wonderful things for me, infinitely more than my boundless desires."[44] As the world sees it, this is all "madness" and "folly"; but "we shall

---

[38] SS 200.

[39] SS 195.

[40] Ged 390.

[41] H 236 (T 222).

[42] H 246 (T 232).

[43] 2 P 253 (G 346 [ET 279–80]).

[44] G 347 (ET 280).

never be able to commit the follies for him that he has committed for us."[45] But "what matter that our *vessels* are broken, since Jesus is *consoled* and since, in spite of itself, the world is forced to *awareness* of the perfumes they breathe forth, perfumes that serve to purify the poisoned air the world is ever breathing".[46]

When she speaks of hoping for yet more, Thérèse is not just thinking, in general, of God's infinite goodness. She is referring specifically to God's mercy outstripping his justice. Her hope and trust carry her to the very hall of judgment, where she appeals to the mercy that is above justice. In her play about the angels, the Angel of the Last Judgment points to the justice that has not been satisfied. On that day, the Angel will claim "vengeance" for the twofold wrong perpetrated upon the "sweet victim" of Calvary, who is not only their God but also their Savior. The Angel has his mind set on vengeance; but the Savior himself, who came to avert vengeance, is not thinking of that. How should he take vengeance for the Cross that men inflicted on him, when it was his very purpose to save his tormentors by this Cross! And so he gives a warning:

> Beautiful Angel, put up your sword.
> It is not your office to judge
> The nature that I redeem.
> I am the messenger of peace.
>
> The one who will judge the world
> Is I . . . and I am called *Jesus*!
> My blood is the welling spring
> In which all my elect shall be purified.[47]

---

[45] S 240 (GC II:882).   [46] S 241 (GC II:883).

[47] O bel Ange, abaisse ton glaive, / Ce n'est pas à toi de juger / La nature que je relève: / De la paix, je suis Messager. / Celui qui jugera le monde, / C'est moi . . . que l'on nomme *Jésus*! / De mon sang, la source féconde / Purifiera tous mes élus.

And, when the Angel of the Holy Face has implored for mercy toward sinners, the answer is given:

> I shall listen to your prayer:
> Every soul shall obtain its pardon,
> I shall fill it with light,
> As soon as it invokes my name.[48]

[48] Ged 484–87. Je veux exaucer ta prière / Toute âme obtiendra son pardon / Je la remplirai de lumière / Dès qu'elle invoquera mon Nom.

THÉRÈSE AND MYSTICISM

THE WHOLE PROBLEM with which we are faced in Thérèse of Lisieux is extremely complex; it becomes especially acute if we ask ourselves whether Thérèse was a mystic and what contribution she made to mysticism. For, as the representative of the little way, Thérèse goes on the defensive whenever anything extraordinary is suggested as part of the means to perfection; she is particularly suspicious of mystical phenomena. Yet one could hardly assert that mystical phenomena never occurred in her own life. On the contrary, we find plenty of them. The outstanding one is the "great miracle", the appearance of the Blessed Virgin, who smiles upon Thérèse and comes to cure her. But even previously, other events had occurred that Thérèse regards as genuine and that we have no reason to doubt. In her earliest childhood came the dream of the two little devils; Thérèse says that it was "nothing extraordinary" but was meant by God to show her "that a soul in a state of grace has nothing to fear from evil spirits".[1] Far more important is the prophetic vision of her father, with his head hidden in a thick veil, which Thérèse saw and described as clearly as one could wish; and the witness of her sisters and the maid at least proves that it was not a case of mistaken identity.[2] The vision is all the more striking in that no one—not even Thérèse—had the faintest notion of its meaning at the time; not until her father falls ill do we receive any explanation. Another "little miracle", in Thérèse's eyes, was the cure of her emotional disturbances at Christmas 1886.[3] She thinks much the same about the sudden fall of snow that came to grace her Clothing on quite a warm day.[4] And what are we to make of the little "tokens of love" with which God sought to lighten her sufferings in Carmel? The birds coming in

---

[1] SS 28.   [2] SS 45–46.
[3] SS 97–98.   [4] SS 156.

through the window to visit her; and the many flowers she receives at odd times? And this continuous stream of happenings that are hardly to be explained in terms of "ordinary providence"? How are we to classify the many answers to her prayers, the first of which was the conversion of Pranzini, the criminal who remained unrepentant until reaching the scaffold?[5] How shall we explain her capacity for reading other souls and almost unconsciously saying just the right word? Or, finally, the whole inner direction of her prayer in the convent, the "semi-night" in which Thérèse became immersed, which was undoubtedly a prior state or variation of the "dark night" of her father, Saint John of the Cross? How are we to account for her being pierced by a searing dart soon after her oblation to divine mercy? Unlike the piercing of Teresa of Jesus, it left no physical trace but was no less unexpected and intense, so intense that she thought she would die of it. Finally, what are we to say of the following experiences during prayer, which she compares—wrongly, it would seem—with what Teresa of Jesus called the "flight of the spirit", by which she felt herself to be as if outside herself? "I felt myself completely hidden beneath the veil of the Mother of God. At the time, I was serving in the refectory, and I remember performing my duties as if it were not I doing them, as though I had been lent someone else's body. I remained that way for one whole week."[6] Nor was it a natural dream in which Thérèse recognized the foundress of the French Carmelites, the Venerable Anne of Jesus, from whom she received an important legacy.[7] It seems much less likely that Thérèse was granted really mystical experiences during meditation, because her meditation normally took the form of Scripture reading. Yet even after taking all these events into account, one cannot say that Thérèse crossed the threshold into what is known as mysticism; her personal way was the little way, free from mystical phenomena.

---

[5] SS 99–100.   [6] N 63–64 (LC 88).
[7] SS 190–92.

Nor does it prevent Thérèse from taking her own line about mysticism. It is not only that her teaching on perfection emphasizes the solid Christian virtues, based upon faith; if that were all, she would simply be stating the wholesome tradition of Christian spirituality that attaches little significance to mystical phenomena. Moreover, she would simply be following the direction of Teresa and John of the Cross. But she goes farther: she *deliberately rejects* mysticism. And here she takes an astonishingly independent line, in direct opposition to the great Spaniards. For, whether they admit it or not, the Spaniards' whole attitude is an invitation to enter the world of mysticism, which they range over and map out with such assurance that one eventually feels as if Christian perfection is impossible without mystical experience. It seems to be the inevitable complement of "mere faith". When the great Teresa, for instance, lays down the steps that lead to the heights of Mount Carmel and draws distinctions that really separate the different "mansions of the soul", she is automatically recognizing a "higher and lower", a "perfect" and a "less perfect". And the map of mysticism sketched with such lucidity and assurance by the two great Spaniards from their personal experiences has set the pattern for all mysticism during modern times.

Although a Carmelite herself, Thérèse refuses to follow this map. She does not directly deny its accuracy any more than she denies that the "great souls" and the "strong in spirit" have their own way. But it is not her way and not the way of "little souls". It is so little her way that she seems here to forsake her indifference. One may well ask whether Thérèse did not first begin to build up her own theory when she realized that the way of the "great mystics" was out of the question for her. However that may be, Thérèse *wishes not to see*. "I do not wish to see the good God here on earth. No. Not in the least. And yet I love him. I also love the Mother of God and the saints very much; but I do not wish to see them either. I prefer to

live in faith.''[8] This is all the more curious in that Thérèse
has seen the Mother of God. But she does not long for this
vision to be repeated. And perhaps one is not wholly wrong
to relate her distaste for visions to the unhappy consequences
of the first one: that slight deviation from the direction of her
mission. Thérèse had paid too high a price for visions to want
any more. The taste of sadness, of falsity even, has remained in
her mouth ever since—a sort of "spontaneous mistrust" (Petitot).[9] And so she draws up a list of reasons why seeing is
not superior to believing, rather the reverse is true. First, there
is her whole conception of love, which is centered on being
one with the Beloved rather than seeing him, upon obedience
rather than happiness. "I am afraid that I cannot quite see what
will be added to me after my death that I do not already have. I
shall see the good God, that is true, but ultimately I am already
united to him completely here on earth."[10] And again, she treasures the poverty of her love, which neither sees nor feels anything supernatural. "Ah, Mother! Those intuitions! If you only
knew the depths of my poverty! I know nothing except what
you also know. I can realize nothing except what I can see and
feel. But, despite this darkness, my soul is bathed in amazing
peace."[11] Finally, she explicitly voices her distrust of visions:
"I can only nourish myself upon the truth. That is the reason
why I have never longed for visions. On earth, one can never
see heaven and the angels as they are. I would rather wait until death."[12] According to Thérèse, then, there can be no true
visions, none that adequately represent the world beyond. Her
opinion on this matter is mistaken; if it were true, God's power
would be limited. In fact, he can provide adequate modes of
revealing his truth in this world and has no more difficulty in
presenting adequate images for those who see than in granting
the believer the means to believe. In this matter—too strongly

[8] N 177 (LC 188).   [9] Pt 92.
[10] N 6 (LC 45).   [11] N 184 (LC 199).
[12] N 117 (LC 134).

impressed perhaps by the Spanish tradition—Thérèse does not realize that a person may be just as obedient in acknowledging a vision as in believing the truth by faith. When her family went on a pilgrimage to Lourdes in May 1890, she wrote to Pauline: "I have no wish to go to Lourdes to have ecstasies. I prefer the monotony of sacrifice."[13] She tells her novices that to hanker after revelations is a venial sin.[14] And she warns her Sisters in advance not to count on her appearing to them. "Do not be surprised if I do not appear after my death and you receive no signs of my blessedness. You know well that it is in the spirit of my little way not to long to see and that I have often said to the good God, the angels and the saints, 'Here below my desire is not to see.' "[15] Or again, when it is suggested that she may be granted a vision at the moment of her death: "Oh no, I have never wished for extraordinary graces. That does not fit in with my little way."[16] There is even a trace of animosity in the firm manner in which she excludes from her little way all who hanker after extraordinary things. The publication of her biography "will be useful to all kinds of souls, apart from those who take extraordinary measures".[17] When one of her Sisters regrets that she has not written more: "It is enough, and it offers something for everyone, except for those who choose an extraordinary way." She also discounts the possibility of a miracle for herself: "It would take a miracle to keep me here in exile, and I do not think Jesus will work so pointless a miracle."[18] She models herself on Mary, who, after the angelic vision, returns to the night of poverty and faith: "I know, O Mother full of grace, that you lived in great poverty in Nazareth. You did not long to leave it; no raptures, miracles or ecstasies lightened your life, O Mother of the Chosen One! . . . O Mother beyond compare, you chose to tread the everyday paths so as to show little ones the way to heaven."

---

[13] S 128 (GC I:620).
[14] Co 223.
[15] N 25–26 (LC 55).
[16] Pt 93.
[17] Pt 91.
[18] S 351 (GC II:1139).

And she comments upon the twelve-year-old Boy's reply to his Mother: "Mother, your Son chose you as an example to souls who were to seek him in the night of faith."[19] The more Thérèse is plunged into this night, the more emphatically she prefers not to see—not even to be heard! "Often I pray to the saints, but the more they are deaf to my voice, the more I love them. . . . For my desire not to see God and the saints but to live in the night of faith is stronger than other people's desire to see and understand everything."[20] We have already mentioned how she criticizes Saint John of the Cross for allowing the soul at the height of love to gaze upon its own beauty. She also broaches a criticism of his mystical theory about the loving death;[21] she herself has no desire for such a death but only for the death of the Lord, which was very different: "Our Lord died as a victim of love; and see what his agony was!"[22] "He died upon the Cross in agony, and yet it was the most beautiful death of love ever beheld. To die from love does not mean dying in transports."[23]

These anti-mystical tendencies are particularly marked during Thérèse's last years, and especially during her last months, when her own way began to take conscious shape and she ventured to treat it as valid doctrine. But they are simply the end-term of that whole teaching on poverty, surrender and littleness that had been hers for so long and is in complete harmony with the Gospels and the mystical tradition. God "has no need of our fine thoughts—has he not his angels, his legions of heavenly spirits, whose knowledge infinitely surpasses that of the greatest geniuses of our sad earth? So it is not our intellects or talents that Jesus has come upon earth to seek. He became the Flower of the fields solely to show us how he loves simplicity."[24] Thérèse has never heard the Lord speaking to her,[25] yet she knows that he is dwelling within her. She prefers his

[19] Ged 429.
[20] N 136 (LC 146).
[21] N 139-40 (LC 148).
[22] N 27 (LC 56).
[23] N 45 (LC 73).
[24] S 187 (GC II:784-85).
[25] SS 179.

silence to his speech. "Jesus charmed feeble souls by his divine words. He was trying to make them strong against the day of trial. . . . But how small was the number of the Lord's friends, when *he was silent* before his judges! . . . Oh! What a melody for my heart is that silence of Jesus. . . ."[26]

If, during her Carmelite period, Thérèse does not encounter any of those extraordinary phenomena that the great Teresa describes in such detail, the same cannot be said of the "night", for that is where she lives almost the whole time. This is something worthy of special attention, particularly since she has described it so fully. During Easter 1896, after the Good Friday when she first spat up blood, God shows her "that there really are souls without faith who, by misusing graces, lose these precious gifts, the only source of true and pure joy".[27] And, since Thérèse asks God that she may suffer vicariously for the sake of these souls, he "allows my little soul to be darkened by the thickest gloom, so that the thought of heaven, so sweet to me up until then, becomes an occasion of torment and agony".[28] This condition is to last until her death, and she declares herself ready to remain in this gloom.

> For as long as you wish, your child is ready to eat the bread of sorrow. She does not wish to leave this table of bitterness at which poor sinners are eating until the day set by you. But may she not say in her own name, in the name of her brethren, "Have pity on us, O Lord, for we are poor sinners"? O Lord, send us away justified! May all those not yet illumined by the torch of faith behold it at last! O Jesus, if it needs a soul that loves you to purify your table they have stained, I desire to eat this bread of trial at this table until it pleases you to bring me into your bright Kingdom. The only grace I ask of you is that I might never offend you.[29]

From time to time, there is a break in the trial: "Occasionally, I grant, a thin streak of sunlight brightens up my dark night,

[26] S 196–97 (GC II:808).   [27] SS 211.
[28] Ibid.   [29] SS 212.

and for a moment the trial ceases; but then the memory of this light, instead of consoling me, makes the gloom still thicker."[30]

> When I want to rest my heart, weary of the surrounding darkness, by the memory of the luminous country after which I aspire, my anguish only increases. It seems as if the darkness, echoing the voices of sinners is mocking me, saying, "You dream of light, of a fragrant homeland, you dream that you will possess the Creator of these wonders for all eternity, you believe that you will one day emerge from this gloom. . . . Go on! Look forward to death, which will give you—not what you hope—but a still darker night, the night of nothingness."[31]

It is no longer the "veil of faith" that separates her from heaven, as it was before; now it is a wall that reaches to the very heavens.

However, this darkness over her soul and over her faith is not what has usually been described, since Saint John of the Cross' time, as the dark night of the soul. It is true that all *feeling* of certainty was withdrawn from Thérèse—but not faith itself. What she endures is the utmost "aridity", by which God withdraws all consolations and warmth from the soul, seeming to abandon it to desperate enterprises for which it has only its own resources. "[Jesus] knows", writes Thérèse, "that, although I have no *joy* of faith, I still try to carry out the works of faith. This last year, I believe I have made more acts of faith than during the rest of my life." Her condition is not one of sheer passivity: "At each fresh challenge . . . , I conduct myself bravely. . . . I run toward Jesus and tell him that I am ready to shed my blood to the last drop as witness that there is a heaven; I tell him that I am happy to be unable on earth to contemplate this beautiful heaven, so that he will open it eternally to the poor unbelievers." Even in the midst of her trial, she is able to sense another, higher joy:

> In spite of this trial, which deprives me of all my joy, I can still cry, "You have given me, O Lord, a delight in all your doings",

for is there any greater joy than to suffer for love of you? The more intense the suffering, and the more hidden it is from creatures, the more it rejoices you, O my God! And if, as is impossible, you were not to notice it yourself, I should still be glad to suffer in the hope that my tears might prevent or atone for one single sin against faith. . . . Oh! Never have I realized so well how sweet and merciful the Lord really is.[32]

The paradox remains: "The road I follow is one that affords me no consolation, yet it brings every consolation."[33] Whatever name one gives to her condition, however one classifies it, it seems impossible to equate it with the true "night", where there is no room left even for these unfelt joys, certainties and hopes. What Thérèse loses is the feeling and triumphant sense of faith but never faith itself. And she is still able to recognize that the voices telling her that God and heaven are illusions constitute a temptation that she must resist with all her might. It is significant that she feels the temptation to be coming from outside herself: "If you only knew what horrid thoughts crowd in upon me all the time! My mind is gripped by the arguments of the worst materialists. O my Mother, has one to think such things, when loving the good God so dearly!"[34] "Some devilish spirit whispers to me: Are you sure that God loves you? Has he told? Is it not just the opinion of certain people who are trying to justify you before him?"[35] But there is no proof that this temptation ever went farther, that subjectively Thérèse actually ceased to believe;[36] the texts clearly contradict this. Admittedly, Thérèse's faith was clouded and became meaningless to her; it was never extinguished. Nor is there any evidence for Father Gottfried Madeline's view that Thérèse for eighteen months believed herself to be damned; what he cites as evidence is contradicted by the texts already quoted. Thérèse is ready *on earth* to do without God if it means that heaven will be thrown open to one sinner. That she was ready to abandon

[32] SS 213–14.
[33] S 139 (GC I:652).
[34] Pt 255.
[35] Pt 256.
[36] Cf. G 448 (ET 357–58).

heaven for the sake of sinners may be true but is unproven. Indeed, it is extremely unlikely, because no one has ever had a greater certainty of her heavenly vocation, and the idea that she might renounce it would stand in open contradiction to the whole of her life; it could only be a theatrical notion, devoid of any real meaning. Nor is there any substantial evidence that she was cast into the condition of the damned, in the passive night of the soul. Even her most extreme statement tells us the opposite: "I no longer believe in eternal life; it seems to me there is nothing beyond this mortal life. Everything is brought to an end. Love alone remains."[37] If love remains, and if Thérèse knows that love remains, that is not the dark night of the soul. Thérèse inappropriately cites the mystery in the Garden, where the Lord "enjoyed all the delights of the Trinity and still his agony was nonetheless cruel".[38] Apart from the fact that we cannot fully comprehend the Lord's example, it cannot be immediately equated with human experience. The real dark night of the soul, as described by John of the Cross and others, allows no room for *toutes les délices de la Trinité*. Thérèse's night remains a sort of "half-night" such as prevails in the "subterranean way where the sun does not shine. . . . I see nothing but a brightness half-veiled, the glow from the downcast eyes in the Face of my Spouse."[39]

Nor is it difficult to detect the reason why the darkening of Thérèse's faith *could* not become complete night. For her to have reached the dark night, God would have had to take her, so to speak, by violence. He would have had to prise her out of the position she had taken up since her "great miracle". The complete night involves complete solidarity with the sinners and the damned; it means identifying oneself with their lot and sharing their fate utterly. But how could Thérèse, knowing herself to be a saint, abandon herself unconditionally to the community of sinners? She would have to relinquish all her

---

[37] G 448, 452 (ET 358, 360).   [38] N 48 (LC 75).
[39] S 139 (GC I:652).

truth. She would have to give up the meaning of her theological existence. For her, this kind of community would be the self-destruction of her being and, in her eyes, the abandonment of her mission to holiness. God might ask it, perhaps, of other saints who are not always meditating on their own sanctity. But not from Thérèse. In its place, and possibly just as painful, he sends her temptations appropriate to the inchoate quality of her life. The need to start all over again from the place where she first began acts as a substitute for total desolation. "Oh, I can never manage it. I am like a child who is continually being offered a piece of cake; it is shown to him from a distance, but as soon as he comes nearer to take it, the hand withdraws it."[40]

Here, the fateful consequences of those early mistakes begin to make themselves felt: the mistake of acclaiming her as a saint immediately after the miracle and her confessor's mistake in declaring her sinless. They were seemingly harmless mistakes, but they now lead to a fateful consequence at this critical moment in her Christian life. Thérèse does everything she can to avoid this consequence, thinking her way around it, twisting and turning in an attempt to find a way out, yet finding herself trapped in the end. In other words, her Carmelite mission demands that she should identify herself with the community of sinners, but her self-conscious sanctity makes such solidarity impossible. She cannot even bring herself to say that she entered Carmel to do penance for her sins. She makes the ambitious declaration that is ultimately so questionable and bitterly harmful: "I chose an austere life to expiate, not my own sins, but the sins of others."[41] Thérèse is not a sinner. That is what she had been told, and she must believe it. And she needs to combine this belief with the humility demanded by the Scriptures. Thérèse, who can never meditate upon the gospel without automatically looking for the place it allots to her, quickly hits upon the solution. In the parable of the prodigal son, she adopts the role of the elder brother. It is the less brilliant role,

[40] N 12–13 (LC 47).   [41] S 349 (GC II:1134).

the humbler one, and yet it allows her to play a part in the drama of redemption without herself having to fall. "Like the father of the prodigal son speaking to his elder son, you say to me, 'All I have is yours.' So your words, O Jesus, belong to me, and I can use them to draw down the favors of the Heavenly Father upon the souls that have been given to me."[42] "God, who is infinitely just, deigns in his great mercy to pardon the faults of the prodigal son; must he not also be *just* toward me, who 'am always with him'?"[43] "But, after all, she is not the prodigal son; there is no point in Jesus making her a feast, since she is with him always."[44] Is this possible? Can a Christian really say such things? "After all, I am not the prodigal son." What must have been going on in Thérèse's heart when she wrote those words? How utterly she excludes herself from the community of the lost, who, like the lost son in the Bible, have to starve, to weep and to repent before embracing the Father! This glorious parable is told for sinners, and she does not share in it! In her sanctity, she contents herself with being the elder son! Nor will she be one of the lost sheep. "Our Lord chooses to leave in the desert the sheep that have not gone astray. What deep things that tells me! . . . He is *sure of them*, they cannot go astray now, for they are love's captives; so Jesus robs them of his visible presence to bring his consolations to sinners."[45] And, alas, she has no share in the consolations of sinners! All she can do is to seat herself "at the table of sinners" and, if not in her own, then "in the name of her brothers, say, 'Have pity on us, O Lord. . . .' "[46]

In Thérèse's wrestling with the mystery of saving grace, the decisive throw comes when she is faced with the figure of the Magdalen. Let us now turn to the Magdalen problem.

It is the first problem she confronts right at the beginning of her autobiography: the mystery of different vocations, and

[42] SS 255–56.
[43] SS 180.
[44] S 190 (GC II:795).
[45] Ibid.
[46] SS 212.

especially the contrast between saints converted from a sinful life and saints who did not need that conversion.

> I have long wondered why God has preferences, why all souls do not receive an equal measure of grace. I was astonished to see him lavishing extraordinary favors on such great sinners as Saint Paul and Saint Augustine, whom he so to speak forced to receive his grace. In reading the lives of the saints, I was surprised to see our Lord caressing certain privileged souls from the cradle to the grave, never allowing any obstacle in their way when coming to him, helping them with such favors that they were unable to stain the immaculate splendor of their baptismal robe.[47]

That is the prelude to the *Story of a Soul*; the dualism between converted saints and those not converted, between the Magdalen family and the Thérèse family. Her first attempt to resolve the dualism is actually less relevant to this contrast than to that between "great" and "little" saints: that since "it is the essence of love to abase itself",[48] if God had only produced "great saints", he would obviously not have abased himself sufficiently, would have shown insufficient love. It is true that indirectly this affords a solution to the Magdalen problem; both the forgiveness of sins and the preservation from sins are forms of God's love and self-abasement. But Thérèse's classical solution of the Magdalen problem does not come till later. It cannot be pretended that Thérèse, who is preserved from sin, stands above Mary Magdalen, who is converted from her sins. A way must be found of producing the opposite result, by which Thérèse's preservation from sin requires of her more humility—because it is a greater act of humility on God's part —than does the forgiveness of sins. Thérèse invents a parable about the doctor's son who trips over a stone and breaks a limb and is then skillfully cured by his father. "Doubtless this child has good reason to love his father. But let us take a different case. The father learns that there is a stone in his son's path and goes before him to clear it away, without anyone seeing him.

[47] SS 13–14.   [48] SS 14.

Certainly, this child, . . . if he should get to know all this, will love him all the more."[49] Without blinking an eye, Thérèse applies this case to herself: "Well now, I am this child, the object of a Father's loving foresight, who did not send his Son to call the *just* but *sinners*."[50] Our attention is roused—Thérèse is not just, but a sinner. What will she make of it? She explains: "He wishes me to *love* him, because he *has forgiven* me, not much, but *everything*. Without expecting me to love him much, like Mary Magdalen, he has made me understand how he has loved me with a marvelous, foreseeing love so that now I love him even unto *folly*."[51] Thérèse, therefore, has also been redeemed, but all her sins were forgiven before she had the time to commit any. The fact that she has not committed any is due to the all-forgiving grace that has saved her in advance, so that she has put sin behind her once and for all. Which explains why Thérèse can venture that most paradoxical of statements: "I know that Jesus has forgiven me more than Saint Mary Magdalen." "Do not believe", she writes to Bellière, "that it is humility that keeps me from realizing the good God's gifts. I know that 'he has done great things in me', and I sing it daily with joy. I know that one 'to whom more is forgiven should love more'."[52] "But, if Jesus could say of Magdalen 'that one loves more to whom more is forgiven', surely it may be said with even more reason when Jesus delivers from sins in *advance*!"[53] And so, in the competition between the lily and the rose, it is Thérèse who has won:[54] "I have heard it said that no pure soul has ever been more loving than a repentant one. Ah, how I should like to give the lie to that statement!"[55] So far everything appears to be in order; but Thérèse's theory has taken her near the edge at another point. She has expounded her own situation in such a way that one finds it difficult to distinguish between her and the immaculately conceived Mother

[49] SS 84.

[51] Ibid.

[53] S 164 (GC II:732).

[55] SS 84.

[50] Ibid.

[52] S 326 (GC II:1085).

[54] Ged 193.

of God. Thérèse is certainly saved, but through the advance working of grace that saved her before she fell. Which means that the word "forgiveness" can only be applied to Thérèse, as to Mary, in a peculiar sense. Thérèse herself did not see the danger she was courting. She so little recognized it that in her "Life of Mary" she connects herself very closely to Mary:

> I am your child, O beloved Mother!
> Do your virtues and love not belong to me as well?
> So, when the white Host descends into my heart,
> Jesus, your sweet Lamb, believes he is dwelling in you!
>
> You make me realize, O Queen of the elect,
> That it is not impossible to follow in your steps.
>
> You teach me to sing the divine praises,
> *To rejoice in Jesus, my Savior.*[56]

Ought we to say it? Thérèse—until her last months, anyway —never had a concrete notion of the reality of original sin and its effects in all who have once incurred it. Even though she is far from identifying herself with the Mother of God, she is unable to appreciate properly the infinite gulf that divides her from Mary. And perhaps this gulf is most clearly revealed in the fact that Mary is never self-conscious in her humility, whereas Thérèse is constantly thinking about her own sanctity, trying to understand it and give it a name. Mary is complete simplicity; Thérèse, after her sanctity has been openly proclaimed, is anything but simple. Her intensely conscious mind sets itself to explain all the secrets of her soul. Even assuming that she had never in fact offended God willingly, the Christian thing would have been to think herself (if it was at all necessary to

---

[56] Ged 427. Et je suis ton enfant, ô ma Mère chérie! / Tes vertus, ton amour ne sont-ils pas à moi? / Aussi, lorsqu'en mon coeur descend la blanche Hostie / Jésus, ton doux Agneau, croit reposer en toi!

Tu me le fais sentir, ce n'est pas impossible / De marcher sur tes pas, ô Reine des élus!

Tu m'apprends à chanter les divines louanges, / *A me glorifier en Jésus, mon Sauveur.*

keep thinking of herself) toward a deeper, unshakable solidarity with all the sinners in the world. At least that was the way of the virginal disciple, John, whom one may similarly imagine to have been preserved from sin rather than converted from it. He is the author of the statement that so perfectly establishes the community of salvation, which Thérèse seems never to have dwelt upon sufficiently: "If we say that we have no sin, we deceive ourselves, and the truth is not in us. If we confess our sins, he is faithful and just and will forgive us our sins and cleanse us from all iniquity. If we say that we have not sinned, we make him a liar, and his word is not in us" (1 Jn 1:8–10).

At one place, Thérèse writes: "I hasten to occupy, not the first place, but the last place. Rather than advance like the Pharisee, I repeat in complete confidence the prayer of the publican. Above all, I imitate the behavior of the Magdalen; her amazing, or rather her loving, audacity, which charms the heart of Jesus, also attracts my own."[57] The audacity she has in mind is illustrated by Thérèse in a poem where she speaks of the Magdalen's "holy audacity" in washing the Lord's feet with penitential tears and then rising to anoint the Holy Face. "And I— the nard with which I shall anoint your face, it is my love."[58] And, in her song "Jesus in Bethany" (where Thérèse identifies Mary Magdalen and Mary of Bethany):

> My incomparable goodness
> Will place the sinner
> And the unspotted soul
> Together on my heart![59]

Here it is the same love and the same audacity that she hymns. It is as though Thérèse is now taking a closer look at the sinner in order to study the meaning of love: her love as well as God's love. Everything that happens here must happen to her

---

[57] SS 258–59.   [58] Ged 381.
[59] Ged 494. Ma bonté sans égale / Placera le pécheur / Et l'âme virginale / Ensemble sur mon Coeur!

as well. She must learn it so as to be able to translate it into other contexts.

> You love Saint Augustine, Saint Magdalen, those souls to whom "many sins have been forgiven because they loved much"; I love them too, love their repentance and, above all . . . , their audacity in love! When I see the Magdalen come forward in the face of this crowd of guests and water with her tears the feet of her adored Master as she touches him for the first time, I feel that *her heart* realized the fathomless depths of love and mercy in *Jesus' heart*, realized, despite her sins, that that heart was ready not only to pardon her but actually to lavish on her the treasures of his divine intimacy and raise her to the highest summits of contemplation.[60]

From here, she could take one of two ways. The first way was to examine her own soul, if not for sins, then for "faults", to have them forgiven in a way that would have enabled her to share the Magdalen's experience. That is the way she indicates in her letters to the missionary she is trying to instruct and influence. "Ah, my dear little brother, since it has been given to me too to realize the love of Jesus' heart, I own that it has driven from my heart all fear! The remembrance of my faults humiliates me, leads me never to rely on *my* strength, which is only weakness; but the remembrance speaks to me still more of mercy and love."[61] But this way is not Thérèse's own. She takes the other way, as we see from the passage at the end of her second manuscript: "It is not because God, in his anticipating Mercy, has preserved my soul from mortal sin that I go to him with trust and love." "Ah! I feel that even if I had every imaginable sin on my conscience, I would go, with my heart broken by sorrow, and throw myself into the arms of Jesus. I know that he loves the prodigal son."[62] "People might think it is because I have been preserved from mortal sin that I have such trust in God. But you must realize, Mother, that even if

[60] S 348 (GC II:1133). [61] Ibid.
[62] SS 259.

I had committed every crime imaginable, I would still have the same trust; all these offenses would be like a drop of water falling into a glowing furnace."[63] So Thérèse discovers that her love could not be increased through the action of repentance. For both forms of love are directed toward divine mercy, both the virgin and the sinner are offerings to the same mercy. As Thérèse now understands this mercy, it is so much an immanent quality of God's that it is just as great and adorable even when it has no matter of sin to work upon. In the face of God's absolute mercy, the innocent and the sinner are equally favored. Ultimately that is the point of Jesus' teaching to the sisters at Bethany: Martha (whose role Thérèse must inevitably undertake) has received the word of Christ that the person who is forgiven more also loves more. It astonishes her, and she reflects that God has delivered her from danger in advance and so has more claim upon her loving gratitude. God recognizes that the pure soul is his love's masterpiece and must therefore love him beyond measure. But if she has attracted the divine glance in advance, if she possesses innocence, the Magdalen has humility for her compensation.[64]

And yet, Thérèse is not altogether satisfied with this somewhat smooth solution. True, she is convinced of her "innocence". That is what she has been told, and, out of obedience, she must believe it. She is so much in the grip of her innocence that it commands her immediate reactions. For instance, a novice says to her that she would rather be reproached when she has deserved it than when she is innocent. Thérèse answers: "For myself, I would rather be unjustly accused, because I having nothing to reproach myself for, and I offer it to the good God; and then I humble myself by thinking of how I am quite capable of doing what I am accused of."[65] Nothing could be more typical of Thérèse than this immediate reaction—innocent!—which she then goes on to bring within

the scope of grace by an act of humility. But the conflict between the harm wrought upon her and the mission entrusted
to her goes too deep to be so quickly smoothed away. A light
is fixed upon her that isolates her more than ever from the
community of sinners. She knows something of the curse at
which Nietzsche cried out in his hymn of night: "It is night
. . . alas, that I should be the light." She longs, not after sin, but
after sinners, seeking to return to communion with those from
whom she has been divided. To sink down forgotten into the
crowd of sinners—only that would bring her peace. "If I had
not been accepted in Carmel, I should have entered a refuge
to live there unknown and despised in the midst of the poor
penitents. It would have given me happiness to be regarded
as one of them; and I should have made myself an apostle to
my companions, telling them my thoughts about the mercy
of the good God. . . ." "But how would you have managed
to hide your innocence from your confessor?" "I would have
told him that I had made a general confession in the world and
been forbidden to repeat it."[66] What a miserable plan of escape,
which would never have worked and could only have led to
petty deceit!

Not until she comes to the very last turning of the road
do several streaks of sunlight penetrate through the mist. Her
ego collapses, and her mission bursts through. Much of what
Thérèse is made to say of herself sounds like an echo coming from afar. She goes on playing the role for which she has
been cast, the model of sanctity, the oracle who has to reply
to skillfully turned questions aimed at revealing her sanctity.
She does not wish to trouble her Sisters and overtax them by
showing them that altogether different side of herself that she
had come to accept. She is even, perhaps, too weary to throw
such old-established habits aside at the last minute. Still, the
truth breaks through. Not that Thérèse can quite bring the old
habits into line with her fresh awareness of sin, an awareness as

[66] H 265 (T 297).

fresh as it was in her childhood; the two attitudes remain side by side. How refreshing and moving, for instance, is her exclamation: "When I think of all the graces that the good God has bestowed upon me, I have to pull myself together so as not to be constantly weeping tears of gratitude. It seems to me that the tears I shed this morning were tears of perfect contrition."[67] Simple, poverty-stricken, unprepared words, still entangled in the plan of sanctity—but somehow, one cannot explain why, the thought of grace leads to tears of repentance. Nor is it quite enough that Thérèse should try to pray along with sinners and share the intentions of their prayers: "Your child, Lord, has recognized your divine light! She asks pardon for her brothers, and, for as long as you wish, your child is ready to eat the bread of sorrow. . . . But may she not say in her own name, and in the name of her brethren, 'Have pity on us, O Lord, for we are poor sinners'?"[68] This is not enough, because even here the distinction between herself and her guilty brethren is not entirely wiped out. But, at the end of Manuscript B, we eventually read: "It cries like a swallow, and, in its sweet song, it recounts in detail all its infidelities, thinking in the boldness of its full trust that it will acquire in even greater fullness the love of him who *came to call, not the just, but sinners*."[69] And she is also reported to have said: "I entrust God with my infidelities; I tell them to him in all their detail, and I think in my daring trust that I achieve all the more power over his heart and draw unto myself even more of his love who is come to call, not the just, but sinners."[70] But both these quotations are more an illustration of the little way than evidence of a deep sense of sin. And the scriptural text is more negatively directed against the self-righteous and the Pharisees rather than addressed positively to sinners. Even here, as always, Thérèse speaks only of "imperfections", "faults" and "infidelities", without even venturing to use the word "sin" of herself.

---

[67] N 138 (LC 147).   [68] SS 212.
[69] SS 198–99.   [70] Esprit 144 (G 423–24 [ET 339]).

But there are two short references that seem absolutely decisive. The first was on the morning of August 12, 1897, when the priest was praying the *Confiteor* as she was preparing to make her Communion. "There I saw our Lord quite near, ready to give himself to me. And this Confession seemed to me a most necessary humiliation. 'I confess to God, to the Blessed Virgin Mary and to all the saints that I have sinned exceedingly.' Oh, yes, I said to myself, it is good that prayers should be offered for my forgiveness. And particularly to God and all the saints. Like the publican, I felt myself to be a great sinner."[71] At last, a month before her death, she feels herself a sinner! Her subsequent reflections upon this experience during the *Confiteor* (if the report is genuine) half takes back what she had said. "How remarkable that I should feel like that at the *Confiteor*. I presume it was on account of being so poorly. I felt so miserable." In any case, whatever we make of this report, she received the grace of repentance for a moment. The other reference is from the evidence of Thérèse's novice mistress, who assures us that Thérèse once burst into tears at hearing the words of Scripture: "No one knows whether he is worthy of love or hatred." One would be glad to believe that at this point she encountered the God of the Old Testament, the God of the burning bush and the God of Mount Horeb, before whom Job writhes and in whose sight the very angels are not pure.

But, having in mind this whole phase of her development, one is less surprised that Thérèse should not have known the dark night. We do not know what her lot would have been if her sense of sin had not been warped and if she had not suffered artificial isolation through misleading talk about sanctity. We do not know to what extent God in his providence adapts his plans to human follies and distributes and somehow guides his commissions in an infralapsarian manner. Thérèse is a saint. That means she fulfilled her mission. The heart of this mission is not to be found at the point where the shadows could

[71] N 137 (LC 147).

fall upon anything essential; despite human weakness, the integrity of her mission remains. What dimensions it would have assumed without these weaknesses is beyond our knowing.

⚜

It is Thérèse's task to proclaim God's mercy and to urge men to boundless, ever stronger trust in God's grace. This she has experienced, this her life has manifested, and her existence is proof of the truth of her theology. She had never encountered the God of strict justice. It is as though she did not know him. And, though she knows from hearsay that he exists, she has no means of realizing this truth, because she uses her own notions as the measure of everything. So this truth remains empty and abstract to her. Consequently one can say that hell has no place in Thérèse's vision of the world. It may form part of the Creed and be a truth of faith that she accepts implicitly, as she believes everything that is of faith. But this does not make it a vital truth for her. Preserved from sin, she stands outside all relationship with hell.

On the first few pages of her biography, she tells of the dream in which she saw two little devils dancing on a barrel, although they had heavy chains around their feet.

> All of a sudden, they cast fiery glances at me and at the same moment appeared to be more frightened than I was, for they jumped from the barrel and went to hide in the laundry, which was just opposite. Discovering that they were so cowardly, I wanted to know what they were going to do, and I moved toward the window. The poor little devils were there, running across the tables and not knowing how to escape my gaze. From time to time, they came nearer and peered through the windows to see if I was still there, and, seeing me there, they began running like madmen.[72]

[72] SS 28.

That is Thérèse's first encounter with elemental evil—"the poor little devils". And she herself draws the lesson from it: "The good God intended to show me that a soul in a state of grace has nothing to fear from evil spirits, who are such cowards that they flee from the glance of a child." From that moment, hell holds no fears for her. However she tries, she cannot screw up any fear of the devil: "Must I really be frightened of the devil? I think not, because everything I do is under obedience."[73] Even more emphatically, she excludes hell altogether from her little way; she is asked: "You do not, then, share the feelings of that hermit who said, 'Though I should have spent long years doing penance, so long as a quarter of an hour remained, so long as I had a breath of life, I should be frightened of being damned'?" "No, I cannot share this fear, I am too little to get myself damned. *Little children do not get damned.*"[74] She is certain of her ultimate safety; the saints protect her. "These vultures are the demons whom the little bird does not fear, for it is not destined to become their prey but the prey of the Eagle."[75] Hell only shows up in her vision of the world when *others* seem in danger of going there. It is simply that *from which* souls must be saved. "I felt myself consumed with a thirst for souls . . . , and I burned with the desire to snatch sinners from the eternal flames."[76] And when her first experiment—with Pranzini—succeeds, she is confirmed in her convictions. Here nothing can frighten her; she advances boldly, unflinching, and strides untouched through the flames. She goes so far as to wish to bear her gospel of love into the center of hell. "One evening, when I did not know how to express my love to Jesus or tell him how much I desired that he be loved and glorified everywhere, I was thinking of how not a single act of love would ever arise from hell. Then I said to God that to please him I would gladly be plunged into hell so that he might be loved eternally in that place of blas-

[73] G 486 (ET 387).   [74] H 263 (T 295).
[75] SS 199.   [76] SS 99.

phemy.''[77] But, as soon as she says it, Thérèse realizes that she is simply experimenting with ideas. "That could never be to his glory, since he desires only our happiness; but a person in love feels the desire to say a thousand foolish things."[78] At the same time, Thérèse's trust in God's mercy is so unlimited, and she is so completely obsessed with this attribute of God, the prism through which she sees all the others, that even the possibility of a sinner being lost is unreal to her. "*Every* soul will require pardon" are the words she puts into the mouth of the child Jesus.[79] It was pride that cast Lucifer into hell; man, too, fell after him, "but he was not abandoned there, without help. The eternal Word, the likeness of the Father, clothed himself in poor humanity, and, by his profound humility, the *whole of creation* was born again."[80]

Thérèse's world remains immune from the effects of elemental evil—a fact that confirms our opinion that her night of the soul never reached the dimensions of the night of the Cross, that point where the Son is brought face to face with the sinner's absolute abandonment by God. In a sense, Thérèse's little way leaves her at the beginning of the Passion; it confines her to the Mount of Olives. That is *her* mystery, which she loves and reverently worships; she herself describes it as the essence, the heart of her devotion. Once more, it is very difficult to say whether she did not go a step farther during the last weeks of all or to decide the point on the way of suffering to which her terrible last agony took her. But she drinks in full measure the chalice for which she had asked: "The chalice is full to overflowing! No. I would never have believed that it was possible to suffer so much. I cannot explain it except by my boundless desire to save souls. . . ."[81] "If this is but the death agony, what then will death be like? . . . But the good God will not abandon me. He has never abandoned me."[82] And now she has taken

[77] SS 112.
[78] Ibid.
[79] Ged 484.
[80] Ged 449.
[81] H 253 (T 238–39).
[82] N 192 (LC 204–5).

a step farther. "One morning during thanksgiving I felt, as it were, the agonies of death. . . ."[83] "I am afraid of being afraid of death. I said to myself with some surprise: What then is this mysterious separation of soul and body? It's my first experience of this. . . ."[84] And how the powers of darkness crowd in upon her—the "evil snakes" that "hiss in her ear".[85] She asks for her bed to be sprinkled with holy water: "The devil is slithering around me, I do not see him, but I feel him, he torments me, holds me in an iron grip and prevents me from feeling the slightest alleviation. He increases my torments, to tempt me to despair. . . . I believe the devil has sought permission of God to inflict the utmost suffering upon me, in order that I should give in, to lose my patience and my faith."[86] She feels to be "as if in Purgatory".[87] She is seriously frightened of losing her reason, remembering her father's suffering, perhaps. She asks the Mother of God to take her head in her hands, so that she can stand it.[88] She says she is not surprised that "so many unbelievers commit suicide".[89] More and more she is deprived of this world's air, the air for herself. "The air of earth is withdrawn from me! When will the good God grant me the air of heaven?"[90] No sooner, Thérèse, than the moment all air is withdrawn from yourself! With this suffering, her plans of love are finally realized: "I, who have desired every form of martyrdom for myself—ah, a person has to be plunged into it to know what it means!"[91] But, all alone, she is being taken at her word in her longing for God alone; her plunge into the "fiery abyss"; her longing to burst forever the shell of sanctity with which she had been encrusted. Now she will live in the sanctity of God. "Is it too much to ask one to close one's eyes? Not to struggle with the chimeras of the night?"[92] If this soul had never had its veil drawn aside, it would have been

[83] N 27–28 (LC 56).
[84] N 176 (LC 188).
[85] N 32 (LC 62).
[86] G 470 (ET 375–76).
[87] N 97 (LC 117).
[88] N 144 (LC 154).
[89] G 469 (ET 374).
[90] N 188 (LC 200–201).
[91] 2 P 828 (G 469 [ET 374]).
[92] S 323 (GC II:1033).

less painfully separated from "that dark despot, the self". But happiness came at last with death, bringing that which mortals cannot themselves achieve: surrender.

CHRONOLOGY

1873   *January 2*: Marie-Françoise-Thérèse born in Alençon and baptized on January 4.

1877   *August 28*: Her mother dies.
August 29: Thérèse chooses Pauline as her second mother.
November 15: Moved to Lisieux, under the direction of Mr. Guérin.

1879   Late in the year, or at the beginning of 1880, first Confession.

1879   (or 1880): The prophetic vision about her father's later illness.

1881   *October 3*: Thérèse enrolls at the Convent School of the Benedictine Abbey as a half-time boarder.

1882   *October 2*: Pauline enters the Carmelite Monastery at Lisieux.
Around the end of the year: The beginning of her persistent headaches.

1883   *March 25, Easter*: Thérèse becomes ill while her father and two older sisters are away.
May 13, Pentecost: The smile of the Blessed Virgin and miraculous healing.

1884   *May 8*: Thérèse receives her First Communion at the Abbey. Sister Agnes of Jesus makes her Profession at the Carmel.
June 14: Confirmed by Msgr. Hugonin, Bishop of Bayeux.

1885 *May 17–21*: During retreat days, in preparation for her second Holy Communion, the beginning of the "terrible sickness of scrupulosity".

1886 *May 31*: She is received in the Abbey as a child of Mary.

October 7: Léonie enters the Convent of the Poor Clares in Alençon for the first time.

October 15: Marie enters the Carmelite Monastery of Lisieux.

End of October: Through the intercession of her "little brother in heaven", Thérèse is healed of her scruples.

December 25: "The Christmas conversion".

1887 *May 29, Pentecost Sunday*: Thérèse asks her father's permission to enter the Carmelite Order.

September 1: She reads the report of Pranzini's execution in the newspaper *La Croix*.

October 31: She visits Msgr. Hugonin to ask permission to enter the Carmelite Order.

November 4–20: Trip to Rome.

December 28: Msgr. Hugonin allows Mother Marie de Gonzague to give an affirmative answer. Nevertheless, her entry is delayed until after Lent.

1888 *April 9*: Thérèse enters the Carmelite Monastery at Lisieux.

May 23: Sister Marie of the Sacred Heart makes her Profession.

June 23: Mr. Martin is missing for four days.

1889 *January 10*: Thérèse receives the habit, under the direction of Bishop Hugonin.

February 12: Mr. Martin is placed in an insane asylum at Caen.

1890 *September 8*: Profession.

September 24: Veiling ceremony.

1891 *October 8–15*: Exercises, conducted by Father Alexis Prou, which strengthen Thérèse on her path.

December 5: Death of the Reverend Mother Geneviève of Saint Teresa, foundress of the Carmelite Monastery of Lisieux.

End of December: Beginning of the influenza epidemic. Thérèse receives permission to have daily Holy Communion.

1893 *February 20*: Sister Agnes of Jesus becomes Prioress. Shortly thereafter, Thérèse is assigned to assist Mother Marie de Gonzague in training the novices.

1894 *July 29*: Death of her father.

September 14: Céline enters the Carmelite Monastery of Lisieux.

End of December: Mother Agnes of Jesus assigns Thérèse the task of writing down her childhood memories.

1895 *June 9, Feast of the Holy Trinity*: Thérèse consecrates herself as an offering to God's merciful love.

June 11: Consecration together with Céline.

October 16 or 17: Beginning of the correspondence with the future White Father, Maurice-Barthélemy Bellière.

1896 *January 20*: Thérèse turns in the notebook containing her childhood memories to Mother Agnes of Jesus (Manuscript A).

February 24: Céline's Profession; she now becomes Sister Geneviève of Saint Teresa.

March 21: Mother Marie de Gonzague is reelected Prioress. She confirms Thérèse in her office with the novices.

April 2–3, on the eve of Good Friday: First cough accompanied by bleeding.

April 5, Easter: The attacks on her faith begin.

May 10: Dream concerning Venerable Anne of Jesus.

May 30: Mother Marie de Gonzague assigns Thérèse a second spiritual brother: Father Adolph Roulland of the Foreign Missions.

September 13–16: Letter to Sister Marie of the Sacred Heart (Manuscript B).

1897   *April 6*: Mother Agnes of Jesus starts to write down Thérèse's last words.

June 3: Mother Marie de Gonzague assigns Thérèse the task of continuing her memoirs (Manuscript C).

July 8: Thérèse exchanges her cell for the infirmary.

July 30: Extreme Unction.

August 19: Last Holy Communion.

September 30: Thérèse dies at about 7:20 in the evening.

Elizabeth of the Trinity

A WORD ABOUT
THIS TRANSLATION

I N HIS FOREWORD, Father von Balthasar apologizes for the
Sprödigkeit of his method—using one of those delightful-
sounding German words that are difficult to render into English. Sometimes translated as "dryness", it carries here the
meaning of "lack of spice". Yet von Balthasar's disclaimer dis-
sembles. As he notes in the same foreword, Elizabeth of the
Trinity's French was not particularly vivid and forceful. Rightly
or wrongly, he makes it less *spröde* in translation than it was
in French, using a more vivid and vigorous German. I have
tried to reflect his word choice, rather than simply inserting
the more conventional style of the existing English translations of Elizabeth's writings. As an example, one might study
the first paragraph of von Balthasar's translation of Elizabeth's
famous prayer to the Trinity at the end of this work. Where
the most recent English translation has "May nothing trouble my peace or make me leave you" (CW 183), Father von
Balthasar writes: "Nichts vermöge meinen Frieden zu stören,
mich herauszuverlocken aus Dir." He has deliberately used the
vivid word *herausverlocken* ("entice", even "seduce") for the
rather colorless "me faire sortir de vous" of the original. The
anonymous Benedictine translator of Father Philipon's study
of Elizabeth's writings translates this phrase as follows: "May
nothing disturb my peace or draw me out of Thee" (53–54),
which corresponds to von Balthasar's own more mundane rendering in the chapter on "Predestination" (*heraustreten*, that is,
"to depart from", p. 377 in the third German edition) and
near the end of the chapter on "Limitlessness" (p. 407 in the
German). A second example comes from the third paragraph
of "Praise of Glory", where the French original has "Une âme
qui permet ainsi à l'Etre divin de rassasier en elle son besoin de

communiquer tout ce qu'il est et tout ce qu'il a, . . ." Father von Balthasar translates *rassasier* (to satiate) as *Stillung gewähren* ("Eine Seele, die dem göttlichen Wesen die Stillung seiner Sehnsucht gewährt"), emphasizing the soul's granting satiation—hinting at the image of a mother suckling her child and thus slightly modifying Elizabeth's original image of the divine Being satiating his yearning to impart himself. Earlier (p. 442 of the German original, near the beginning of the chapter on "Praise"), von Balthasar uses the verb *stillen* to translate this passage—the use of a second verb relativizes the role played by "granting" (*gewähren*) in the above-mentioned passage. In this latter instance, instead of granting *satiation* (noun), the soul permits God *to satiate* (verb) his hunger—but the image of the mother's breast is still present in the background. Another example, in a direct quotation from Scripture, further illustrates von Balthasar's forceful choice of words: early in section II of the chapter on "Predestination", he translates a phrase from John 4:14 as "springing up into eternal life" as *emporsprudelt*, literally, "bubbling up" (the Douai-Reims version has "springing up"; the Vulgate has *salientis*).

One might also note the instances where he translates the same words of Elizabeth at two different places. In such cases he does not reach back to repeat his earlier translation; rather he retranslates as the moment seems to require. See the passages at the beginning and end of the chapter on "Adoration" (pp. 420 and 435 in the German), where he translates a quotation from p. 73 of *Écrits spirituels* [ET 55]).

The reader should thus keep in mind that it is Hans Urs von Balthasar's words through which Elizabeth of the Trinity speaks, both in his German text and, to the best of this translator's ability, in the present translation of his rendering. I have, however, occasionally departed from one feature of von Balthasar's German, which was found in medieval English but is uncommon in modern English: the use of synonymous and parallel nouns or verbs as a literary device. In some instances, where these doublings are strictly synonymous, they have been reduced to a single word in order to achieve a more readable English idiom.

Psalm numbers are given first according to the Vulgate (Septuagint) numbering. This translation retains von Balthasar's constant use of the historical present tense as a reminder that Elizabeth and other voices from the past are voices in the present. Several typographical errors in the German edition's references to Elizabeth's *Écrits spirituels* have been silently corrected.

DENNIS D. MARTIN
NOVEMBER 9, 1989

ABBREVIATIONS

Where only page numbers are given = *Écrits spirituels d'Elisabeth de la Trinité. Lettres, retraites et inédits*, prepared by R. P. Philipon, O.P. (Paris: Éditions du Seuil, 1949). [English translation: Sister Elizabeth of the Trinity, *Spiritual Writings: Letters, Retreats, and Unpublished Notes* (New York: P. J. Kenedy and Sons, 1962)].

S   The Carmel of Dijon, *La Servante de Dieu Elisabeth de la Trinité, 1880–1906: Souvenirs* (Paris: Éditions St.-Paul, n.d.). [Partial English translation: *Reminiscences of Sister Elizabeth of the Trinity, Servant of God*, translated by a Benedictine of Stanbrook Abbey (Westminster, Md.: Newman Press, 1952; originally published London, 1913)].

P   Marie Michel Philipon, O.P., *La Doctrine spirituelle de Soeur Elisabeth de la Trinité*, with preface by R. P. Garrigou-Lagrange and numerous unpublished documents (Paris: Desclée de Brouwer, 1958). [English translation by a Benedictine of Stanbrook Abbey as *The Spiritual Doctrine of Sister Elizabeth of the Trinity* (Westminster, Md.: Newman Press, 1947)]. Cited according to the 4th French edition.

CW   Élisabeth de la Trinité, *J'ai trouvé Dieu: Oeuvre complètes*, ed. by Conrad De Meester, O.C.D. (Paris: Editions du Cerf, 1979–1980). [English translation: Elizabeth of the Trinity, *The Complete Works* (Washington: ICS Publications, 1984–)]. Citations will be to the page number of the first volume of the English translation and to the document number in the second and third volumes

(II = vol. 1b of the French edition; III = vol. 2 of the French edition).

ET   English translation of work cited.

FOREWORD TO THE
SECOND EDITION (1970)

A N ACCOUNT OF THE SPIRITUAL MISSION of Elizabeth of the Trinity, the young Carmelite of Dijon (1880–1906), complements and extends the interpretation of Thérèse of Lisieux's mission. Because we wish to direct the reader's attention entirely to the teaching of Elizabeth of the Trinity, we make no effort here to repeat the biographical material presented in the *Souvenirs* and in the account by Father Philipon. The most important dates may be found in the "Chronology" at the end of this book. Even though we still have no critical edition of Elizabeth's writings,[1] they are so clear and their content so well shaped that corrections and additions would bring no significant surprises to light. The purpose of the present work is to let her fundamental insights speak for themselves, to spread them out in a clarifying mosaic of texts. Only at the edges—and then gingerly—will the framework be expanded theologically. We can only ask the reader's indulgence for the missing spice that biographical anecdotes and sweeping synthesis might have added. Omitting them seemed the best way to do justice to the explicitly doctrinal mission of Elizabeth of the Trinity. Only slight changes have been made to the text of the first edition.

---

[1] [Publication of the critical French edition was completed in 1980. See the preceding bibliographical abbreviations—TRANS.]

INTRODUCTION

I N RECENT TIMES no religious order has been granted such clear graces for mission as has the Carmelite Order. Such divine favors admonish us and counter recent trends in the world and the Church. In an era of churchly projects and campaigns, they call us back to the one thing necessary, to contemplation, without considering whether it will succeed or be effective. In an age of psychology, we are called back to anonymity, not merely to the anonymity of the veil but deeper into pure liturgical adoration of God for his own sake, where the worshippers seem to be indistinguishable from each other. In an age of emphasis on religious personality, we are called back into the life of a supernatural mission, a mission for which each personal ability and preference can at most serve as material to be used, a mission that demands a readiness to sacrifice one's entire nature.

The well of pure contemplation, which is the innermost source and mover of all life in the Church, must either be kept clean or be restored to purity. Great women of prayer like Antoinette de Geuser, Elizabeth of the Trinity, Josefa Menendez and Edith Stein now take their places beside Thérèse of Lisieux and Charles de Foucauld. The Carmelite nuns among this group carry out a dual commission, oriented first toward the Carmelite life itself but also, through Carmel, toward the entire Church.[1] The Carmel portion of this mission focuses on a place of singleminded adoration without respect of persons—even if the person be so venerable as the great Mother Teresa [of Avila]. Unlike the theorists of mystical theology outside the Order, little Thérèse [of Lisieux] and, even more, her

---

[1] Members of various religious orders encouraged and inspired Elizabeth, especially Jesuits, Benedictines (Dom Vandeur's commentary on prayer, *O Mon Dieu: Trinité que j'adore* [1923]) and Dominicans, to say nothing of secular clergy. A wide spectrum from among the religious orders have given testimony of her mission. See P 19 (ET 12–13).

three younger sisters in religion know how to move relatively quickly past the person of the great reformer of the Order to focus on what she had in mind. In this they avoid what may be the greatest danger of modern Carmel: the temptation to focus too much on the psychology of the religious and mystical personality. Prevented from entering the Order, Antoinette de Geuser was unable to give full measure in this regard. Edith Stein, who perhaps lived out the mission in its greatest purity, was probably too closely tied—against her better inclinations —to the realm of analytical thought. Elizabeth of the Trinity, however, was able to extend with precision a trajectory stemming from her older sister of Lisieux.

Much has been written about these two missions, which run in both parallel and countervailing directions, supplementing and separating each other. Seven years younger than Thérèse, Elizabeth outlived her by nine years and thus was able to read Thérèse's obituary and autobiography and to make their teachings part of her own life. She did this with an inimitable and lively power of assimilation that immediately grasped what was essential and shaped it to her own form so as to leave not the slightest visible joint, indeed, in such a way that her own shape revealed its clarity and contours even more compellingly. Not for a moment was Elizabeth distracted by Thérèse. Thérèse pointed more exactly to a few things that Elizabeth had known in a general way. One might say that Elizabeth made more definite certain background aspects only indistinctly sketched out in Thérèse's life and work. Indeed Elizabeth may have more firmly integrated into the pure form of Carmel certain Franciscan tendencies in Thérèse (overflowing gifts of heaven, showers of roses).

Thérèse is an expansive, unique person who makes everything she touches Christian and humanly lovable. Elizabeth's world is narrow and lofty, her humanness is more pale and less compelling by itself. Only in its very retreat behind ideas embraced with absolute passion does her humanness gain force. Her phrasing is more conventional, and she lacks access to the images and metaphors that flow richly for Thérèse. Her language fades rather like a shadow flees before the illuminating dawn of the single all-saying, all-filling Holy Word. Yet the fragility of the external frame cannot hide the incomprehensible power of the inner form: perhaps to a greater degree than that of Thérèse, the structure of Elizabeth's cosmology [Weltbild], what one might call her theological content and pattern of thinking, has an integrated, flawless texture. The narrow heights require stern discipline: Elizabeth thinks only the single necessary thought for which she has space. For the sake of its purity, she unflinchingly leaves aside everything not immediately relevant, even if that means dropping entire segments of the gospel. Her world is the consummate vision as transmitted by Paul's hidden revelation, the "mystery", and by John's logos and apocalypse. The Synoptic Gospels and the Old Testament lie embedded as silent presuppositions within these. If Joachim of Flora's (d. 1202) "gospel of Spirit" ever applied to anyone, it would fit here: more than under the mystery of the Trinity, Elizabeth stands under the shadow of the Holy Spirit and his final illumination of the mystery of incarnation and redemption, his conclusive glorification of the Trinity's redemptive history of revelation.

Yet even here Elizabeth does not lose herself in the breadth and expanse of the Pauline world. Bypassing the colorful life of his contacts with the churches, his guidance and analysis, she places herself once and for all firmly in the center of his contemplative gaze. As a Carmelite, she places herself immovably, like Mary of Bethany, at the feet of the Lord; yet not at the feet of the incarnate Lord, receiving divine words from his human mouth like Francis of Assisi or even the great Teresa of Jesus. Instead she sits at the feet of the risen and glorified Kyrios [Lord], whom Paul "no longer regarded from a human point of view" (2 Cor 5:16), saying indeed that "the Lord is the Spirit" (2 Cor 3:17). Unblinking and unblinded, she gazes into the central light as it flares up into the "great mystery" proclaimed by the letter to the Ephesians. Her steady perseverance is rewarded by increasingly clearer, less distorted, bolder revelation. Elizabeth is the one who stays, who does not move on. She stays even when she or any other person can no longer see how the mystery can fail to contradict itself. Far from pointing out contradiction, taking nothing away from the unity of what she has seen and believed, she prefers to fall silent, postponing to the next world the vision of reconcilability.

She does not perceive herself to be a theologian. In no sense is it her task to speculate or construct theories out of revealed concepts. Her power lies in reflecting (*speculari*), in gazing (*theōrein*), in glimpsing the depths of the simple word. These glimpses fully satisfy her, for she could never fully chart the depths of the word by taking soundings. She permits the word to stand, and, as she adores, its unforeseen dimensions reveal themselves. At most she notes parallel words[2] or joins them to each other in a chain[3] or translates the meaning of the Old Testament, especially the Psalms, into the conceptual world of the New Testament.[4] Her exegetical efforts remain shy and scarcely developed. She desires, not theology, but adoration; yet adoration of the word in its revealed character. This requires contemplation of the word, contemplation born of "the mind of God" as it is implanted in the believer.[5] Her mission is not narrowly doctrinal, rather, corresponding to her Carmelite existence, it is a mission of life, a mission realized in silence, prayer and suffering. This part of her mission remains invisible, as is true of all missions in the Church, especially the contemplative ones, whose real fruit remains hidden under God's guidance and can never be described even in outline here on earth. Still, in some missions, especially in the active ones, a portion (which can never be sharply distinguished from the other, invisible, part) is outwardly visible. In some instances this occurs even with contemplative callings: when testimony of hidden life in God must be given. Elizabeth belongs to those missions that lie pre-

---

[2] 211 (ET 157); CW I:143.   [3] E.g., 224f. (ET 166f.); CW I:151f.
[4] E.g., 220f. (ET 163f.); CW I:149.   [5] 223 (ET 166); CW I:151.

cisely on the line between visible and invisible. Her calling is found in an invisibility of contemplation that points to a visible activity. A certain visibility of thought can point to this invisibility of life, to thought's origin, possibility and end. Thus Elizabeth's mission is located in the invisibility of the transcendent world toward which the vapor trail of existence directs all eyes even as it visibly disappears in the dusk.

Although every strictly contemplative life in a general sense is a testimony to the invisible, there are still explicit commissions of word and formulation. It is to these that Elizabeth's belongs. The objection that might be raised here—the paucity of her own ideas, her firm dependence on other people's spirituality—misses the decisive point. For in every expression of her mission there rings forth something that can be found in none of her sources, no matter how much richer and more complex they may be. The narrow heights, that is, her conscious or unconscious training and trimming of thoughts, are born, not of a cramped intellect or limited power of comprehension, but of an almost exaggerated concentration on her goal. The outcome is a work of the highest spiritual, even theological, style that has been achieved, not by outward compression, but rather by inward growth and shaping. All of this glows with a boldness that one searches for in vain among her theologically more sophisticated sources of inspiration: it partakes of a splendid simplicity and, yes, one-sidedness. Unerringly the one thing necessary is rooted to the spot until it becomes apparent that this one thing was all things, the pearl that justifies giving up everything else. Whatever a comparison of Elizabeth's writings with unpublished papers of Father Vallée may yet reveal —perhaps a greater influence than has been visible so far—it cannot detract from that unique quality of her spiritual teaching that defies analysis: its source in a genuine and grace-filled commission.

Having established this much, several misgivings arise, similar to those raised by the mission emanating from Lisieux. We should not simply ignore them. We must ask, in a different manner than with Thérèse, about Elizabeth's spiritual authenticity and its opposite, an inner superficiality that nearly always leads to outward *kitsch*. It is not a matter of the misfortunes that made Thérèse's temporary artificiality nearly inevitable. Elizabeth's youth followed the most normal patterns imaginable: we see few if any extraordinary graces of prayer, and no imprudent word from a confessor or spiritual director seems ever to have warped anything about her. Yet that which she herself would have characterized as her chief danger, indeed her chief flaw—*la sensibilité*—not only caused her much trouble but also left its imprint in many ways on her conduct of her mission. It takes nothing away from Elizabeth's stature to have mentioned this danger. In large part she came to terms with it, and, through persistent effort and the work of grace in prayer and suffering, what was inauthentic about her was nearly completely consumed and cast off. That she chose the right path is clear from the way an idea triumphed in her life, even more so by the way God took her seriously, took her at her word in the name she chose for herself. For her, *sensibilité* meant for her primarily a prickly sensitiveness, the soul's vulnerability in regard to all things of this world. This carried a dual danger: on the one hand, a certain high-strung sensitiveness with a sublimating tendency to become lost in thoughts and feelings; on the other hand, a vulnerability toward everything worldly, or, as her religious commitment became dominant in her life, an almost passionate abandonment of everything worldly. Her inclination toward the transcendent and her determined wish never to settle down in this world, to walk on tiptoes on this earth, if not to hover over it—these tendencies cannot simply be attributed to "grace". Rather, they were based in her "nature" and were, for the most part, indifferent or even opposed to her mission and to grace. Christianity is neither flight from the world nor high-strung sublimation; the Son of God, his Mother and his apostles stood firmly on earth, courageously accepted their commission from God to go into the world and lived the other world in this world.

The two powerful Christian figures who marked off Elizabeth's path and gave her spiritual help and strength both lived in an exemplary balance of nature and grace, worldly realism and heavenly idealism. These were the first prioress at Dijon, whom she knew before she entered the monastery, Marie of Jesus, and the person who really formed her spiritual perception of the world, Father Vallée.[6]

In her writings and talks, Marie of Jesus appears as a strong woman who draws her power from the gospel and the liturgy; she is intelligent and kind. In keeping with her office as prioress and novice mistress, her teaching, although the same as Elizabeth's in many ways, is more varied and yet more balanced than that of the young nun. Although it was she who steered Elizabeth toward Carmel and although her visit with Elizabeth three months before Elizabeth's death brought much edification to Marie of Jesus, the interior paths followed by the two women still remained essentially divergent.[7]

In a decisive conversation (spring 1900), Father Vallée clarified for Elizabeth the nature of interior graces and taught her about the indwelling of the Holy Trinity in the soul of the recipient of grace. After she had entered the convent, he once more provided integrated teaching during a retreat in October 1902. Elizabeth found herself then in the grip of intense struggles that Father Vallée could not comprehend. He did not see her again until shortly before her death. A fiery preacher, zealous for the purity of contemplative ideals in monastic communities and a powerful man of prayer, Father Vallée did not have an exceptional intellect. In his published lectures on the soul of Christ (which are not identical with what Elizabeth would have heard), he reveals a fine balance between the down-

---

[6] Alongside these one might mention Mother Germaine of Jesus, who trained and strengthened Elizabeth as a novice, repressing her sensitivity. Marie of Jesus had already left the Dijon Carmel by the time Elizabeth entered and thus had no personal role in her formation.

[7] See Marie de Jésus, O.C.D., *Gestalt und Lehre, Nach der Chronik des Karmels von Paray-le-Monial*, trans. by E. Berbuir (Düsseldorf: Patmos, 1951).

to-earth Jesus of the Synoptic Gospels and the Christ of the Pauline and Johannine writings, a balance thoroughly interpenetrated with Thomistic concerns. With precise alternation, his lecture series deals first with a theme from the earthly life of the Lord and then with one from speculative Christology. In the second series (speculative Christology), significant parallels to the thought of Elizabeth are visible, except that she ignores completely the Thomistic aspects, retaining only the Pauline-Johannine perspective. From the first series (the Synoptic Jesus), she has, for all practical purposes, taken nothing. Yet there is more to the relationship. Vallée's comments are explicitly christocentric. With all his strength, he places the God-Man in the center, shows him to be the Lord of the world and the source of all God's gifts of grace. He carefully works out the relationship of the human and divine natures, emphasizing the inner experiences of the human nature insofar as they remain open to the divine in all their natural and obedient capacities. With awe, he attempts to think his way into this world of inner experience, and out of it he draws all the experiences of the saints—he bases all "life in the presence of God" upon the christological presence of the divine nature in the human. He gives attention to the origin of the word of Christ in the Father's gaze, he inquires after the manner in which the Son knows us, works in us and heads the various types of members of his body. Vallée's spirituality is centered in the pivotal concept of Thomas Aquinas: the humanity of Christ as the center of creation, the head of the body, the *instrumentum conjunctum*, the keystone of all gifts of grace.

None of this is central for Elizabeth. Although her love for the incarnate Lord, for Mary and the saints, for the Church and sacraments, is fully Catholic, she places her emphasis elsewhere. She shifts to the center aspects of Christian doctrine that are present but not highlighted in Father Vallée's work. One can document many, perhaps most, of Elizabeth's essential insights in Vallée, but what was a note, formula, term or word in his work becomes an expanded world in hers. She has taken single stones from Vallée and built with them a finished house whose originality is obvious at a glance. Of course, in the Church it is difficult to delineate sharply one doctrinal mission from another. Charismatic, literary and human influences weave back and forth, and this is as God would have it. But each mission that leaves a deep impress has its own center, and the contents of Christian doctrine appear each time, as in a kaleidoscope, in a clearly distinguishable pattern.

The foregoing discussion of Elizabeth's *sensibilité* was necessary because her emphatic "transcendence" separates her from those who inspired and influenced her and gives her a completely different center of gravity. The most delicate question in this regard is the extent to which this "transcendence" is part of her commission and the degree to which it grows out of her sensitive nature, which so easily lost itself in the depths of prayer. This characteristic remained to the end, and, in her final suffering, she had much more difficulty finding the path to complete indifference than Thérèse of Lisieux had had. Desiring to die, with every inch of her being she strained to be set free and to be with Christ, to be off and away into the bottomless abyss of God! She understood it to be her apostolate to infect as many as possible with an immense longing for the infinite. This is impenetrable for us. All that one can say is that her mission breaks through in the final phase so victoriously, and is so pure and persuasive, that all the peculiar inclinations of her nature are incorporated without dissonance in the closing scene of life.

The same *sensibilité* has another side. Her powerful ability to resonate with the thought of other masters makes it easy for her to appropriate their material and offer it as her own. Thérèse of Lisieux read very little apart from Scripture. Elizabeth read much and did so with a hunger for learning and instruction. In those writings that have already been published, one sees repeated citations: Teresa of Jesus, John of the Cross, Catherine of Siena, Angela of Foligno, Jan Ruysbroeck (whom she knew and freely excerpted from Hello's account), Lacordaire, the Areopagite, Augustine, Francis Xavier, Msgr. Gay and a large number of anonymous "pious authors". She also frequently cites Thérèse of Lisieux and, naturally, Father Vallée. Much of the material from her early period in the monastery comes across as lifted mechanically from her reading. Worse still, she often seems, rather naïvely, to expect her lofty sentiments to arouse a cry of amazement from both the simple readers of her letters (her mother, sister, women friends and acquaintances) and from the priests among her friends.[8] For a minute she may linger on the lofty heights, but she cannot maintain her perch with complete believability. She has put on clothes that are too large for her, and she cannot walk naturally. Likewise, sometimes her flights into the sublime border on banality and *kitsch*. Yet before rejecting this out of hand, we must first consider how young she was and then take note that a great mission only rarely develops *organically* with the person commissioned to it. Often it happens that the outlines are sketched in their full extent from the beginning, while the person must gradually assume the shape of her task. One grows into the outline. Of course every analogy to natural, organic or intellectual growth breaks down at this point. The commission does not presuppose the unfolding of inner capabilities, as in the case of a natural gift, rather it requires a process of conforming to an ideal granted to the person's nature from above and beyond. When this overwhelms one's nature, the grace-aided effort to conform to what is required can at times seem unnatural. It can also be dangerous to think that what one *should* do is the same as what one *can* do (with the aid of grace) or to observe one's own Christian achievement, even if this is done without guile. In her early years in the monastic life,

---

[8] This is rather clear in the questionnaire she filled out as a postulant (see below, p. 493). In response to the present passage in this book's first edition, I received a communication from the Carmel in Dijon saying that Elizabeth probably read too little rather than too much. Before her entry into the monastery she had been educated more in the fine arts than intellectually—it was her feelings rather than her mind that had been encouraged.

Elizabeth was not completely free from the resonance of personal satisfaction. This may explain why her mission, so fully directed toward the greatest objectivity and depersonalization, was accompanied up to the very end by the theme of the personal and the subjective. In the famous prayer, "O mon Dieu, Trinité que j'adore" (O My God, Trinity Whom I Adore), the words "I" and "mine" occur forty-three times. It is not really a prayer of adoration but a petition for the ability to adore, a prayer that moves exclusively back and forth between the "I" and God, a prayer in which "Thou" and the Church are absent. Even though Elizabeth's thought and prayer open themselves more and more to the total plan of salvation, the Church has no special profile in her realm of thought. The narrow space she occupies means that much must remain covered by a veil.

Yet these questions and reservations fade away in the end. Elizabeth's mounting passion for God's word, the steadily more victorious breakthrough of Holy Scripture to complete dominance in the last months—all this demonstrates that genuine hearing and doing have triumphed over mere reading. The "Last Retreat" and "Heaven on Earth", her spiritual testament, reveal her at the peak of her self-assured capability. The effect of the Holy Spirit and of the progressive suffering that hollowed her out and cleansed her are palpable. She has shed all spiritual vanity, and a pure consuming fire burns in itself and consumes itself in praise of the glory of divine grace. It is here alone that one should grasp Elizabeth's words—all her earlier statements are preparation and beginnings. Here the word is "pure and flawless before God", as her favorite passage from Paul demands, a fire that sparks others into flames of adoration, glorification and service before the eternal throne.

PREDESTINATION

I

WHAT HAPPENED IN ELIZABETH'S LIFE often happens in the lives of those who are called: everything needed for the moment of calling, insight and commissioning has been carefully assembled from all sides, even though the person was unaware he was doing this. The elements as well as the underlying atmosphere, perhaps even the outlines of the central insight itself, were all present. It is all obvious in hindsight, even though these things were concealed at the time from the person about to be struck by inspiration—mainly because teachers, friends, books and her own prejudices distracted her and kept her from looking in the right direction. Thus a number of elements, harmoniously integrated, were long present in Elizabeth's consciousness: Carmel's apostolic contemplation, the inclination of the entire spirit toward eternity, the presence of God in the soul, love for the crucified and eucharistic Lord and the deeply felt yet still abstract idea of God's triunity sketched out in the name of this love, love for Holy Scripture, especially for Paul and his letters. All these were present but had not crystallized around the one enfolding and unfolding center.

Lightning must have struck at the end of 1904. It is possible but not demonstrable that the scales fell from Elizabeth's eyes as the result of a suggestion from an older nun, who, according to a later recollection (spring or summer 1905), commented on the place in Ephesians where Paul described the Christian calling with the words *in laudem gloriae gratiae ipsius* [to the praise of the glory of his grace] (Eph 1:6). Elizabeth is supposed to have been deeply impressed and, after returning to her cell where she tried unsuccessfully to find the passage, went back once more to the Sister to ask her to show her the words. This new insight slowly took root in her, and, on January 1, 1906, according to Father Philipon's account, she first gave herself the new name: "I would like to share with you a great secret: it is my dream to be 'the praise of glory'."[1] This account must be corrected slightly, since the "new name" appeared already in a Christmas letter of [January 1904]—and not in an offhand or accidental way.[2] But much more important is the realization that her gripping and transforming intuition lies, not in the three words from the opening of the letter to the Ephesians, but in the awesome vision that unfolds in this passage and has its center in the words of verses 4–6: "He [God the Father] has chosen us in him [that is, in Christ] before the foundation of the world, that we should be holy and blameless before his face; in love he has predestined us to adoption as children through Jesus Christ to himself, according to the pleasure of his will, to the praise of the glory of his grace." These are words of destiny. Elizabeth quickly noticed a reflection of these in Romans (8:29–30): "Those whom he foreknew, these he also predestined, to be conformed to the image of his Son, that he might be the firstborn among many brethren; moreover, those whom he predestined, these he has also called, and those whom he called, these he has also justified, and those whom he justified, these he has also glorified." These two texts, each of which can stand in the place of the other, each reflecting the other, made up the load-bearing framework of Elizabeth's spiritual edifice until her death.

The decisive stimulus appears to have come, not from her Carmelite Sister, but, according to her own account, from reading the encyclical Pius X issued on October 4, 1903. Under the title "Instaurare omnia in Christo" [To renew all things in Christ], she wrote about it in verse to her Prioress:

Mother, do you remember? In his beautiful encyclical, the Chief Shepherd expressed this wish, and my heart gathered like a mys-

---

[1] P 128 (ET 83–84).

[2] 110 (ET 82). [Von Balthasar was correct in revising Philipon's account. Subsequent evidence brought forward by Conrad De Meester in the definitive edition of Elizabeth's *Complete Works* moved the date of this important letter even earlier: January 25, 1904. See CW I:47 and II:L 191, n. 1—TRANS.]

tical flower, and now I wish to give it to you. May this divine
wish of our pastor indeed become a reality in me. For that reason
I have taken it as my motto: "Renew everything in you, my Lord
and my Savior." This most beautiful pattern, given [to the Pope]
by Wisdom herself, is the same as that which God has in eternity.
Paul repeats it constantly in his writings: it is the "excess of love",
the abundance of mercy. Let us listen to his word by being silent,
Mother. He wants to proclaim to us the festive decree, "So that
we might be pure and holy in his presence, God has chosen us
in him [Christ] according to his eternal decree." But we have
sinned, our misery is immense. What will become of us if God
does not come to us? "Rich in mercy", he remains our Father;
the Son's prayer soothes his wrath. And "so that the praise of his
glory might shine forth, he will justify us through redemption."
From now on we can see the brightness of his face, for he has
called us "children for the sake of his Son".

The poem continues, drawing on John 17 and Colossians 3 in
praise of *Instauratio in Christo*.[3]

According to Prioress Germaine of Jesus, these verses were
written in 1904. They fit well with the previously mentioned
January letter of that year. In that letter, besides the name
"Praise of Glory", Elizabeth notes for the first time that "Saint
Paul" proclaims "in his glorious Letter nothing but the mystery of the love of Christ", following this with the great closing passage of the dogmatic part of the letter to the Ephesians
(3:14-19). From this point onward, nearly all Elizabeth's letters or writings mention either Ephesians 1:4-6[4] or Romans
8:29-30—whether the passages fit or not.[5] It is as if she were

---

[3] S 431-32; CW III:P89.

[4] The passage from Ephesians is cited or explained in S 429 (CW III:P89) and
in *Écrits spirituels* 111, 115-16, 127, 128, 130, 160-61, 175, 199, 211, 225, 235-
36 (ET 83, 85, 86, 96 [twice], 98, 120, 132, 149, 157, 161, 167, 175); CW I:103
(twice), 128, 141, 143, 152, 158, 180; II:L 226, L 227, L 238, L 239, L 244, L 299,
L 331; III:PN16, P89. In February 1904, significantly enough, only Ephesians
1:7-8 is cited in a nondogmatic, personal-ascetic context (see S 77; cf. *Spiritual
Writings*, 59 [CW II:L 225]).

[5] The passage from Romans appears nearly as often: 112, 124, 155, 157, 174,

blinded by the light of this mystery, obsessed with its urgency. Only when viewed from this vast context—no broader horizon exists—does the full significance of her "new name" become apparent. Without this background, the choice would float in a vacuum; with this background, it is filled to bursting with the whole mystery of divine predestination. For Elizabeth, the entire Carmelite mission finds its dogmatic foundation and justification in this mystery. Her entire subjective striving for prayer, contemplation and passion fits within it. Above all, in this mystery Elizabeth is set free to enjoy a clear awareness in faith of what previously had been a faint hint of the meaning of creation, redemption and the Church. The mystery of predestination becomes from this time onward the horizon from which and toward which she lives, the standard for all her individual and concrete steps, the ordering framework for all ecclesiastical teaching and doing, the decisive goad for all decisions and sacrifices.

One must listen carefully to Elizabeth herself and avoid interrupting her or tiring of her repetitions. One must permit oneself to float on the waves on to which she leads the way, without thinking that one already knows what she has seen. Above all, one must resist the prejudices stemming from the heavy burden carried by the history of the systematic theology of predestination. Elizabeth is ignorant of the history of theology. She approaches the word of Paul with the lightheartedness of a child of God, and the arrow of that word pierces her heart of hearts. Elizabeth's happiness in this experience has nothing to do with the brooding and spiritual terrors that so often attack those who fall into this mystery—from Augustine and Gottschalk to the Reformers and Jansenists. A child encounters the abyss of predestination, and this abyss seems to

195–96, 198, 207, 217, 236, 240 (ET 83, 94, 116, 117, 131, 147, 149, 155, 162, 175, 178); CW I:98, 105, 107, 127, 141, 147, 158, 161; II:L 228, L 231, L 240, L 249, L 300, L 304, L 306, L 307, L 308, L 312, L 315, L 324; III:P93, P105 (twice), P106, P122.

her to be a single light worthy of adoration. Let us listen to her own words.

> When we consider our eternal predestination, how contemptible visible things appear! Listen to what Paul says: "Those whom God knew in his foreknowledge, these he has also predestined that they might be conformed to the image of his Son." But that is not all. You will see that you are also among the ones he has known. "And those whom he knew, these he has also called." Baptism has made you into an adopted child, has marked you with the seal of the Holy Trinity. "And those whom he has called, these he has also justified." How often you have become this through the sacrament of penance and through all God's stirrings in your soul, even those you were unaware of! "And those whom he has justified, these he has also glorified." Now this is what awaits you in eternity. But remember that the degree of our glorification will correspond to the degree of grace in which God finds us at death. So you must permit him to complete in you the work of predestination. To this end listen once more to Paul, for he wishes to give you a plan for your life: "Stride along in Jesus Christ, well-rooted in him, built up in him, fortified in faith, and growing in him with thanksgiving" (Col 2:6–7).[6]

> "Those whom God knew in his foreknowledge, these he has also predestined to be conformed to the image of his divine Son. And those whom he has predestined, these he has also called, and those whom he has called, these he has also justified, and those whom he has justified, these he has also glorified. What more should we say? If God is for us, who is then against us? . . . Who can separate me from the love of Jesus Christ?" This is how the mystery of predestination, the secret of divine election, appears in the enlightened view of the Apostle. "Those whom he knew." Were we not among this number? Cannot God say to our soul what he once said through the mouth of his prophet: "I have passed by you and have regarded you. I have seen that the time has come for you to be loved, I have spread my garment over you, I have sworn to protect you, I have made a covenant with you, and you have become my own" (Ezek 16:8)? Yes

[6] 174 (ET 131); CW I:127.

indeed, we have become his own through baptism, for that is what Paul was saying with the words: "He has called us." Yes indeed, called in order to receive the seal of the Trinity; at the same time as we became, in the words of Peter, "participants in the divine nature" (2 Pet 1:4), we received "a beginning of his being" (Heb 3:14). For "he has justified us" through his sacraments, through direct contacts with the foundation of our soul, "justified also through faith" (Rom 5:1) and "according to the measure of our faith in the redemption given us through Jesus Christ". Finally, he wants to "glorify" us, and, to that end, Paul says, "he has made us worthy to have a part in the inheritance of the saints in the light" (Col 1:2); but we shall be glorified to the degree that we "have been conformed to the image of his divine Son". Let us therefore contemplate this adored image, let us remain forever in its rays so that it can impress itself on us, and then let us approach everything in the same attitude as our blessed Master. Then we shall accomplish the great "will" with which God "in himself" decided "to bring all things together in Christ" (Eph 1:9–10).[7]

"God has predestined us to adoption as children through Jesus Christ, in union with him, according to the decision of his will, in order to let the glory of his grace shine forth, through which he has justified us in his beloved Son, in whom we have redemption through his blood, the forgiveness of sins, according to the riches of his grace, which has flooded over us in all wisdom and discernment" (Eph 1:5–8). According to the word of the Apostle, the soul who has truly become a child of God is moved by the Holy Spirit himself. "All who are led by the Spirit of God are children of God" (Rom 8:14). And again, "We have not received the spirit of servitude, which would make us fearful again, rather the spirit of adoption as children, in which we cry, Abba! Father! And truly, this spirit confirms to our spirit that we are children of God; but if we are children, then also heirs, I say, heirs of God and co-heirs with Christ; but we must suffer together with him, so that we may be glorified with him" (Rom 8:15–17). So that we might reach these depths of glory, God

[7] 195–96 (ET 147); CW I:105–6.

has created us after his image and likeness. "Behold", John says, "what great love the Father has bestowed on us, that we should be called and should be the children of God, and it is not yet revealed what we shall be. We know that when he appears, then we shall be like him, for we shall see him as he is. And whoever places this hope in him, sanctifies himself, just as God himself is holy" (1 Jn 3:1-3).[8]

If you knew what inexpressible happiness my soul tastes in pondering the fact that the Father "has predestined me to be conformed to his crucified Son"! Paul has proclaimed to us this divine election, which seems to be my lot. . . . Courage! Let us look to the Crucified One and shape ourselves like this divine image![9]

I wonder how any soul who has fathomed the love in God's heart can be anything but happy, despite all suffering and pain. Remember "that he has chosen you before the foundation of the world, to be spotless and pure in his presence in love" (Eph 1:4). Once more, it is Paul who says that—so you need not fear struggle and temptation.[10]

"*Nescivi!*" (Song 6:11), "I knew nothing more!" I desire to know nothing more, except one thing: "to know him, him, the fellowship of his suffering, the conformity of his death" (Phil 3:10). "Those whom God knew in his foreknowledge, these he has also predestined, to be conformed to the image of his divine Son," the one who was crucified for love. If I ever become completely conformed to this divine model, completely taken up in him and he in me, then I shall have fulfilled my eternal calling, for which God chose me *in principio* [in the beginning], and which I shall carry out *in aeternum* [in eternity], when I fall into the lap of my Trinity and become the unending song of praise of his glory, the *laudem gloriae ejus*.[11]

As we can see, Elizabeth weaves around her central text a cluster of other texts that become intelligible to her in the light of the mystery of predestination. For example, she favors the

[8] 199-200 (ET 149); CW I:107.   [9] 155 (ET 116, 117); CWII:L 324.
[10] 175 (ET 132); CW I:128.   [11] 207 (ET 254-55); CW I:141.

text from Philippians regarding the heavenly calling that shaped the entire life and work of the Apostle: "I desire to know him, him and communion with his suffering and the conformity of his death. . . . I chase after this goal and desire to attain the place for which God destined me when he chose me. . . . My whole aim is to forget what lies behind me, and, intent on that which lies before me, I dash for the goal, toward the calling to which God called me in Christ Jesus" (Phil 3:10, 12–14).[12] In the same way she uses John 17, where the basis of election in Christ becomes especially visible in our Lord's prayer: " 'I sanctify myself for them so that they may be sanctified in truth' (Jn 17:19). Here I come face to face with the 'mystery concealed from the ages and the generations', the mystery, according to Paul's words, that 'Christ is for us the hope of glory' (Col 1:26–27). Paul adds that insight into this mystery has been given to him (Eph 3:4). Therefore from him I wish to learn so that I can attain the 'knowledge' that, according to his words, 'surpasses all other knowledge, the knowledge of the love of Jesus Christ' (Eph 3:19)."[13] For Elizabeth, everything is ordered and illuminated by the light of her fundamental text.

II

Believing men and women live out of the eternal election that establishes their future creation "before the foundation of the world" but places in Jesus Christ their predestination to conformity with the image of the Son, their redemption through the blood of Christ and their standing before God in purity and holiness. They live from election toward predestination, redemption and holiness, in an orbit that begins in and returns to the utter eternity of the triune God. They live as pilgrims within time yet without abandoning this fundamental chosenness. Were they not chosen, they could not proceed from God

[12] 197, see also 235 (ET 148, 174); CW I:106, 158.
[13] 231 (ET 171); CW I:155.

as a creature, for they are created *in order* to be conformed to the image of God's Son. And unless they came from election, they could not march toward that to which they have been predestined by the power of grace and the Son's redemption, toward the image to which they are conformed. The links in the chain described by Paul are so interlocked in God that the chain cannot be torn apart: the one foreknown is predestined, the one predestined is called, the one called is justified, the one justified is glorified. This is a chain located within eternity, within God's plan, which, because it is God's, is just as immutable and immovable as God himself. To live the Christian life within time, one must fit into the great orbit extending from eternity to eternity; one must remain within it, not slip out of it; one must adjust one's temporal path to fit the eternal plan. Contrary to all earthly appearances, the space in which the believer moves is fundamentally eternal; the believer's homeland is where God is, the house of God, the city of God, the communion of the saints. The "time" in which the believer lives is fundamentally an "incipient eternity", a "steadily progressing eternity",[14] just as the "earth" on which the believer lives is at bottom an "anticipated heaven", a *ciel anticipé*.[15]

Thus contemplation of the end for which man was created, the famous *contemplatio de fine*, coincides with contemplation of human origin in God's predestination: "I reflect on our eternal predestination. . . , on the purpose for which God has created the soul".[16] *Faith*, the foundation of Christian life, is what happens when both origin and goal—the entire invisible and eternal world that is the truth behind our temporal life—come together for us in our presentness.

> "To approach God, one must believe" (Heb 11:6). It is Paul who talks like this. Furthermore, he says "faith is the presence

[14] 186 (ET 141); CW I:94.

[15] 58, 62, 79, 102, 223, 241 (ET 45, 47, 60, 77, 166, 178); CW II:L 111, L 133, L 123, L 199; I:151, 161.

[16] 173, 175 (ET 131, 132); CW I:127, 128.

of things hoped for and the evidence of things not seen" (Heb 11:1). This means that faith makes future blessings so certain and present that they take up existence in our soul and are available to her before we can enjoy them. John of the Cross says that faith serves as feet to make our way to God, that faith is an obscured possession for us. . . . In his conversation with the Samaritan woman, the Lord was referring to faith when he promised to give to all who would believe in him a "spring of living water that would bubble up into eternal life" (Jn 4:14).[17]

If, on the one hand, faith, for Elizabeth, is essentially characterized by this productive anticipation of eternal life, on the other hand, it is also faith in the self-creating *love* flowing from eternity. This corresponds to the thought of Saint John: "We have known and believed the love that God has for us" (1 Jn 4:16). In Elizabeth's words:

> This is our great act of faith, this is the means to return God's love with love, this is the "hidden secret" (Col 1:26) in the Father's heart of which Paul speaks and into which we ultimately penetrate, making our entire soul tremble. If she has learned to believe in the colossal love that is above her, . . . then it makes no difference to her whether she senses God or not, it makes no difference to her whether he gives her desire or pain—she believes in love. Indeed, the more she is tested, the more her faith grows, because faith pushes through all obstacles in order to relax in the lap of endless love, which can do nothing but a work of love.[18]

This faith, it goes without saying, is precisely the living, loving and therefore "saving faith"[19] that itself believes in love and is itself an act of love. Yet it is more, it is a response to and a stake in the eternal love that has revealed itself to faith from the beginning. It is an act that carries *hope* in itself, according to the words of Saint John: "We shall see him as he is, and whoever has this hope in him, he sanctifies himself, as God

---

[17] 193–94 (ET 145–46); CW I:101.   [18] 194–95 (ET 146); CW I:101–2.
[19] 195 (ET 146); CW I:102.

himself is holy" (1 Jn 3:3).[20] Therefore this hope is identical with love.

Faith, hope and love, all three are experienced as living gifts of God from eternity, as something that we could not do from ourselves but which he has granted us out of the stores of his grace so that we might respond to the eternal calling and predestination. "He lives in our soul so that he himself can be our faithfulness. In ourselves we are nothing but nothingness and sin. But he alone is holy, and he dwells in us to save us, to cleanse us, to change us into himself. Remember the brilliant challenge of the Apostle: 'Who can separate me from the love of Christ?' (Rom 8:35). . . . 'For if I am weak the power of Christ dwells in me' (2 Cor 12:9)."[21] Often Elizabeth's heart fails her in the face of the immensity of her calling. "Then I throw myself upon him whom John called 'Faithful' and 'True' (Rev 19:11) and beg him to be my faithfulness."[22] "I do not fear my weakness, for that is what gives me confidence, for 'the Mighty One' (Is 9:6) is in me, and his strength is all-powerful. 'It accomplishes', Paul says, 'more than we can hope' (Eph 3:20)."[23] Thus loving and hoping faith becomes a genuine participation in eternal life by the power of God indwelling the chosen soul through grace. She is the *pistis* (faith) because the *pistos*, the Faithful One, is present in her. "Those who follow the Lamb wherever he goes are the beings who already here below belong to the people pure as light. Already they bear on their brow the name of the Lamb and of his Father. They bear the name of the Lamb through their likeness and conformity to him whom John calls the 'True and Faithful One', who appears in a 'bloodstained garment'. These beings are also faithful and true, and they also wear garments stained red with blood from their constant offering of themselves. They bear the name of the Father because he lets the beauty of his perfections shine forth from

[20] 200 (ET 149); CW I:107.
[21] 92 (ET 70); CW II:L252.
[22] 134 (ET 101); CW II:L256.
[23] 162 (ET 121); CW II:L333.

them.'"[24] Ultimately the truth of faith is to offer one's self, to prefer God's love to all forms of self-love, and to let God's truth shape one's existence. "He is the 'Beginning', who speaks within us; and has he not said: 'He who has sent me is the Truth, and all that I have heard from him I declare to you' (Jn 8:26)? Let us ask him then to make us genuine in our love, that is, to make us creatures of sacrifice, for sacrifice is simply love turned into deeds: 'He loved me and delivered up himself for me' (Gal 2:20)."[25] "Let us therefore be sacrificed ones, that is, genuine in our love."[26] "What is more beautiful than truth, the truth of love? 'He has loved me and delivered up himself for me.' That, my child, is what it means to be true."[27]

Faith, love, hope contain within themselves the truth as life, as something really carried out: the divine and eternal carried out for us and at the same time the Son's sacrifice carried out in us—our conformity to his image. Sacrifice is not an addition to faith, rather it is simply the fulfillment of eternal predestination in us through faith, through which the eternal becomes present in us. It is an *abiding* in the orbit that begins with God's fore-knowledge and, in glorification, flows back to the beginning. This abiding not only expresses for John the basic attitude of a Christian but also substantiates predestination within time. "Whoever abides in him remains without sin. Whoever sins has not seen or known him" (1 Jn 3:6). For Elizabeth, it is an abiding in the God of heaven, in the Trinity: "The Trinity is our dwelling place, our Father's house, from which we shall never depart. The Lord once said, 'The servant does not abide in the house forever, but the son abides there forever and ever' (Jn 8:35)."[28] Abiding implies keeping and preserving: " 'If any-one loves me, he will keep my word and the Father will love him and we shall come to him and make our home in him' (Jn 14:23)."[29] She speaks constantly of being firmly established, in

[24] 218 (ET 162); CW I:148.

[25] 132 (ET 99); CW II:L250.

[26] 108 (ET 81); CW II:L214.

[27] 175 (ET 132); CW I:128.

[28] 187 (ET 141); CW I:94.

[29] 189 (ET 143); CW I:96.

the double sense of a settled place and a steady line of sight. In her prayers she desires to "attach myself to God forever and remain in his great light".[30] "It is his will that we should be rooted in him, that we dwell where he dwells, in the unity of love, that we follow him like a shadow."[31] And the Son desires "that I, like the Father, live in an eternal now, without a before, without an after, completely within the unity of my being in this eternal now . . . to adore him for his own sake (Ps 71:15 [72:15]), that is the eternal now, in which the praise of glory must be established."[32] She wishes not only "to be fixed in God without distraction"[33] but also to be the soul that "fixes her gaze on God in faith and simplicity",[34] who gazes on the unchanging God, for this is the attribute under which she loves to contemplate God. Very early, before she entered religion, God was "the Unchanging One" for her.[35] In prayer she asks to be permitted "to be rooted in you, the unmoving and peaceful one, as if my soul were already in eternity: let nothing darken my peace, let nothing cause me to depart from you, O my Unchanging One!"[36] In the same way she likes to quote the words from the letter to the Hebrews in which Moses is called "firm in faith, as if he had seen the invisible" (Heb 11:27).[37] Once more she refers back to predestination to substantiate this rootedness:

"We have been predestined through the decision of him who created all things according to the purpose of his will, so that we might be the praise of his glory" (Eph 1:11-12). It is Paul who proclaims this divine election, . . . he also shows us the purpose of our calling: "God", he says, "chose us in him before the foundation of the world, that we might be holy and spotless before his face in love" (Eph 1:4). If I compare these two descriptions

---

[30] 81 (ET 62); CW I:83.   [31] 186 (ET 141); CW I:94.
[32] 226 (ET 168, 169); CW I:152-53.   [33] 205 (ET 153); CW I:112.
[34] 204 (ET 153); CW I:112.   [35] 44 (ET 32); CW III:L70.
[36] 80 (ET 61); CW I:183.
[37] 194-95, 214 (ET 146, 159); CW I:101, 145.

of the divine decision, which in itself is "eternally immutable", I conclude from them that I must, in order to carry out my office as praise of glory worthily, keep myself before his face no matter what happens; more than that, I must keep myself "in love", that is, in God himself, for "God is love" (1 Jn 4:16). It is contact with the divine being that will then make me "spotless and pure" in his eyes.[38]

If, from the perspective of faith, the Christian life is an abiding, a refusal to depart from the eternal, from the perspective of pure creatureliness, it is a once-for-all entry into this eternal circle. Elizabeth wrote to someone preparing for the priesthood: "Like that High Priest 'without father, without mother, without ancestry, without beginning of days, without end of life, image of the Son of God' (Heb 7:3) of whom Paul speaks in the Letter to the Hebrews, so through sacred anointing you become a being who no longer belongs to this earth, a mediator between God and souls, appointed 'to show forth the glory of his grace'."[39] Thus we need to "fence in" our free will in God, a free will that in its creatureliness has no finally fixed form. Through this cloistering of the will, for the first time we enter the realm of true—because eternal and divine—freedom. "So that my will might be free, I must enclose it within the will of God."[40] This is the content with which Elizabeth fills Teresa of Jesus' image of the "castle"—it is not so much an inner fortress of the soul as it is, in a Pauline and apocalyptic sense, all earthliness surrounded and enclosed by the heavenly world. The Carmelite ideal is found "in living together with God in the impregnable fortress"[41] where the soul can " 'serve God day and night in his temple' (Rev 7:15). . . . Inner and outer trials are unable to force the soul from the holy fortress in which the Master has confined her."[42] This presupposes a primarily Christian and supernatural understanding of *freedom*: participation in the freedom of God in his eternal plan. The

[38] 211 (ET 157); CW I:143.   [39] 113–14 (ET 84–85); CW II:L 232.
[40] 230 (ET 171); CW I:155.   [41] 190 (ET 144); CW I:97.
[42] 217 (ET 160, 161); CW I:146, 147.

free person is the one who lives liberated from herself and all things, who lives for the "one thing necessary", who "has locked up her will in the will of God".[43] "The freest soul is the one who has most forgotten herself."[44] "In the midst of everything and against every resistance, she is ready to adore God for his own sake forever, for she is free, freed from herself and from everything",[45] so that in the end she partakes of the mysterious freedom of God that permits him to be bound only by himself, that is, by his love: "God is free from everything except his love."[46] The soul has been eternally imprisoned within this mystery of eternal love. "He captivates me, he chains me forever in silence, in the deep mystery."[47] In her great prayer she even asks to be swept away, to be charmed, by love: "Enchant, captivate me, so that I can never again escape the circle of your radiance!"[48] And, in her letter to her priest-friend, she mentions Saint Catherine of Siena: "We wish to ask her to draw our souls to God until we are completely captivated by him and unable to break out of the circle of his radiance."[49]

Now this captivity in the orbit of the divine plan is anything but a narrowing or numbness of the mind. Instead Elizabeth understands the eternal as a perfect broadness, and she sees abiding in God as a steady march. The phrase "walk in the presence of God" would express what she means, except that it has become too pale. What she has in mind is a walking with firm step into a space that is always open, a walking that stays on the road of those "works that God has prepared, so that we might walk in them" (Eph 2:10). It is a walking that takes place under his gaze, in the radiance of his presence. "God said to Abraham, 'Walk in my presence and be perfect!' (Gen 17:1). Paul, who steeped himself in the divine plan, discloses the same with the words, 'God has chosen us before the foundation of

---

[43] 173 (ET 131); CW I:127.

[44] 170 (ET 129); CW I:125.

[45] 233 (ET 173); CW I:157.

[46] 101 (ET 76); CW II:L 199.

[47] S 426; CW III:P88.

[48] 81 (ET 62); CW I:183.

[49] 102 (ET 77); CW II:L 199.

the world, that we might be spotless and holy before his face in love' (Eph 1:4). The same saint will light my way so I don't go astray when I march forth on the glorious road of the presence of God, where the soul travels 'alone with the Alone', directed by the 'power of his right arm', under the 'refuge of his wings' (Ps 90:4 [91:4])."[50]

> "*Instaurare omnia in Christo*." . . . So that I might personally realize this divine plan, Paul comes to my aid and designs a rule for my life: "Walk along in Jesus Christ", he says to me, "rooted in him, built up on him, strengthened in faith . . . and growing more and more in him through thanksgiving" (Col 2:6–7). To walk in Jesus Christ means to leave oneself behind, to lose sight of oneself, to say good-bye to oneself in order to penetrate deeper into him minute by minute, so deep that one is rooted there and can face every event and thing with the challenge: "Who can separate me from the love of Christ?" (Rom 8:35). . . . Then says the Apostle, "Our mortality is swallowed up into life" (2 Cor 5:4).[51]

Elizabeth does not underestimate the effort needed for this "marching in the depths of God". Although it is the mystical way, it is also an ascetic path through tough daily battle with one's faults. It is truly a step-by-step path that cannot be traveled by flying or by being carried. It most certainly is a path, not an already attained goal. "Pride cannot be eliminated with a stroke of the sword. To be sure, certain acts of heroic humility, as one finds them in the lives of the saints, can knock it down with a fatal blow or at least significantly weaken it, but for the most part one must see to it that it dies daily: '*Quotidie morior*' (1 Cor 15:31), 'I die daily', Paul cried out. This teaching on mortification or dying to self applies to all Christians ever since Christ said, 'If any one wants to follow me, let him take up his cross and deny himself' (Lk 9:23). It may seem grim but is actually wonderfully sweet if one keeps in mind that the aim of this death is to replace our wretchedly sinful life with

[50] 225 (ET 167); CW I:152.　　　　[51] 233 (ET 173); CW I:156–57.

God's life."[52] "So 'march forth in Jesus Christ'; you need this
broad way, you have not been created for the narrow byways
of this world. Be 'rooted in him' and therefore uprooted from
yourself, . . . be 'built up in him', far above all that passes you
by, built up into purity, into the light; be 'firmly established
in faith', that is, . . . feed your soul with the great truths of
faith that reveal to her the riches of God and the purpose for
which God created her."[53] "Marching forth" means, for Elizabeth, to set oneself in motion within the plan of God. It is
dominated from the start by the determination to go as far as
God wishes and not to stop before his will has been fulfilled:
"Pray that I will be faithful so that I may fulfill his plans for
me to the end, that I may carry out his complete will."[54] In its
fullest sense "marching forth" thus is equivalent to holiness:
" 'Be holy, for I am holy' (Lev 19:2): under the light of this
word I shall direct my steps during my entire spiritual journey.
Paul expounds this word for me when he says, 'God chose
us before creation, so that we may be spotless and holy in his
presence in love.' "[55] The effect of the idea of divine predestination on Elizabeth is clearly that of an immediate and en-
compassing response, a Yes, a departure and a hurrying along.
This effect is precisely what Paul (and all of Holy Scripture)
wanted to achieve through the revelation of the mystery of
predestination. Elizabeth grasps the revelation of this mystery
precisely in the manner and meaning with which the Scriptures
give it to believers: as the loftiest unveiling of divine love—
and as nothing else. It has been promulgated for one purpose
alone: to gather together the human response of love, incorpo-
rating it perfectly into God's plan of love. Men and women can
perceive from the immutability of the divine plan how much
their response must be a total one, given in the realm of the
unchangeable.[56] "It seems to me that the Apostle's words are

[52] 169 (ET 128); CW I:124–25.
[53] 175, cf. 160–61 (ET 131–32, cf. 120); CW I:127–28; cf. II:L 331.
[54] 68 (ET 51); CW II:L 149.   [55] 130 (ET 98); CW II:L 244.
[56] 211 (ET 157); CW I:143.

directed to this soul, made imperturbable in her faith in the
God of love: 'Because you believe, you will be filled with an
inexpressible joy, and you shall be glorified' (1 Pet 1:8)."[57]

III

A spirituality built entirely upon the idea of predestination,
which constitutes the core of Elizabeth's message, needs more
precise explanation and justification. Striving to ground her total devotion to God in faith, beyond the limits of her own subjectivity and beyond the demands and boundaries of her own
striving and groping, Elizabeth has unintentionally reached the
last, most objective and limitless outlook of Christian faith, the
last horizon of Christian revelation (and Christian dogma).
Even when overpowered by the abundance of light, she can
do nothing except direct her personal path into this vision and
to let it merge with the path of God that winds its way high
above it. She does this in faith and thereby also in obedience.
She follows the word of Holy Scripture with precision by permitting it to have its full force of illumination, adding nothing
that is essentially alien to it, taking away nothing that belongs
to its essential wholeness. Thus she understands predestination
to be exactly what Paul obviously wished to have understood:
our election to holiness and to the praise of the glory of grace,
as brethren of Christ, who is the Father's first, original and
comprehensive Chosen One. Any consideration of predestination that bypasses Christ and his redemption to poke around
arrogantly in rash speculation "behind" the household of salvation in Christ; any consideration of predestination that loses itself in allegedly obscure depths unknown and contradictory to
the "revelation of the mystery" (Eph 3:3)—all such teachings
are outside the bounds of Christian faith-obedience. Christian
theology knows no predestination except that in Christ, the

[57] 215 (ET 160); CW I:146.

Alpha and the Omega of the world, the source and goal of the
Father's entire work of creation, according to Scripture. Although Elizabeth does not refer to it, Paul pointedly explains
the dialectic of election (Rom 9–10) against the backdrop of
the Christian promise to Israel and within God's aim of saving
Israel (Rom 11:26). For Paul, the revelation of the mystery is
the final, unsurpassable proof of God's all-encompassing love
and loving foreknowledge. All that comes to pass within the
plan of salvation—separation and decision, demarcation and
erecting of "walls that separate", election of one and condemnation of another—all this serves God's loving providence. If
one trembles with awe at this point, the starting point for every work of God, then one is being awed by the "excess of
love" (Eph 2:4) that Elizabeth praises tirelessly. If she has any
merit in this regard, it is certainly not because she has con-
structed a speculative account of the idea of predestination—
nothing could be more alien to her nature. Instead she has with
simplicity withstood the human mind's almost uncontrollable
urge to speculate on this matter, she has imperturbably held on
to the clear content of the word. Indeed, it is precisely in this
standing fast and *not* going forward, *not* thinking further, *not*
drawing the seemingly *obvious* conclusions, that she has found
faith's full secret. She has found not only what God requires
but also the very content of the mystery; she has found both
illumination and reward in the mystery.

One notices immediately that Elizabeth innocently includes
herself among those Paul had in mind, among those enclosed in
God's plan of love. After citing Romans 8:29, she says, "How I
love these thoughts of this great Saint Paul, my soul reposes in
them! I think about the Lord's excess of love. He has known,
called and justified me, and, waiting for him to glorify me, I
desire now to be an unceasing praise of his glory."[58] "If you
only knew what inexpressible happiness my soul tastes at the
thought that the Father has predestined me to be conformed

[58] 151 (ET 113); CW II:L 304.

to the image of his crucified Son: Saint Paul tells us about this divine election, which seems to be my portion."[59] One might think that Elizabeth has received a kind of "assurance of salvation" based on a personal, inner revelation (in the sense of the Council of Trent, ss 6, c 12). Although this cannot be entirely ruled out, it seems more likely that she bases the above words solely on the objective revelation of God through Paul. In them one sees that she does not understand the whole idea of predestination in an individualistic way, rather always in a social, ecclesial, communal way. Thus, on the basis of the same evidence, she can address others as ones Paul had in mind. One example is her young priest-friend, shortly before his first Mass: "In the Letter to the Romans, Paul says that those 'whom God has known in his foreknowledge, he also predestined to be conformed to the image of his Son'. These words certainly seem to me to refer to you. Are you not this predestined one, whom God has chosen to be his priest? . . . *Tu es sacerdos in aeternum*! [You are a priest forever!] Everything about you will be, as it were, a copy of Jesus Christ, the high priest, and you will reflect him eternally before the Father and the faithful."[60] Two months before Elizabeth's death, she wrote to her friend Françoise, explaining Romans 8:29: "You will see that you are also included among those God has 'known'." The proof that Françoise is one of the "called" lies in the seal of holy baptism.[61] Similarly, in a letter to a friend of her sister: " 'Those whom he has known': Are we not among this number? Cannot God speak to our soul as he once spoke through the voice of his prophet [to Jerusalem] (Ezek 16:8)? . . . Yes we have become his through baptism . . . , also justified through faith and 'according to the measure of our faith'."[62] A year earlier she had written to her sister: "I have read marvelous things in Paul about our adoption as children. Immediately I thought of you. . . . You, a child of God, doesn't that make you tremble

[59] 155 (ET 116); CW II:L324.   [60] 112 (ET 83); CW II:L231.
[61] 174 (ET 131); CW I:127.   [62] 195-96 (ET 147); CW I:105.

with joy? Just listen to what Paul says." [63] She wrote to a friend, after quoting Romans 8:29: "Both of us belong among these 'known ones'; let's not take our happiness too lightly!" [64] She said much the same in a letter to an older woman, [65] as well as in a letter to a young former novice: "I know how much my little sister needs protection in the middle of immense Paris. Paul says that 'we are chosen in him before the foundation of the world, to be pure and spotless in his presence in love.' How I shall pray him that this great decree of his will might be fulfilled in you!" [66]

For Elizabeth, predestination is just as certain as it was for the author of the Letters to the Ephesians and the Romans. And, as for Paul, it is for her no delimiting individualistic matter but an inclusive and social reality. As God's universal plan before the foundation of the world is unveiled before their eyes, nothing could be farther from the mind of Paul or Elizabeth than to count certain individuals in (and thereby count others out). Instead, God's universal plan of salvation, which begins with the choosing of the saints in Christ, merges with the *instaurare omnia in Christo*, with God's will to incorporate all things in heaven and on earth in the Head, Christ, the Savior and Redeemer of the world. To worldly thinking, the "election" of one seems unavoidably to require the "rejection" of the other —yet precisely this is alien to believing thinking based on the word of Scripture, because biblical election, as personal and definite as it may be, always has a social and vicarious sense (most brilliantly seen in Romans 9–11). Just as Christ is a predestined one not for himself alone but for his brothers, so no one will be saved for himself alone, rather, only together with his brethren. Indeed, his own salvation necessarily contributes to their salvation. Thus the entire theology of predestination culminates in the announcement of the choosing, each for the other, of the two great social bodies of humanity: the people

---

[63] 128 (ET 96); CW II:L 239.   [64] 157 (ET 117); CW II:L 315.
[65] 124 (ET 94); CW II:L 249.   [66] 160–61 (ET 120); CW II:L 331.

of the promise standing in the stead of those who were out-side the promise, and the heathen who have come to salvation standing in the stead of the once rejected and impenitent Jew-ish people. That is the biblical way of talking about this truth. To make an individualistic, "delimiting" and "enumerating" form of predestination *primary* is foreign to the Scriptures and fundamentally reorganizes the biblical point of view. First, the problem of the rewarding of one and the punishing of another (which belongs at another point theologically) would have to be placed next to, indeed be equated with, the unclouded orig-inal clarity. Moreover, it would require a distinction between God's primary will to save (general) and secondary will to save (limited and dependent on human behavior). All this would surround the sphere of predestination with fearful clouds of darkness. The translucent web of Paul's words would have to be torn apart, with part of it applied to the first, merely con-ditional, will of God and a part to the second, unconditional but no longer universal, will of God. In the process, Paul's claim would be robbed of all its force. When the discussion slips into this individualism, making it possible for believers to ask each other who among them has been "chosen" and who has not (what is *impossible* for Christians to ask became possible in a final sense with the Reformers), it is high time for the Church to reject as firmly as possible an "assurance of salvation" understood in this manner, regardless of whether it claims to be based on "faith alone" or on the signs of "works". An individualistic (and therefore psychological) concept of as-surance of salvation has as little to do with revelation as does the individualistic, static, "enumerating" view of predestina-tion that goes along with it. To use them is to narrow the shining vistas of revelation from the start and to darken them with the gloomiest of shadows. If Elizabeth has any merit, then it is this: to have found her way back through the tangle of distinctions to the original glory of the revealed mystery. This original glory refuses to surround the "we the chosen" with the question marks of "I" and "you" or to restrict the saving will of God with a *still* more absolute divine will for justification.

This simple Carmelite nun has not the slightest thought of drawing conclusions from Paul that would lead in the direction of a false Origenist gnosis. She has no inclination to depart from simple trusting faith to follow a detour into a secret knowledge of the ways and judgments of God. But faith itself is built up and strengthened in an unexpected way through the words she has heard, so that it can form once more, as in the Scriptures, an indivisible living unity with love and hope. Faith has no need for any additional secret whose gloominess prevents it being embraced together with hope and love. It also has no need to draw an endpoint on the Church's or God's horizon of hope at the outset, to demand the impossible of Christian and ecclesial love: to abandon at the outset a portion of brethren (even if their number and names are unknown). *Spes non confundit, caritas omnia credit, omnia sperat* [hope does not make people perplexed; love believes all things, hopes all things], and the God who earnestly and eagerly desires the salvation of all men (1 Tim 2:1–4) commands the Church and her members to pray with the same earnestness and eagerness for the salvation of all people. This means the Church must believe in the light of God's love that such salvation is possible and must hope for it. Only someone who does not know the nature of living faith can object that "fear and trembling" gets short shrift here in describing the process of salvation—one's own as well as another's. No one is above judgment, as long as he remains a sinner. But fear in the New Testament can be understood only as one—indispensable, to be sure—function of the Comforter (Jn 16:8–11).

The Church and her believers and saints live and pray in love and hope that are open and inclusive rather than limited. In obedience they are called to prayer and to life. They are not to use their own speculation to delimit their love and hope eschatologically. Conceptual systems that require or imply eschatological limits restrict the wide-angle vision granted by the "revelation of the mystery" just as much as others that, in the opposite direction, transform revelation's open faith, love and hope into a finite system of knowledge (the *apokatastasis*). The false limitations of the one are simply the antithesis to the false limitations of the other. Both overlook through their abstract speculation the fact that every divine revelation is given to challenge a person in his practice of the inner life. All four Gospels demand faith and immediate following in response to the word of God. (Matthew 25 is the climax of this insistence on decision in the face of the absolute crisis of the Cross!) Such insistence on practice is equally evident in the Pauline mystery, whose unveiling calls the "we" of the Church to nothing less than an immediate dying and rising again with Christ for the salvation of the world—that is, for the salvation of all those not yet conformed to the image of the Son. Once the idea of election loses its ecclesial, social and practical character, it ceases to be biblical and Christian election. So long as it remains a Christian doctrine of election, there can be no "I" outside of the ecclesial "we" and there can be no Calvinist-Jansenist "we" outside of human solidarity with the least of sinners. When these perspectives are kept in view, predestination begins to bear fruit, the fruit Paul speaks about to his community and that Elizabeth spontaneously offers as the only possible response: a complete Yes to God's unveiled word of love, a response of pure love to God and every neighbor. And, finally, we come to the piece that completes the picture: where pure Christian love for God and every neighbor is present, it can only be a response to *this* revelation of a mystery without boundaries and limits.

If one must use the loaded concept of "assurance of salvation", then one ought to say that the one and eternally predestined One, Jesus Christ, possesses complete assurance of salvation; yet through him, the "we" of the Church possesses it in the same degree. (The mediating role of the Church-as-community, significantly enough, was suppressed in the old predestination theology.) The individual then is called upon, within the Church and her certainty of salvation, to "walk" in the footsteps of the one who not only has salvation but is salvation. With this walking in salvation, she must be satisfied. For just as the eternally predestined One possesses certainty to the degree that he knows his loving obedience to the Father was turned into action, so the person predestined in the Lord and his Church is predestined precisely in the degree to which he helps to carry out this "walking in spotlessness and holiness before his face" through grace.

Elizabeth understood that this was her Carmelite calling: "As a virgin engaged to the Lord in faith, as a mother saving souls, to *multiply* the number of 'adopted children of the Father', the coheirs with Christ. How that enlarges the soul! It is like embracing infinity."[67] Thus the real, full, yet vicarious response to revelation is given by the one who, as the original cell of the Church gave the Yes of *life* on behalf of the entire human race (*loco totius generis humani*—Thomas Aquinas): "Following Jesus Christ, at a distance that separates the finite from the infinite, there is the creature, who fully corresponded to the divine election of which the Apostle speaks and who stood forever 'pure, spotless, blameless' before the eyes of the thrice-holy God."[68] "There is a creature who understood these gifts of God, who lost not so much as a crumb of them, who was so pure, so luminous, that she almost seemed to be the light itself."[69] "I weep for joy at the thought that this completely transparent, perfectly radiant being is my mother."[70] She it is who responds to the speaking God, who does not fall from the orbit of predestination but holds, guards and realizes everything, and who, because she was a completely "enclosed garden", became the wide-open mediatrix for all those who linger in the open. The closedness unlocks, the staying attracts, the perfect becomes a love-standard for failure. With Paul, John and Mary, Elizabeth grasped that what is Christian must be understood from

[67] 102 (ET 77); CW II:L 199.
[68] 238 (ET 177); CW I:160.
[69] 201 (ET 151); CW I:110.
[70] 146 (ET 109); CW II:L 298.

above and within, just as it comes into the world from above and within and will be realized from above and within. From Christ come his Mother and his Church, from the Church come his saints, from the saints comes faith, from faith come life and the world. Christianity is pure, transparent and luminous when it proceeds unsullied from God and announces itself integrally in the world. It then becomes intelligible to the pure eye of faith, unproblematic and free of agonizing brooding: "This is the message that we have received from him and also proclaim: God is light and in him there is no darkness at all. If we say that we have fellowship with him but walk in darkness, then we lie and do not the truth; but if we walk in the light as he is in the light, we have fellowship one with another, and the blood of Jesus his Son cleanses us from all guilt" (1 Jn 1:3–7).

The word of Paul challenges Elizabeth not only to believe theoretically in the light of God but to walk in it and thereby to become herself a radiant, community-building light. It is an invitation to recognize the gravity of election and to forget herself as "I", to place herself completely in the service of the saving will of God that shines forth from the crucified Son. The weakness and sinfulness of which she remains conscious only goads her to greater service.

> If, despite trusting faith, I fall each moment, I shall let him help me to my feet. I know that he will forgive me, more than that, that he will "strip" me, that he will "rob" me of all my misery, of all that blocks God's work; that he will take away with him all my "abilities", take them "captive", in order to "triumph over them in himself" (Col 2:15). Then I shall be entirely absorbed into him; then I can say, "I no longer live, my Lord lives in me" (Gal 2:20); then I shall be "holy, pure, spotless in the eyes of the Father".[71]

This process, a human response yet within God's comprehensive word of election, is a matter of utmost *seriousness* for Eliz-

---

[71] 232 (ET 172); CW I:156.

abeth. And even though the joy of discovery may have made her a bit too generous with words in announcing her "find", on her deathbed she continually insisted on the seriousness of this calling. "In the light of eternity one sees things restored to their proper places. . . . How earnest a matter life really is!"[72] "The Master urges me, he speaks to me only of the eternity of love. It is so weighty, so serious!"[73] And in one of her last letters, which she could only dictate, she told her physician: "Yes, the dear Lord entrusts you to your little patient, who, according to him, will be the invisible angel who will lead you on the path of duty to the goal to which every creature born under God must attain. In this last hour of my exile, on this beautiful evening of my life, how solemn everything seems to me in the light that shines from eternity!"[74] She took her response seriously, as she herself was taken seriously by God.

With this seriousness she knew that she and her Yes were enclosed within divine election. For her, the leap into the divine circle was a leap out of herself. She was able to call her life an "anticipated heaven" because she desired to live "above that which perishes, above herself",[75] because in that daily dying through which she knew herself to be preserved and saved from her own evil, she was separated from what condemned her (Rom 8:1). She loved to recall the words of the Psalmist: "With the help of God I shall be without blemish and keep myself from the guilt that is in me."[76] Likewise she cherished the words of Saint John of the Cross: "In the substance of the soul, where neither devil nor world can enter, God gives himself to the soul."[77] "In order to live in that way 'above the veil' (Heb 6:19), how one must be tightly shuttered against earthly things!"[78] Above the veil, however, even saints occasionally become dizzy in the face of the *exceedingly great light*

---

[72] 162 (ET 121); CW II:L 333. [73] 164 (ET 122); CW II:L 335.
[74] 165 (ET 123); CW II:L 340. [75] 223 (ET 166); CW I:151.
[76] 122, 219 (ET 92, 163); CW II:L 249; I:148.
[77] 188 (ET 142); CW I:95. [78] 131 (ET 99); CW II:L 250.

that shines forth from the revelation of the mystery. They are overwhelmed by an excess of responsibility that seems to emanate from that light. Thus Elizabeth writes to her friend the young priest: "Request of him that I might be at the peak of my calling and that I *not abuse the grace* he lavishes on me. If you only knew how that often worries me. In those instances I can only cast myself upon the one whom John calls the 'Faithful', the 'True', and beg him to be my faithfulness."[79] It is a fear of having climbed too high—at least in the context of this world. The height of calling, as well as knowledge, is scaled by way of a corresponding peak of faithfulness, of nonabuse of divine trust, as well as of simple sacrifice and pain. From this pinnacle supercharged with mystery all the Church's light flows. None of that light is kept from the Church, and thus everything must be exceedingly pure.

But the "cooperation" required of a chosen one is no willful, freely invented deed that someone lacking imagination doubts he can fulfill. When one responds to the mystery of predestination with the sole question, "How can one respond to the honor of this calling?",[80] the questioner is referred to the power of the word of revelation: " 'The word', Paul says, 'is living and effective, more piercing than a two-edged sword; it reaches to the division of soul and spirit, of joint and marrow' (Heb 4:12). It is God's word itself that denudes the soul, for the word's character and property is to effect and create what it makes known—if the soul permits it to."[81] This act of letting it happen is that "keeping of the word through which the soul is sanctified in truth, according to the Lord's desire: 'Sanctify them in the truth; thy word is truth' (Jn 17:17)."[82] Few have ever exposed themselves so unreservedly to the *word* in its entire breadth and depth in order to let sanctification take place in them as did Elizabeth of the Trinity.

---

[79] 134 (ET 101); CW II:L 256.
[80] 236 (ET 175); CW I:158.
[81] 229 (ET 170); CW I:154.
[82] Ibid.

IV

The center of the doctrinal mission of Thérèse of Lisieux[83] was to relate human sinners to divine mercy in a new way, based on the interpenetration of justice and mercy within the Godhead, indeed, on the primacy of love over justice as a form of love. This relationship was established in the New Testament, and Paul's teaching on faith and works was intended to help people appropriate it. Elizabeth's mission appears then as a straightforward continuation and unfolding of Thérèse's. Thérèse also concerned herself with a form of "certainty of salvation", for she spoke constantly of her future heaven, which she desired to bring down to earth in a shower of grace. She also spoke of a type of trust in the ever-greater compassion of God, trust accessible not only to her as a chosen "saint" but to all "little souls" who came after her. In Thérèse's case, too, it was a matter of social grace in the highest degree, since she considered an election *for herself alone*, for the single individual that she was, to be a contradictory, absurd and certainly highly unchristian matter. Indeed, she understood precisely that her grace of election placed her as a woman of prayer and mediator in the heart of the Church, as a means and instrument of God's love for all brothers and sisters. Yet the manner in which Thérèse carried out her mission carried with it so many of her personal characteristics that its revelatory content slipped slightly out of focus. The temerity of the "little child" who threw herself into God's arms and conquered his heart contained a bit too much self-consciousness, a bit too much Pauline demonstrativeness, despite all its Christian theological correctness.

Elizabeth's mission moves through that level of Paul's character, leaving it behind so that everything could be absorbed into the message itself and into the universality of the mystery of Christ. Elizabeth seems to take each of the "teachings"

---

[83] Thérèse of Lisieux, *The Story of a Soul: The Autobiography of St. Thérèse of Lisieux*, 2d ed. (Washington, D.C.: ICS Publications, 1976), 173–82, 195, 200.

of Thérèse and reset them into their framework in revelation. They may lose a bit of the sparkle of novelty, but they are more firmly attached to their original niches in God's word. She does this, for example, in a chapter from "Heaven on Earth"[84] where she collected Scripture texts about "Adoption as Children". She begins with Ephesians 1:5-8, which refers to predestination to adoption as children in Jesus Christ; then she moves to Romans 8:14-17, where the child of God is moved by the Holy Spirit, who calls out to the Father and drives out the spirit of fear, testifying to his spirit that he is a child of God and coheir with the Son, with whom he must suffer in order to be glorified with him. Then she draws on the words in 1 John 3:1-3, regarding adoption as children through the Father's love, whom we shall resemble on the basis of this adoption because we shall see him as he is, being sanctified in the assurance of this hope just as he is holy. "That is the measure of the holiness of the children of God—to be holy as God is holy, holy from the holiness of God and this by contact with him." Then she lets everything come together in Johannine worship in spirit and in truth, "which means *through* Jesus Christ and in him, for he is the one who truly worships in spirit and in truth."[85] Here, finally, she finds room for Thérèse of Lisieux' favorite quotation: "Now we really are daughters of God and understand from our own experience the truth of Isaiah's words, 'You shall be carried at the breast and upon the knees they shall caress you' (Is 66:12)."[86] When Elizabeth makes use of such Thérèsian words as "Cast your soul on the waves of trust and surrender, and take note that whatever perplexes and frightens does not come from God", she is careful to frame these words with a reference to the divine decree of Ephesians 1:11 and Romans 5:20: "Where sin abounds, grace abounds much more."[87] Precisely this central text from Paul, which, in the

---

[84] [Retitled "Heaven in Faith" in the definitive edition of her *Complete Works* —Trans.]

[85] 199-200 (ET 149-50); CW I:107-8.

[86] 201 (ET 150); CW I:108.   [87] 94 (ET 71); CW II:L 224.

widest possible context of salvation history, repeatedly praises
the predominance of Christ's redemptive grace over the entire
Adamic system of original sin and condemnation (Rom 5:12–
21), becomes for Elizabeth the specific "locus" for Thérèsian
grace: "Never permit yourself to be depressed by the thought
of your failures. The great Saint Paul says, 'Where sin abounds,
grace abounds much more.' Thus it is the weakest, indeed, the
most guilty soul who has the best grounds for hope, and this
act by which she surrenders herself and throws herself into the
arms of God, glorifies him more and gives him more joy than all
her introspections and examinations of conscience, which only
cause her to dwell on her weakness, even though she possesses
within herself a Savior who comes at every moment to cleanse
her."[88] Near the end of the same letter, Elizabeth's Thérèsian
inspiration becomes obvious: "Have courage, Madam and Sister, I entrust you most particularly to a little Carmelite who
died at age twenty-two in the odor of sanctity and who called
herself Thérèse of the Child Jesus. Before she died she said that
she wanted to spend her heaven doing good on earth; that her
mission was to broaden souls, to launch them onto the waves
of love, trust and self-surrender; she said of herself that she had
found happiness when she began to forget herself. With me,
ask her daily to obtain for you the knowledge that the saints
possess."[89] Again and again we find her connecting the idea
of adoption as children with the idea of predestination: "Isn't
it very consoling to think that the one who will judge us also
lives in us in order to save us continually from our wretchedness and to forgive us. Paul says this explicitly: 'He has justified
us freely by his blood' (Rom 3:24–25). How rich we are in
divine gifts, we who are 'predestined to adoption as children'
and are thus 'coheirs of his inheritance of glory'! He chose us in
him from all eternity to be holy before him in love."[90] Again,
drawing on another passage from Paul:

---

[88] 123 (ET 92–93); CW II:L 249.   [89] 125 (ET 94); CW II:L 249.
[90] 127 (ET 95–96); CW II:L 238.

You should strike the word "discouragement" from your dictionary. The more you sense your weakness and incapacity for recollection, the more the Master hides himself, so much more you should rejoice, for then you are the one who gives, and is not "giving better than receiving" for the one who loves? God said to Paul: "My grace is sufficient for you, for strength becomes perfect in weakness" (2 Cor 12:9), and that great saint understood it when he cried out "I glory in my weaknesses, for when I am weak, then the power of Christ lives in me." What difference does it make what we feel? He is the Immutable One, who never changes. He loves you today as he loved you yesterday, as he will love you tomorrow, even when you hurt him. Remember that "one deep calls to another"—that the abyss of your misery attracts the bottomlessness of his mercy.[91]

Thus the "gift of fear", which has made many a theologian uneasy, disappears from the teaching of both Thérèse and Elizabeth.[92] "She seems to have been untouched by the fear of hell that is experienced by so many other holy souls."[93] " 'God is rich in mercy because of his excess of love' (Eph 2:4). Don't be afraid of the hour that we must all pass through. Death is like a child falling asleep at his mother's heart. The night of exile will finally be over, and we shall enter upon 'the possession of the inheritance of the saints in light' (Col 1:12). . . . If we would give God more space in our soul each day, what great confidence that would give us for the day we appear before his infinite holiness!"[94] Both Thérèse and Elizabeth are filled with the New Testament Johannine and Pauline concept of "confidence" (parrēsia) in the face of the Day of Judgment. And their confidence does not rest solely on personal election but is a disposition they have been given for the sake of demonstrating it to others—to the fearful and perplexed.

In this disposition the mystery of holiness once more becomes a reality in the Church. Or perhaps a specific mystery of holiness is involved here. There are some people in the

[91] 146–47 (ET 110); CW II:L 298.   [92] P 227 (ET 162–63).
[93] P 228 (ET 163).   [94] 94–95 (ET 71–72); CW II:L 224.

Church who, through a special calling, are entrusted by God with a special mission, and this calling lifts them above the valleys into the vicinity of God and requires of them the sort of total cooperation expressed by Jesus Christ in the evangelical counsels: to leave the whole world in order to follow the call singlemindedly and to live out the heavenly will. But these people receive their commission for others, not for themselves alone. They are supposed to be a city on a hill, in order to protect and influence those living in the valleys. They are supposed to let the light they receive on the heights reach others. They are supposed to permit others to experience as social and ecclesial assurances those certainties of faith that they have been given, for these things were not intended for them personally but for them as one member among many, standing in indissoluble solidarity. They are supposed to show what complete love, complete trust, complete confidence look like and to offer not only an example but an outstretched hand that pulls the others up higher. Yet precisely these attitudes are what keep these helping beings at a distance from us. Because they have the love that drives out all fear, for that very reason they are different from the rest of us who cannot help being fearful, because we are sinners and "whoever is fearful, he is not perfected in love" (1 Jn 4:18). The hand that reaches out to us says only one thing: See how easy it is to love; hand yourself over, give yourself up, and you will see how much easier love is than fear!

DOÑA SEVENSWORDS: There is only one thing necessary, that is the folk that we are necessary to. Forward! . . .

THE BUTCHER'S DAUGHTER: . . . While you are there and talking, how jolly, I cease to exist, I don't feel it worthwhile existing. . . .

DOÑA SEVENSWORDS: . . . But it is nonsense, I tell you! The sea bears you up, it's delightful! There is hardly any effort to make, the water is warm. Who could get tired?

There is nothing to be tired for. Don't go and tell me you are tired?

THE BUTCHER'S DAUGHTER: No, I'm not tired.

DOÑA SEVENSWORDS: There is only one thing necessary, and blow all the rest. What good is it to peer so much and walk about everlastingly like a connoisseur with a pot of color in hand, retouching here and there?

And when a thing is finished to pack his little toucher-up outfit to go and tinker somewhere else?

There is only one thing necessary, and that is someone who asks everything of you and to whom you can give everything. Forward! . . .

I hope you are not tired?

THE BUTCHER'S DAUGHTER (*almost spent*): No, no, I am not tired. . . .

DOÑA SEVENSWORDS: Let us go now quietly at our ease. It is delightful to soak in this kind of liquid light that makes us into hovering godlike beings, (*in thought*) glorified bodies.

No more need of hands to grasp with or feet to carry you.

You go on, like the sea-anemone's breathing, by the mere expansion of the body and the kick of the will.

The whole body is one sense, a planet watching the other planets in the air.

(*Aloud*)

I feel immediately with my heart every beat of thy heart.

(*Here the Butcher's Daughter drowns*)

The water bears up everything. . . . And all that is no longer outside one, you are inside; there is something that unites you blissfully with everything, a drop of water mingling with the sea! The Communion of Saints![95]

---

[95] Paul Claudel, *Le Soulier de satin*, Fourth Day, Scene 10; English translation by John O'Connor, *The Satin Slipper* (New Haven: Yale University Press, 1931), 298–300.

Let us read Elizabeth's letters with these sounds echoing in our ears: "There is a Being who is Love and who wants us to live in fellowship with him. He is there with me, he keeps me company, helps me endure, teaches me to overcome my pain in order to rest in him. Do as I do, *fais comme moi*, and you will see how that transforms everything!"[96] "I want to be completely at his service, completely vigilant in faith, so that the Master can take me wherever he wishes. . . . What a blessing my beloved silence is! . . . Someone wrote to me recently: 'Faith is a face-to-face encounter in the dark.' Why should that not be true of us, if God indeed is in us and he simply wants to take us as he took the saints?"[97] "I ask myself why the soul that has sounded the depths of love for her in God's heart should not be forever happy, despite all suffering and pain. Think about it: he has chosen you before the creation, to be 'spotless and pure in his presence in love'!"[98] The perfect divine security with which Elizabeth romps in the ocean of heavenly love and with which she encourages those who swim fearfully after her to relax and surrender their fears—this security is not private but ecclesial and social. It is given copiously so that it can be given away, hauled up from the Catholic Church's ancient well of confidence and certainty, and rightly so, because she has brought forth the single necessary response: a complete loving surrender to this security. Wherever this effort of love is made with seriousness, inadequate as the effort always is, the guarantee is given: the colossal message will be heard and received undiminished *because* an unreserved answer has been given to a limitless word.

[96] 183–84 (ET 138–39); CW II:L 327.
[97] 98–99 (ET 74–75); CW II:L 165.
[98] 175 (ET 132); CW I:128.

LIMITLESSNESS

EVERYTHING YET TO BE SAID about Elizabeth's spiritual world grows out of the roots described in the preceding pages. She herself understood and expressed her vocation as unmistakably Carmelite in nature. From the beginning, "standing before God spotless and pure" meant to her a standing or kneeling in the silent surrender and receptiveness of Mary the Mother of Jesus and Mary of Bethany, with all her senses opened up to the received word. Her mission was to contemplate at the well in order to channel its flowing waters to the Church.

Here, however, we want to see Elizabeth's gift of grace as she herself saw it: not as one instance among many, whose pattern is well known and long established, rather, as something unique and unrepeatable, uncomprehended and inexpressible. This is true of every encounter with the one and only God, for the brightness of God's solitude covers each of his approaches to his creatures. Whenever the soul hears herself being called by name, as did Mary Magdalen at the tomb, the most personal and unmistakable primal meaning of the personal God resonates in the sound of one's name. And anyone called by Carmel to pass beyond all limits, to move *to the margin* where there is nothing except the limitless God, will find all her accustomed props knocked down so that she can face unprotected the experience of being "alone with the Alone". One cannot describe God, one cannot even describe an encounter with God. One can only follow with one's eyes from afar as someone gets up and goes forward, farther and farther, until she reaches the shore of infinity and kneels there where nothing but God remains, in order to enter silently the vision of endlessness. Such a one can stammer about what she encounters, but her babbling falls far short of what she encounters, and our stammering account of her speech is even farther removed from what she encounters. Elizabeth's statements lack literary charm. Her words are most compelling when they fall silent in the infinite Word who is God and who became audible in the revelation of Jesus Christ. What she actually says from her standpoint at the edge of the world remains fragmentary and must be interpreted by the Church's words, as she intended it to be.

Living in the orbit of the divine decree, Elizabeth has been bowled over with elemental force by the limitlessness of God. For her, *infinity* is no empty word devoid of imagery, and it is no experience of nothingness beyond the familiar finite world. For her, it is a spiritual disposition, a physical experience and an ever more inescapable need. She does not encounter God as a Someone who, among other attributes, also happens to possess infinity. She encounters Limitlessness and knows that it is God. She sees the edge, the margin, and beyond it the abyss and by letting go, she knows: God is here. She does not confuse her experience of the disappearing boundary with God, she does not swoon at this experience. But the experience points to Something and Someone beyond all limits of earthly life, and this Inexpressible One is God. God lives in inaccessible light, since he is eternal and unbounded. But, in revealing himself, he has crossed the threshold from infinity to time and thereby opened the door to infinity for the creature. "You will see the heavens opened" (Jn 1:51). There comes a moment when the creature no longer merely sees by faith Infinity-become-finite. Instead, raised beyond her limits, she must stagger into the bottomless ground of infinity without perishing. Nor may the crossing of the boundary be postponed until death. In the midst of the finite, the creature must, through faith in Infinity-become-incarnate, practice being a citizen of the infinite world. This is surely what faith is. The creature cannot be fitted to the world of God without faith being present. The creature must be ready to take the step across the boundary, no matter how deadly it appears to a finitude without faith. Long before entering it in death, the creature must learn to love and explore as his home what appears to be the most alien of places.

Elizabeth's language is saturated with images and ideas of limitlessness. She lives on this horizon. As a young girl, before she entered the convent, she was already full of an "infinite thirst for him"[1], which she later described more precisely as a "thirst for the infinite".[2] Sunday morning church bells invite her "to climb above this earth into the regions of infinity, where there is nothing but him",[3] "indeed, let us leave this earth and everything perceived by the senses, let us live already in heaven now. . . . I sense myself called by him to live in endless fields where union with him takes place."[4] "Let us be carried to those regions where only he remains, he alone."[5] Later, in Carmel, God and love are "like an ocean into which I plunge, in which I lose myself",[6] "everything disappears, and I lose myself in him like a drop of water in the sea."[7] Again and again she describes an expansiveness large enough for every movement, every unfolding and fulfillment: "Our home is limitlessness, where we can move around no matter what",[8] it is " 'the broad place' of which the Psalmist speaks" (17:22 [18:19]).[9] "God carries me to the depths of that divine being in which through grace we already live and where I want to be so deeply buried that nothing can ever convince me to leave."[10] She continually quotes the words of Paul about "the spirit searching the depths of the Godhead" (1 Cor 2:10), calling these depths unfathomable,[11] yet describing the Christian life as a steady and deeper penetration into them day by day.[12] Walking clearly and courageously does not prevent (rather seems to require) losing one's footing and letting oneself float in the abyss of love. The soul is "on the path to the

---

[1] 43 (ET 31); CW III:L 49.   [2] 69 (ET 52); CW II:L 169.

[3] 44 (ET 31); CW III:L 49.   [4] 45 (ET 32); CW III:L 54.

[5] 46 (ET 33); CW III:L 58.   [6] 73 (ET 55); CW II:L 177.

[7] 76 (ET 58); CW II:L 190.   [8] 100 (ET 75); CW II:L 185.

[9] 219, 228, 242 (ET 163, 170, 179); CW I:148, 154, 162.

[10] 107 (ET 80); CW II:L 214.

[11] 140, cf. 110 (ET 105, cf. 82); CW II:L 274, cf. L226.

[12] 222 (ET 165); CW I:150.

abyss",[13] "on the slope of love",[14] which exists already this side of finitude as love and as a response to the love of God. Because, through revelation, she is called before God to be his image and is challenged to offer an adequate response of love, the soul encounters limitlessness in herself. There is within her a "path to the abyss" on which she walks toward that place where the infinite meets her. Yet her "inner abyss"[15] is not a second infinity alongside God, rather, it is distinct from God primarily as an abyss of incapacity, an expression of hopeless finitude in the face of God's endlessness.[16] It is in this sense that Angela of Foligno could say that "the abyss of God's infinity turns to face the creature's abyss of nothingness and that God embraces this nothingness".[17] Elizabeth had sensed such an "embrace of infinity" very early on.[18] Now she can summarize:

> Push farther and farther into this deepness. For here is the wilderness into which God wants to entice the soul in order to talk with her, as the prophet sang (Hos 2:14). In order to hear the password, one dare not camp on the surface, rather one must penetrate by recollection deeper and deeper into the divine being. "I keep going", Paul exclaimed (Phil 3:12). In the same way we must descend daily to the path of the abyss, the abyss that is God. Let us slip down this slope in a confidence bursting of love. "Deep calls on deep" (Ps 41:8 [42:7]). Here, all the way down, the divine crash [le choc divin] occurs. The abyss of our nothingness, of our wretchedness, finds itself confronting the abyss of mercy, of limitlessness, of God's All. Here we find the strength to die to ourselves and, losing every trace of our own way, to be changed into love. "Blessed are those who die in the Lord" (Rev 14:13).[19]

"Swallowed up" [abîmée][20] in this way, the soul encounters the great Solitary. "The Eternal Being lives in an eternal, enormous

[13] 190 (ET 143–44); CW I:97. [14] 191 (ET 144); CW I:97.
[15] 241–42 (ET 179); CW I:162. [16] 169 (ET 128); CW I:124.
[17] 171 (ET 129–30); CW I:126. [18] 102 (ET 77); CW II:L 199.
[19] 187–88 (ET 141–42); CW I:95. [20] 41 (ET 29); CW III:J156.

solitude that he never leaves even when he takes care of the needs of the creature. For God never departs from himself, and this solitude is nothing other than his divinity."[21] Yet this is also our "Father's house from which we shall never depart".[22] It is the "spacious abyss . . . of the unfathomable Trinity",[23] into which the self-silenced soul sinks. "When the Creator sees the beautiful silence that reigns in his creature, sees her recollected in his inward solitude, he permits her to pass over into that immeasurable solitude that is nothing but himself."[24] It is God's "endlessness that surrounds the cosmos from all sides"[25] in the "fathomless abyss",[26] in genuine eternity: "He requires of me that I live in the eternal present, without before and without after, completely within the unity of my being in this eternal now"[27] and therein "to do nothing but what is eternal".[28]

This is the essence of the one who is called and consecrated: already here below to live, not in temporal, but in eternal space, to be someone who has died to this world and to finitude. Her day of death is not that of the physical departure from her body, but in the strictest sense it is the day of her Yes to God. "Dying away" and "mortification" are not the language of asceticism for her, rather they are expressions of her existence. The meaning of her life is found completely in the eternal and unending. Thus one cannot say that her existence can be meaningfully explained and proven from the perspective of finitude. One's death is the ultimate offense to unbelief and even seems ultimately offensive to most Christians living in the world. In truth, the saint is a person of the beyond. That she remains on this side only makes sense as a way to open a window so that something of the customs and laws, something of the air of the beyond can drift over into this world. What the ancient monks knew has nearly drifted out of the consciousness of

---

[21] 227 (ET 169); CW I:153. [22] 187 (ET 141); CW I:94.
[23] 243 (ET 180); CW I:162. [24] 229 (ET 170); CW I:154.
[25] 104 (ET 78); CW II:L 202.
[26] 200, 202 (ET 150, 151); CW I:108, 110.
[27] 226 (ET 168); CW I:152. [28] 230 (ET 171); CW I:155.

modern cultural Catholicism. Missions like those of Elizabeth
or Charles de Foucauld are great voices of admonition within
time and the Church, calling on Christians not to settle down
within finitude but to permit dying with Christ to happen to
them so that, "having died", they might lead a "life hidden
with Christ in God" (Col 3:3).

When Elizabeth first becomes acquainted with her cell, she
has an immediate impression of falling barriers and disappearing bars. She is pleased that her relatives are traveling through
beautiful lands. "But look, the horizons of Carmel are much
more beautiful: they are limitlessness. And I have in God all
the valleys and lakes and all the scenic views."[29] "Everything
is full of wonder in Carmel. You find God in the laundry room
as well as in prayer. He is simply everywhere. You live him,
you breathe him. My horizon grows from day to day."[30] "I
don't know how to describe my happiness. There is nothing
left here except him. He is everything, he suffices, one lives
from him alone. . . . It is as if the gate of heaven had opened
up."[31] "Endless vistas open up in the life of a Carmelite."[32]
And, since access comes by way of her own silence, the limitlessness of God becomes a great *quietness*. "The tranquil Trinity",[33] even more so *peace*,[34] is God's name; that peace "above
all activity of the mind" known not only by Paul and John
but also by Dionysius the Pseudo-Areopagite, who celebrates
God as the endless reconciliation beyond all the quarrels and
contradictions of finitude. "Everything is peaceful, everything
has quieted, how good the peace of God is! This is what Paul
was talking about when he said that it surpasses all thought."[35]
"He reigns in the soul through the fullness of peace and the
repose that he spreads out within",[36] "he holds the soul immovably and peacefully in his presence, as if she already were

[29] 53 (ET 41); CW II:L 87. [30] 53 (ET 41); CW II:L 89.
[31] 56–57 (ET 43, 44); CW II:L 91. [32] 86 (ET 66); CW II:L 209.
[33] 223, 241 (ET 166, 179); CW I:150, 162.
[34] 76 (ET 58); CW II:L 190. [35] Ibid.
[36] 112 (ET 84); CW II:L 231.

in eternity."[37] For Elizabeth, this repose in endless peace is the simplest, most natural movement of the grace-filled creature, since "all streams of the soul lose themselves in the sea of divine love and have already become as broad as the sea."[38] To rest in God is the opposite of strenuous spiritual exercises.[39] "Ah, if you only could learn to know God a little bit, then prayer would not bore you. For me it is recreation, relaxation. One turns in simplicity to the one whom one loves."[40]

The tranquil soul becomes a place of peace for God himself. What has been freed from earth becomes a heaven for God, where he can live, the "de-finitized"[41] soul becomes a container for divine limitlessness. "Release my soul, make her into your heaven, your beloved dwelling and the place of your peace",[42] "a bottomless abyss into which God can overflow and lavish himself";[43] for "God hollows out deep chasms in my soul, chasms that he alone can fill."[44] Opening herself and offering herself to infinity, she is ready to be possessed by limitlessness. The most forceful words rush toward her as she tries to express this: she wants "to let herself be taken" by God. Already before entering the convent she said, "May I be hidden in you! May all I do be done in your sight! Take me, Master, take all of me!"[45] She wants to "be submerged",[46] to "be overtaken", as if by an invading superior power or by an elemental force

[37] 232 (ET 172); CW I:156.

[38] 158, quoting John of the Cross (ET 119); CW II:L 293.

[39] 181, 66 (ET 137, 50); CW II:L 301, L150.

[40] 78, cf. 181 (ET 59, cf. 136–37); CW II:L 123, cf. L301.

[41] 221: infinisé (ET 164: "becomes infinite"); CW I:149.

[42] 80 (ET 61); CW I:183. [The German text has befreie (liberate) for the paci-fiez of Elizabeth's famous prayer to the Trinity. This may be a typographical error for befriede (pacify), although befreien can carry the sense of "release" and therefore "relax" or "make tranquil". It is conceivable that the author intended to take account of the subtle interrelationship of these two concepts—TRANS.]

[43] 204 (ET 153); CW I:112.   [44] 77 (ET 58); CW II:L 190.

[45] 41 (ET 29); CW III:J156; cf. S 422, 83, 86; CW III:P83.

[46] 81 (ET 62); CW I:183.

(the word *envahir* occurs again and again in her writings),[47] to "be buried" (*ensevelir*),[48] to "lose" herself in God and to God.[49] She loves to see in God the "consuming fire" that eats up her finitude to prepare her for eternal life;[50] she wants to be God's prey.[51] The passion with which she throws herself into the flames is particularly visible where she struggles with all her strength to be free of the earth, doing so with an intensity that is striking because it has no equal in our times (one finds a parallel in Novalis). Furthermore, the passion with which she abandons the world seems to us to fit so oddly with her loving devotion to her fellow creatures.

In this, Elizabeth ought to be a beacon for us. Already before entering the monastery she speaks of her "longing for heaven" and of how grateful she would be if God took her to himself before she could enter Carmel.[52] And when it became apparent that she was really approaching death, her momentum became precipitous: "The Master compels me to separate myself from everything that is not himself."[53] She speaks constantly of her departure, as simply as if she were merely walking from one room to another: "Before I leave I'd like to send you a note. . . ."[54] "Everything speaks to me of my departure to 'my Father's house'."[55] She has already begun to float above, and it is hard for her to keep her feet on earth. She "flies away";[56] 'she already draws breath from a divine atmosphere, only her body is still here, her soul lives above the clouds and fog";[57] she

[47] 61, 63, 65, 69, 72, 81, 83, 97, 105, 106 (ET 47, 48, 50, 52, 54, 62, 64, 73, 79 [twice]); CW II:L131, L136, L151, L169, L172; I:183; II:L183, L158, L124 (twice); S 422, 425; CW III:P83, P88.

[48] 110, 114 (ET 82, 85); CW II:L191, L232.

[49] 46, 97, 159, 166 (ET 33, 74, 119, 124); CW III:L58; II:L158, L293, L341.

[50] 81, 140, 159, 191 and frequently elsewhere (ET 62, 105, 119, 144, etc.); CW I:183; II:L274, L293; I:98.

[51] 69, 81 (ET 52, 62); CW II:L169; I:184; S 426; CW III:P88.

[52] 47 (ET 34); CW II:L55.   [53] 131 (ET 99); CW II:L250.

[54] 161 (ET 120); CW II:L331.   [55] 159 (ET 119); CW II:L293.

[56] 77, 163 (ET 59, 122); CW II:L225, L335.

[57] 124 (ET 93–94); CW II:L249.

rises like a balloon that has been cut free, and nothing can catch her. "She climbs, she raises herself above the senses, above nature; she surpasses even herself, she soars over all joy as well as all suffering; she glides through everything, never again to rest until she has pushed through to the inner being of him who himself will give her 'the repose of the spacious abyss'."[58] She almost seems to view with a sort of pleasure the wasting and burning her sickness causes her. "I feel death destroying me. But faith tells me that it is love who is destroying me and slowly wearing me away. My joy is immeasurable, and I give myself as prey to love."[59] "I feel in my whole being the work of destruction. The way of the Cross lies open, and, as happy as a bride, I walk it alongside the divine Crucified One."[60] "That calls for pain, for everything that we are must be destroyed so that God himself can take its place."[61] "Indeed, the holy God has glorified himself in this soul because he destroyed everything in her in order to clothe her with himself, and because she has lived out daily the words of the forerunner: 'He must increase and I must decrease' (Jn 3:30)."[62]

Elizabeth perceives Christian existence as a steady self-opening and broadening of divine space. Unlike Augustine, who thought that the soul could only stagger into and out of the momentary flashes of light from beyond this world, Elizabeth marches with steady steps *into the divine depths*. To be sure, it is a march of faith that sees not yet walks in the certainty that every step of one who loves is a step into the limitlessness of God—not only in the privileged quiet of Carmel and in the life of contemplation but also in the middle of the world where the same life of love cannot help but succeed, because nothing can deter one who truly loves from walking in God. This thought returns again and again, illuminated from all sides. For herself, she prays: "Let nothing disturb my peace or make me leave

[58] 242–43 (ET 179–80); CW I:162.   [59] 172–73 (ET 130); CW I:126.
[60] 145 (ET 108); CW II:L 294.   [61] 148 (ET 111); CW II:L 298.
[62] 238 (ET 177); CW I:159–60.

you, my Changeless One; indeed, let every minute carry me deeper into the abyss of your mystery!"[63] "Each moment is granted us so that we can 'push our roots' deeper into God (to use Paul's words), to make our likeness to the divine image more telling and our union more intimate."[64] "The soul who penetrates the depths of God and lives there . . . becomes with each movement, with each of her yearnings, with each of her actions, as ordinary as they may be, more firmly and deeply rooted in the one she loves."[65] " 'Walk in Jesus Christ' means to depart from oneself, to lose sight of oneself, to abandon oneself in order to penetrate deeper into him with each passing moment, so deep that one is rooted into him . . . and all of one's incomplete, commonplace and natural life is destroyed. The soul who is emptied of herself in this way, who has been 'clothed with Jesus Christ', no longer has to fear contact with the external world, nor is she anxious about inner difficulties; far from hindering her, they actually 'push her roots deeper into love' (Eph 3:17)."[66] And the fact that Elizabeth offers instructions about this sort of life to her friends and relatives in the world means that she was convinced that these guidelines could be lived out. She herself had lived this way before entering Carmel, and she thus speaks from experience.[67] It is possible in the active life to live completely with God.[68] As an example she offers the Mother of God, who remained a perfect woman of worship in the midst of daily work and service to others.[69] A loving soul can do the same,[70] even to the point that the roles of Mary and Martha interpenetrate each other and no longer need to be played by two different persons. "Don't you find", she writes to a priest, "that even while seemingly occupied with Martha's duties the soul can remain deep in con-

---

[63] 80 (ET 61); CW I:183.   [64] 162 (ET 121); CW II:L333.

[65] 222 (ET 165); CW I:150.

[66] 233, cf. 204 (ET 173, cf. 153); CW I:156-57, cf. I:112.

[67] 41, 43 (ET 28-29, 31-32); CW III:J140, J156, L49.

[68] 125-26 (ET 94-95); CW II:L235.   [69] 202 (ET 151-52); CW I:110-11.

[70] 193 (ET 145); CW I:99.

templation with Mary, bending over the well like someone dying of thirst? This is the way I understand the apostolate of the Carmelites and of the priesthood: both can give off rays of God and bring them to souls if they linger without interruption at the divine spring."[71] To another priest: "I want to be an apostle together with you out of the depths of my beloved solitude in Carmel, to work for God's glory—and to that end I must be completely filled with him. Then all power will be given to me: a glance, a wish will become an irresistible prayer that can obtain everything, for then, so to speak, one offers God to God. May our souls be one in God, and, while you carry him to people, I shall remain, like Mary, silent and adoring before the Master, praying him that he will make your words fruitful. Apostle, Carmelite—they are the same thing!"[72] This is the ancient concept of the radiant contemplation, which the desert monks and Dionysius the Pseudo-Areopagite already knew but which first revealed its full inner dimension of apostolic action in modern times—through the great Teresa and little Thérèse. We must reflect on the degree of comprehensiveness and significance attained in the modern era if the ancient formula, *in contemplatione activus* [active in contemplation] is to take on life. In this way it can be expanded to serve as an effective bulwark against modern churchly activism and against the myopia of many Christians who, thinking pure contemplation outdated, insist on a "world-oriented" spirituality. The Carmels of our time possess the antidote against feeble and anxious efforts to be relevant—namely, the insight that pure contemplation and the complete spiritual death it demands is the most effective way to help the Church in the world. Because the soul who has set out for God's limitlessness encounters no barriers in that limitlessness, it is there that she can locate her sister soul and help her. Although the spirituality of Christian antiquity and the Middle Ages experienced the two commands of love of God and of neighbor in a palpable tension with each other—

[71] 97 (ET 73–74); CW II:L 158.   [72] 106 (ET 79); CW II:L 124.

turning from the world to God and from God again back to the world—today's Carmelite finds her neighbor directly in God. "Souls need not communicate in writing, they press forward to the limitlessness of God only to rediscover themselves there and to throw themselves into the same adoration."[73] "Whoever lingers at the spring of living water can bubble over in all directions without ever emptying her soul, for, after all, she has communion with the Infinite."[74] " 'Our walk is in heaven' (Phil 3:20). And I thought that my soul would have to go as far as that to find yours."[75]

II

At this point, where love of neighbor finds its place within the love of God, we can see that Elizabeth's experience of God's infinity is not an acosmic, empty, worldless experience. She is anything but a nature mystic or pantheistic mystic who is miffed at the boundaries imposed by finitude or who impatiently rattles the bars of the imprisoning world, seeking to escape so she can venture forth into a supposed divine unlimitedness. The proof of this lies in the complete absence of any "negative theology" in Elizabeth, a theology that tries to express God's limitlessness by denying him all the names and characteristics of finite being. What Elizabeth seeks in limitlessness is not the God of philosophy, a God of distance and unapproachability, rather, she seeks the God of Jesus Christ, the God of perfect nearness and familiarity—because the creature has an inner need and yearning to linger at home with this God. One can see in Elizabeth's case how much the experience of God in Christianity is diametrically opposed to pagan mysticism in this crucial area, no matter how much Christian experience makes use of concepts and expressions similar to those of pagan mysticism. The exuberant experience that John of the

[73] 104, cf. 107, 147 (ET 78, cf. 80, 110–11); CW II:L 202, cf. L214, L298.
[74] 105 (ET 79); CW II:L 124.   [75] 131 (ET 98); CW II:L 250.

Cross sets out to describe with virtually neoplatonist words is an experience of a directly present, absolute and limitless love that is consuming in its purity. This love demands an immediate and unconditional response, and this love accomplishes the same in the willing soul. That response obtains for the soul a share in the boundlessness of God as the flame and sword of infinite love destroy all barriers of created love.

Limitlessness is, for Elizabeth, a familiar home from the start, not "inaccessible light", but light that is accessible, uncovered and proffered through the revelation of the Son of God. Already in the Old Covenant, "God said: 'Be holy for I am holy', but he was hidden in his inaccessible light. It was necessary for the creature's sake that he climb down all the way to the creaturely, that he live the creature's life, so that the creature, following step by step in God's path, could climb up to God and make himself holy with God's holiness."[76] We would know nothing of true limitlessness if the Son had not flooded the world with the fullness of his infinity by taking on limits. He is the word, the revelation, but he is such only because he is also grace, communication and incorporation. And only for that reason does the fullness of the Godhead dwell in him. "I want to keep myself as close as possible to God, who possesses the whole secret, so that I can learn everything from him. 'The speech of the Word is the infusion of the gifts of grace.' "[77] Although Elizabeth's mysticism is an explicit mysticism of infinity, it is just as unquestionably *christological* mysticism, since limitlessness invades finitude only at one place—the Incarnation, Passion and Eucharist of the body of God in Christ. Therefore to exist at the margin, at the point where the world opens up to God, is to exist in Christ, who, as mediator between finite and infinite, is the locus of infinity's opening to finitude. Continual existence "in transit" there is a steady resting and communication with Christ. The experience begins for Elizabeth with Holy Communion, where the communication of infinite

[76] 231–32 (ET 171); CW I:155.   [77] 98–99 (ET 74); CW II:L 165.

love takes place most intimately. "Nothing speaks more of the love hidden in the heart of God than the Eucharist. Here one finds union, here one finds consummation: he is in us, and we are in him. Is that not heaven on earth, heaven in faith?"[78] The experience of Holy Communion broadens itself into an extra-sacramental, lasting communion spreading through all of Christian existence. "No matter what, let us constantly communicate with this word become flesh, with Jesus who lives in us and wishes to tell us the whole secret."[79] "To live from him! Then every offering, every sacrifice, becomes divine; the soul sees the one she loves in everything; everything carries her to him in an uninterrupted heart-to-heart communication."[80] Already as a child, before Carmel, when she once fell sick, she said: "I can't go to Holy Communion, but God needs no sacrament in order to come to me—it seems to me as if I have him in any case. How good this presence of God is!"[81] "I feel as if he communicates eternal life to me."[82] "I feel as if all the treasures of the soul of Christ belong to me."[83] More and more her entire existence becomes a sacrament to her, a communication of the life and suffering of the Lord. "Let us make a continual Holy Communion out of our days!"[84] "Life in Carmel is communion with God from morning to evening, from evening to morning. If he did not fill our cells and halls, how empty everything would be!"[85] It is a "communion with the soul of the Lord, a conforming to all his motions"[86] and, through him, "a kind of continual communion with the triune God",[87] "since all things that come to us are like a sacrament that offers God to us".[88] "Each incident, each event and each suffering, as well as each joy, is a sacrament that gives us God, and the soul can no longer distinguish among these

[78] 98 (ET 74); CW II:L 165.

[80] 63 (ET 48); CW II:L 136.

[82] P 160 (ET 108).

[84] 72 (ET 55); CW II:L 172.

[86] 97 (ET 74); CW II:L 158.

[88] 135–36 (ET 102); CW II:L 264.

[79] 64 (ET 48–49); CW II:L 145.

[81] 48 (ET 34); CW III:L 62.

[83] P 164 (ET 111); CW II:L 91.

[85] 79 (ET 60); CW II:L 123.

[87] 92 (ET 70); CW II:L 252.

things, rather she passes beyond them to repose above all in her Lord himself."[89] When in the end Elizabeth once more has to do without Holy Communion, it is really no pain for her, since she has accustomed herself so much to a constant spiritual communion with her Lord. Christ dwelling in her constitutes for her each moment the *admirabile commercium*,[90] the wonderful exchange of divine and creaturely life, without which no Christian can be for a single moment a Christian. In this crossing of the specific sacrament's boundaries into the boundless life it transmits, Elizabeth once more joins her sister Thérèse of the Child Jesus, who prayed for the same grace: "Ah, I cannot receive Holy Communion as often as I would like, but Lord, are you not all-powerful? Dwell in me as in a tabernacle, never remove yourself from your little host!"[91]

Once more, especially in the last, pain-filled months of her life, the presence of the infinite in Jesus Christ changed for Elizabeth. Where once the "excess of love" emanated toward her from the humanity of the Son, overpowering her with awareness of his eternal presence, at the end it is always the *suffering of Christ* for her and in her that becomes the gateway to limitlessness. Here the depths of God for the world become palpable. The moment at which Jesus left the world and his own to enter into suffering is the moment at which he most loves her, the moment of transition into infinity, the moment at which love visibly once more assumes the measure of infinity.[92] Moreover, suffering itself is "something divine, so much so that the saints themselves must envy us".[93] It is the "proof of love", it is "love in action".[94] "I see that suffering is the revelation of love, and I hurry toward it. I am sure to meet my Lord there and live with him."[95] Suffering stretches one, ex-

[89] 190 (ET 143); CW I:97.   [90] 123 (ET 93); CW II:L 249.

[91] *Story of a Soul: The Autobiography of St. Thérèse of Lisieux*, 2d ed. (Washington, D.C.: ICS Publications, 1976), 277.

[92] 156, 160, 162 (ET 117, 120, 121); CW II:L 315, L 331, L 333.

[93] 90 (ET 69); CW II:L 207.   [94] 132 (ET 99); CW II:L 250.

[95] 154 (ET 115); CW II:L 323.

pands one's soul: "All the elect . . . must pass through this great
affliction, must learn pain that is as immense as the ocean, as
the prophet said (Lam 2:13). Before contemplating God with
uncovered faces (2 Cor 3:18), they have shared the descent of
the Son into nothingness. Before they are transformed from
glory into glory into the image of the Divine Being (2 Cor
3:18), they are conformed to the image of the incarnate Word,
who was crucified for love. A soul who wishes to worship
God day and night in his temple must be prepared to participate in deed and in truth in her Lord's Passion." [96] For it is
here and nowhere else that she acquires actual conformity. "In
the hours in which she feels the fearful emptiness, God hollows out the soul to create more room for receiving; he creates a soul who, so to speak, is as limitless as he is himself." [97]
This is implied in the secret of predestination from eternity,
since we "are predestined to be conformed to the image of the
Son", the "one who died", and the one from whom—because
he bore all guilt and pain—"neither tribulation, nor distress,
nor persecution, nor hunger, nor nakedness, nor the sword
can separate; as it is written: for your sake we are slaughtered
every day, we are counted as sheep for the slaughter" (Rom
8:29, 32–36). For Elizabeth, the face of crucified love shines
ever more powerfully from within the limitlessness of God,
and thus the general, and at the same time neutral, dying away
from the world toward God steadily becomes deliberate dying
with Christ. One can see how the word *passer*,[98] so loaded with
meaning for her and applied not only to the "great passage" of
the soul to God but also to the transitory nature of things, also
moves into a mysterious proximity to the Passion of Christ.
For the Lord, the hour of his "departing out of this world to
the Father" is, after all, precisely the hour of his descent into
the abyss of suffering, the "definition of his death". [99] Yet it is
also, for him and for the one who follows him, the expression

---

[96] 216 (ET 160–61); CW I:146.
[97] 122 (ET 92); CW II:L 249.
[98] 191 (ET 144); CW I:97.
[99] 126 (ET 95); CW II:L 238.

of his great passion for the glory of the Father.[100] To be permitted to suffer thus becomes a sign that the believer has entered into the endless orbit of predestination: "We enter our path to the Cross singing, a hymn of thanksgiving rises from our soul to the Father, for those who walk the way of suffering are the ones 'he knew and predestined to be conformed to the image of his divine Son', the one crucified for love."[101]

Because infinity is in Christ and because we know and are shaped into Christ in suffering, therefore—and not for reasons of philosophy or because we yearn for it—limitlessness is our homeland.[102] Through Christ, infinity becomes a livable and inhabited infinity. In the last months of Elizabeth's life, she perceives the mysterious unity of the mountain of the Cross and the mountain of the Apocalypse, on which the heavenly lamb stands with his companions. The mountain of suffering darkness and abandonment is the same as the mountain of election to heavenly fellowship, to the city of God and the city of saints. This is the way Elizabeth liked to describe limitless heaven, based on Ephesians 2:19.[103] Her understanding of eternity is a social one, and the texts of Paul that she piles one upon another confirm this communion in the eternal: " 'Through baptism', Paul says, 'we have been grafted into Jesus Christ'. 'God has shown us to seats in heaven in Jesus Christ, in order to reveal the riches of his grace to the coming ages,' 'You are no longer guests and friends, rather you are the city of the saints and the house of God.' The triune God is our house, our home, our Father's house, from which we shall never be able to depart. The Lord said this himself: 'The servant does not always remain in the house, but the son remains forever.' "[104] It is thus no abstract infinity but *the infinity of an excess of presence*: the presence of Christ, the presence of the triune God,

---

[100] 205 (ET 154); CW I:141.   [101] 198 (ET 149); CW I:107.

[102] 96, 187 (ET 73, 141); CW II:L 193; I:94–95.

[103] 108, 128, 131, 134, 153, 187 (ET 81, 96, 98–99, 100, 115, 141); CW II:L 191, L239, L250, L256, L323; I:94.

[104] 187 (ET 141); CW I:94.

the presence of all the saints. These together, by being present, indeed truly by the wonder of their existence and their love engender the sense and experience of limitlessness. What is really endless is love. The ever-repeated wish to lose herself in God, in the Endless One,[105] is thus, not a metaphysical desire, but a simple movement of love, yet it is such a great gesture that the word *infinity* is the absolute truth, not a mere exaggeration. "To lose oneself" must be understood here in the sense of the Lord's commandment—in the loss of one's own soul lies the key to entry into the kingdom of love, in which the "I" indeed, but not a single "Thou", is lost. On the feast of All Saints, 1906, as Elizabeth thought she was dying (she continued dying for nine more days), she wrote to a friend these last words: "I have hope that I may find myself tonight among the 'great multitude' that John saw standing round the throne of the Lamb, serving him 'day and night in his temple'. We shall see one another again in this chapter of the Apocalypse, . . . in the vision into which I am going to lose myself forever."[106]

---

[105] 46, 97, 159 (ET 33, 74, 119); CW III:L 58; II:L 158, L293.
[106] 166 (ET 124); CW II:L 341.

ADORATION

I

BECAUSE LIMITLESSNESS IS A THOU, and the Thou is limit-lessness, movement into infinity must be a movement of worship. Predestination is the framework, limitlessness the destination, of this movement; adoration is its essential content, action, fullness and significance. With gentle passion, Elizabeth circles round the vision of worship in the book of Revelation; it touches the innermost part of her soul and challenges her to give everything.

"And day or night they never ceased calling out 'Holy, Holy, Holy is the Lord God Almighty, who was, and who is, and who is to come!' . . . And they fell down and adored, and they threw their crowns before the throne, saying 'Worthy art Thou, our Lord and God, to receive glory, and honor, and power . . .' " (Rev 4:8, 10–11). How can I imitate in the heaven of my soul the unceasing adoration of the saints in heaven's glory? How can I carry out this hymn of praise, this unbroken worship? . . . The soul must first fall down, plunge into the abyss of her nothingness . . . , then she will be able to worship. Adoration, heavenly word! I believe I can describe it as the ecstasy of love. Adoration is a love that is smothered and buried by the beauty, power and infinite grandeur of the Beloved. It falls into a kind of swoon, into a silence that is deep and complete . . . , the most beautiful song of praise that sounds forth eternally in the unity of the tranquil Trinity. Adoration is "the last effort of the soul that has flooded its banks and can speak no more" (Lacordaire). "Adore the Lord, for he is holy" (Ps 98:9 [99:9]). And: "They shall adore him forever for his own sake" (Ps 71:15 [72:15]).[1]

Worship is not a voluntary act that the creature decides to undertake after thinking it over. It forces itself upon the creature wherever eternal love, in its inexpressible impact on a person,

[1] 222–23 (ET 165–66); CW I:150–51.

in its incomprehensible presentness, permits itself to be seen. "Crushed by happiness",[2] the soul falls to the ground, buried under what Paul called the "excess of love" (Eph 2:4) and what Elizabeth took as a maxim for her life: "There is a word of Paul that is like a summary of my existence, that could be written over each moment of my life: '*Propter nimiam caritatem!*' [from excessive love]. Yes, all these rivers of graces—they arise from his having loved me all too much."[3] This phrase is always on her lips.[4] This "all too much" says more than even the idea of limitlessness does; it destroys all relationships by surpassing them all; it mocks every coming to terms, accommodation and habituation; it throws one off every well-worn track and enforces every capitulation; it is a word that can be spoken only in the midst of tears and with choking voice by one who knows he has been conquered and is finally ready to surrender all his freedom. For a moment, perhaps, one might want to turn aside, as Peter did after the marvelous catch of fish, solely to avoid burdening this excess of love, to disappear silently from the "impossible": "Lord, depart from me." But one knows that flight has already been overtaken, that the net of love has closed and only one eternal destiny remains: "Lord, not only my feet but also my hands and my head!" The loving one does not enter the kingdom of eternal love exulting in having found the crown of all yearnings, rather, she enters humbly, dumb-struck, because love has unimaginably surpassed all her expectations and even herself. One can endure the unbearable: the presence of love. To describe this Unbearable as bliss, as the ecstasy of love, is miserably inadequate! For love is indeed too great and this "too" carries in it something painful that only the loving one knows—the arrow, the thorn of all blessedness. And how inadequate it would be to describe this pain as a failure to respond, as a failure to offer something in return, as the

[2] 157 (ET 118); CW II:L 325.   [3] 180 (ET 136); CW II:L 280.
[4] 99, 108, 113, 147, 151, 175, 180, 194, 214, 232, 234 (ET 75, 81, 84, 111, 113, 132, 136, 146, 159, 172, 174); CW II:L 165, L 191, L 232, L 298, L 304; I:128; II:L 280; I:101, 145, 156, 157.

disappointment at oneself who, even in the highest degree of devotion, has nothing worth giving to love. The excess of love surpasses not only the self to whom it is given, indeed a greater and more worthy self would still have nothing worth giving in response to this exuberance. The characteristic excessiveness belongs to love itself—it is excessive in comparison with itself. Each one encountered by this wonder and bathed in its flood simply must enter into adoration in the face of love's superiority and its radiant triumph.

All the elements of worship that are considered here must be viewed in this context. They are comprehensible outlines within an incomprehensible, overwhelmingly powerful light. Elizabeth lived in this light and related everything to it. Unlike John of the Cross, she lacked the poetic gifts needed to celebrate in song the central fire of the living flame of love. Her ideas are often borrowed, her words are often flat and undefined. She speaks best when she clothes herself in the words of Scripture. But that from which she lives and toward which her weak words point—adoration—is powerful and authentic. It fills the many hours that she spent huddled alone before her God in the little chapel and at the end, in her sickness, in a corner of the tribune overlooking the choir. Adoration filled her to the limit with the mystery she contemplated: the indisputable present-ness of God, before her and in her, in the nakedness, surrender and self-sacrifice of eternal love. Nothing but contemplation and awe, beyond all satisfaction and bliss for herself, nothing but being for, being with, being a response and being at love's disposal. And this astonishing silence is heaven on earth. In it, presence, not bliss, makes a down payment on an eternal heaven in which bliss will be found simply in the repeated and everlasting wonder of presence. "On Mount Carmel, in silence, in solitude, in a prayer that never ends and survives all interruptions, the Carmelite lives as if already in heaven: for God alone. The same God who some day will be her blessedness and will satiate her in glory, bestows himself on her here and now, never leaves her, lives in her soul, more than that, forms a single entity with her. Therefore she thirsts for silence so that she can listen relentlessly, so she can steadily penetrate deeper into his limitless being. She is one with the one she loves, she finds him everywhere. She sees how he shines forth through everything."[5] "Often this need for silence is so great that one wishes only to sit like Mary at the Master's feet, to sit yearning to hear everything, to press deeper into the mystery of love that he has come to reveal to us."[6]

The solitude that throws itself like a shining veil around the mystery is not emptiness and absence but rather a fascination with the presence of the Beloved. Already before Elizabeth entered Carmel, she wrote: "Since I cannot abandon the world to live with you in your solitude, give me at least solitude of heart! Let me live with you in intimacy! May nothing distract me from you, my life will be a constant prayer. . . . Create a Carmelite within me, for this is possible inwardly, and I will that it be so."[7] However Elizabeth found herself fully in her element only when she had her personal days of retreat after she entered the monastery. "I shall be ten days in complete solitude; I shall be able to pray for many hours more than normal and walk through the monastery with my veil lowered; my life will be much more that of a desert hermit. . . ."[8] "I am God's little recluse. . . ."[9] Yet it is not so much external aloneness that constitutes the perfection of being alone with the Alone [*solus cum Solo*],[10] rather it is the inner claustration that coincides with love, with love's exclusiveness, with its flaming jealousy. "There is a divine jealousy for your soul, the jealousy of a bridegroom. Keep him in your heart, alone and separated. Let love be your 'cloister'; carry him with you everywhere, and thus you will find solitude even in the midst of a crowd of people."[11] Love itself is solitude; all external sep-

---

[5] 62 (ET 47); CW II:L 133.   [6] 97 (ET 73); CW II:L 158.
[7] 40 (ET 28–29); CW III:J 138.   [8] 129 (ET 97); CW II:L 244.
[9] 148 (ET 111); CW II:L 298.   [10] 150 (ET 112); CW II:L 302.
[11] 159 (ET 119); CW II:L 293.

arateness, all asceticism of silence and recollection is merely a preparatory exercise of what flows from perfected love itself, because that is what love *is*: exclusivity. This is so much a part of the essence of love that it survives miraculously even when love becomes communication and community. Love is able to enclose in her circle more and more being, indeed, everything she left outside for the sake of the One, she finds again within the One who is everything. What on the outside would have been distracting, indeed literally a dissipation, now becomes in the interior an integration into the One, making the most recollected and detached soul precisely the most communicative soul, since the detached soul is the one who most closely approaches the solitary Sun of love.

In a Christian view, solitude is a duality: solus *cum* Solo. Solitude is an existence-for-another, a mutual "standing-before-each other" in love. That is what the word "*pre*-sence" (*présence*) meant for Elizabeth, as it is also expressed in the fundamental text from Paul: "Chosen to be spotless and holy in his *presence* [before his face] in love". "The eye of the soul, opened to faith's enlightening, discovers the present God who lives in her. In her turn, she is so present to him that he guards her with jealous care."[12] They are present for each other as in an "eye-to-eye",[13] "heart-to-heart" encounter,[14] whose electric pulse is the "immensity of love that washes over us from all sides".[15] It is a presentness that envelopes and captivates from all sides, leaving no way of escape: "I feel as if I am wrapped up in the mystery of the love of Christ, and when I look back, I see how divine love has pursued my soul. O how much love there is! It is as if I am crushed under its weight. So I fall silent and adore."[16] "I feel so much love over my soul! It is like an ocean into which I plunge and disappear, it is my vision on earth while waiting for the face-to-face encounter in light. He is in

[12] 210 (ET 156); CW I:143.   [13] S 431; CW III:P85.

[14] 63, 68, 116, 138 (ET 48, 51, 86, 104); CW II:L136, L149, L299, L267.

[15] 103 (ET 77); CW II:L199.   [16] 65 (ET 49); CW II:L151.

me, I am in him, I only have to love him, let myself be loved by him, and to do this forever, no matter what—to awaken in love, to move in love, to fall asleep in love; soul in his soul, heart in his heart, so that he might cleanse me by his touch and free me from my misery."[17]

We must interpret from this vantage point what Elizabeth says about the soul as the place of God and, consequently, as the hidden heaven. Although her words closely recall those of the Fathers of the Church, they have a different scope. She does not have in mind, as they did, the soul's character as image and likeness or the reflection of the divine archetype in its human image when the image has been cleansed through virtue and turned to consider itself. She does not even have in mind an Augustinian "journey inward" by which one is drawn toward the pure spirit of God by way of the most spiritual things of the world. Even though the entire patristic (and through it also the neoplatonic) tradition hovers in the background, from the outset she has in mind the gospel mystery of the *indwelling of God through grace* and the nearness and intimacy that this indwelling engenders in the innermost soul. The Pauline and Johannine indwelling and interdwelling of Father and Son in the Holy Spirit and the mutual indwelling of God and the soul in the Holy Spirit form the center of the Christian revelation of grace: "God in me, I in him: let that be our motto. How good is this presence of God in us, in the hidden holiness of our soul! It is there that we always find him—even if we no longer feel his presence, he is still there, indeed he has drawn even closer to us!"[18] "How good it is to be in this presence of God! In the very depths, in the heaven of my soul, I find him, because he never leaves me. God in me, I in him, that is my life! Except for the beatific vision, we possess him just as much as do the saints above, and we are able never to leave him, never to let ourselves be distracted from him."[19] "From

---

[17] 73 (ET 55); CW II:177. [18] 45 (ET 33); CW III:L47.
[19] 48 (ET 34–35); CW III:L62.

now on I want to live only *within*, in the cell that you build in my heart."[20]

The first way to describe this presence of grace is to speak of the presence of God "in the soul", which is thus a place for God. This comes from the Pauline image of the soul as a temple of God. With hints of the great Teresa of Jesus over-shadowing her, Elizabeth likes to express this image in terms of an inner "castle" or "holy fortress".[21] Often she deliber-ately equates temple and castle,[22] or, linking the "impregnable fortress" with the mystery of predestination, she speaks of "a calm and tranquil standing in the presence of God as if my soul were already in eternity",[23] recalling Psalm 61 [62]: "In God my soul is silent, from him I expect salvation; he is the rock in which I find salvation, my strong fortress, and I shall not be moved."[24] But the emphasis lies no longer on being fixed in God, rather, on God's dwelling within the enclosed domain sanctified by his presence, which thereby becomes "heaven". From this point onward, Elizabeth speaks of the "heaven of the soul",[25] intending thereby to express two further aspects of God's indwelling by grace: (1) the anticipation of the be-yond in the here and now, extending even to a reflection of a heavenly inhabitant's behavior and manners, although the di-rect vision remains veiled in faith; and (2) the fact that the presence of God in the soul is an unmediated one (*amesōs* was a favorite expression of the Greek fathers) and thus deserves in the truest sense to be called presence or immanence.

It will have become clear how little the God who is present is determined and enclosed by the soul's "place". It is not God who is fixed in place, it is not God who has moved; rather it is the soul who has arrived at the place of God, because

[20] 41 (ET 29); CW III: J140.

[21] 217, 232, 241 (ET 161, 172, 179); CW I:147, 156, 162.

[22] 217 (ET 161); CW I:147.   [23] 232 (ET 172); CW I:156.

[24] 241 (ET 178–79); CW I:161.

[25] 200, 212, 213, 220, 222, etc. (ET 150, 158, 159, 163, 165, etc.); CW I:108, 144, 149, 150, etc.

the veils and distances between her and God have fallen away and because she has come in from the "outside" and has left her estrangement to come home, not to herself, but to her homeland and her natural center in God. *God in the soul* has acquired the deeper meaning of *the soul in God*. "This is the life of Carmel: To live in him!"[26] "Let us belong entirely to him, let the divine elixir of life so penetrate us that God becomes the life of our life, the soul of our soul; let us remain conscious day and night of his divine activity."[27] The term "center of the soul" (which Elizabeth borrows from John of the Cross), that innermost part of her where she encounters and touches God,[28] simply means the "border" between the created person and God, a border that eliminates all boundary and aloofness in the inexplicable phenomenon of mutual presence. "He is always with us; remain with him always, in all your doing and suffering. Even if your body collapses, remain beneath his gaze. Behold him present, living in your soul!"[29] "Since God is in us, he demands only to take possession of us as he has taken possession of the saints."[30] All perfection consists, according to her basic text from Paul, in that nakedness and stripping off of every husk, which is the very heart of presentness. God required of Abraham that he "walk in my presence and be perfect", and the eternal election of God's love desired that we should be "without spot, holy in his presence".[31]

We can now see why Elizabeth links presence with simplicity and *unity*. Presence is the evaporation of every boundary set by multiplicity, namely, the boundary and multiplicity between soul and God and the boundary and multiplicity found within the soul herself. Here she picks up the patristic and neoplatonic view of union (*henōsis*) as an integration of the powers of the soul in their simple essence, as a coalescing of many words into a single, silent word, as the uniting of the soul and God.

[26] 63 (ET 48); CW II:L 136.   [27] 106 (ET 79); CW II:L 124.
[28] 188–89 (ET 142–43); CW I:95–96.
[29] 87 (ET 66–67); CW II:L 138.   [30] 99 (ET 75); CW II:L 165.
[31] 225 (ET 167); CW I:152.

The second day of the "Last Retreat" is devoted entirely to this mystery:

> The Lord said [to the Father]: "I shall keep my strength for you" (Ps 58:10 [59:9]). My rule prescribes for me: "Your strength will be in silence." Keeping one's strength for the Lord thus means to unify one's whole being in inner silence, to recollect all one's powers so that they can be engaged exclusively in the exercise of love, to possess an eye that is "single", a clear eye that lets light stream in. A soul who bargains with herself, who is preoccupied with her own feelings and useless thoughts, who clings to all sorts of wishes—such a soul dissipates her powers. She is not oriented to God, her instrument is out of tune, and when the Master strokes it, he can coax no divine tones from it—instead it sounds human and dissonant. The soul who reserves anything for herself in her innermost self, whose powers are not completely enclosed in God, can be no perfect praise of glory . . . , for unity does not reign in her. Instead of pursuing her praise in all simplicity no matter what happens, she has to devote herself constantly to collecting the strings of her instrument that have been scattered in all directions. A beautiful inner unity is indispensable for the soul if she is to live here below the life of the saints, that is, the life of the spirits, the life of simple beings. That is what the Lord meant when he spoke to Mary of the one thing necessary.[32]

This line of thought, although it definitely has Thomist and Platonist overtones, focuses on unity as the gospel's demand: on the need to collect all that is one's own in order to receive the simple fullness of the word and of grace. "The blessed in heaven . . . behold God in the simplicity of his being, 'they know him', according to Paul, 'as he himself is known' (1 Cor 13:12), that is, through intuitive vision, in a simple look, and therefore 'they are changed from glory to glory through the

---

[32] 208-9 (ET 155-56); CW I:142-43. [Elizabeth uses the word *réunir* to express "bringing into harmony" the strings that have been "lost" (*perdues*). Von Balthasar translates this literally as "collecting" (*sammeln*) the strings that have been "scattered" (*verstreut*)—TRANS.]

power of his spirit in his own image' (2 Cor 3:18). . . ."[33]
And this becoming like him is necessarily a growing simplifi-
cation, since God is the most perfectly simple being. "The soul
who penetrates to the depths of God and lives in them, who
thereby does all things in him, with him, through him and for
him, with the clarity of vision that gives her a certain similarity with simple being—this soul . . . is an unceasing praise
of glory."[34] "The Divine Being lives in an eternal, immeasurable solitude, . . . and this solitude is simply the Godhead itself. So that nothing wrests me from this inner silence, I must
constantly renew my detachment, separation, nakedness. If my
desires and fears, my joys and sorrows, and all the stirrings
that arise from these four emotions, are not perfectly directed
toward God, then I am no longer alone, then noise arises in
me. Thus I need to quiet, to rock to sleep, the faculties of
the soul; I need unity of being."[35] The unity that Elizabeth
has just described as the essence of eternal bliss, as assimilation
of the heavenly vision to divine solitude, this unity was the
original plan for the world and something of it was realized in
the original pattern of paradise:

"It would give God's heart infinite joy if people sought to do
in the heaven of their souls what the blessed in heaven do: to
cling to him in that simple gazing that brings the creature close
to her original state of innocence. 'According to our image and
likeness': that was the dream of the Creator! To see himself in
his creature, to see his perfections, his full beauty, reflected as
in clear, spotless crystal: Is that not a kind of extension of his
own glory?"[36]

The essential step beyond this idea of simplicity follows at
this point. Elizabeth continues immediately: "Through the simplicity of the soul's gaze as she contemplates God, she finds herself separated from everything that surrounds her, separated
above all from herself. Now she begins 'to shine with the

---

[33] 211–12 (ET 158); CW I:143–44.   [34] 222 (ET 165); CW I:150.
[35] 227–28 (ET 169); CW I:153.   [36] 212 (ET 158); CW I:144.

knowledge of the glory of God' (2 Cor 4:6), which permits the Divine Being to reflect himself in her, and all his characteristics are communicated to her."[37] The soul does not consciously and explicitly pursue the unity of the soul, a "perfect self-possession".[38] Indeed, this unity ultimately rests, not in the soul, but in God, the sole true unity, and the soul's full self-possession coincides with her full self-oblivion, with her final ascent into the single unity that is God. Elizabeth never tires of this subject: "I would that your soul were completely set free to cling completely to God, . . . the secret of peace and happiness lies in self-forgetting, in no longer being preoccupied with oneself, . . . in self-surrender, a boundless trust."[39] "May the gravity of love lead you to a complete forgetting of yourself, to the mysterious death of which the Apostle spoke: 'I live, yet not I, Christ lives in me.' "[40] "The saints are those beings who are forever forgetting themselves, who so lose themselves in the Beloved, without any attention to themselves, without any regard for creatures, that they can say with Paul: 'I live no more, Christ lives in me.' "[41] Elizabeth interpreted her own name, "Elizabeth of the Trinity" as "Elizabeth the Vanishing".[42] She opens her "Last Retreat" with the words of John of the Cross: "Nescivi!" [I knew not].[43] In this freedom, self-detachment and self-divestment, she also glimpses the essence of true virginity.[44] "Oh blessed death in God! Oh gentle, sweet loss of oneself in the beloved Being!"[45] "To hear God, one must 'leave one's fathers' house', that is, leave all that constitutes natural life. One has to 'leave one's nation', which is harder, for 'the nation' is this entire world and at the same time a part of ourselves: our life of feelings, memories, impressions, in short, one's self. We have to forget it, abandon it. When this rift opens up, then the soul is free and the king desires her beauty (Ps 44:12-13

[37] Ibid.
[38] 208 (ET 155); CW I:142.
[39] 121-22 (ET 91-92); CW II:L 249.
[40] 135 (ET 101); CW II:L 264.
[41] 74 (ET 56); CW II:L 179.
[42] 71-72 (ET 54); CW II:L 172.
[43] 207 (ET 154); CW I:141.
[44] 219 (ET 163); CW I:148.
[45] Ibid.

[45:11–12]); for her, beauty is unity, namely, God's unity."[46]
Forgetting and ignoring follow, not on annihilation, but on an
act of the most sublime sort. Elizabeth borrows a phrase from
Paul to comment on the bride's cry in the Song of Songs: "I
choose not to know anything" (1 Cor 2:2) except "to know
him, the communion of his suffering, the conformity with his
death" (Phil 3:10).[47] Thus one ignores one's way into Christ
and into his redemption, a Christian ignoring of self, including
one's sins and faults.

At this point Elizabeth incorporates once more the "little
way" of Lisieux into her own thinking, and she does it in the
same manner as Thérèse, in close conjunction with the Letter
to the Romans and Paul's teaching on justification. "Never let
yourself be depressed by thoughts of your own failings and
wretchedness. Paul says: 'Where sin abounded, grace did more
abound' (Rom 5:20). The weakest soul, indeed the most guilty,
is precisely the one who has the greatest grounds for hope, and
her act of forgetting herself in order to throw herself into the
arms of God glorifies him more and makes him happier than
all her introspection and examination of conscience—for in
the latter she merely finds a way to dwell on her weaknesses,
whereas in her heart she already possesses a Savior ready at
any moment to cleanse her."[48] One can see from this powerful
passage the great unity of Elizabeth's spiritual teaching. The
Savior's presence and the redemption and cleansing he brings
require nothing but a glance, a simple turning toward him; and
this act of self-forgetting simultaneously becomes for the soul
the forgiveness of her sins and a recognition of the overwhelming power and endless scope of grace. Through this act she admits both her guilt and God's grace, entering into the eternal
plan of divine predestination.

Do you know the fine passage where Jesus says to his Father:
"You have given him power over all flesh, that he might give

---

[46] 228 (ET 169); CW I:153–54.   [47] 207 (ET 154); CW I:141.
[48] 123 (ET 92–93); CW II:L 249.

them . . . eternal life" (Jn 17:2)? That is what he wants to accomplish in us. He desires every moment that you leave yourself behind, that you give up all cares, in order to retreat into that solitude that he has selected for himself in the depths of your soul. He is always there, even when you do not notice him. He is waiting for you and wants to carry out the "marvelous exchange" spoken of in the liturgy: the exchange of life between bride and Bridegroom. Through his steady touch, he wants to free you from your failings, your faults, from all that bewilders you. Has he not said: "I came, not to judge, but to save" (Jn 12:47)? Let *nothing* obstruct your way to him. Don't let it bother you that you are either passionately enthused or depressed—it is the law of this world that we waver between one emotional state and another. You must simply trust the fact that he never changes, that he is always bending over you in kindness. . . . You may think it hard to forget yourself. Don't let that bother you! If you only knew how easy it is! I'll let you in on my secret: think about this God who lives in you, whose temple you are (Paul says that, and we can believe it). Little by little the soul accustoms herself to living in his sweet fellowship; she realizes that she carries within herself a little heaven where the God of love has set up housekeeping. And then it will seem to her as if she were breathing the divine atmosphere, indeed, I might say, she remains on earth only in her body, while her soul already lives above the clouds and the mists in him who is unmovable. Don't tell me that this is too sublime for you, that you are too wretched; for that would only be one more reason to turn to the one who saves. We are not cleansed through being stuck in our misery, rather by looking at the one who is nothing but purity and holiness. Paul says that we are predestined to be conformed to his image. When you are hurting, think of it this way: the divine Master goes to work with the chisel in order to complete his work, therefore, hold still under his hand as it works. After the Apostle had been raptured to the third heaven he was much aware of his weaknesses and complained about them. But God's answer was: "My grace is sufficient for you, for power is made perfect in weakness" (2 Cor 12:9). Take courage then, Madame and dear Sister; I entrust you most especially to a little Carmelite who died at the age of twenty-two in the odor of sanctity and who bore the name Thérèse of the Child Jesus. Her mission is to broaden souls so that they can throw themselves onto the billows of grace, of trust, of abandonment. She said that she found happiness when she began to forget herself. Won't you call on her daily, so that she can grant you this knowledge of the saints? . . .[49]

If Elizabeth thus incorporates the approach taken by Thérèse and Paul into her overall vision and lets it play a role, even though a subordinate one, she also expresses the same thing in ideas reminiscent of Augustine, who in turn simply restates Paul's thoughts in a different form:

The freest soul is the one who most forgets herself. If someone asked me about the secret of happiness, I would say that it consists in no longer taking account of oneself, in constantly denying oneself. . . . Pride is love of ourselves. The love of God should be so powerful within us that it squeezes out all other love. Augustine says that we have two "cities" within us: the city of God and the city of the self. As the first grows, the second dwindles. A soul who lives in faith under the gaze of God, who has the "single eye" of which the Gospel speaks, the purity of intention that looks to God alone, such a one also lives in humility. . . . If you perceive in yourself the stirrings of pride, don't get worked up over it, for pride is being aroused even in your concern about pride. Instead, place your weakness at the Master's feet like Mary and ask him to free you from it.[50]

Both forms of description—the Thérèsian-Pauline and the Augustinian—converge in the same gospel image of contemplative surrender and surrendering contemplation.

This remains the fundamental mystery of Christian existence, and all asceticism is a path toward it. This mystery of adoration of the divine presence forms the rule for every form of existence—for the contemplative life in a strict sense as well as the active life. The presence is heaven, and any distinction

[49] 123–25 (ET 93–94); CW II:L 249.
[50] 170–71 (ET 129); CW I:125–26. [Elizabeth writes "Magdalen" in the last sentence of this quotation. Von Balthasar has changed it to "Mary"—TRANS.]

between faith and celestial vision takes a back seat in light of it. Elizabeth was well aware of this double meaning of the word *presence*: the presence of a person and the temporal presence that contrasts with the absence of pastness and futureness. The presence of God in the soul is such that it makes the Eternal Being a "being-there", and it is thereby already a form of eternity: a presence of genuinely eternal life and genuinely eternal "always-now" surrounded by timeboundedness. " 'Be perfect, as your Father in heaven is perfect.' If the Master permits me to hear these words in the depths of my soul, then it is because he desires that I live, like the Father, in an eternal presence, without a Before, without an After, indeed, completely bound up together in the unity of my being in this eternal Now. And what is this Now? David gives me the answer: 'Let him be adored forever for his own sake' (Ps 71:15 [72:15]). That is the eternal law in which the 'praise of glory' must stand firmly and immovably." To be able to do all this, the soul must for the sake of God forsake all merely natural life. "Then she will adore her God for his own sake forever and live according to his image in the same eternal Now in which he lives."[51]

II

The adoration granted to the Christian here below remains an adoration in faith, not in heavenly vision. What is this *faith*, and how is it related to adoring worship? First, faith is a human person's encounter with God's naked presence and present being. Insofar as this is not an encounter with a limited and created being, this act of faith surpasses all objective and all subjective this-worldly experience and situations, all evidence and criteria that give off a natural and worldly light. Faith is primarily night, and God's presence and worship of him must take place in this night.

[51] 226–27 (ET 168, 169); CW I:152–53.

"Faith", Paul says, "is the presence of things hoped for, the proof of things not seen" (Heb 11:1). If the soul has recollected herself in the clarity that this word creates in her, what does it matter whether she feels or feels not, whether she is in night or in light, whether she enjoys or enjoys not? She is somewhat ashamed to distinguish between these things anymore, and, if she is affected by them, she despises herself deeply for her littleness of love and quickly looks to the Lord for liberation. She "extols him" . . . above all the sweetness and consolation that flow from him, for she has determined to transcend everything in order to join herself with her Beloved.[52]

The place of mutual presence now lies beyond all these circumstances, and its location can only be found by transcending all these situations. He proves himself in his reality, in his constancy, in his presentness (that is the meaning of the Pauline word in Hebrews) by remaining transcendent, and this proof becomes compelling for the soul by her own act of transcendence. "The eye of the soul, open to the light of faith, discovers the presence of her God, who lives in her, and she in turn is present to him. . . . Now outer storms or inner turmoil can rage as they will, she can even be robbed of her honor: 'Nescivi!' God might conceal himself and withdraw from her his palpable grace: 'Nescivi!', or with Paul: 'For his love's sake I have lost everything' (Phil 3:8)."[53] "Every incident, every event, every suffering, as well as every joy, becomes a sacrament that gives her God. For that reason, the soul no longer makes any distinction between these things, she passes beyond them to lasting repose in her Lord on the other side. She exalts him high on the mountain of her heart, higher than all his gifts, higher than all the consolations that flow from him."[54] "Taste and touch no longer hold attraction for her, it makes no difference to her whether he gives her joy or pain—she believes in his love. The more she is assaulted, the more her faith grows, for she pushes through all barriers so that she can

[52] 214-15 (ET 160); CW I:145-46. [53] 210 (ET 156-57); CW I:143.
[54] 190 (ET 143); CW I:97.

rest in the lap of eternal Love, who can do nothing but love. Fully alert in her faith, the Master's voice can whisper to her in her innermost soul the words he whispered to Mary Magdalen: 'Go in peace, your faith has saved you.' "[55]

Faith is primarily a transcending of all criteria of the world and the soul—and not merely a transcending of reason but of all of life, of the entire human experience, including most particularly the richest and innermost experience: intuition. But this transcending does not take place in a vacuum, rather it follows and submits to a law—the law of the word and revelation of God, who thereby proves beyond all this world's words his divinely present being and who demands adoring submission to that proof of his presence. In this sacrifice of all worldly criteria, faith is a powerful act of *obedience*. We can now see that God's presence to the soul in the night of faith defines itself more precisely as the presence in the soul of a clear divine *will* that serves her as a point of reference beyond all worldly things. It is even more than that: it is nourishment from which she as a believer lives. It is thus the immanence of the Divine Being in her. Elizabeth often returns to this truth, for it is an essential part of her faith's insight.[56] The central thought here is that there is no real distinction between God's will and God's being, and therefore, whoever has elevated God's will to the innermost law of her being possesses God's being at the center of her being.

How can one glorify God? It is not hard, for God lets out the secret when he tells us: "My food is to do the will of him who sent me" (Jn 4:34). Therefore throw your arms tightly around every expression of the will of the Master who is worthy of adoration, consider each pain as well as each joy as having come directly from him, and your life will be an unbroken communion, because everything will become a sacrament that gives God to you. And that is the complete reality, for God does not split

[55] 195 (ET 146); CW I:102.
[56] 86–87, 92, 136, 197–98, 237 (ET 66, 70, 102, 148, 175–76); CW II:L 138, L 252, L 264; I:106–7, 158–59.

himself into parts: his will is his entire being. He is completeness in all things. And things, in a sense, are only the rays of his love. Now you see how you can glorify him in these scarcely bearable situations of suffering and exhaustion.[57]

Carrying out this pure will of God involves renunciation of everything that is not this simple, naked will, yet, because it is present as the eternal, unchanging will in every situation, every situation becomes the sacrament of faith. Precisely in the sacrifice demanded lies the reward: the offering of the blood of eternity, indeed, a giving of the Divine Being under the form of any matter or concern whatsoever. What prohibits us from being profound or exalted in a worldly sense, what points us to simple, daily obedience, is indeed most profound, because it grants us fellowship with God in his essence continually, not merely in exceptional moments. "This exaltation of the soul to God in the midst of all things grants us a kind of continual communion with the Holy Trinity simply through the fact that we do all things under their gaze."[58] Not only does this obedience bring us all things by virtue of bringing us God in all things, but it also grants us participation in the trinitarian unity between Father and Son, for the Son himself willed to have the Father in himself on earth precisely in his continual doing of the Father's will. " 'My food is to do the will of him who sent me.' The Lord said it first, and the soul who communicates with him enters into the movement of his divine soul, and it becomes her sole purpose to do the will of this Father who 'has loved us with an everlasting love' (Jer 31:3)."[59] "During his thirty-three years, this will was his daily bread to such a degree that he could say as he died: 'Everything is finished.' Yes, all your commands, your entire will is completed, and therefore 'I have glorified you on earth' (Jn 17:4). In fact, when the Lord spoke to his disciples about food they knew not, food that consisted in doing the will of him who sent him, he could

[57] 135–36 (ET 102); CW II:L 264.   [58] 92 (ET 70); CW II:L 252.
[59] 86–87 (ET 66); CW II:L 138.

say: 'I am never alone' (Jn 8:16), 'he who sent me is always with me because I always do what pleases him' (Jn 8:29). Let us therefore eat lovingly this food of God's will."[60] " 'I have taken your precepts as my portion forever, for they are the pleasure of my soul' (Ps 118:111 [119:111]). That is what the Lord's soul sang, and therefore it must echo in the soul of the bride. By her faithfulness to the inner and outer commandments, she gives witness to the truth and can say: 'He who sent me has never left me alone. He is always with me, for I always do what pleases him.' And because she never leaves him, but instead senses him so powerfully, she is able to send forth the secret power that redeems and saves souls."[61]

Faith is so much a matter of simple obedience that Elizabeth repeatedly and firmly turned back the suggestions of relatives that she might, because of her faith-intimacy with God, presume somehow to cross normal borders. A woman she knew asked her "to try to enter into contact with" a dead relative. Elizabeth responded: "If you only knew how much we live from bare faith here in Carmel, how powers of imagination and feelings are excluded from our relationships with God! I gladly join myself with your dear one who has passed on, enter into communion with her, find her once more in the One who is her sole life. Each time I draw close to God, my faith tells me that I thereby also approach her. . . . She is, after all, fixed in pure love, nothing distracts her from God. And thus I am closer to the dead than to the living."[62] On another occasion, a novice who had left the monastery asked her "to request a sign" from the Lord, "to tell us whether we shall see one another again", whether she would be returning; but here too the answer was: "I cannot do that. That is not part of my commission. To do that, it seems to me, I would need to abandon my self-abandonment."[63] Faith is the opposite of magic and occultism. It is the renunciation of all curiosity, of

[60] 198 (ET 148); CW I:106. [61] 237 (ET 175–76); CW I:159.
[62] 153–54 (ET 115); CW II:L 323. [63] 159 (ET 119); CW II:L 293.

all forays into divine secrets: it is pure subordination to his will.

Closely related to the obedience that characterizes faith, and which, according to Elizabeth, claims each moment of the believer's existence, is *vigilance*. Faith must be watchful in the sense that it remains ready at any moment to bring transcendence to completion, to offer a sacrifice in the night, to prefer the divine to all of one's own reality. Faith must be on the lookout for the presence of the divine will and being that lies hidden in this sacrifice, on the lookout for the communion offered in all situations. "Let us rouse our faith, let us consider that he is there, within, that he is counting on our faithfulness!"[64] "May I be fully present there, completely awake in my faith, completely adoring, completely surrendered to your creative power!"[65] "I want to be completely at his disposal, so that the Master can take me wherever he wants."[66] "Pray that I may be completely faithful, fully alert, that I might walk the way of the Cross as bride of the Crucified!"[67] "The Lord hides himself thoroughly, but I rouse up my faith and am all the more satisfied not to enjoy his presence, so that *he* might experience the joy of my love."[68] "To arm herself against natural love, the soul must be fully vigilant in her faith, with her eyes firmly fixed on the Master."[69] "Paul orders us to be 'fortified in faith', in a faith that never lets the soul doze off, a faith that keeps her totally alert under the eye of the Master, fully recollected under his creative word."[70]

It is in this vigilance, this standing at attention, this purity and holiness of the act of faith that Elizabeth finds the final characteristic of faith, one that appears to contradict the first characteristic and yet is really in full harmony with it. Already here below faith involves a *vision*—a vision, not of God's essence, but of his love. This love is the full range of God's saving work

[64] 74, cf. 195 (ET 56, cf. 145–46); CW II:L 179; cf. I:101–2.
[65] 80 (ET 61); CW I:183.   [66] 98 (ET 74); CW II:L 158.
[67] 150 (ET 113); CW II:L 304.   [68] 148 (ET 111); CW II:L 298.
[69] 227 (ET 169); CW I:153.   [70] 234 (ET 174); CW I:157.

as the soul views it in the world but also as she sees and experiences it in herself, in her life, love and faith. The bread of life that she eats in faith does not disappear without leaving its traces in her. The eternity in which she makes her home while sojourning on the foreign shores of time gleams so brightly that it can be seen even in letting go of time, in the night of transcendence. "Through every sacrifice and every immolation, the soul sees him whom she loves."[71] "I feel so much love on my soul, like an ocean into which I plunge, in which I lose myself! Love is my vision on earth in expectation of the vision face to face in eternal light."[72] "Faith is the face-to-face encounter in the night. . . . Let nothing distract us from the gaze of his love."[73] "We are already living in the supernatural and divine world through faith. . . . His love, his 'excess of love' . . . that is my vision on earth."[74]

Ultimately, Elizabeth finds two texts that powerfully support this idea and permit this entire train of thought to merge with the idea of predestination and of an eternity that is already possessed in this life. The one comes from John, for whom faith rests on a living relationship with the incarnate Son, on recognition and experience of love, which in turn calls forth love and self-surrender. The other comes from the Pauline view of Old Testament faith as an "unshakable" standpoint so firm and fixed that it becomes the equivalent of seeing the invisible:

"To see God, one must believe", Paul says (Heb 11:6), and he repeats: "Faith is the substance of things hoped for and the proof of things not seen" (Heb 11:1). That means then that faith makes future blessings so certain and present that they become reality and exist in our soul through faith before we can enjoy them. John of the Cross says that faith is possession in a condition of darkness. Faith alone can give us true light about him whom we love. And our soul must choose faith as the means to reach a happy union. . . . In conversation with the Samaritan woman, the Lord pointed to faith when he promised to give those who

[71] 63 (ET 48); CW II:L 136.   [72] 73 (ET 55); CW II:L 177.
[73] 96 (ET 73); CW II:L 193.   [74] 109 (ET 81); CW II:L 191.

believe in him a fountain of living water bubbling up into eternal life (Jn 4:14). . . . "We have known the love God has for us, and we have believed in it" (1 Jn 4:16). That is the great act of our faith: the means to repay God's love with love. Through faith we press forward all the way to the "hidden mystery" in the heart of the Father of which Paul speaks (Col 1:26), and our whole soul trembles for joy. When she manages to believe in this "excess of love" (Eph 2:4) who bends over her, then one can say of her what we find written about Moses: "He was unshakable in his faith, as if he had seen the invisible" (Heb 11:27). She is not content with a taste and a touch, . . . she believes in his love.[75]

"This should be the attitude of a 'praise of glory' who wants to strike up a hymn of thanksgiving in the midst of everything: to be 'unshakable in faith as if she had seen the invisible', unshakable in faith in the excess of love: 'We have known the love God has for us, and we have believed in it' (1 Jn 4:16)."[76]

To be sure, the difference between this life's vision (in the night) and the next world's vision (in light) cannot be denied, and no one, least of all Elizabeth, has any thought of doing so. However, if earthly faith draws its full power and form from its eternal Object and his eternal presence, then it should surprise no one that the "night" that surrounds faith here below is not simply something negative, rather it is a mysterious participation in an eternal feature of love.

John, the disciple whom Jesus loved, is to open the "eternal doors" slightly today so that my soul can rest in holy Jerusalem, in the "sweet vision of peace". He tells me: "There are no lamps in the city, because the glory of God has illuminated her, and the Lamb is her lamp" (Rev 21:23). If my inner city is to have some sort of similarity and conformity to the city of the "immortal king of eternities" (1 Tim 1:17), then a great illumination from God should be granted me, and I must extinguish every light, so that, as in the holy city, the Lamb will be my only lamp. And behold, now faith appears to me, that beautiful light of faith!

[75] 193–95 (ET 145–46); CW I:101–2.   [76] 214 (ET 159–60); CW I:145.

> This alone shall light my way as I go to meet the Bridegroom.
> The Psalmist says that "God hides himself in the darkness", yet
> he seems to contradict himself when he says that "light envelops
> him like a garment". Still, out of this apparent contradiction I
> see that I must forge ahead into the sacred darkness, turn all
> my faculties into emptiness and night, if I am to meet my Lord.
> Then the light that clothes him like a garment will also wrap itself
> around me, for he wants his bride to shine with his light and
> exclusively with his light, the "splendor of God" (Rev 21:11).[77]

Here we find the key to the paradox of light and darkness in
earthly faith and the paradox that the darkness of this faith originates in the light of eternal vision and faith. "No light except
God's light"—the eternal vision implies precisely this sort of
exclusivity. The denial of all other lights is derived from the
eternal vision, and this denial takes place in this life in the nega-
tions of suffering that stretch all the way to the night of the
Cross and its obedience. Thus faith itself, not merely knowledge granted by faith, will be completed in the heavenly vision.
" 'When that which is perfect comes' (clear vision), then that
which is 'imperfect' (seeing through faith) 'will attain its full
perfection' (1 Cor 13:10)."[78] Faith is ultimately a characteristic
and requirement of love, and love, after all, is eternal. "For the
time being we want to 'believe in love' with John (1 Jn 4:16),
and, since we possess it in ourselves, what does it matter if the
nights manage to darken our heaven?"[79]

Adoration as a living exercise of faith, as an abiding before the
mystery of the presence that can only be recognized when faith
is surpassed, as a knuckling under of human love surrendering
to endless love—adoration as an ultimately indescribable act, is
possible only as *participation*. We have already seen that communion with the Son is participation in his communion with the
Father.[80] Thus it is evident that the original adoration is that
of the Son before the Father, the act from which all types of
transcendent faith originate. "The Divine Worshipper" makes

---

[77] 213-14 (ET 159); CW I:145.   [78] 194 (ET 146); CW I:101.
[79] 129 (ET 97); CW II:L239.   [80] 86-87 (ET 66); CW II:L138.

it possible for the soul to become a praise of the Father[81]—he who lives in the soul as Savior and Redeemer teaches her his own adoration.[82] For "he alone is the true worshipper in spirit and in truth" (Jn 4:23).[83] The most hidden depths of Elizabeth's spiritual teaching reveal themselves in this christological and, through Christ, trinitarian foundation for adoration, all of which circles back to her starting point in the doctrine of predestination. Just as Paul understood this teaching solely in a trinitarian manner, so too Elizabeth can only interpret the praise of glory, which she knew to be her name and her calling, in a trinitarian manner: the phrase simply makes explicit the trinitarian meaning of Christian worship, the trinitarian meaning that unifies the Christian actions of faith, love, surrender and humiliation.

Indeed, one final prospect comes into view, one that Elizabeth did not expressly catch sight of but that extends the trajectory of her thoughts, even focuses them into a sort of compact center. The idea of predestination was to be believed only because it was applied socially, not individually. What is predestined in Christ is first of all the Church; her individual members are predestined insofar as they themselves are the Church. But the idea of indwelling grace is the prerequisite for this social vision—in grace there can be no solitary self with a private, distinguishable destiny. Each person is mysteriously socialized into the Church by the indwelling of God's grace, without ceasing to be a person. Without slipping into pantheism or pan-Christism, grace is able to universalize the self. This becomes most clearly visible in the mystery of the Mother of God as she is universalized to a real symbol of the *Ecclesia*, the mediatrix of all grace and the flawless bride "without spot or wrinkle". Yet it also takes place, in analogy to the Virgin, in all other graced persons, especially in those who have given themselves

[81] 237 (ET 176); CW I:159.
[82] 81, 107 (ET 62, 80); CW I:183; II:L 214.
[83] 201 (ET 150); CW I:108.

up once for all through vows. For to the same degree that the innermost self is "indwelt" by a yet more inward Trinity of God—*Deus trinus interior intimo meo* [triune God deeper than my depths]—so also that self is opened toward the Church and toward the most intimate fellowship of the saints. Indeed, this can be suggested in no other way but as a mutual interdwelling of persons in the trinitarian God who interdwells all. A Plotinian *solus cum Solo* [alone with the Alone] cannot lend adequate force to this idea; but where the Christian *Solus* unveils the hidden trinitarian fellowship, one comes inescapably to the point we have just suggested. Here, finally, the proclamation of ecclesial predestination converges with the proclamation of ecclesial grace. Both belong together, and together their immense radiating light leads the soul into deeper adoration and grateful service. Something of the relational character of the Divine Persons has penetrated the creaturely person through "participation in the divine nature", rousing the creature to adventures in love that cannot be imagined by natural means.

PRAISE

I N ADORATION THE SOUL BECOMES SIMPLE. Recollected in the act of transcending all multiplicity, her unity is possible through the unique unity of God into which she passes. The same movement that makes the soul simple also makes her mirror God. Completely transparent in herself, retaining nothing of the opaque image of the world, she becomes an image of the simplicity and transparency of God, who thus recognizes himself in her.

Elizabeth demands to be completely absorbed into the sacrifice of the Son, "so that I might be completely pure, completely transparent—so that the Trinity can be reflected in me as in crystal. The Trinity loves so much to gaze on its beauty in my soul. This moves the Trinity to give even more, to flow even more fully into me."[1] Elizabeth took this metaphor from Teresa of Jesus,[2] but it is so vivid for Elizabeth that whenever she sees the sun shining through glass, she thinks of God shining into the soul. She sees the holiness of the presence of God, the "crystal that radiates God", in other souls as well, especially in those of children. It is in this holiness and presence that one can worship God.[3] The imagery prepares the way for a deeper insight, namely, that God does not see a second image confronting himself but rather sees reflected in the soul his own essence, which he has given to the soul and in which she participates. "To be conformed to the image of the Son" was the plan of predestination; but the image of the Son is the same as the image of the Father. " 'Get rid of the old man and put on the new . . . according to the image of the one who created him' (Col 3:9−10). This image is God himself. He makes his will known explicitly on the day of creation: 'Let us

---

[1] 61 (ET 46); CW II:L 131.   [2] 63 (ET 48); CW II:L 136.
[3] 84 (ET 65); CW II:L 197.

make man after our own image and likeness'. . . . In a letter, Peter says that we have 'become partakers of the divine nature' (2 Pet 1:4), and Paul admonishes us 'to hold firmly until the end that beginning of his essence that he has shared with us' (Heb 3:14)."[4] "Those who are glorified . . . see God in the simplicity of his essence. Paul says that 'they know as they are known' (1 Cor 13:12)—they are known by him, that is, by direct, simple vision, and therefore, the great saint continues, 'they are changed from glory to glory by the power of his spirit into his own image' (2 Cor 3:18). Thus they become a nev-erending 'praise of glory' for the Divine Being, who sees in them his own glory."[5]

The transformation spoken of in this last passage from Paul is no "moral" transformation accomplished by making the copy similar to its exemplar, rather it is virtually a "physical" change in which the sovereign power of the exemplar is expressed in the copy in a steadily more glorious manner, causing the exemplar to shine forth from the copy. Elizabeth understood this very well. She knows that "we love God with his own love",[6] and that the faithfulness with which we keep God's commands is no new, independent human word in response to God's word in us, rather it is itself part of and powered by God's command within us.[7] It is the grace of God itself that streams forth from the soul's faith and obedience, indeed, this grace shines from the very darkness of the soul. "My inability, my loathing, my darkness, my faults themselves speak of eternal glory. Suffer-ings, whether of soul or body, boast of my Master's glory."[8] This only illustrates how little the "glory" emanating from the soul is her own, how that which is most disgraceful about her has the task of proclaiming the glory and honor of God. A single glory of God shines through shadows as well as light.

[4] 169–70 (ET 128); CW I:125.   [5] 211–12 (ET 158); CW I:143–44.
[6] 61 (ET 46); CW II:L 131.   [7] 220 (ET 164); CW I:149.
[8] Ibid.

And only the soul that seeks not to shine by herself but permits God to reflect himself in her, is a praise of his glory.[9] "The whole Trinity bends" over her so that " 'the glory of God's grace' can shine forth" in her.[10] Elizabeth writes to a priest: "Like that high priest 'without father, without mother, without ancestry, without beginning of days or end of life, like that image of the Son of God' (Heb 7:3), of whom Paul speaks, so you too, through holy anointing, shall become a being who no longer belongs to the earth, a mediator between God and man, called to radiate 'the glory of his grace' through your participation in the 'exuberant grandeur of his power' (2 Cor 4:7)."[11] We encounter the same reversal again and again: what a man can really give to God is what he has received as a gift from God. God also expects as part of man's response that man's being be absorbed by the gift of grace, so that he can become capable and worthy of eternal life through participation in the full measure of that gift. "David sang, 'What shall I repay the Lord for all the blessings I have received from him? This: that I take up the cup of the Lord!' (Ps 115:12–13 [116:12–13]). If I take hold of this cup, reddened with the Lord's blood, and with joyful thanksgiving add my blood to the sacrifice, then it in a certain sense loses its limitedness and is capable of being a glorious praise to the Father. My suffering then becomes a message proclaiming the glory of the eternal!"[12]

Thus the "Praise of Glory" can be described as "a soul who resolutely gazes at God in faith and simplicity. She is the reflection of all that he is; she is like a bottomless abyss into which he spreads himself and pours himself forth; she is like a crystal through which he shines and through which he can contemplate all his perfection and brightness. A soul who can permit the Divine Being to satiate in her his hunger to give all he is

---

[9] 243 (ET 179–80); CW I:162.   [10] 111 (ET 83); CW II:L 226.
[11] 113–14 (ET 84–85); CW II:L 232.   [12] 221 (ET 164); CW I:149.

and has is in truth a praise of the glory of all his gifts."[13] She offers God, not herself, but "she offers God to God."[14] Again, this indicates that the "praise of glory" has never left the divine orbit that travels from foreknowledge and predestination to glorification and back. In that circle, it is God's own grace that praises and glorifies the one and solitary love that encloses within itself all communication and dividedness, burying them in its solitude, in its endless silence and contemplation. Elizabeth frequently uses, in all innocence, the phrase "pure love" (*amour pur et désintéressé*),[15] seeing in it the essence of the praise of glory. The purity she is referring to is not a denial of hope within love but a perfect transparency for divine love. It is the crystal shining with no light of its own, rather with sunlight alone, yet—unlike any earthly crystal—without refracting it. It takes place in that absolute relationship to its object that only Christian and ecclesial obedience can transmit; it takes place in accepting and passing on the full and pure divine will.

Because God's grace permits such a high degree of purity and accuracy, the image reflected in the soul can only be a trinitarian one. If the image is a true one, it can only come from the Son, with and through whom the Father recognizes his image, accomplished through the Holy Spirit, who is the realization and efficacy in everything. As Elizabeth follows this path, she remains fully within her Pauline trajectory. The soul is "one with Christ in order together with him to be a praise of the Father's glory",[16] indeed, she even speaks of "equality" [*pied d'égalité*].[17] "I no longer want to live my own life, rather I want to be transformed into Jesus Christ so that my life is more divine than human, so that when the Father bends down to me he can recognize in me 'the image of his beloved Son, in whom he has placed his entire good will' (2 Pet 1:17)."[18]

---

[13] 204 (ET 153); CW I:112.
[14] 106 (ET 79); CW II:L 124.
[15] 203 (ET 152); CW I:112.
[16] 221 (ET 164); CW I:149.
[17] 193 (ET 145); CW I:99.
[18] 191 (ET 144); CW I:98.

[I want to be] "a living, striking image of the 'Firstborn', of the eternal Son, of him who is the perfect praise of the glory of the Father".[19] "The goal is 'to be transformed in Jesus Christ', as Paul insists: 'Those whom God has known in his foreknowledge he also predestined to be conformed to the image of his Son.' For that reason, I have to search out this divine model and make myself so much like him that without ceasing I can express it in the sight of the Father."[20] When he sees this sight, the Father feels the same as when he sees the Son. "When the Father leans over this soul, his adopted daughter so conformed to the image of his Son, the 'firstborn among all creatures' (Col 1:15); when he recognizes her as one of those 'whom he has predestined, called, justified', then he thrills in his paternal heart and determines to crown his work—to 'glorify her', to transport her into his Kingdom so she can sing the praise of his glory in endless eternities there."[21] These are the souls who stand on the mountain of the Lamb and already "here below come from the race of those who are as pure as light and who carry the name of the Father and the Son written on their brow —the Son's name through conformity with him; the Father's name because he radiates into them the beauty of his perfection, because all divine qualities are reflected in them, because they are the harp strings that vibrate with the 'sound of the new song of praise' (Rev 14:3)."[22]

The more the trinitarian meaning of mirroring God shines forth and the more the Father's face becomes translucent with the mystery of God's presence, so much more must this mirroring be christologically shaped. For Elizabeth, the concluding christological phase of her spirituality clearly grows out of the trinitarian phase, just as at the end of Dante's *Paradiso* the face of the God-Man shines forth from the vision of the three interlaced circles. Increasingly, conformity to the image

[19] 208 (ET 155); CW I:141.
[20] 236 (ET 175); CW I:158.
[21] 217 (ET 162); CW I:147.
[22] 218 (ET 162–63); CW I:148.

of Christ becomes for her conformity to the suffering and crucified Christ. In this way her loftiest thoughts and speculations
are realized and made incarnate. She has been taken at her word,
and it becomes clear that it is the word of the Crucified. "Let
us therefore be sacrificed souls, that is, those who are genuine
in their love! 'He has loved me. He has given himself for me'
(Gal 2:20)."[23] Suffering is proof of election, the truth of God's
predestination.

> All these chosen ones, who "hold palms in their hands" and
> "bathe in God's great light", first had to pass through the "great
> tribulation". They had to learn to know the "pain as endless as
> the ocean" of which the prophet speaks, and, before they could
> "gaze upon the glory of the Lord with unveiled face", they had to
> participate in the humiliation of his Christ. Before they could be
> "changed from glory to glory in the image of the Divine Being",
> they were conformed to the incarnate Word, the one crucified
> for love. The soul who wishes to "serve God day and night in
> his temple" . . . must be determined to take part earnestly and
> effectively in the Passion of her Lord. She is a redeemed one
> who must herself buy back the freedom of other souls, and her
> song therefore runs as follows: "I glory in the cross of Jesus
> Christ" (Gal 6:14), "with Christ I am nailed to the cross" (Gal
> 2:19), "I suffer in my body what is lacking in the suffering of
> Christ, for his body, the Church" (Col 1:24). "The queen stands
> at your right hand" (Ps 44:11 [45:9]). That should be the posture
> of such a soul. She walks the path to Calvary at the right hand
> of her crucified, annihilated, humiliated King, who nonetheless
> remains strong, quiet and full of majesty, and who walks toward
> suffering, in Paul's powerful words, to manifest the "glory of his
> grace" (Eph 1:6).[24]

Always from the perspective of predestination, always asking
how "one could ever respond to the dignity of such a calling",[25] Elizabeth discovers and joyfully affirms the necessity

[23] 108 (ET 81); CW II:L214.   [24] 216 (ET 160-61); CW I:146-47.
[25] 236, 203 (ET 175, 152); CW I:158, 111.

of suffering. The bride must be pierced with the very sword that pierced the Bridegroom—for that makes them like each other. "Thus she makes her way hither, rejoicing with the Master at every sacrifice, happy in the knowledge *that the Father has known her*, because he crucifies her together with his Son."[26] The sword on which the bride sacrifices herself is, however, simply the sword of God's word (Heb 4:12), the sword of the commandment and of obedience. "Love has to end in sacrifice. Paul tells us that when he says of the Lord: 'He loved me and gave himself for me.' Thus his holy will is the sword that sacrifices you moment by moment. Learn this with the Lord in Gethsemane, where his crushed soul cried 'Let your will be done, not mine.' "[27] From Gethsemane, the path then continues through the Stations of the Cross all the way to participation in the last stages of his suffering:

> When the hour of humiliation, of annihilation, comes, the soul recalls this short phrase: "*Jesus autem tacebat*" [Jesus then was silent]. She says nothing, "keeping her entire strength for the Lord" (Ps 58:10 [59:9]), the strength that one can draw only from the well of silence. When the loneliness comes, the abandonment, the anxiety of the Lord's great cry: "Why have you forsaken me?", then she remembers the prayer: "That they might possess the fullness of my joy in themselves" (Jn 17:13). Drinking to the dregs the cup prepared by the Father, she finds divine sweetness in its bitterness. When she has often repeated the "I thirst"—I thirst to possess you in your glory—she says at the end, "It is finished"; "Into your hands I commend my spirit." . . . Then the holy God will be glorified in her because he has destroyed everything in her to clothe her with himself and because she earnestly lived out the words of the Baptist: "He must increase, I must decrease."[28]

The last months of Elizabeth's life were completely given to this mystery. "Pray that my likeness to the image I worship may

[26] 236 (ET 175); CW I:159.   [27] 143 (ET 107); CW II:L291.
[28] 237–38 (ET 176–77); CW I:159.

grow more perfect each day. *Configuratus morti ejus* [conformed to his death] (Phil 3:13), that is the thought that pursues me, that gives me strength in suffering. If you only knew what a work of annihilation I feel in my whole being! The way of the Cross stretches out before me, and I am glad to walk it like a bride beside the divine Crucified One."[29] "How mysterious and hushed indeed is my small cell with its bare walls—from which a cross of black wood with no corpus stands out. It is my cross, on which I must offer myself every moment in order to be conformed to my crucified Bridegroom. Paul told us: 'What I desire is to know him . . . and the fellowship of his suffering and conformity with his death' (Phil 3:10)."[30] As her physical pain increases, this idea increasingly captivates Elizabeth, surrounding her like a powerful wall that encloses everything and leaves no exit. She had often reflected on the words of Msgr. Gay—that the obedient and cosuffering Christian was like another humanity [*une humanité de surcroît*] for the Lord.[31] Now these words take on their full truth. And her prayer for conformity, which she had written down two years earlier, is fulfilled in these last months:

"O my beloved Lord, crucified for love, I want to be a bride for your heart, to cover you with glory, to love you until death! But I sense my weakness, and so I ask you to clothe me with yourself, let my soul move with all the movements of your soul. Inundate me, invade me, replace me with yourself, so that my life is nothing but a radiating of your life, . . . another humanity in which you renew your whole mystery."[32]

Now everything rushes toward the mystery of the *Mass*, in which the sacrifice of the Bridegroom is inseparable from that of the Bride, the Church, who offers the Son to the Father and who receives back the life of the Sacrificed One from the

[29] 144–45 (ET 108); CW II:L 294.   [30] 148 (ET 111); CW II:L 298.
[31] 81, 93, 107, 134 (ET 62, 70, 80, 101); CW I:183; II:L 259, L 214, L 256.
[32] 81–82 (ET 61–62); CW I:183.

Father, taking it into herself and thereby permitting the Father to sacrifice her with the Son. She would not dare offer the Son, would not dare affirm the unity of life in the mystery of the one flesh of Holy Communion, if she were not ready to hang as his flesh on the Cross. Elizabeth wants her life's offering to disappear into the mystery of the Eucharist. She wrote to a priest: "I ask you, as a child might ask her father, to consecrate me at Mass and to offer me as a host of praise to God's glorification. Consecrate me so well that I am no more myself but am he, so that, when the Father sees me, he sees him; that I may be 'conformed to his death', that I may suffer in myself 'what yet remains lacking in his Passion, for his body, the Church'. Plunge me into the blood of Christ that I may be strong with his strength."[33] To her mother she writes: "God is pleased to offer his little host, but this Mass that he says with me as bread and with love as the priest could go on for some time yet."[34] "Lord whom I adore, you desire a host, for in your love you wish to be continually renewing your life, to be continually becoming man among men, so that sacrifice and adoration may rise to the Father. . . . My heart is your lowliest sacrament: come, glorify the Father in it in silence and recollection."[35] And once more, basing and subsuming everything under the decree of predestination:

Rejoice in the thought that we are known in eternity by the Father, as Paul says, and that he wants to rediscover the image of his crucified Son in us. How indispensable suffering really is if God's work is to take place in the soul! God infinitely longs to enrich us with his graces, but the measuring cup comes from us, through the degree to which we let ourselves be sacrificed through him, to be sacrificed in joy and thankfulness like the Son and with the Son's words: "Shall I not drink the cup that the Father has prepared for me?" He called the hour of his Passion "his hour". It was for that hour that he had come, the hour he

---

[33] 145 (ET 109); CW II:L 294.   [34] P 174 (ET 119); CW II:L 309.
[35] S 428; CW III:P91.

yearned for with all his might. If a great pain or a little sacrifice offers itself to us, then we want to think like him that it is our hour, the hour in which we can prove our love to him who, in Paul's words, "loved us all too much".[36]

II

The whole process of becoming like the Son can be grasped only when understood as the work of the mysterious Third Person of the Trinity, the *Holy Spirit*. The whole thrust of Elizabeth's thought is directed toward him, even though she never succeeds at describing his work precisely. In a sense she can only point to the place, the presence and the work of the Spirit; she knows only what Paul tells her—how much everything converges upon this center, the Spirit. Yet she remains unaware of how much her whole mission takes place under the sign of the Spirit. Her mission occurs more specifically under the Spirit as the Third Person, with the characteristic spirituality that distinguishes the Spirit from the Father and the Son, and less specifically under the activity of the Spirit made known in the "seven gifts" and characteristic of all holy living in the Church.

Elizabeth knows that the Holy Spirit of love carries out and directs all God's activities in the world.[37] He does this because he "seals and completes the unity of the Trinity" in the inner life of God. From within this unity he can effect the outworkings of union in the world and in souls, "pouring himself out" in order "to lead in the light of faith to those heights where one lives from peace, from love, from union".[38] He is also the "consuming fire" that burns up all that is ungodly in the soul, changing everything changeable into himself. The souls who have within them this fire, "think much less about the unfin-

---

[36] P 175 (ET 120); CW II:L 308.   [37] 202 (ET 151); CW I:110.
[38] 96 (ET 72); CW II:L 193.

ished work of destruction and self-surrender than about tumbling into the flaming hearth, which is the Holy Spirit himself, the very love that binds the Father and his Word together in the Trinity. Through faith, they enter into him and in simplicity and joy are lifted high above things and sense impressions into sacred darkness, where they are changed into the divine image."[39] One must ask the Spirit to kindle the fire of union with the Son,[40] because the Spirit is given the task of carrying out the will of the Father with regard to the Son: "to restore all things in Christ, in heaven and on earth. Heaven is within us, and the Holy Spirit desires to renew it in the heat of his flames."[41]

Elizabeth explained the role of the Spirit in its larger context to her sister:

> Little sister, do you know how rich you are? Have you ever measured the depths of love? I want to show you the constant tenderness that hovers over your soul day and night. Your faith will see in a simple glance the hidden mystery that is at work in your heart. The Holy Spirit has chosen you for his temple; you don't belong to yourself any more, and that is your majesty. Linger silently under the divine touch, so that he can impress on you the Redeemer's image. You have been predestined to this likeness by a mysterious decree of the Creator, and, in truth, you are no longer yourself, you are he, and the change is taking place all the time. Give God thanks for this most sublime decision; let your whole being collapse into adoration, and, whatever happens, always believe in love![42]

To perceive the *completion* of the Father's eternal plan (conforming us to his Son's image) as the work of the Holy Spirit is Elizabeth's vantage point for revelation—thus her viewpoint is primarily that of the Spirit. Neither the Father's creating nor the Son's human person described in the Synoptic Gospels ulti-

---

[39] 192 (ET 144); CW I:98.   [40] S 424; CW III:P86.

[41] S 430; CW III:P89.   [42] S 442; CW III:P93.

mately captivates her; with Paul she can say that she no longer wants to know the Son according to the flesh. She knows him as the spiritualized and glorified one, as John and Paul know him; as the one continually revealed anew to the world in the sacraments and Holy Eucharist, which indeed are works of the Spirit; and as the indwelling of the individual soul, which also comes from the Spirit. As much as Elizabeth longs to leave earth to enter eternal endlessness, it is not the inner mystery of the Trinity, the relation of the three Divine Persons to each other, that concerns her—she scarcely expends a word on that. Rather, her interest lies in the "household" (*oeconomia*) of the Trinity, which reveals itself outwardly and pulls creation into its eternal orbit through this window, becoming ultimately the point at which this world becomes a praise of the all-perfecting grace of the Father in conformity to the Son through the work of the Spirit. After all, it is said of the Spirit that he will glorify the Son (Jn 16:14), that is, he will bring to consummation the glorification of the Father through the Son in the world. Whoever places her life under the sign of *doxa* (praise) by that act also lives under the sign of *pneuma* (Spirit).

To live under the sign of the Spirit, for Elizabeth, is to circle around the mystery of the soul's transformation in God, a mystery that can be seen only indistinctly but which can be hinted at by approaching it from two sides at once: close *unity* in lasting *distinction*, indeed, close unity in steadily deeper detachment of adoration. The indwelling of the Holy Spirit in our spirit, as spirit of our spirit and soul of our soul, requires the boldest, most fearless words. To describe the way the Holy Spirit imparts from himself the innermost personal activity of our spiritual life: the gift of faith, of hope, of the love "that is poured out in our hearts through the Holy Spirit", of the prayer that he prays in us to the Father; to describe the transformation of a person into a member of the Body of Christ, into a living stone of his temple, indeed, into "one spirit with him" (1 Cor 6:17)—all this demands bold words, which Christian mystics of all ages and Elizabeth too have not hesitated to use. Again and again she speaks of identity and identification,[43] fusing,[44] being changed into the other Thou,[45] crossing over into God[46] in a departure from oneself and an entry into God's sphere—to the point that the soul radiates forth nothing but God and God's characteristics, until she reaches an "equality with God" (*égalité*),[47] a "deification".[48] Yet this grand language is held in check by another series of stark phrases that speak of steadily deeper humiliation in one's own nothingness, in one's own abyss, in a movement so unconditional that it can only be understood as following Christ's footsteps: "Who is like God? If we behold the Son humbling himself before his holy Father, then we too wish to vanish, we wish to humble ourselves in order to be like him."[49] "If we are to live constantly in his presence, we must humiliate ourselves, we must always put ourselves in last place in order to be like Jesus. Humiliation should be our constant dwellingplace."[50] "He loves to encounter the soul in this posture of self-destruction, of holy humility. For then he comes to meet her with his fullness and lets her be intimate with him."[51]

Ultimately we encounter the mystery of the "double abyss", a mystery that cannot be further resolved, a mystery of which Elizabeth speaks as if it were a unity. "Let us plunge to the bottom of the double abyss: God's boundlessness and our own nothingness. Then our song will rise more perfectly and praise the glory of the Almighty."[52] The abyss remains a double one

[43] 62, 70, 189, 207, 224 (ET 47, 53, 143, 155, 167); CW II:L133, L164; I:96, 141, 151.

[44] S 427; CW III:P91.

[45] 189, 191, 192, 221 (ET 143 [twice], 164–65); CW I:96, 98 (twice), 149; S 438; CW III:P109, etc.

[46] 223 (ET 166); CW I:151.   [47] 140 (ET 105); CW II:L274.

[48] 105 (ET 79); CW II:L124; S 431; CW III:P85.

[49] S 441; CW III:P118.   [50] S 439; CW III:P120.

[51] S 441; CW III:P118.   [52] Ibid.

and yawns ever wider—as the otherness and the infinite distance between the creature and the Creator reveal themselves more and more in self-revelation and self-communication. Yet the yawning gulf is also being covered over and forgotten as the Son of God clothes himself with it, deifies it, makes it the expression of the Trinity's inner distinction of Persons in a unity of essence. Precisely that which distinguishes the creature from God now becomes that within which the creature is like God: otherness in unity. And it is the Holy Spirit who makes the creature's dissimilarity resemble the original disparity between image and exemplar, who raises the disappointment of otherness into the rapture of a loving exchange that "forgets the distance"[53] by drawing distance into unity, making distinction a function of maximal union.

This passionate, rhythmic contrasting of union and disparity, of the abyss of all and the abyss of nothingness, synchronizes with an emphatically Carmelite rhythm. We should not be surprised to find it in Elizabeth. It is no "natural mysticism", rather it is a christological and pneumatological mysticism nourished on the Pauline and Johannine Scriptures. It takes seriously the foundation of all creation in Christ the incarnate God, since from the beginning the creature was created into a framework provided by the identity in one person of two extremes: the glorified divine nature and the crucified, rejected human nature. Elizabeth learned about this "mystery" from Paul,[54] about the Son as firstborn of all creatures,[55] placing all others in his shadow.[56] The creature not only has its origin in God's eternity (according to Scriptures on both Christology and predestination) but also finds in eternity—in God's free will from eternity and for all eternity—a participation in the eternal inner dynamic of the triune God, in the eternal procession of the

[53] S 427; CW III:P91.

[54] 109, 211, 231, 232–33 (ET 81, 157, 171, 173); CW II:L 191; I:143, 155, 156.

[55] 217 (ET 162); CW I:147.   [56] 186 (ET 141); CW I:94.

Persons. Elizabeth knows this deep insight from John of the
Cross, who in turn borrowed it from Scholastic theology. "Our
Holy Father says that the Holy Spirit raises the soul to such
marvelous heights that she is able to exhale the same breath of
love that the Father breathes with the Son and the Son with
the Father: the breath that is nothing other than the Person of
the Holy Spirit."[57] In eternity a man is not an alien spectator
watching events as they unfold before him; rather, through the
lumen gloriae [light of glory] that inhabits him and that is itself
divine, he is able to participate in the eternal event of eternal
processions, that is, in self-occurring love itself. Elizabeth always views the Trinity as an *open* space that she can enter and
into which she can be absorbed. She cites a phrase from Father
Vallée: "May the Holy Spirit bear you to the Word and the
Word to the Father, and may you be perfected in the One, as
was true of Christ and our saints."[58] In her own words she
writes: "Deliver yourself up to the Holy Spirit, so that he can
change you into God and impress on your soul the image of
divine beauty in which the Father sees nothing but his Son
when he bends over you."[59] And thus she can say of the feast
of the Holy Trinity: "This feast of the Three is all mine; as far
as I am concerned, there is none that can compare to it. It is
a feast of silence and adoration. Never before have I grasped
so well the mystery and the entire calling that lies within my
name."[60] This is her lasting destiny, into which she enters and
disappears:

> In a night of peace, in lofty silence
> My craft rode gently on ocean endlessness,
> The world lay mute beneath the heavens' spaces
> And listened for the word of eternity.
> Then, unforeseen, high billows rose,
> The storm-tossed skiff sank, and

[57] 100 (ET 76); CW II:L 185. [58] 60 (ET 46); CW II:L 113.
[59] 128 (ET 96–97); CW II:L 239. [60] 60 (ET 45–46); CW II:L 113.

The Trinity drew me into an embrace,
I found in its abyss my landing.
No one can carry me back to shore,
For I range freely in boundlessness,
No bars block my recreation,
My endless life lives in the Holy Three.[61]

---

[61] S 439-40; CW III:P115. [This literal translation of Father von Balthasar's rhymed German version is, of course, some distance removed from Elizabeth's original verses. For that reason we give both Elizabeth's original French and von Balthasar's German version here: ". . . Par une nuit paisible, en un profond silence, / Il voguait doucement sur l'Océan immense, / Tout était en repos sous la voûte des cieux / Et semblait écouter 'la grande voix de Dieu'. / Mais il survint soudain plusieurs lames profondes / Et le si frêle esquif disparut sous leurs ondes! / C'était la Trinité qui m'entrouvrait son Sein / Et j'ai trouvé mon centre en l'Abîme divin! / On ne me verra plus sur le bord du rivage, / Je plonge en l'Infini, c'est là tout mon partage, / Mon âme se repose en cette immensité / Et vit avec ses Trois comme en l'éternité! . . ." "In einer Friedensnacht, in hohem Schweigen / Glitt sanft mein Kahn auf Meerunendlichkeit, / Die Welt lag stumm unter den Himmelsräumen / Und lauschte auf das Wort der Ewigkeit. / Da hoben unversehns sich tiefe Wogen, / Der schwanke Nachen tauchte unter, und / Dreifaltigkeit hat mich in sich gezogen, / In ihrem Abgrund fand ich meinen Grund. / Man kann ans Ufer mich zurück nicht holen, / Im Grenzenlosen rege ich mich frei, / Im Unbeschrankten kann ich mich erholen, / Im Ewigen leb ich in den Heiligen Drei."—TRANS.]

SERVICE

I

THE GLORY OF GOD adored by men and women, who become a praise of glory through grace, is the glory of a love that shines gratuitously. Love is the heart of triune life, and created and redeemed ones circle around the love God lavishes from within his inner life. In dedicating herself to praise of the Trinity, Elizabeth gives herself to praise of love. She wants to suffer the "martyrdom of love".[1] Like little Thérèse, she wishes to offer herself, not as a sacrifice to God's righteousness, but as a sacrifice to God's love. "Consecrate me on December 8th to the power of love, that I might in truth be a 'praise of glory'."[2] "Consecrate your child to almighty love, so that love might reshape her into a 'praise of glory'."[3] She knows that the Fountainhead, the ancient Source of all love, is enthroned in her innermost being,[4] that love alone unites her with God,[5] that love of God "attracts him and draws him to his creature".[6]

This love, which is God and which God gives, is a cleansing and redeeming force simply by its presence;[7] its presence and touch alone can make the unholy holy. That is the power, the radiance, the apostolate of God's love. The cleansed and sanctified soul is equipped with the same power of love in which it participates. In this mutual presence, she is not only irradiated with God's light, she is infected by it: "You are the light of the world." When Elizabeth, as powerfully as Thérèse of Lisieux before her, praises the apostolic character of love, of a life surrendered and sacrificed in the service of God, she is following a clear Carmelite tradition. "I want to be totally silent,

[1] 146 (ET 109); CW II:L 287.   [2] 133 (ET 100); CW II:L 250.
[3] 134 (ET 101); CW II:L 256.   [4] 132 (ET 99); CW II:L 250.
[5] 189 (ET 142); CW I:95–96.   [6] 189 (ET 143); CW I:97.
[7] 72–73 (ET 55); CW II:L 172.

to be complete adoration, so that I can penetrate constantly deeper into God and be so filled with him that through prayer I can give him to those poor souls who know nothing of God's gifts."[8] She wrote to a priest: "Together with you I would like to be an apostle from within the depths of my beloved Carmel's solitude; I want to work for God's glorification, and to that end I need to be completely filled with him. Then I shall be all-powerful: a glance, a wish, will become an irresistible plea that gains everything—for in a sense it is now God that one offers to God."[9] She wants "to be the little vessel at the well, at the fountain of life, in order to give to souls by overflowing with floods of limitless love."[10] The priest and the Carmelite nun alike live "precursor-lives", "preparing the path for the One whom the Apostle called 'a consuming fire'. Under his touch our soul becomes a flame of love that spreads to all parts of Christ's Body, which is the Church."[11] "The Carmelite nun found the one thing necessary: God, who is light and love; and, since she wraps the world in her prayer, she in truth is an apostle."[12] Thus Elizabeth is convinced that the offices of Mary and Martha are not mutually exclusive. Not only does the active life need its own contemplation and that of others if it is to be fruitful, but the contemplative life also possesses in itself at least as much activity as the active life; indeed, the closer the soul clings to contemplation, the more activity it possesses.[13] Love that serves God is always also service to God's works, the souls.

The idea of cooperation, even of coredemption, now comes into view. To speak of grace is also to speak of work, to speak of redemption is also to speak of coredemption. This is all included in the concept of participation and communion that is the essence of redeeming grace. The one who is God's holy temple must "actively participate in the Passion of the Lord,

---

[8] 61 (ET 46); CW II:L 131.   [9] 105–6 (ET 79); CW II:L 124.

[10] 109 (ET 82); CW II:L 191.   [11] 132–33 (ET 100); CW II:L 250.

[12] S 422; CW III:P 83.   [13] 97 (ET 73–74); CW II:L 158.

for his freedom has been bought, and he must in turn buy the freedom of others."[14] Elizabeth understands this necessity to have been established already in the plan of predestination: "The Father has determined to make into his partners in the great work of redemption those whom he 'knew and predestined to be conformed to the image of the Son', to the image of the One crucified for love."[15] If this were not the case, what would be the meaning of conformity with the Son? If God denied men and women his grace's effective power, demonstrated from the Cross, would he not be holding back the most precious gifts of his grace? How blind are they who pit grace and works against each other, as if grace-filled fruitfulness were not itself the proper work of a Christian! Elizabeth enjoys borrowing from Paul the title of a mother of souls and applying it to her own apostolate. As a Carmelite, she has a "dual mission: to be both virgin and mother: virgin because espoused to the Lord in faith; mother as a savior of souls, who increases the number of the 'Father's adopted children, Christ's coheirs' (Rom 8:17)."[16] She uses this title when addressing her sister,[17] her friends,[18] even her own natural mother: "My darling little mother . . . it seems to me that my love for you is not only that of a child to the best of mothers, but beyond that the love of a mother to her child. I am the Mama of your soul. Do you like that?"[19] And these are not empty words for her: she devotes herself, she prays and sacrifices. She also teaches—as best she can. Above all she strengthens, offering herself as a supporting pillar. She even dares, in the name of this strength, to ask of her mother the highest form of Christian trust. Lovingly and solid as a rock, she stands next to this frightened woman who is inclined to self-pity and pulls her to her feet. She writes out in advance a prayer for her mother to say upon receiving the news of her death.

[14] 216 (ET 161); CW I:146. [15] 240 (ET 178); CW I:160–61.
[16] 102 (ET 77); CW II:L 199. [17] 129 (ET 97); CW II:L 239.
[18] 158, 168 (ET 119, 127); CW II:L 293; I:124.
[19] 178 (ET 134–35); CW II:L 273.

Like little Thérèse, she promises aid from beyond the grave. To a friend she says: "When I am on the other side, will you permit me then to help you, even to scold you when I see that you are not offering all to the Lord? This I would do because I love you."[20] To a fellow nun: "If, from the lap of eternal light I should see that you are slipping out of your singleminded preoccupation as a Carmelite, then I would come immediately to call you to order. You would not object, would you?"[21] Her assistance is primarily assistance in prayer: "In heaven it will be my task to attract souls by helping them to depart from themselves so that they can cling to God in a completely simple and loving movement, to keep them in a great inner silence that permits God to impress himself on them and to change them into himself."[22] All the way into eternity Elizabeth retains her own style. Her apostolate is shaped by the specific character of her contemplative mission. It is a mission that has its origin on the other side, in predestination, and therefore it cannot be ended or placed in doubt by death. She was of earth only because she was already of heaven, and thus after death she can persevere unchanged, both in her inner activity and in her outer radiance. She left behind a note for her Prioress: "Reverend Mother, consecrated for me from eternity, now that I am leaving you, I bequeath to you the calling that I held within the bosom of the Church Militant and which I shall from this point onward fulfill without ceasing in the Church Triumphant: to be a 'praise of the glory of the Holy Trinity'."[23]

II

The concept of grace bearing fruit underlies the idea of service. To understand fruitbearing as "merit" expresses only the relationship between the graced person and herself. It does not

---

[20] 163 (ET 122); CW II:L 333.   [21] 164 (ET 122); CW II:L 335.
[22] 163 (ET 122); CW II:L 335.   [23] P 285 (ET 210); CW I:180.

express her relationship with God and only indirectly touches on her relationship with her neighbor. If, on the other hand, one has grasped the insight that the believer is predestined by the Father to conformity with the Son so that she can work for the salvation of all the brethren to the glory of God the Father, then one's life of grace appears as service to God and men and women. She has received grace for the sake of service together with the Son; her being graced is the fruit of service and thereby also the seed of new service. And, since grace is God's light in the creature, this service is from the outset twofold in character: service toward God as a "praise of the glory of his grace" and service toward men and women as a coredeeming radiance. The more pure the service to God, so much more powerful is the service in the world. Thus Paul, writing to the Philippians, debates which service is more useful for himself: to leave this life and be with Christ or to stay and preach to them. Deciding for the latter is no expression of an either/or choice, rather it is an expression of two sides of the same, inseparable service. Grace is participation in a divine disposition, in the inner selflessness of God's threefold outpouring. Eternal happiness can thus only be an entry into the finality of God's selfless humility, into the bliss of not existing for oneself.

In her last months, Elizabeth learned from the Apocalypse that heaven, the eternal "praise of glory", is service. She talks about soon joining the throng of those who "with palm in hand serve God day and night in his temple while he wipes all tears from their eyes" (Rev 7:17).[24] In heaven she will carry out the office of praise forever. "A 'praise of glory' is a being who never stops giving thanks. All her actions, movements, thoughts and desires root her deeper in love and echo the eternal Sanctus. In glory's heaven the souls never rest, whether by day or by night. They call 'Holy, holy, holy, is the Lord God almighty', and 'they prostrate themselves and worship him who lives in all eternity' (Rev 4:8-9). In the heaven of her soul, a

[24] 152 (ET 114); CW II:L 313.

'praise of glory' begins already her eternal office. Her song of praise continues without end, for it is under the influence of the Holy Spirit, who accomplishes all things in her."[25] The "Last Retreat" is full of images from the Apocalypse. Indeed, she chooses and comments with fondness on those that portray the great liturgy of thanksgiving carried on by the entire heavenly court before the throne of the Father and the Son. A certain festiveness that attaches itself to Elizabeth's simple, warm words seems to echo the liturgy of the other side and grants to her a distant kinship with the great "liturgist" among the Church Fathers: the unknown monk who called himself Dionysius the Areopagite. Hierarchy in heaven, as on earth, makes the entire creaturely world, drenched with the light of redeeming grace, appear as a single universe of service. This is explicitly so because the fundamental idea of service is located in the heavenly world, and the earthly world reflects in a transient way the forms of eternal serving. Life is service, but so is theology and so is mysticism. We must reappropriate what was taken for granted at the end of the patristic era when the gospel poured its waters into the stream of the neoplatonic vision of life. After centuries of egocentric asceticism and in the middle of an era of psychology, this must be won back as the Catholic position proper to God's revelation.

That is the reason why Elizabeth emphasizes so powerfully the place of *office* within the monastic framework. Far from being opposites, office and charism actually coincide. Every charism in the Church is an office, and the priestly office, the priestly order and hierarchy, is a form of charismatic grace. For all her reverence for the priestly office, Elizabeth's independence in her friendships with priests is nonetheless striking. One is surprised at how she places her office as a Carmelite nun side by side with that of the priest and permits each to interpenetrate and complement the other.[26] She understands "the apostolate of the Carmelite [in the same manner] as that of

[25] 204-5 (ET 153); CW I:112.   [26] P 194-215 (ET 135-53).

the priest. If they keep themselves close to their divine source, both can radiate God and impart him to souls."[27] "At the moment of consecration, the priest raises the host to the Trinity, at the moment of communion he turns to the people to distribute to them the bread of life. To offer Christ to the Trinity, to impart him to the world—that is the dual mission of the priest on earth. To live it out fully, he must have the soul of Christ himself. For that reason the entire Church, particularly the contemplatives, must stand behind him. A multitude of life offers itself silently to that end: the purest, the most crucified ones in the monasteries."[28] By doing this, they fill an ecclesial office, indeed, a specific ecclesial office. Ecclesial vows are a commitment to sacrifice, a dedication that gives that sacrifice an explicitly universal ecclesial meaning. "How good the Lord is! He bestows so much on my soul that it seems as if he has only me to think about, only me to love. But this takes place so that I in turn can offer myself up for his Church and for all that matters to her."[29] Again and again she asks priests to consecrate her and transform her together with the great Host, Christ, as a "little host of praise", so that her entire being down to its very roots might become praise and service.[30] "Consecrate me tomorrow with him at Holy Mass. Baptize me in the blood of the Lamb, so that, being virginal in all that is not he, I might love him with rising passion until I reach that unity to which God predestined us in his eternal, immutable purpose."[31] This consecration of love is for Elizabeth the office of her existence. Everything takes place within the context of the Church and within the narrower context of her Order, yet in a natural way, devoid of any theoretically based sense of importance. For her, the Church is the "law of God" within which the Christian lives;[32] beyond that, she is the Bride of Christ, his Body within which each limb moves naturally. Her Order's rule is for her

[27] P 196 (ET 137); CW II:L158. [28] Philipon's words, P 203 (ET 143).

[29] 142 (ET 107); CW II:L275. [30] 130 (ET 97–98); CW II:L244.

[31] 115 (ET 85); CW II:L234. [32] 165 (ET 123); CW II:L340.

"the form in which God wants me to be holy",[33] a form that radiates holiness by imparting it moment by moment to those who observe it. It is in this sense of office that she loves to address her Prioress as a "priestess" who consecrates her and offers her to God.[34] Yet divine love alone occupies center stage. It completes her priestly office in all forms of ecclesial life, much as Elizabeth has already understood the entire Christian life to be a sacramental process. Whatever God holds out to her is full of grace, full of the most authentic presence of God. Everything becomes a sacrament for her until she senses herself becoming a sacrament of God.[35]

Though something perilously exuberant lurks in such thoughts, a firm fence remains, keeping her within the Church's order and fetching all straying notions back into line: the word of God in Holy Scripture. More than anything else, the word of Scripture is an ecclesial place for Elizabeth. As it was for the Church Fathers, so too for Elizabeth: to think and speak as a Christian is to think and speak within the thought and speech of the divine Logos as he became flesh in the letter of Scripture. Her asceticism is the asceticism of the Scriptures; her mysticism is the mysticism of the Scriptures. She stakes everything on a phrase from Paul that she does not exactly tear from its context in heretical fashion but which she likewise refuses to dilute or flatten because *she herself* could not see any other way to bring it into accord with other phrases that she permitted to stand with all their breathtaking depth and their unimaginably divine brilliance. Elizabeth wants to see Scripture read and contemplated with the "mind of God" (*sens de Dieu*),[36] with a subjectively supernatural power of comprehension that alone would be capable of grasping God's objectively supernatural, infinite mind. Each word of Scripture seems to overwhelm her, to surpass her greatest expectations, to compel her to bow in adoring silence. In each word she recognizes God, and she receives each one

---

[33] 69 (ET 52); CW II:L 169.   [34] S 436; CW III:P100.

[35] S 428; CW III:P91.   [36] 223 (ET 166); CW I:151.

with the same veneration as she receives the divine Son. In prayer she becomes intimate with the word. She knows how it sounds, where to find it, how meaning builds on meaning and word piles onto word in a supernatural science of harmonics and craft of composition that God permits his children to practice. It is on Paul and John that the brightest light shines; it is to them that the Lord's words apply: that they would perform greater works with words than he himself (Jn 14:12). These two, who supervise the gospel of the Spirit in which the Spirit guides the Church into the depths of the Word-made-man, direct Elizabeth's theological reflections.[37] Father Arintero, O.P., noticed this: "What I marvel at most about her is her deep sense for the great mysteries of Christian life; . . . this sensitivity— so similar to that of the Apostle—has permitted her to become a faithful expositor of the finest and most profound passages of his letters."[38] Msgr. Paulot, who also interpreted the theological teaching of Thérèse of Lisieux, emphasized much the same: "That a young woman of twenty-three or twenty-four years should attain this understanding of the word of God without formal studies, that she should know how to expound the mystery of grace with flawless orthodoxy, can only be explained through an essential kinship of her soul with the things she explained, a deep affinity that she undoubtedly experienced before she ventured to speak of these things."[39] She lives in the word to such a degree that she never sees heaven anywhere but in this word. As she was dying, she wrote to her physician: "We shall meet again in the light that these pages [of Saint Paul] bring to those who read them with the faith of God's children."[40] To a friend she wrote: "We shall see each other again in that beautiful chapter of the Apocalypse [chapter seven] and in the last one, the one that carries my soul high above the earth into that vision in which I shall lose myself forever."[41]

[37] 213 (ET 159); CW I:144–45. [38] S XXXII (P: ET xviii–xix).
[39] S XXXV. [40] 165 (ET 123); CW II:L 340.
[41] 166 (ET 124); CW II:L 341.

All her thought is and increasingly becomes scriptural thought. Even though her lack of theological education does not permit her to uncover in the word of Scripture hitherto hidden truths by means of theological deduction, she is able to think her way into the depths of the word (which, after all, is the purpose of adoring contemplation). In that way she brings to light with no lesser degree of certainty the hidden abundance of truth, grace and call to action. And the more she responds to this truth by her life, so much more the hidden light shines forth.

III

Christian life as receiving and contemplating the word, as a continual adoration of grace present in us, as service to the Church, even as the Church's service itself—all this would be inconceivable and unreal without *Mary*, the Mother of the Lord. She is the sign of recognition to which Elizabeth looks in order to live and think rightly, the model of loving faith that Elizabeth embraces with childlike love. In Mary, Elizabeth grasps the great silent objectivity and detachment that is her ideal; in Mary, she comprehends the sublime office of woman, marching as bride beside the crucified Bridegroom, Christ and the Church together.

Elizabeth never tires of reflecting on Mary's adoration as she waited: her perfect inner conversion; the two-in-oneness of Mother and Child that is a physical portrayal of the two-in-oneness of the soul and God; her silent listening for the silent Word. "What must have been going on in the Virgin's soul as she, after the Incarnation, sheltered within her the Word-made-flesh, the grace of the Father! How great must have been her silence, her recollection, her adoration, as she sank to the bottom of her soul in order to embrace the God whose Mother she was!"[42] She is the perfect worshipper:

[42] 84 (ET 64); CW II:L 183.

The Virgin's attitude in the months between the Annunciation and the birth is a model for contemplative souls, whom God has chosen so that they might live "interiorly", so that they might live at the bottom of the bottomless depths. In what peace, with what inner recollectedness Mary approached all things and let them approach her! How the most mundane things were deified by her—for the Virgin remained an adorer of the grace of God in the midst of everything. That did not keep her from giving love to her neighbor. Scripture says that she hurried eagerly through the mountains of Judaea to be with her cousin Elizabeth. The unspeakable vision within her never impeded her outer loving.[43]

Mary joins action and contemplation because she is the model of that simplicity engendered by faith through ascent to God.

There is a creature so pure, so transparent, that she seems to be made of light. *Speculum justitiae* [mirror of righteousness], a creature whose life was so simple, so lost in God, that one can scarcely talk about it. *Virgo fidelis*, the faithful Virgin, who "kept all things in her heart," who stood so pure and recollected before God in the mystery of his temple that she attracted the good pleasure of the Holy Trinity to herself: "Because he has regarded the lowliness of his handmaiden, from this time onward all generations shall call me blessed." The Father bent down over the beauty she herself did not recognize and chose her to be the Mother of the One whose Father he was in all eternity. And then the Spirit of love stepped forth, the Spirit in charge of all of God's work. The Virgin gave her *Fiat*: "Behold the handmaiden of the Lord, let it happen to me according to your word", and the most sublime of mysteries took place: by the descent of the Word into her, Mary becomes forever the prize of God.[44]

"Her soul is so simple and its stirrings so deep that one cannot grasp them. She seems to portray on earth the life that the Divine Being, the simple Being lives. That is why she is so

[43] 202–3 (ET 151–52); CW I:110–11.
[44] 201–2 (ET 151); CW I:110.

transparent, why she shines so much that she seems to be made of light. Yet she is only the mirror of the Sun of Righteousness, the *Speculum justitiae*. 'She kept all things in her heart': her entire story can be told in so few words. She lived in her heart, in such depth that no glimpse can force its way in."[45] " 'No one has seen the Father, except the Son and those to whom the Son reveals him.' I think one could also say that no one has penetrated into the depths of the mystery of Christ except the Virgin. John and Mary Magdalen gazed deep into this mystery; Paul often talks about 'insight that has been given to him' (Eph 3:4), and yet, how the saints are covered by shadows when one looks at the brilliance of the Virgin! . . . She, she is the indescribable one! The mystery that she 'kept in her heart and pondered' is a mystery that no tongue can tell, no pen can transcribe."[46] In this sense she is the perfect image of divine simplicity in the world, a simplicity that means both imagelessness and the sharpest possible focus.

Now we also see that she was the perfectly predestined one. "Next to Jesus Christ, certainly at that infinite distance that separates the creature from God, there is a being who was the greatest praise of the glory of the Holy Trinity. She responded integrally to that divine election the Apostle talks about; she was always 'pure, spotless, blameless' (Eph 1:4; Col 1:22) in the eyes of the thrice-holy God."[47] Her eternal predestination shines forth most clearly in the Passion, into which she was drawn completely and in conformity to her Son: "How marvelous it is to contemplate her during her protracted suffering, so tranquil, veiled in a majesty full of gentle strength. For she had learned from the Word himself about the suffering of those chosen by the Father as burnt offerings, as his partners in the great work of redemption; how 'those whom he knew and predestined to be conformed to the image of his Son', who was crucified for love, must suffer."[48] She is a

[45] 239 (ET 177); CW I:160.   [46] 208 (ET 155); CW I:141.
[47] 238 (ET 177); CW I:160.   [48] 240 (ET 178); CW I:160–61.

teacher of sorrows, the "queen of martyrs", who teaches "the last verses of his song, the sounds only a Mother's ears could hear, to those who complete Christ's suffering in suffering with him."[49]

And thus under the Cross she is the "priestly Virgin, whom every priest should call upon and contemplate continually. She will obtain for us 'the knowledge of the glory of God reflected in the face of Christ' (2 Cor 4:6)."[50] "Draw close to her heart, for this priestly Virgin is the 'Mother of divine grace', and in her love she wants to make you into that 'faithful priest after the heart of God' (1 Kings 2:35) of whom the Holy Scriptures speak."[51] Through her, the simple Carmelite can also become a "mediator together with Christ".[52] In this role as a perfect and effective image, Mary becomes "Heaven's Portal" for everyone, helping us all over the threshold of eternity and gently saying these mysterious words to those who enter: "*Laetatus sum in his quae dicta sunt mihi: in domum Domini ibimus*" [I was glad when it was said to me: We shall go into the house of the Lord] (Ps 121 [122]:1).[53] Janua Caeli was Elizabeth's favorite greeting for the Mother of the Lord. It was also the name she gave to a statue that, as a girl, she venerated at home. During her illness, she asked her mother for it so that she could carry it with her through the cloister or into the tribune overlooking the choir, even though it was almost too heavy for her emaciated arms.[54] *Janua Caeli* was a path and entrance to the Trinity for her. She also had a picture of the Mother of God that portrayed her in relationship to each of the three Divine Persons: "In the solitude of our little cells . . . I often like to contemplate this precious image and join myself to the soul of the Virgin as the Father covered her with his shadow, the Son took on her flesh, and the Holy Spirit came forth to accomplish the great mystery. The entire Trinity is at work, the

[49] 239–40 (ET 178); CW I:161.   [50] 112 (ET 84); CW II:231.
[51] 113 (ET 84); CW II:232.   [52] 134 (ET 101); CW II:L256.
[53] 240 (ET 178); CW I:161.   [54] P 188–89 (ET 131–32).

God who empties himself and overflows. What purpose could life in Carmel possibly have if not thus to be surrounded by God?"[55]

[55] P 186 (ET 129); CW II:L 246.

TEXTS

Postulant's Questionnaire (1901)

What is your ideal for sanctity?
To live from love.

What is the quickest way to attain it?
To make oneself as small as possible, to surrender oneself without reserve.

Which saint do you love most?
The disciple Jesus loved, who rested his head on Jesus' breast.

Which part of the Rule speaks most directly to you?
Silence.

What is the dominant trait of your character?
Sensitiveness.

Your favorite virtue?
Purity. "Blessed are the pure in heart, for they shall see God."

The fault you most abhor?
Egoism in general.

Give a basic definition of prayer.
The union of one who is not with the One who Is.

What is your favorite book?
The soul of Christ—it reveals to me all the secrets of the heavenly Father.

Do you have a powerful yearning for heaven?

I often long for that, but, apart from the beatific vision, I already possess heaven in my innermost soul.

In what disposition would you like to die?

I would like to die loving and thus collapse into the arms of the one I love.

What form of martyrdom would you desire most?

I love them all, especially the martyrdom of love.

What name would you like to bear in heaven?

The Will of God.

What is your motto?

God in me and I in Him.[1]

The Prayer to the Holy Trinity (1904)

O my God, Trinity, whom I adore, help me to forget myself completely so that I may be rooted in you as firmly and peacefully as if my soul were already in eternity. Let nothing disturb my peace or entice me out of you, O my Changeless One; carry me moment by moment deeper into the depths of your mystery! Pacify my soul, construct out of her your heaven, your favored abode and the place of your repose. Never do I want to leave you alone there, rather, I want to be fully present, totally alert in faith, full of adoration, completely surrendered to your creating work.

O Christ my Beloved, crucified for love, gladly would I be a bride of your heart; I would so like to cover you with glory, to love you until I die of it. But I sense my weakness, and

[1] 51–52 (ET 40); CW III:PN12.

thus I ask you: clothe me with yourself, unite my soul with all the movements of your soul. Inundate me, invade me, replace me with yourself so that my life is nothing but a radiating of yours. Enter me as adorer, renewer and savior. O eternal Word, speech of my God, I want to listen to you all my life, to make myself teachable so that I can learn everything from you and fix my gaze on you in the midst of all nights, in the midst of all voids, in the midst of all powerlessness, abiding under your great light; O my beloved star, charm me so that I can never leave the circle of your radiance.

O all-consuming Fire, Spirit of love, come upon me from above so that something of an incarnation of the Word takes place in my soul, that I might be another humanity for him, a humanity in which he can renew his whole mystery. And you, Father, bend down to your poor little creature, cover her with your shadow, glimpse in her nothing but the Well-Beloved in whom you have placed all your good pleasure.

O my Three, my all, my bliss, limitless solitude, immensity in which I lose myself; I deliver myself to you as your prey. Bury yourself in me so that I might bury myself in you until I can at the end gaze in your light at the abyss of your grandeur.[2]

Praise of Glory (1906)

A praise of glory is a soul who abides in God, who loves him with pure and selfless love, without self-seeking in the enjoyment of this love, who loves him beyond all his gifts, who would love him even if she received nothing from him and who desires the best for her Beloved. But how can one really will and wish good things for God except by fulfilling his will, since it is his will that directs everything to his greater glory?

A praise of glory is a silent soul who holds still like a harp under the mysterious touch of the Spirit so that he can entice

[2] 80–81 (ET 61–62); CW I:183–84.

from her his divine tones. She knows that suffering is the string that produces the finer sounds; thus she is pleased to see that string on her instrument, so that God's heart might be deeply moved.

A praise of glory is a soul who gazes in unblinking faith and simplicity at God. She is a reflection of all that he is, a bottomless abyss into which he can pour himself and overflow. She is also a crystal through which he can shine and in which he can contemplate all his perfections and shining brilliance. A soul who satisfies the divine Being's yearning to impart all that He is and has, such a soul is in truth a praise of the glory of all his gifts.

A praise of glory is, finally, a being who persists in constant thanksgiving. All her deeds, her actions, her thoughts and her desires root her deeper in love and are like an echo of the eternal Sanctus. . . . Some day the veil will fall, and we may cross the eternal threshold where we shall sing in the lap of eternal love. God will give us a new name, the one he promised to the victor. What will it be? Praise of glory.[3]

---

[3] 203-5 (ET 152-53); CW I:112-13.

CHRONOLOGY

1880　*July 18*: Elizabeth Catez is born in a military officer's family at Bourges. The family moves to Dijon a bit later.
　　July 22: Baptism.

1887　*October 2*: Elizabeth's father dies.

1891　*April 19*: First Communion. The Prioress of the Carmelite convent, Marie of Jesus, gives Elizabeth the name she later used in religious life: de la Trinité [of the Trinity].

1894　Elizabeth vows perpetual virginity.

1897　Elizabeth wants to enter the Carmelite community; her mother says no.

1899　*January*: A retreat for girls held by Father Chesnay, S.J. Elizabeth's first profound grace in prayer. "I want to be a saint—for You!" She begins keeping a spiritual diary.
　　February: She reads Teresa of Avila's *Way of Perfection*.
　　March 26: Her mother approves in principle Elizabeth's plans to become a nun.

1900　*January*: While on retreat Elizabeth resolves to live as much like a Carmelite as possible while still in the world.
　　February: Decisive encounter with Father G. Vallée, who helps Elizabeth interpret her inner experiences and explains to her the gracious indwelling of the Holy Trinity in her soul.

1901   *June*: Marie of Jesus moves to Paray le Monial, where she founds a new Carmelite community. Her successor is Germaine of Jesus, who will be Elizabeth's Prioress until she dies.

August 2: Elizabeth enters the Carmelite convent; she becomes a postulant.

September: Beginning of a friendship with Abbé Chevignard, who at the time is still a seminarian.

December 8: Elizabeth is clothed as a novice.

1902   *October*: Retreat, with conferences by Father Vallée regarding the soul of Christ. Elizabeth struggles with intense inner trials. Father Vallée no longer understands her state of soul.

1903   *January 11*: After protracted spiritual struggle, Elizabeth takes her permanent vows in complete peace.

January 21: Elizabeth takes the veil in festive celebration.

November: Elizabeth reads the main writings of John of the Cross.

1904   Elizabeth reads the encyclical of Pius X: *Omnia instaurare in Christo* and writes a poem about it.

January: The first mention of the name *Laudem gloriae* in a letter.

November 21: She composes the prayer, "O mon Dieu, Trinité que j'adore". Toward the end of the year she reaches a final clarification of her spiritual doctrine.

1905   *Spring*: Her failing health requires that she be released from choir office and brings mitigation of the Order's Rule.

Fall: Elizabeth recognizes "Praise of Glory" in a final sense as her personal calling.

1906   *January 1*: She chooses Saint Joseph, patron of the dying, as her special patron.

January: Retreat preached by a Jesuit father.

Lent: Saint Paul reveals to her her imminent death. Severe stomach illness. From this point onward, Elizabeth daily expects death.

Late March: She transfers to the infirmary, where she will live the rest of her days.

Palm Sunday: Extreme Unction and Viaticum.

Good Friday: A sudden improvement, which, however, is followed by new setbacks in May.

Late July: Reunion with Marie of Jesus.

Summer: She studies and contemplates the Revelation of Saint John; she writes "Heaven on Earth".

August 15–31: "Last Retreat of a Praise of Glory".

October 15: Father Vallée visits for the last time.

October 29: Her last conversation with her entire family present.

November 1: The community assembles at her deathbed. Frightful agony for nine days.

November 9: Death.